T0391907

The Universal Republic

The Universal Republic

A Realistic Utopia?

Mathias Koenig-Archibugi

OXFORD
UNIVERSITY PRESS

OXFORD
UNIVERSITY PRESS

Great Clarendon Street, Oxford, OX2 6DP,
United Kingdom

Oxford University Press is a department of the University of Oxford.
It furthers the University's objective of excellence in research, scholarship,
and education by publishing worldwide. Oxford is a registered trade mark of
Oxford University Press in the UK and in certain other countries

Published in the United States of America by Oxford University Press
198 Madison Avenue, New York, NY 10016, United States of America

British Library Cataloguing in Publication Data
Data available

Library of Congress Control Number: 2024932678

ISBN 9780198921127

DOI: 10.1093/9780198921158.001.0001

Printed and bound by
CPI Group (UK) Ltd, Croydon, CR0 4YY

Cover image: Lequeu, Jean-Jacques. 1794. *Élévation géométrale du temple
de la Terre*. Paris: Bibliothèque nationale de France (BnF).

Contents

Acknowledgements

This book has been in the making for many years, and I am delighted to be able at last to thank in print the scholars and friends who offered comments and encouragement along the way. Max Afnan, Hans Agné, and Jens Steffek read previous versions of the entire manuscript and offered many valuable suggestions, as Farsan Ghassim and Mirko Heinzel did on specific parts.

I have been fortunate that many fine scholars commented on work in progress that eventually became part of this book. Heartfelt thanks to Seebal Aboudounya, Roy Allison, Filippo Andreatta, Daniele Archibugi, André Bächtiger, Michael Barnett, Eugenia Baroncelli, Richard Beardsworth, Alexandra-Maria Bocse, Chris Brown, Barry Buzan, Luis Cabrera, Marco Clementi, Michael Cox, Ben Crum, Katerina Dalacoura, Lisa Dellmuth, Caroline Elak, Pilar Elizalde, Viktor Elm-Schulin, Eva Erman, Benjamin Faude, Katrin Flikschuh, Rainer Forst, Mervyn Frost, Thomas Gehring, Marta Golonka, Robert Goodin, Max Grömping, Alessandro Guasti, Tom Hale, David Held, Kimberly Hutchings, Ryan Jablonski, Markus Jachtenfuchs, Leigh Jenco, Robert Kissack, Faradj Koliev, Friedrich Kratochwil, Chandran Kukathas, George Lawson, Daniel Laqua, Zoe Lefkofridi, Simon Lightfoot, Christian List, Catherine Lu, Magnus Lundgren, Kate Macdonald, Terry Macdonald, Franziska Maier, Raffaele Marchetti, Karolina Milewicz, Irene Morlino, Claus Offe, Heikki Patomäki, Riccardo Pelizzo, Wan Peng, Ulrich Preuss, McKenzie Ratner, Christine Reh, Berhard Reinsberg, Anke Schmidt-felzmann, Jan Aart Scholte, Ulrich Sedelmeier, Karen Smith, Duncan Snidal, Theresa Squatrito, Jonas Tallberg, Henning Tamm, Luke Ulaş, Laura Valentini, Soetkin Verhaegen, Carl Vikberg, Oliver Westerwinter, Jonathan White, Alexandra Zeitz, and Michael Zürn. Many thanks also to the readers for Oxford University Press. Luka Bareis and Marco Pinfari provided excellent research assistance. I had the privilege of having Luis Cabrera, Farsan Ghassim, Alessandro Guasti, and Tom Hale as coauthors on publications that are summarized in this work.

I am fully responsible for all remaining shortcomings. No doubt there are plenty of them, and I can only repeat what Anacharsis Cloots, author of *La république universelle*, wrote shortly before he was arrested during France's revolutionary Terror: *effectivement, si mes principes sont universels, mes talents ne le sont pas.*

Dominic Byatt of Oxford University Press has been a truly wonderful editor, and his steadfast encouragement and good humour are deeply appreciated. I am also grateful to the other members of the excellent publishing team, notably Phoebe Aldridge-Turner, Rajalakshmi Ezhumalai, and Anthony Mercer.

I owe the greatest debt to my wife and best friend, Nicola. Her kindness and support throughout the gestation of this project have been essential. She and our children, Francesco and Fabrizio, accepted patiently my prolonged travels in the land of utopia. This book is dedicated to her as a small token of my love.

List of Figures

List of Tables

1
Introduction

Can humanity achieve collective self-government in a highly interdependent world? Catastrophic climate change, biodiversity loss, the dangers of natural and bioengineered pandemics, war and displacement, the risks generated by thousands of nuclear warheads and by novel technologies, the persistence of poverty and inequality, and other global challenges remind us daily about the weaknesses of the international institutions expected to address common concerns and how unjustly power and vulnerability are distributed in the world today. This book examines whether a democratic world state is a possible and desirable solution to the problem of governing the planet that we all share.

The scale and urgency of the challenges that such a world state would be expected to meet in the twenty-first century should not make us forget that the questions examined here have divided political thinkers throughout history. Seven centuries ago, Dante Alighieri declared that the fulfilment of the mission of the human species—achieving ever deeper knowledge—required peace, and peace in turn required the establishment of world government under a wise and disinterested ruler who would decide 'in those matters which are common to all men and of relevance to all' (Dante Alighieri c.1312/1996, 25). His contemporary Marsilius of Padua argued that universal empire was legitimate in so far as its authority rested on the revocable consent of the people subject to its rule—including 'the workmen or craftsmen or the rest of the labourers' (Marsiglio of Padua c.1339/1993, 6, 39–43). Writing around the same time, Pierre Dubois retorted that any attempt to establish a world government would bring war rather than peace.[1] Instead, he offered what may well be the oldest proposal for an international organization aimed at resolving disputes between European sovereigns before they escalate into war (Dubois c.1306/1956, 78–79).

---

[1] His reasoning is worth quoting at length because it anticipated many later arguments: 'I doubt if there is a man of sound mind who thinks that in this day and age there can be a single temporal monarch for the whole world, who would rule all things and whom all would obey as their superior. If there were a tendency in this direction there would be wars, rebellions, and dissensions without end. There would be no one who could quell these disturbances because of the multitude of people and the distant areas involved, local differences, and the natural inclination of men toward strife' (Dubois c.1306/1956, 121–122).

The Universal Republic. Mathias Koenig-Archibugi, Oxford University Press. © Mathias Koenig-Archibugi (2024). DOI: 10.1093/9780198921158.003.0001

These early explorations set the tone for the debate in subsequent centuries. Key writers of the Enlightenment rejected the imperial discourses common in previous centuries and redefined the idea of a world state in ways that still profoundly shape current debates. Immanuel Kant maintained that the establishment of a 'world republic' (*Weltrepublik*) or 'state of peoples' (*Völkerstaat*) was demanded by reason. However, he eventually settled for what he called a 'negative surrogate', that is a voluntary association of free states that would not wield coercive powers itself. The reasons for this evolution in his thinking are debated among scholars, but arguably it was at least partly driven by concerns about the achievability of a world republic (states 'do not at all want this') as well as its viability (the danger of a 'soulless despotism' eventually lapsing into anarchy).[2] Another Prussian Enlightenment thinker, Anacharsis Cloots, was far less cautious. He stated that the only legitimate sovereignty was the sovereignty of humankind as a whole. Hence, a 'republic of the united individuals of the world', centred around a legislative assembly of popularly elected representatives from every part of the globe, was indispensable to bring the principles of the Declaration of the Rights of Man and of the Citizen of 1789 to full realization (Cloots 1792/1979, 1793/1979).[3] Cloot's ideas emerged at a time when many shared the conviction of his political associate Thomas Paine that 'nothing of reform in the political world ought to be held improbable. It is an age of Revolutions, in which everything may be looked for' (Paine 1791/1995, 198). Toussaint L'Ouverture combined his call for the destruction of slavery with an appeal to overcome 'the barriers that separate the nations, and unite the human species into a single brotherhood' (L'Ouverture 1797/2019, 28). Paine himself believed that, '[f]or what we can foresee, all Europe may form but one great republic' (Paine 1792/1995, 262). However, Kant was not the only cosmopolitan thinker of the age to be wary about a global state. Condorcet, for instance, offered public support to Cloots and the principles he proclaimed for the 'great society of the human race' (Mortier 1995, 298–299), but in a posthumously published manuscript the universal republic is curtly dismissed as a 'puerile illusion' (Condorcet 1793/1976, 287).

---

[2] The cited words are in Kant (1795/1996, 328, 336). Other important statements are in Kant (1775–76/2012, 229; 1784/2007, 114–115; 1793/1996, 309; 1797/1996, 487–488).

[3] While Kant died in his Königsberg home at the age of 79, Cloots was guillotined on Paris' Place de la Concorde at the age of 38 for energetically promoting his ideas as a member of the National Convention, to which he was elected after the solemn conferral of French citizenship in 1792. In the speech that led to Cloots' arrest, Robespierre accused him of lacking patriotism by preferring the title of citizen of the world to the title of French citizen, and condemned 'his extravagant opinions' and 'obstinacy in speaking of a universal republic' (Robespierre 1793/1979, 654).

Intellectual and political interest in world government became particularly intense between the 1930s and the 1950s, gaining endorsements from campaigners and politicians as diverse as Rosika Schwimmer, Barbara Wottoon, Albert Einstein, Jawaharlal Nehru, Winston Churchill, Léopold Sédar Senghor, and Martin Luther King, Jr. (Wootton 1943; Churchill 1947/2003; Einstein 1947, 1948/2007b; King, Jr. 1964/2012; Bhagavan 2012; Billion 2021; Threlkeld 2022). Gathered for the Fifth Pan-African Congress of 1945, Kwame Nkrumah, Jomo Kenyatta, W. E. B. Du Bois and other anticolonial leaders declared: 'We demand for Black Africa autonomy and independence, so far and no further than it is possible in this "One World" for groups and peoples to rule themselves subject to inevitable world unity and federation' (Fifth Pan-African Congress 1947, 5). Following several decades of neglect, scholars have started to devote serious attention to the topic since the early years of the current century, prompting some authors to celebrate a 'resurgence' of the idea of world government or at least renewed debate (Craig 2008; Cabrera 2010b; cf. also Weiss 2009).

As during the Enlightenment, cosmopolitan theorists remain divided on whether a democratic world state is the best way to realize the principles they advocate. While some embrace the notion (e.g. Cabrera 2004; Höffe 2007; Marchetti 2008; Martí 2010), others reject it (e.g. Habermas 2006, 134; Appiah 2007, 163; Archibugi 2008, 110). This rejection is often rooted in concerns that are shared by thinkers across a broad spectrum of intellectual traditions, notably that '[t]he prospect of world government would be an invitation to prepare for world civil war' (Waltz 1979, 111–112) or 'a forbidding nightmare of tyranny' (Arendt 1970, 81). It is common for political philosophers to stress that the realization of the principles they advocate does not involve the establishment of a world state (e.g. Pogge 1992, 63; Held 1995, 230; Walzer 2000; O'Neill 2001, 181; Nussbaum 2006, 313; 2019, 137; Benhabib 2007, 448; Miller 2007, 26; Gould 2009, 25; Sen 2009, 408; Stevens 2009, 98; Pettit 2010b, 156; 2022, 141; Pavel 2015, 139; Laborde and Ronzoni 2016, 286; Unger 2022, 3).

Disagreements about whether a democratic world state is an ideal worth pursuing are partly rooted in disagreement over the interpretation and importance of values such as equality, freedom, community, identity, and tradition. But the disagreements are also driven by different understandings of the *empirical* realities of world politics. Perceptions of empirical circumstances and constraints determine which global institutions are deemed achievable and viable. But they also play a part in judgements on which ones are (more) desirable. Take for instance the contemporary republican school of political theory inaugurated by Philip Pettit (1997) and Quentin

Skinner (1998). Despite adopting the ideal of nondomination (understood as robust freedom from arbitrary interference) as their common starting point, republican thinkers disagree on which institutions are best suited to promote that ideal, with some supporting protections for state sovereignty, some favouring a global republic, and others preferring an intermediate arrangement or something else altogether. Miriam Ronzoni (2017) suggests that this wide divergence is due to each author prioritizing only one or two of the three desiderata that ideally should guide republican institutional design: (1) bringing informal power under rule-governed control, (2) avoiding excessive concentration of power, and (3) promoting an active and vigilant citizenry. Ronzoni argues that republican global institutional design requires a careful exercise of balancing that gives full attention to all three desiderata. I would emphasize that the extent to which different institutions further those goals cannot be ascertained purely through philosophical analysis: rather, it requires systematic engagement with empirical research. The same can be said about debates on institutional design within other traditions in international political theory.

Despite the importance of systematic empirical evidence for assessing the idea of a world state, such evidence plays only a marginal role in most contributions to the debate. Some leading political theorists dismissed the idea of a world state simply by referring to what Kant had written two centuries earlier (Held 1995, 230; Rawls 1999b, 36). When some prominent social scientists touched upon the question of global democracy, they did so impressionistically, without adopting the systematic approach they have applied to other topics (R. Dahl 1999a, 1999b, 2001; Keohane 2003, 2006, 2015). To be sure, there are exceptions to this generalization, such as the important work of Michael Zürn (2000, 2016, 2018) and Robert Goodin (2010, 2012, 2016, 2022). Also relevant are studies that empirically demonstrate and systematically explain the democratization of aspects of global politics, even when they do not address world state formation as such (e.g. Payne and Samhat 2004; Scholte 2011; Tallberg et al. 2013; Stevenson and Dryzek 2014; Grigorescu 2015; Schimmelfennig et al. 2020; Agné 2022). Overall, however, empirical research on these questions remains scarce, especially considering the wealth of data on democracy, statehood, and other relevant phenomena that has become available since the time of Kant and Cloots.

This book builds a bridge between normative and empirical analyses by identifying the factual assumptions that underlie prominent positions on democratic global governance and by evaluating those assumptions against relevant empirical evidence. In this endeavour, I align with the terminological preferences of the early proponents of global democratic statehood and focus the analysis on the *universal republic*, sometimes abbreviated to UR for conciseness (Cloots 1792/1979; L'Aurora 1796/1956; Hugo 1848/1875; Garibaldi *c.*1871/1934; Woodhull 1872/2010). For the purposes of this investigation, 'universal republic' denotes a political entity with the following features. First, it is a *state*. To be a state, a political organization must have the authority to create collectively binding rules on an important (but not necessarily comprehensive) range of issues, to enforce compliance with those rules using means of coercion when necessary, and to access the resources it needs through some form of taxation. A state does not need to have a monopoly of legislation, coercion, and taxation over its territory—these powers can be shared across multiple levels of governance. However, it needs to have sufficient authority and resources to be able to protect individuals and groups from the power wielded by other individuals and groups. States perform legislative, executive, and judicial functions, although how these functions are distributed among different organs can vary greatly. The second feature of the universal republic is that it is a *democratic* state. For operational purposes, I consider democratic a state that meets the conditions stated by Robert Dahl (1998, 85–86): it has robust institutional protections for the right of citizens to form and join organizations, to exercise freedom of expression and to access alternative sources of information, and all adult citizens must be able to control the acts of key state officials by choosing between competing candidates and holding them accountable through free, fair, and frequent elections.[4] These are minimal conditions, and the implications of 'thicker' forms of democracy will be considered later in this book. I also assume, with Cloots and others, that the citizens of a universal republic would have a direct relationship with its institutions, as opposed to an indirect one that is fully mediated through the national layer of government. The third feature of the universal republic is that it aims to be *globally inclusive*. Its democracy entails a global *demos* (List and Koenig-Archibugi 2010). This does not necessarily mean authority over the whole global population from the beginning—at least some UR advocates assumed it would emerge from a gradual enlargement process (Cloots 1792/1979; Woodhull 1872/2010). But I assume that two conditions must be met for a political entity to qualify as UR. First, it must be open to including on an equal basis all populations that express a wish for membership, as long as their representatives in UR institutions are

---

[4] This definition concerns specifically the democratic character of *state institutions*. Hence, its adoption does not imply a position on what democracy is in general, whether it manifests itself in social processes and practices beyond formal institutions, and what forms democracy beyond the state could take. These questions are investigated in depth by Agné (2022, 33–93) and they will become especially relevant in Part II of this book, where polycentric forms of global democracy are considered.

chosen through free and fair elections. Second, the universal republic needs to control sufficient resources to be able to protect its citizens from coercion and harm initiated by outsiders.[5] In practice, this requires that a 'critical mass' of states have transferred authority to the UR, including the authority to obtain resources through taxation. The fourth feature of the universal republic is that it is a *federal* state. Most decisions would be taken within lower jurisdictions, at national and subnational levels. As Goodin (2012) pointed out, virtually all proposals for world government take the form of a federal arrangement, where authority over some issues is *constitutionally* reserved for layers of government that encompass a more limited circle of citizens and are closer to them. Constitutional entrenchment means that authority cannot be claimed unilaterally by the higher level of government. However, I assume that the division of competences would emerge from a constitutional deliberative process rather than from theoretical postulates.

In sum, this book examines the viability, achievability, and comparative desirability of a universal republic in the light of relevant empirical facts. But how can the facts to which we have access help us answer questions about something that has never existed? John Rawls described the essence of the problem:

> [T]he limits of the possible are not given by the actual, for we can to a greater or lesser extent change political and social institutions and much else. Hence we have to rely on conjecture and speculation, arguing as best we can that the social world we envision is feasible and might actually exist, if not now then at some future time under happier circumstances. (Rawls 1999b, 12)

If the realization of an ideal is feasible in this broad sense, then it is a 'realistic utopia' (Rawls 1999b, 11–12). But how can we ensure that the 'conjecture and speculation' Rawls regarded as necessary are sufficiently disciplined and stringent? What follows are some reflections on the overall strategy adopted throughout the book, leaving the details about the methods to later chapters. The strategy combines elements of 'classical' and 'scientific' approaches to the study of global politics. Hedley Bull defined the scientific approach as aspiring 'to a theory of international relations whose propositions are based either upon logical or mathematical proof, or upon strict, empirical

---

[5] Kant (2016, 69–70) appears to have hinted at this condition in this remark: 'A world republic would in any case be one where no individual state would have enough forces to fight the great republic if necessary...'

procedures of verification' (Bull 1966, 362). By contrast, he saw the classical approach as being

characterized above all by explicit reliance upon the exercise of judgment and by the assumptions that if we confine ourselves to strict standards of verification and proof there is very little of significance that can be said about international relations, that general propositions about this subject must therefore derive from a scientifically imperfect process of perception or intuition, and that these general propositions cannot be accorded anything more than the tentative and inconclusive status appropriate to their doubtful origin. (Bull 1966, 361)

Among the questions 'of significance' that classical authors have been willing to tackle is the possibility and desirability of world government. Bull himself discussed it in *The Anarchical Society* as one of the conceivable alternatives to the states system (Bull 1977, 244–245, 252–254). Hans Morgenthau and other classical Realist writers also engaged deeply with the problem of a world state (Schwarzenberger 1951; Schuman 1952; Morgenthau 1954, 469–485; Herz 1959; cf. Scheuerman 2011), as have other authors writing in a classical vein (e.g. Ewing 1947; Zimmern 1953; Claude 1956; Wight 1959/2022, 1991; Aron 1966, 1972; Falk 1975). By contrast, authors oriented towards the scientific approach have been more reluctant to engage with the topic. This may well be because they found it too speculative and unamenable to rigorous empirical hypothesis-testing. By tackling questions about fundamentally different forms of world order, this book follows in the footsteps of classically oriented scholars of international relations.

On the other hand, advocates of the scientific approach had a point when they criticized their opponents for frequently leaving their assumptions implicit rather than stating them explicitly, and for remaining ambiguous about which variables and observations play a part in reaching a judgement and how they are combined (Kaplan 1966; Singer 1969). Even when they do not settle questions with appeal to authority, the reliance of classically oriented scholars on 'intuition' and 'judgement' makes it difficult to evaluate to what extent they transcended preconceptions and biases—and what Singer (1969, 78) derided as 'the old faith in the folklore and conventional wisdom of a particular time and place'.[6]

---

[6] Social scientists do not have a strong record in forecasting societal change. However, there is some evidence that social scientists who rely on data-based modelling as a basis for their forecasts tend to be somewhat more accurate compared to those who rely on intuitions or theoretical considerations (Grossmann et al. 2023).

For these reasons, this book examines some of the questions that classically oriented scholars were and are willing to address with some of the methods privileged by scientifically oriented researchers. Such methods have several advantages. First, the collection of relevant data is more systematic, with inclusion criteria determined in advance of the analysis. This reduces the risk that findings are driven by particularly prominent but not necessarily representative cases, experiences, and informants. Second, the procedures involve transparency and auditability regarding assumptions, research design, and data. In short, it should be possible for others to replicate the results by applying the same research protocol to the same data. Third, systematic and transparent procedures help make knowledge more cumulative by enabling other researchers to modify and improve the ingredients of the research and check whether and how any conclusions change. This is especially important for the question addressed in this book. I have no choice but to make a substantial number of assumptions that some readers may find dubious or unpersuasive. Each step of the argument aims to present such assumptions as clearly as possible and put other researchers in a position to replace them with alternative assumptions if they wish. While I present some substantive conclusions on the questions at hand, this project has the equally important aim of offering a basis for future conversations that may end up overturning its original conclusions.

With its focus on the empirical dimensions of global political integration and democratization, this book closely relates to two strands of research in the recent literature. The first strand identifies and explains developments that can be seen as increasing the democratic quality of politics beyond the state.[7] These studies may lead to the conclusion that global democracy is possible simply because it already exists—at least to some extent and in some contexts. The second strand finds elements of global statehood in the current international system.[8] Again, these studies may suggest that a world state is possible simply because, in some way, it is here already. Both strands are very important and several of the findings generated by them

---

[7] The literature is substantial and includes, for instance, Payne and Samhat (2004); Nanz and Steffek (2005); Scholte (2005, 2011); Bäckstrand (2006); T. Macdonald and K. Macdonald (2006, 2020); Steffek, Kissling, and Nanz (2007); T. Macdonald (2008); K. Macdonald and T. Macdonald (2010); K. Macdonald (2012); Jönsson and Tallberg (2010); Krisch (2010); Steffek (2010); Steffek and Hahn (2010); Tallberg and Uhlin (2012); Little and Macdonald (2013); Tallberg et al. (2013, 2014); Kuyper (2014); Stevenson and Dryzek (2014); Grigorescu (2015, 2023); Stevenson (2016); Koenig-Archibugi and Macdonald (2017); Kuyper and Squatrito (2017); Squatrito (2018); Martens, van der Linden, and Wörsdörfer (2019); Schimmelfennig et al. (2020); Agné (2022).

[8] Studies positing the existence of global statehood are fewer and more heavily qualified than those finding instances of global democracy (Shaw 2000; Chimni 2004; Albert and Stichweh 2007; Goodin 2012).

play an important role in the assessment of achievability conducted here (see especially section 4.4.). However, this book is distinctive in its focus on the *combination* of global statehood and democracy, which is a defining feature of the universal republic. This is important because the elements of global democracy that already exist are largely disconnected from global statehood, and the existing elements of global statehood are mostly disconnected from global democracy. Consider for instance Goodin's argument that the 'defining features of statehood are found, in at least rudimentary form, at the global level today' (Goodin 2012, 153). Specifically, he points out that international organizations and perhaps even individual states are 'legally permitted' (Goodin 2012, 158) to intervene against governments that violate *jus cogens*—by committing aggression, genocide, crimes against humanity, war crimes, slavery, and torture. This point does not settle the questions addressed in this book. First, today participation in enforcement action remains essentially a voluntary choice, which points at a qualitative difference between how law enforcement works in the contemporary international system and how it is supposed to work in a state. The universal republic would be expected to enforce its laws in a less haphazard way than what we have now. Second, what legal authority there is today is not usually wielded in line with democratic principles. As Hans Kelsen (among many others) pointed out when the United Nations was created, 'The veto right of the five permanent members of the Security Council places them above the law of the United Nations, establishes their legal hegemony over all the other Members, and thus stamps the Organization with the mark of an autocratic regime' (Kelsen 1946, 1121).

The starting point of this investigation is thus the observation that supranational authority and democratic processes are both present in the contemporary system, but that they would need to be joined more closely as well as strengthened to give rise to something like the universal republic. To be sure, thoughtful contributors to the debate on world order have questioned whether strengthening global statehood is necessary for, or indeed even beneficial to, global democracy. This important question is addressed in Part II, especially Chapter 7.

The book has two main parts, which are devoted respectively to the feasibility and the desirability of the universal republic. The two questions are tackled in this order because the alleged infeasibility of a democratic world state is often treated as a 'normative argument-stopper', a dialogical device that Southwood and Goodin (2021, 966) describe as follows: 'If a proposed policy makes infeasible demands, then the merits or demerits of that policy are of no practical consequence. It is irrelevant how desirable or undesirable it would be to successfully realize the policy—it simply cannot be the case that we ought, practically speaking, to bring it about.' As Southwood also put it, the function of feasibility assessments is to determine whether a particular course of action is 'deliberation-worthy', i.e. whether it should be included among 'the set of options that are candidates for consideration within practical deliberation' (Southwood 2022, 130). The feasibility of a democratic world state has been questioned by authors who reject it on principled grounds as well as authors who are sympathetic to the idea. Among the former is Anne-Marie Slaughter (2004, 8), who dismissed world government as 'both infeasible and undesirable'.[9] Among the latter is Hans Kelsen, who declared: 'There can be no doubt that the ideal solution of the problem of world organization as the problem of world peace is the establishment of a World Federal State composed of all or as many nations as possible. The realization of this idea, however, is confronted with serious and, at least at present, insurmountable difficulties' (Kelsen 1944a, 5).[10] A third position does not declare a global democratic state to be infeasible, but more modestly points out that its proponents have not done enough to show it might be viable, given the ubiquitous problem of institutional design failing to attain its intended goals (Pavel 2015, 139).

The conception of feasibility adopted in Part I has two dimensions. The first dimension is *viability*, which can be defined as having a reasonable chance of persisting over time and working in the intended way. This concept is similar to the notion of stability, which Gilabert and Lawford-Smith (2012, 820) define as 'the extent to which its continued presence does not clash with general empirical truths about how people are or can be in their social life as they apply to the circumstances in which the scheme is instantiated'. The second dimension of feasibility is *achievability*, which refers to the existence of transition paths from the status quo to the intended end state. Chapter 2 discusses three issues. First, it elaborates on and makes more precise these understandings of viability and achievability, in general and in relation to the problem at hand. Then it presents an overview of various

---

[9] For a similar stance see Unger (2022, 3) and Isensee (2003), who applies to the world state the remark about perpetual peace uttered by the Prussian army's chief of staff: 'just a dream and not even a beautiful one' (Isensee 2003, 31).

[10] Nevertheless, Kelsen went on to describe a path to global judicialization, after which 'we can try to make a further step; we can hope to succeed in organizing a centralized executive power, a world police, and later perhaps a world administration under a world parliament' (Kelsen 1944b, 389). Kelsen regarded 'the organizational unity of a universal legal community, that is, the emergence of a world state', as the logical outcome of his 'pure theory of law' (Kelsen 1967, 328; more fully in Kelsen 1920, 249–257). Hersh Lauterpacht (1950, 456–463) held a similar position on world federation.

arguments that cast doubt on the feasibility of a world state—specifically a democratic world government—by invoking motivational, structural, or institutional constraints. The chapter concludes with a discussion of the challenge of gauging empirically the feasibility of such an unprecedented institution.

Chapter 3 presents an empirical assessment of the viability arguments reviewed in Chapter 2. The method involves two steps: first, I use a machine-learning method called lasso (least absolute shrinkage and selection opera-tor) to build statistical models of democratic survival that considers a range of geographical, economic, cultural, and social variables to predict the longevity of democratic institutions in most countries of the world over a period of 120 years; second, I simulate the expected longevity of democracy in a hypothet-ical state that is assumed to have values of the current world on each of those variables. Such a hypothetical 'world state' is the universal republic. The start-ing point is a model including variables with good data coverage over time and space, which is then modified to take into account several other variables related to the arguments reviewed in Chapter 2.

Chapter 4 considers achievability arguments and is methodologically more diverse. Arguments about structural constraints are again assessed through a statistical simulation based on the political experiences of countries, this time aimed at deriving a simulated counterfactual predicted level of democracy of a hypothetical world state given the cultural, economic, and social condi-tions of the world as we know it. Arguments about motivational constraints are assessed through the evaluation of a mass of evidence, collected mainly through public opinion surveys but also through text analysis and coding of the institutional design and funding of international organizations.

The evidence presented in Part I provides reasons for regarding the univer-sal republic as achievable and viable, and thus 'deliberation-worthy'. Hence, Part II proceeds to assessing its desirability. The aim here is not to develop a novel set of principles that should guide global institutional design. I draw on the existing philosophical literature to formulate a set of normative postulates that can provide a coherent framework for assessing institutional arrange-ments in the light of relevant empirical information about the world. As such, the chapters in this part are an exercise in what Charles Beitz dubbed 'normative political science'.[11] Chapter 5 develops an argument about what makes the universal republic a normatively attractive institutional ideal. The

---

[11] Beitz (1998, 831) explains: 'Cosmopolitanism need not make any assumptions at all about the best political structure for international affairs; whether there should be an overarching, global political orga-nization, and if so, how authority should be divided between the global organization and its subordinate

argument proceeds in three steps: first, it presents a set of normative postulates that can guide institutional assessments; second, it examines empirical facts about the world that require a global extension of democratic governance; third, it discusses how the institutions of the UR could fulfil that requirement.

The last two chapters of the book reflect the circumstance that the universal republic is not the only solution that has been proposed for combining global governance and democracy. Two other broad approaches have received a substantial amount of attention (Archibugi, Koenig-Archibugi, and Marchetti 2012). One is the 'negative surrogate' that Kant settled for: a voluntary association of states with domestic republican institutions. Here it will be called a confederation of democracies. Chapter 6 examines several arguments on why a confederation of democracies would be normatively superior to a UR or vice versa, discusses the empirical assumptions of such arguments, and assesses them based on empirical data. The other approach is polycentric democracy. This concept encompasses a more diverse set of institutional proposals, which share the vision of democratic practices being instituted in a large variety of transnational settings, both governmental and nongovernmental, without an overarching and unified institutional structure. Chapter 7 develops a conceptual and empirical argument on the advantages of a UR over polycentric democracy in translating popular preferences over global policies into collective decisions.

To conclude this introduction, it is advisable to say something also about what the book does not aim to do. In previous work I considered the question of whether global democracy is possible, reaching the conclusion that it is not impossible (Koenig-Archibugi 2011b, 2012b). As Zürn (2018, 233) rightly points out, rejecting impossibility claims does not tell us much about whether something is likely. Zürn (2016, 2018) himself discussed which cosmopolitan institutional model is more likely to be realized in the light of contemporary trends. This is a valuable exercise, but this book will not follow in its track by gauging the likelihood that a universal republic may come about in the foreseeable future, in absolute terms or relative to the two other institutional models considered here (the confederation of democracies and polycentric democracy). This might be seen as a weakness by some (e.g. Shapiro 2016, 111), but I would disagree. I think that the main contribution that social

---

political elements, is properly understood as a problem for normative political science rather than for political philosophy itself.'

science can offer to the political practices of citizens, groups, and officials in relation to the universal republic is to help them decide whether the notion is 'deliberation-worthy' and, if it is, to help them decide whether it is normatively attractive enough to deserve their support. They will then take care of the rest.[12]

---

[12] As noted earlier, social scientists do not seem to have a strong record in forecasting societal change anyway (Grossmann et al. 2023).

PART I

IS THE UNIVERSAL REPUBLIC POSSIBLE?

2
Arguments on possibility

Most authors who have written extensively about a democratic world state have either implicitly assumed that it is possible or explicitly suggested reasons for believing that it is. However, such authors constitute only a small minority among the writers who have addressed questions of world order. More common are statements denying the feasibility of a world state, especially one taking a democratic form (e.g. Bull 1977, 252; Riker 1995, 513; Doyle 2000, 20; Hoffmann 2003, 34; Kingsbury, Krisch, and Stewart 2005, 27; Kamminga 2006, 37; Keohane 2006, 77; Lovett 2016, 34; Shapiro 2016, 111; Mearsheimer 2018, 122–123; Pettit 2022, 141). Sceptics nowadays tend to abstain from the kind of sarcasm displayed by Frederick the Great in a letter to Voltaire on the plan for European federation proposed by Charles-Irénée Castel, abbé de Saint-Pierre: 'The thing is most practicable; for its success all that is lacking is the consent of Europe and a few similar trifles' (Aldington 1927, 161). However, the notion of a democratic world state is frequently brushed away without further elaboration, possibly because the reasons are considered quite obvious. But some authors are more specific and argue that a democratic world state is impossible because of the absence, at the global level, of some supposedly necessary *conditions* for democracy (R. Dahl 1999b, 927; Buchanan and Keohane 2006, 416).[1]

This chapter does three things. The first section develops an interpretation of possibility as feasibility. Based on recent literature on feasibility, I will propose an approach to thinking about the feasibility of the universal republic that is usable for empirical analysis. Given that this notion of feasibility involves the operation of constraints, the central sections of the chapter reformulate common arguments about the world state in terms of a set of constraints on feasibility. The focus is on three types, which are labelled motivational, structural, and institutional constraints. The final section discusses the challenge of evaluating such constraints empirically.

---

[1] Some authors do not rule out that a world state may emerge, but deny that it would be organized democratically. For instance, Zolo (1997, 166) claimed that a 'world government which developed out of existing international institutions and which based itself on the cosmopolitan model would of necessity be a despotic and totalitarian Leviathan, condemned to resort to the use of crushing military measures in response to the inevitable proliferation of violence'.

The Universal Republic. Mathias Koenig-Archibugi, Oxford University Press. © Mathias Koenig-Archibugi (2024). DOI: 10.1093/9780198921158.003.0002

2.1 Possibility as feasibility

The nature and conceptualization of political possibility has been debated extensively by political philosophers during the past two decades. In this section, I discuss some of the key distinctions and insights that emerged from this debate and that have been particularly relevant in structuring the analysis presented in this book. Most of the debate revolves around the concept of *feasibility*, and I will adopt this conceptualization while coming back to its relationship with other notions of possibility in due course.

The first distinction is between *viability* and *achievability* as two dimensions of feasibility (Wright 2010, 20–25). To assess the viability of a hypothetical institutional order, we need to determine whether, once it is established, it would continue to work in the way envisaged by its proponents. To assess its achievability, we need to determine whether there is a plausible path of political change that would lead from the status quo to the alternative order. Some authors express similar ideas using different words, such as 'stability' instead of 'viability', and 'accessibility' instead of 'achievability' (Rawls 1999a, 434–441; Buchanan 2004, 61; Cohen 2009, 56–57; Gilabert and Lawford-Smith 2012, 812–813). The distinction between assessing viability and assessing achievability was very clear to Rousseau when he commented on the abbé de Saint-Pierre's plan: 'although the plan was very wise, the means for executing it make one feel the author's simplicity ... he saw rather well the effect of things if they were established, but ... he judged the means for establishing them like a child' (Rousseau 1782/2005, 56–57).[2]

The second distinction is between conceiving feasibility as a binary condition, where a state of affairs is either possible or impossible, and conceiving it as a matter of degree. Treating feasibility as a matter of degree enables observers to rank alternative proposals according to how feasible they are (Gilabert and Lawford-Smith 2012, 812).

The third distinction is between hard and soft constraints on feasibility. Gilabert and Lawford-Smith (2012) distinguish between hard and soft constraints based on two criteria. First, hard constraints rule out outcomes, while soft constraints make them less likely. Second, soft constraints are in principle malleable and dynamic, in the sense that, even when they cannot be overcome today, they might at some later time. Gilabert and Lawford-Smith (2012) classify as hard constraints those stemming from logic as well

---

[2] More than two centuries later, Philippe Schmitter berated proponents of cosmopolitan democracy for deficient thinking on both counts: 'What is even more discouraging than a credible idea of the end-product is the almost complete absence of any idea of the process whereby the world might get there' (Schmitter 1999, 940).

as physical and biological laws, and as soft constraints those stemming from economic, cultural, and institutional circumstances.

A feature of most recent conceptualizations of feasibility is that they are agent-centric, as they treat an outcome as (more) feasible if there are agents that can bring it about through their actions. A particularly influential approach is the 'dispositional' account, which in one formulation states: 'For any agent a, it is feasible for a to achieve an outcome O if and only if (i) a would be reasonably likely to succeed in achieving O if a were to try; and (ii) it is not the case that a is robustly disposed not to try to achieve O' (Southwood and Goodin 2021, 5; based on Brennan and Southwood 2007; Southwood 2016; Stemplowska 2016). This account posits two individually necessary and jointly sufficient conditions in order for it to be feasible for an agent to achieve an outcome. Condition (i) focuses on the likelihood of an outcome occurring without declaring it unfeasible just because the agent doesn't try, or try hard enough, to bring it about. Lack of motivation as such does not rule out feasibility. Condition (ii) recognizes that sometimes agents are unable to try. The condition would not be necessary if, as Gilabert and Lawford-Smith (2012) maintained, 'trying is something that people can always do' (considering that trying to act is different from actually acting). Stemplowska (2016), however, argues that sometimes it is impossible for people even to try. In this account, motivational failure can occur not only because of mere unwillingness to try but also because of genuine motivational inability (e.g. phobias), and in such cases the action should not be considered feasible. If an agent is affected by such motivational inability, we can say that she is *robustly* disposed not to try—this is the meaning intended in the wording of condition (ii) above. Distinguishing between mere unwillingness and motivational inability is challenging, however. Stemplowska (2016) proposes the following test: motivational failure is an instance of genuine motivational inability when there exists no conceivable (positive or negative) incentive that would bring the agent's motivational state in line with what is needed to perform the action in question. Conversely, if the agent is responsive to incentives, then failure to try should be interpreted as an instance of mere unwillingness and not rule out feasibility.

Agent-centric accounts are helpful to clarify the essential elements of feasibility, but they are not without complications (Southwood 2018, 4). One is that most outcomes of interest to political theorists cannot be achieved by individuals but can be produced only by the actions of multiple agents (if at all) (Stemplowska 2016). Hence, we need to distinguish the likelihood that collective action would be reasonably likely to succeed in achieving an outcome from the likelihood that agents succeed in acting collectively. This adds complexity to assessments of feasibility.

Another complication is that it is not clear whether a question about the possibility of an institutional arrangement in a particular context can be reframed as a question about action, such as whether a group would be reasonably likely to succeed in realizing or maintaining that arrangement if it were to try. Southwood (2018, 4) notes that, for instance, 'the question of whether democracy is feasible in Equatorial Guinea seems to be a different question from, and not settled by, the question of whether it is feasible for any individual or group agent to realise or maintain democracy in Equatorial Guinea'. I do not aim to contribute a novel solution to this ongoing research agenda. However, for the purposes of this book I will assume that this action/institutions problem can be mitigated by avoiding an assumption that seems to come with at least some agent-centric accounts of feasibility, which is that achieving the outcome in question must be the explicit goal of the agents when they perform the relevant action. Avoiding this assumption seems especially plausible when considering the viability/stability of institutional arrangements. It seems intuitively straightforward to say that an institution is viable when it is feasible for agents to perform actions that, in aggregate, contribute to maintaining the institution, even when the actors are not necessarily motivated by the goal of ensuring the survival of the institution (although they may be). Since at least Mandeville's *The Fable of the Bees*, much modern social theory invokes precisely such an understanding of stability and change of social institutions (Sugden 1989; Smith 2006). When we consider the achievability of political institutions, on the other hand, it seems less straightforward to detach it from action that specifically aimed at creating the institution. At least, this seems the case with formal institutions, which almost always entail an element of intentional design beyond purely spontaneous evolution. This is perhaps clearest in relation to constitution-making. On the one hand, participants in constitution-making are driven by a variety of motivations—which Elster (2018) divides into three groups: reason, interests, and emotions. On the other hand, it seems right to say that a constitution is achievable only when the relevant political actors would be reasonably likely to obtain a constitution if they were to make an intentional attempt at creating one, rather than treating it as an emergent by-product of other activities.

We can now apply these ideas and concepts to the feasibility of the universal republic. The starting point is the distinction between achievability and viability. The next step is the identification of the agents that would play a crucial role in making the UR achievable and viable. For analytical purposes, it is plausible to assume that the set of agents relevant to achievability is not identical to the set that is relevant to viability. For the analysis of achievability,

I focus on the agents that are most likely to play a decisive role in intentionally bringing the UR about. In principle, there can be two kinds of scenarios. In the first scenario, the key agents are governments as agents authorized to act on behalf of states, which would transfer authority to a new central entity while also shaping its institutional design. In the second scenario, non-state actors create a new institutional structure and then, bypassing states, persuade populations to transfer their allegiance to the new institutions. The second scenario is not unthinkable. For instance, Falk and Strauss (2000, 209) urged civil society organizations to 'bypass their sovereign intermediaries and act directly to create an international organization' and specifically a 'Global Peoples Assembly' (see also Monbiot 2003). They conjectured that such an assembly created independently of states but with delegates directly elected by citizens around the world would, over time, acquire increased popular legitimacy, benefit from sociopolitical and ideological dynamics of empowerment, and eventually be accepted by states themselves as a legitimate global legislature. While this is an interesting perspective, in this book I will adopt what many would consider the more conventional and realistic scenario mentioned above, which assumes that the establishment of the UR would consist of a transfer of authority from states, including the authority to obtain resources from social actors through some form of taxation. This does not necessarily mean that every state needs to actively pursue its establishment. The universal republic can be established if it is supported by a critical mass of states, where the quantification of the critical mass needs to be left open for the time being. Once the critical mass of states has transferred authority to the UR, other states may decide to join—for instance, because of what Gruber (2000) has called 'go-it-alone power'.[3]

This discussion yields the following test of achievability:

Achievability (binary): *The universal republic is achievable if and only if (i) a critical mass of states would be reasonably likely to succeed in transferring authority to it if they were to try; and (ii) those states are able to try to transfer authority to the universal republic.*

Here and in the following I use the more concise expression 'are able to try' as a shorthand for the more precise 'it is not the case that they are robustly disposed not to try' (Southwood and Goodin 2021).

---

[3] I make a further assumption, in agreement with Bummel (2021, 327): 'the nuclear armament at the disposal of some states means that the consolidation of the system of states into a single worldwide unit by the exercise or threat of military force by a hegemonic power is impossible in practical terms'. This does not necessarily rule out hegemonic leadership as a potential transition path towards the universal republic (Belic and Miklosi 2023).

As noted above, Gilabert and Lawford-Smith (2012) argue that, when the constraints are soft rather than hard, it makes sense to think of feasibility also as a matter of degree. (To recall, hard constraints rule out outcomes, while soft constraints make them less likely, and are malleable.) I follow Stemplowska (2016, 282–283) in positing that the variation of achievability tracks the varying likelihood of successful action rather than a potentially robust disposition not to try, which either exists or not (although the latter could be in principle be a matter of degree as well). On that basis, we can formulate a scalar version of the achievability condition:

Achievability (scalar): *The universal republic is more achievable when (i) a critical mass of states would be more likely to succeed in transferring authority to it, provided that they try; and (ii) those states are able to try to transfer authority to the universal republic.*

Moving now on to viability, the identification of the relevant agents is somewhat more complex, for two reasons. First, as noted above, the viability/stability of an institutional arrangement is ensured not only by actions that have the explicit goal of maintaining that arrangement, but also by actions that contribute to maintaining it more indirectly, notably by any action that complies with the rules constituting or deriving from the institutional arrangement, regardless of what motivates it. Second, once a UR is established, its survival depends not only on the actions of its member states but also on those of individual citizens and the groups they belong to. The UR effectively creates a 'domestic' political system whose stability depends on the willingness and ability of a wide range of actors—individuals, interest groups, political parties, social movements, ethnic and religious groups, 'local' governments, and so on—to interact with one another and with the organs of the UR according to the 'rules of the game'. Based on these considerations, I formulate the following viability conditions:

Viability (binary): *The universal republic is viable if and only if (i) a critical mass of citizens and groups would be reasonably likely to succeed in complying with its rules, provided that they try; and (ii) those citizens and groups are able to try to comply with the rules of the universal republic.*

We can also formulate a scalar version:

Viability (scalar): *The universal republic is more viable when (i) a critical mass of citizens and groups would be more likely to succeed in complying with its rules if they were to try; and (ii) those citizens and groups are able to try to comply with the rules of the universal republic.*

Recall how Gilabert and Lawford-Smith (2012) distinguished between hard and soft constraints: (i) hard constraints rule out outcomes (binary test), while soft constraints make them less likely (scalar test), and (ii) soft constraints are in principle malleable and dynamic, in the sense that, even when they cannot be overcome today, they might at some later time. More specifically they classified as hard constraints those stemming from logic as well as physical and biological laws, and as soft constraints those stemming from economic, cultural, and institutional circumstances. These distinctions are helpful in structuring the debate on the feasibility of the universal republic.

We can start by noting that the review of arguments presented in the remainder of this chapter will show that they generally do not point at hard constraints as they are understood here. In the social sciences, examples of statements about *logical* possibility are the impossibility theorems proved by axiomatic social choice theory (Arrow 1951; List and Pettit 2002) and the so-called 'impossible trinity' of fixed exchange rate, free capital movement, and independent monetary policy that derives from the assumptions of the Mundell–Fleming model in international economics. The arguments reviewed in the following do not suggest that the universal republic is a logically contradictory notion, hence what is at stake is not its logical possibility. In principle, it is possible to make a case against the *metaphysical* possibility of the universal republic. One argument is grounded in a specific conception of the political: 'The political entity presupposes the existence of an enemy and therefore the co-existence with another state. As long as a state exists, there will thus always be in the world more than just one state. A world state which embraces the entire globe and all of humanity cannot exist' (Schmitt 1932/1996, 53; cf. Kojève 1943/2000, 126). A related line of argument is that (a) the universal republic would require a global *demos*, (b) a global *demos* would require a shared global identity, and (c) a global identity is metaphysically impossible because every collective identity needs an external 'Other' and thus can never be global. Metaphysical impossibility arguments against global democracy will not receive further consideration here, because they have been thoroughly analysed and persuasively refuted by Wendt (2003), Abizadeh (2005), and Bartelson (2008, 2009).

These considerations suggest that the debate on the feasibility of the universal republic is mainly about the nature and severity of soft constraints. For this reason, some proponents of world government have emphasized the central role of motivations. The clearest statement is due to Albert Einstein. Responding to scepticism directed against his advocacy for world government, he retorted: 'Eventualities which depend solely upon the decisions of men should never, in advance, be labelled "impossible". In the sphere of human activity, everything depends on the strength of men's convictions' (Einstein 1946/2007, 380). Winston Churchill displayed a similar attitude with more rhetorical flourish in the famous speech he delivered in Zurich in 1946: 'We must build a kind of United States of Europe ... The process is simple. All that is needed is the resolve of hundreds of millions of men and women to do right instead of wrong and to gain as their reward blessing instead of cursing' (Churchill 1946/2003, 428).

Of course, Einstein was right to insist that physical possibility is different from social possibility. Physicists regard the impossibility of travelling faster than light as an objective constraint that operates independently of people's beliefs about the existence of that constraint; the possibility of social events, on the contrary, depends in part on beliefs about their possibility. Specifically, the possibility of global democracy is not independent from people's beliefs about the possibility of global democracy; nor is it independent from people's beliefs about its desirability (Koenig-Archibugi 2011b). However, sceptics can legitimately retort that individual beliefs about possibility and desirability are shaped not only by immediate processes of social communication and deliberation, but also by structural and institutional circumstances that are in the background of belief formation. Such sceptics may concede that the relevance of such circumstances is not naturally given but instead activated by the very *political* arrangements that a world government is meant to supersede—or, as David Axelsen (2013) nicely put it, that 'anti-cosmopolitanism is created by the state'. That may provide a strong argument for the *un*desirability of the current global political order. But it only reinforces the point that there are substantial—perhaps insurmountable—obstacles to global political transformation.

For our purposes, it is useful to disaggregate the broader category of soft constraints into three groups: motivational constraints, structural constraints, and institutional constraints (Zürn 2000, 2016, 2018; Koenig-Archibugi 2012b). *Motivational constraints* concern the beliefs and preferences of individuals, social groups, and power-holders in relation to actual and hypothetical global political orders. *Structural constraints* refer to social relationships that have a significant degree of sticking power, notably ethnic and religious identities, language, and unequal access to economic resources. *Institutional constraints* refer to rule systems that may hinder or promote the development and functioning of global democratic institutions, such as the political regimes of the countries that would be components of the broader world polity. These three constraint types are not independent from each other. Most importantly, structural factors such as ethnicity, religious identities, and language can affect motivations. Motivations can also be affected by institutional arrangements. It is also likely that motivational factors, in turn, influence the long-term prospects of structural and institutional factors. Despite those interdependencies, it is still useful to distinguish between the three types because they reflect different degrees of *malleability*. Motivational constraints are more malleable than structural constraints, with institutional constraints arguably falling in between. If we use the scalar versions of the feasibility conditions stated earlier, we can say that structural constraints have a deeper impact on feasibility understood as agents being able to attempt actions that realize or maintain the UR and being likely to succeed if they try.

A different way of putting this is to say that departures from the status quo are *less* feasible if they require more things to be different from how they actually are. This notion can be expressed in the language of possible worlds. Let's call our existing world W_E. We can imagine a hypothetical world where a large majority of citizens and political leaders consider the UR to be both possible and desirable, but which otherwise is not much different from our world. In other words, we relax the motivational constraint. Let's call this alternative world W_M. We can also imagine a hypothetical world, W_S, where cultural and language diversity as well as economic inequality are much lower than they are in our world. This would involve relaxing structural constraints. Given the deep-rooted causes of cultural diversity and economic inequality, we would expect W_S to be different from W_E in *many other ways*, notably in relation to political, social, family, and educational structures as well as modes of production and exchange. The differences between W_E and W_S would be greater than between W_E and W_M—or, to put it differently, W_E would be *closer* to W_M than to W_S.

Institutional conditions are arguably in an intermediate position between motivational conditions and structural conditions. To imagine a world, W_I, in which all countries are governed democratically would entail numerous differences with W_E, but those differences would not be as large as those entailed by W_S. Furthermore, one could plausibly (but more speculatively) argue that W_E would be more distant from W_I than from W_M.

In section 2.5, we will return to the question of how the types of constraints relate to the tests of achievability and viability presented in this section. At this point, it is useful to contrast the approach to feasibility developed so far with a different approach to evaluating the prospects of a world state. Shapiro (2016) berated proponents of world government who simply argue that it is not utterly impossible. 'The social science question is: What evidence supports the claim that posited developments are likely or even plausible? A credible political argument would include specifying changes that could move the world toward the new order, identifying coalitions that could be formed to achieve ... those changes, and supplying an account of how they could be held together in light of the likely opposition' (Shapiro 2016, 111). In previous work, I sketched potential pathways to global democracy based on the main actors who may be driving the process (Koenig-Archibugi 2012b). I refrain from doing so here, and focus the analysis on constraints rather than drivers of transformation. If the constraints turn out to be quite loose, the prospects of change depend on the vagaries of rough-and-tumble politics, with coalitions forming and breaking in largely unpredictable ways, creating openings for arguments and persuasion. It may be worth noting that this approach is not radically different from the position defended by Shapiro himself in a different context: 'there is no single path to democracy, and, therefore, no generalization is to be had about the conditions that give rise to it. Democracy can result from decades of gradual evolution (Britain and the United States), imitation (India), cascades (most of Eastern Europe in 1989), collapse (Russia after 1991), imposition from above (Chile), revolutions (Portugal), negotiated settlements (Poland, Nicaragua, and South Africa), or external imposition (Japan and West Germany) ... Perhaps there are other possibilities' (Shapiro 2003, 80).[4]

The next three sections provide a survey of arguments holding that the pursuit of the UR or analogous schemes faces very substantial motivational, structural, and/or institutional constraints.

2.2 Motivational constraints

Motivational constraints concern the beliefs and desires of individuals, social groups, and those in control of state authority in relation to actual or hypothetical global orders. The argument to be considered in this context is that the universal republic is unfeasible because pivotal agents do not want its establishment and/or would not accept the UR's rules if it were established.

Traditionally, the attention has been focused on the political leaders of states. In this book, we will use the shorthand 'governments' when referring to them. The abbé de St Pierre attempted to show that it was in the self-interest of Europe's rulers to transfer authority to a 'European union', but Rousseau retorted that they would never accept such constraints: 'I ask whether there

---

[4] Similarly, Munck concludes that 'the accumulated empirical research does support the view (1) that there is more than one path to democracy and (2) that democracy can emerge under all sorts of conditions' (Munck 2015, 98, references omitted).

is in the world a single sovereign who, limited in this way forever in his dearest plans, would without indignation put up with the mere idea of seeing himself forced to be just, not only with Foreigners, but even with his own subjects' (Rousseau 1782/2005, 54). According to Kant, reason demands that states 'form an (always) growing *state of nations (civitas gentium)* that would finally encompass all the nations of the earth. But, in accordance with their idea of the right of nations, they do not at all want this, thus rejecting *in hypothesi* what is correct in *thesi*' (Kant 1795/1996, 328). Kelsen, who was very supportive of the idea of a world federal state in principle, noted that 'The government of a sovereign State is by its very nature inclined to resist any restriction upon its independence; and to become a member of a federal State means giving up completely one's independence' (Kelsen 1944a, 10; cf. also Mangone 1951, 41). Hedley Bull was adamant that 'There is not the slightest evidence that sovereign states in this century will agree to subordinate themselves to a world government founded upon consent' (Bull 1977, 252).

More recently, authors argued that it is citizens, and not just their governments, who reject the idea of world government (Duchacek 1986, 165; Rabkin 2005, 131; Pettit 2010b, 156). Laborde and Ronzoni (2016, 285) assert that '[t]he idea of replacing states with a global republic seems as unpopular as ever'. Miller is sceptical that many people would be prepared to accept the authority of a global democratic body such as a global parliament and to submit to the decisions taken by majorities: 'They might well think that they were exposing themselves to the risk of domination by a coalition of delegates from different places that might form along lines of economic interest or political ideology' (Miller 2010, 150). Nye is more specific about who might feel threatened by whom:

> treating the world as one global constituency implies the existence of a political community in which citizens of around 200 states would be willing to be continually outvoted by more than a billion Chinese and a billion Indians ... Minorities acquiesce in the will of a majority when they feel they participate in a larger community. There is little evidence that a sufficiently strong sense of community exists at the global level or that it could soon be created. (Nye 2002, 17).

From this perspective, attempts to bring about a cosmopolitan polity are destined to be resisted forcefully. As Martin Wight put it in the 1950s, '[t]hese dry theories and formulas of dusty dons and German professors about human commonwealths and *civitates maximae* can become politically explosive' (Wight 1991, 48).

In response, cosmopolitan authors often point out that the main instances of moral progress that occurred over the past centuries, such as the abolition of slavery and the extension of suffrage to women, resulted from the efforts of groups that succeeded in shifting wider perceptions of normative appropriateness towards emancipatory goals. Gerard Mangone argued in 1951 that '[t]o develop a cosmopolitan democratic outlook ... demands the mobilization of shock troops, imbued with a confidence in their mission, positively planning and executing a total campaign to win the minds and hearts of all people to fundamental principles of government and human conduct' (Mangone 1951, 217). An increasing number of social movements today can be considered part of a 'cosmopolitan avant-garde', as they aim to transform global social, economic, environmental, and political structures in ways that are guided by principles of global justice (Ypi 2012). Proponents of global democratization hope that activist groups will have a transformative impact on global political structures (Marchetti 2008; Archibugi and Held 2011; Cabrera 2010a, 2020).

However, sceptics retort that support for world government is lacking not only among the citizenry as a whole, but also among political movements. According to Sørensen (2013, 897), '[n]o major political faction in the world today argues in favor of a world state; there is simply no constituency for the visions of [its proponents]'. For Sørensen, the main reason for this is clear: 'The threat of interstate war no longer warrants a world state.'

An aspect that straddles motivational and structural constraints is the existence or absence of a 'collective identity' among the members of an existing or hypothetical state. For our purpose, the notion of collective identity should be disaggregated into motivational and structural elements. The motivational element of collective identity refers to the belief that a group—in this case, humankind as a whole—should be able to govern itself through democratic institutions and be subject to the authority of those institutions. From this perspective, the establishment and survival of the universal republic would be, to borrow the well-known expression of Ernest Renan, 'un plébiscite de tous les jours', a daily plebiscite (Renan 1882/2018). My approach of feasibility assumes that the universal republic is feasible only if this motivational element is present to a very substantial degree—or, to put it the other way round, the universal republic is impossible if motivational constraints are insurmountable. The analysis of viability offered in Chapter 3 *assumes* that this motivational condition has been fulfilled (otherwise the UR would not exist), whereas the analysis of achievability in Chapter 4 examines the possibility that it may be fulfilled in the foreseeable future.

By contrast, the structural dimension of collective identity reflects the widespread view that identification is not just a matter of 'free-floating' motivations, where people change their mind (or not) after listening to reasons and arguments for and against political proposals. Collective identities are instead taken to be deeply rooted in features that cannot (and perhaps should not) be changed easily, such as ethnic, cultural, religious, and linguistic belonging. Such factors are sometimes deemed 'prepolitical'. From this perspective, the infeasibility of the universal republic derives not just from the fact that people *now* do not identify sufficiently with humankind to sustain a global state, but more deeply from the fact that they will continue to lack that identification so long as the world remains as ethnically, culturally, religiously, and linguistically diverse as it is now. In this view, structural constraints limit the degree to which motivational constraints can be relaxed. Moreover, even if the motivational constraints were to loosen enough to allow the establishment of the universal republic, its survival as a democratic polity would be threatened by the structural diversity that would persist in the world population, by undermining the motivation to make the universal republic work. This type of argument is considered in more detail in section 2.3.

2.3 Structural constraints

Some authors who express scepticism about the possibility of a world state go beyond claiming that almost no politically relevant agent wants it now, by arguing that its establishment and survival would be undermined by deeper structural features of the social world. This section examines four such features: size, cultural heterogeneity, economic inequality, and the absence of (healthy) competition between polities.

The first structural obstacle to the possibility of a global state is the *size* of the population and territory over which it would have authority. It is a recurrent theme in Western political thinking that statehood becomes unstable and prone to collapse if its dimensions are excessive. The main classical source for this argument is Aristotle, who wrote that 'experience shows that a very populous city can rarely, if ever, be well governed' (Aristotle 1995, 2104–2105). Grotius cited an analogy from Aristotle in rejecting Dante's call for a universal monarchy: 'as a ship may attain such a size that it cannot be steered, so also the number of inhabitants and the distance between places may be so great as not to tolerate a single government' (Grotius 1646/1925, 552). According to Botero (1584, 53), 'states of large extension do not last long, because it happens that the prince does not have enough prudence to foresee all inconveniences and address all disorders that in a large empire necessarily are many and intense'. Kant concurred, noting that 'as the range of government expands laws progressively lose their vigor' (Kant 1795/1996, 336) and 'if such a state made up of nations were to extend too far over vast regions, governing it and so too protecting each of its members would finally have to become impossible' (Kant 1797/1996, 487).

A strand of thinking stresses specifically the problems that size poses to republican or democratic government. Montesquieu famously maintained that 'it is in the nature of a republic to have only a small territory; otherwise, it can scarcely continue to exist' (Montesquieu 1748/1989, 124).[5] In a 1793 pamphlet, Henri Bancal denied the viability of the universal republic advocated by Cloots because of the huge distances involved—but he added a proviso: 'Invent balloons that can travel over the earth as fast as we travel through a European state, and then I will no longer believe your project a chimera' (cited by Bevilacqua 2012, 562). Some contemporary authors share the view that there is a link between territorial size and forms of government (Kohr 1957; Wesson 1978, 207–210; Benhabib 2004, 220). Also Dahl, who had co-authored an earlier pivotal study on the topic (Dahl and Tufte 1973), seemed to be thinking of size when he worried that 'the opportunities available to the ordinary citizen to participate effectively in the decisions of a world government would diminish to the vanishing point' (R. Dahl 1999a, 22).

In turn, proponents of world government tend to dismiss the size argument. Already in 1871, Victoria Woodhull, the women's rights campaigner and advocate of what she called a 'Universal Republic' (Woodhull 1872/2010), pointed out that 'England has possessions in very many latitudes and longitudes of the world. Over these possessions a governing control is exercised, which control foreshadows the possibility of a government that shall control every country in all latitudes and longitudes' (Woodhull 1871, 83).

Size is closely linked to, but distinct from, the issue of *cultural heterogeneity*. Diversity of ethnicity, religion, and language has often been invoked as the key obstacle to political unification. In the tenth century CE, Abu Nasr al-Fārābi saw in the diversity of human societies an insurmountable obstacle to deliberation and legislation for the whole of the inhabited world (Orwin 2014). Four centuries later, Nicole Oresme rejected a world state on the

---

[5] A prominent opponent of the ratification of the Constitution of the United States of America quoted this passage by Montesquieu approvingly and made a point that is worth pondering with the benefit of hindsight: 'The territory of the United States is of vast extent; it now contains near three millions of souls, and is capable of containing much more than ten times that number. Is it practicable for a country, so large and so numerous as they will soon become, to elect a representation, that will speak their sentiments, without their becoming so numerous as to be incapable of transacting public business? It certainly is not' (Brutus 1787/1981). See also Hume (1772/1994, 64–65).

grounds that, 'because of the diversity of regions, temperaments, inclinations and customs of peoples, it is advisable that their positive laws and their governments should be different'. He also maintained that 'the division and diversity of languages is incompatible with social conversation and political life' (cited by Heater 1996, 191). With the consolidation of national states in early modern Europe, this became the predominant view.[6]

Contemporary authors voice similar concerns. Eric Posner argues that 'The problem with a world government is that the global population is far too heterogeneous to govern. People living in different parts of the world have different values, interests, loyalties, and ideas about governance. Heterogeneity frustrates world governance, and the plausibility of world government is receding with the passage of time' (Posner 2009, 9; see also Posner 2006, 541). Miller concurs: the idea of world government 'seems to run contrary to the sheer diversity of human cultures, and to the wish of people everywhere to belong to communities that are able to determine their own future paths' (Miller 2007, 25–26).

As with the problem of size, some authors think that cultural diversity is a problem especially for democratic forms of governments. James Stuart Mill asserted that 'Free institutions are next to impossible in a country made up of different nationalities. Among a people without fellow-feeling, especially if they read and speak different languages, the united public opinion, necessary to the working of representative government, cannot exist' (Mill 1861/1991, 428). Anne-Marie Slaughter is among those who voice similar concerns today: 'the diversity of the peoples to be governed makes it almost impossible to conceive of a global demos' (Slaughter 2004, 8; similarly Isensee 2003; Pettit 2010b; Bellamy 2019).

These arguments overlap with those positing motivational constraints, as they similarly emphasize the unwillingness of people to accept supranational rule, but they go further in interpreting this unwillingness as rooted in deep and pervasive cultural differences. It is such differences that explain why people lack the will to accept the right of transnational majorities to rule for the whole (Isensee 2003, 24). As argued by Miller,

> a democracy whose authority is acceptable to all requires that the majority should not attempt to impose a wholly alien worldview on the minority. The obvious example is a society divided along religious lines, where the division is such that if the majority is allowed to get its way it will force upon the minority (or minorities) beliefs and practices that the latter find intolerable. Here there must either be substantial convergence in the beliefs of the various groups or, alternatively, the

---

[6] A notable exception is Jan Amos Komenský (Comenius), who developed an elaborate plan for a form of global deliberative democracy in the seventeenth century (Comenius 1990, 1993, 1995).

> majority at least must subject its own beliefs to an overriding principle of toler-
> ance. More generally, we can say that for democracy to be possible, there must be
> something like a Rawlsian overlapping consensus on basic principles of justice so
> that the minority can count on the majority to constrain its use of power within the
> bounds set by these principles. (Miller 2010, 145–146)

A shared language is often seen as especially important. Miller (2007, 26) maintains that 'it is hard to see how a world state could be subject to effective democratic control. Current nation-states are only able to practise democracy in an attenuated form—periodic elections and some government responsive-ness to public opinion—and achieving even this level of democracy requires a democratic public who speak the same language (or at a minimum, par-ticipate in official bilingualism) are exposed to the same mass media, form parties and other political associations, and so forth.'

Some cosmopolitans agree that a shared identity is a prerequisite for a functioning democratic polity but deny that there are insurmountable obsta-cles to the development of a widespread globalist identity. A 'global nation' is conceivable and to some extent already in the process of emerging (Damluji 2019; see also Nanz 2006; Patomäki 2012; Bummel 2021).

The third structural factor that has been invoked as an obstacle to world state formation is *economic inequality*. The link between democratic gover-nance and economic equality has attracted the attention of political thinkers for centuries. Many writers agree with Rousseau that 'no citizen [should] be so very rich that he can buy another, and none so poor that he is compelled to sell himself' (Rousseau 1762/1997, 78). However, the potential role of *global* economic inequality in hindering global democracy has been noted in more recent decades. This is arguably the result of growing of global inequality between the early nineteenth century and the late twentieth century. Figure 2.1 shows the evolution of global inequality over the past two centuries, with the Gini index growing from around .60 to over .70 and then declining again from around 2000.

Milanovic (2016) points out that two hundred years ago global inequal-ity was not much higher than inequality within the US and other indus-trializing countries; then, they diverged for several decades, with global inequality growing and US inequality diminishing; then, US inequality began to increase again around 1980, while global inequality has declined since around 2000.

Global inequality can be broken down into two components: inequality among countries and inequality within country. As Milanovic (2012) sug-gests, inequality within countries can be interpreted as the component of global inequality due to class, whereas inequality among countries can be

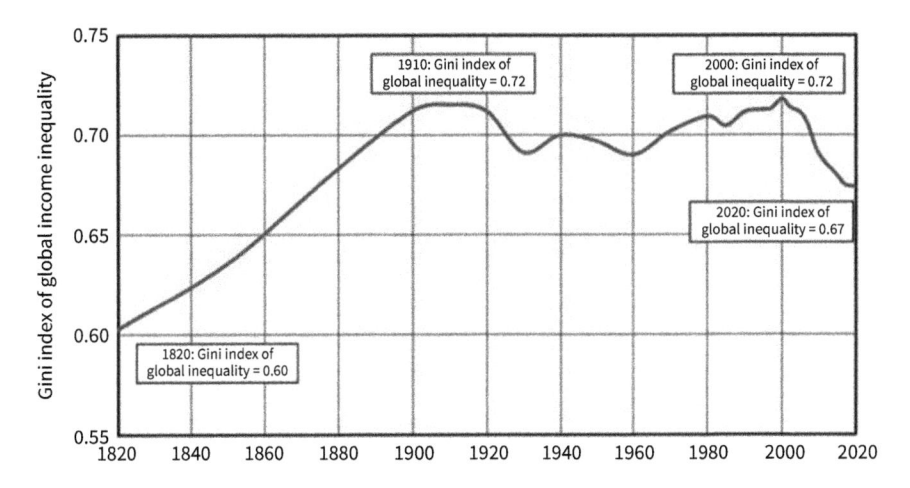

Figure 2.1 Global income inequality, 1820–2020: Gini index.

Source: Lucas Chancel and Thomas Piketty. 'Global income inequality, 1820–2020: the persistence and mutation of extreme inequality'. *Journal of the European Economic Association* 19, no. 6 (2021): 3025–3062. Reproduced by permission of Oxford University Press on behalf of the European Economic Association.

seen as the component of global inequality due to location. It is very relevant for the debate on global democracy that not only the level of global economic inequality has increased during the nineteenth and twentieth centuries, but that the share of it due to inequality among countries has substantially increased compared to the share of it due to inequality within countries. Figure 2.2 shows the proportion of global inequality that can be attributed to the location and the class component (Chancel and Piketty 2021). The graph shows that two hundred years ago class mattered much more than location in determining one person's place in the global income distribution. For instance, it mattered more if someone was a landowner or a landless peasant than if someone lived in England or in India. During the twentieth century, the relative importance of class and location has been reversed: location grew to matter as much, if not more, than class in determining one's place in the global income distribution (see also Milanovic 2016; Goda and Torres García 2017).[7] The importance of within-country inequality has then increased again since the 1980s.

The perception of a growing divergence in living standards between world regions since the nineteenth century has added concerns about economic

---

[7] I use the words 'class' and 'location' as convenient shorthands. An economic class can be defined as a set of individuals who stand in a similar property relationship with an asset that gives them income (e.g. capital and labour). Under that definition, unequal possession of the right to live and work in countries that provide opportunities for higher incomes should be seen as generating class divisions. Concretely, ownership of a passport can be as relevant as ownership of capital in defining a person's class position in global society.

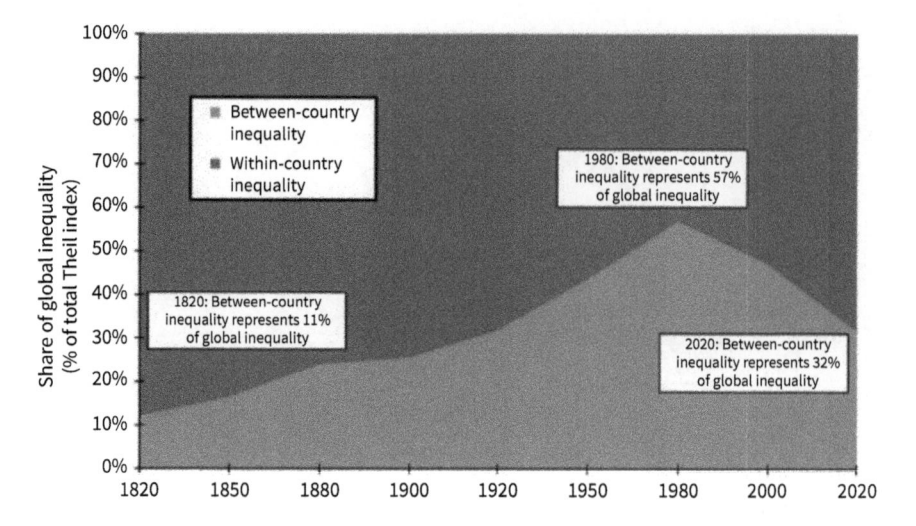

Figure 2.2 Relative shares of within-country and between-country components of global inequality, 1820–2020.

Source: Lucas Chancel and Thomas Piketty. 'Global income inequality, 1820–2020: the persistence and mutation of extreme inequality'. *Journal of the European Economic Association* 19, no. 6 (2021): 3025–3062. Reproduced by permission of Oxford University Press on behalf of the European Economic Association.

inequality to the traditional views on cultural diversity. Raymond Aron anticipated the findings of recent global inequality researchers by noting that, '[i]n a humanity on the way to unification, inequality between nations takes on the significance that inequality between classes once had' (Aron 1961/2002, 48), and he countered the case for a world state by pointing out that 'the wealthy nation would refuse to accept majority rule, and the poor majority would refuse to submit to any other principle of government' (Aron 1972, 238). Yunker (2011, 67) concurs that 'economic differences among nations constitute a major impediment to world government'. According to Milanovic, 'Reduction of material inequality between individuals in the world is a requirement for the existence of a global community of interests and values, however weak, because such a community cannot be based on vastly different levels of material welfare' (Milanovic 2021b, 42; see already Carr 1945; Bull 1977, 293). Miller (2010, 145) also notes that democracy is impossible in 'a class-divided society in which the division of economic resources is zero-sum'. Thomas Schelling ruefully noted that, if established, a world state would have the features of apartheid South Africa rather than that of a well-functioning democracy (Schelling 1992, 200). Dingwerth (2014, 1125), a supporter of global democratization, argues that 'reforming the formal structures is unlikely to add much to democratic governance unless we also address the most important structural obstacles to participation and control'.

A further argument to be considered is that a world state would lack an important mechanism supporting democracy, i.e. competition between independent states. The competition argument is distinct from the size argument, although they are sometimes combined (Vaubel 2008). The idea of a beneficial effect of interstate competition on freedom was already put forward in the eighteenth and nineteenth centuries. Montesquieu foreshadowed an *exit mechanism* when he remarked that the ability of merchants to shift mobile assets across jurisdictions promoted 'goodness of government' within them (Montesquieu 1748/1989, 389). Kant foreshadowed a *competition mechanism* by arguing that interstate rivalry prompted rulers to protect the civil liberties that underpinned the economic and hence military strength of the state (Kant 1784/2007, 117). Lord Acton foreshadowed an *epistemic mechanism* when he wrote that, by 'multiplying centres of government and discussion', 'the distribution of power among several States ... promotes the diffusion of political knowledge and the maintenance of healthy and independent opinion' (Acton 1877/2007, 241). In more recent times, the link between a multiplicity of states and political freedom has been emphasized by Wesson (1978). According to Jones (2003, 118), the link was an essential ingredient of what he called 'the European miracle'. The absence of these three mechanisms often underlies the fear that 'the great accumulation and concentration of power in a *cosmopolis* would create grave dangers of global despotism and lack of accountability' (Laborde and Ronzoni 2016, 286).[8]

It should be noted that this perspective has coexisted with a different interpretation of the relationship between international anarchy and domestic regimes. Erasmus had already pointed at the basic mechanism in the early sixteenth century: 'Now there are some who suspect that the princes are being very devious here; under the pretext of a Turkish war, they will plunder the towns, countryside, and people, overthrow the rule of law, suppress the liberties of the state, remove the authority of parliaments ...' (Erasmus 1530/2005, 263). The analysis of Downing (1993) confirms that interstate conflicts contributed to the end of medieval constitutionalism and the emergence of absolutism in parts of Europe. In more general terms, the argument is that the real or contrived threat posed by the existence of other polities and the absence of a supranational pacifier leads to militarization and autocracy,

---

[8] This brief review focuses on arguments about political freedom, but international competition has been linked to social progress more generally. For instance, writing in 1911 Lassa Oppenheim was confident that a federal world state had become possible, but he denied its desirability: 'So far as we can foresee, the development of mankind is inseparably bound up with the national development of the different peoples and states. In these conditions variety brings life, but unity brings death. Just as the freedom and competition of individuals is needed for the healthy progress of mankind, so also is the independence and rivalry of the various nations' (Oppenheim 1921, 13). See also Aurobindo (1950); Isensee (2003); Bostrom (2006); Scheidel (2019).

justified as necessary to the survival of the political community. Among recent authors, Thompson (1996, 147) highlighted the possibility that it 'is not democracies that create the possibilities of peace, but peace that creates the possibility of democracy'. Based on previous research finding a positive association between the number of land borders circumscribing a country and its involvement in wars (Starr and Most 1978), Midlarsky (1995) used the number of sea borders as a proxy for low threat of war and found that lower threat was positively associated with higher democracy scores. This alternative perspective would imply that the lack of competitors/rivals would make a world state more rather than less likely to retain democratic features. This is a key expectation stemming from Daniel Deudney's theory of world government: given that it 'would not face the competitive pressures of an interstate anarchy, then it follows that an important set of pressures for hierarchical centralization would be absent' (Deudney 2007, 276–277).[9]

A final argument against the possibility of a global democratic state is that historical experience shows that state-building and democratization cannot proceed simultaneously, but the former must precede the latter by a considerable amount of time (Brown 2002, 246). This does not seem to be a historical necessity. For instance, Charles Tilly (2000, 7) identified two ideal-typical paths to democratization. In the strong-state path there is an early expansion of governmental capacity and an authoritarian phase, followed by the emergence of democracy. For Tilly, most European countries followed this path. In the weak-state path, there is an early expansion of democracy and later an increase of governmental capacity. Switzerland exemplifies this path, but also the United States can be seen as a case where state-building and democratization progressed simultaneously. But the argument that prior experience of independent statehood facilitates both democratization and democratic resilience deserves to be considered in the empirical analyses that follow.

2.4 Institutional constraints

The final set of constraints refers to the institutional features that a world government would need to have in order to function and survive as a democracy. Two dimensions have attracted most attention. First, there is the question of which distribution of authority between the global and

---

[9] In his analysis of H. G. Wells' advocacy of world government, Partington (2003, 237) points out that, '[r]ather than create uniformity, Wells believed world union would lead to diversity, as the lack of necessary international competition would free individuals and groups to experiment with different modes of lifestyle and production'.

the other levels of government—notably existing states—would increase the chances of stable democratic processes. Second, there is the argument that global democracy would be possible only if all subordinate levels of government were democratically governed too. These questions will be considered in turn.

Some sceptics maintain that the delegation of authority to international organizations has already reached the maximum level permitted by motivational and structural constraints—this position has already been considered. Among those who regard further authority transfers possible in principle, there are areas of both agreement and disagreement about what division of competencies would be best for democratic stability. There is wide agreement that any viable world state would need to have a *federal* structure. Federalism entails that the constituent units of a world state would retain important constitutionally protected areas of competence. Where opinions diverge is the range of issues over which a world state would have authority (Zürn 2016). Some proponents of world government want its authority to be strictly limited to the prevention of international war (e.g. Russell 1959, 68–69). Others would prefer the central level of governance to be competent for a wider range of tasks, such as the promotion of human rights, stewardship of the global commons, and global distributive justice. Proponents of both positions invoke both normative principles and empirical beliefs about the conditions under which a federal system can obtain and maintain popular support.

The second question concerns the institutional homogeneity of a world state. Some authors are very sceptical that a global polity could be democratic if it included non-democratic states as component members. Miller (2010, 149) points out that, '[s]ince many of the world's peoples are governed undemocratically, it would be problematic, to say the least, to attempt to hold free elections to a global assembly in those territories'. Proponents of global democratic institutions offered a variety of answers to this problem. Some advocate a union of democracies as a stepping stone towards global democracy to be achieved when the conditions are right (e.g. Hobson 1934, 148; Streit 1938; Einstein 1948/2007b; Thompson 1987, 273–274; Falk and Strauss 2001; Pasternak 2012). Others favour the inclusion of nondemocratic countries in global democratic institutions from the beginning (Leinen and Bummel 2018, 374–376). The 'cosmopolitan democracy' approach advocates a gradual process in which international and domestic democratization support each other (Archibugi 2008; Archibugi and Cellini 2017). This issue raises the question of the viability of a world state that meets the criteria of electoral democracy at the global level but where democratic rights are unevenly guaranteed across its territory. In essence: how viable would a democratic world state be if some component states remain governed undemocratically?

2.5 Assessing feasibility arguments

The arguments surveyed so far invoke 'facts', about the motivations of agents as well as structural and institutional factors that form the background of those motivations. In this section, I will first draw a connection between those alleged facts and the tests of achievability and viability formulated earlier in this chapter and then discuss the challenges involved in assessing the connections with empirical data.

Recall the test of achievability formulated in a previous section:

Achievability (binary): *The universal republic is achievable if and only if (i) a critical mass of states would be reasonably likely to succeed in transferring authority to it if they were to try; and (ii) those states are able to try to transfer authority to the universal republic.*

The focus of the achievability assessment is on states and the constraints on their actions. Condition (i) leads us to ask what may prevent states from transferring authority if they took a decision to do so. Based on our previous survey of feasibility arguments, the most plausible candidate is the opposition of the citizens of the state, or the most influential part of it—what Southwood and Goodin (2021) call 'core constituents'. For instance, such core constituents might succeed in deposing the government before the transfer of authority is completed. Condition (ii) prompts us to ask whether states are able—in the sense of not robustly disposed not to try—to transfer authority to the universal republic. Recall the test proposed by Stemplowska (2016) to determine whether a disposition is robust: motivational failure is an instance of genuine motivational inability when there exists no conceivable (positive or negative) incentive that would bring the agent's motivational state in line with what is needed to perform the action in question. The arguments in the previous section can be interpreted as positing that states have a motivational inability to transfer authority. Such a position can have various foundations. First, one can argue that the inability can be rooted in the very essence of states: they 'are unitary actors who, at a minimum, seek their own preservation and, at a maximum, drive for universal domination' and '[o]nly if survival is assured can states safely seek such other goals as tranquillity, profit, and power' (Waltz 1979, 118, 126). In this view, states are *robustly* disposed not to transfer authority because no incentive could outweigh the loss of autonomy. Second, the argument can be that states are under the direct control of their core constituents and those constituents are robustly disposed not to allow the transfer of authority. The distinction between motivational and structural constraints is relevant here. If the opposition to empowering a UR were based only on individual beliefs and preferences, positive or negative incentives might be able to soften such opposition. By contrast, if the resistance is rooted in deeper patterns of cultural diversity and economic inequality, the core constituents may maintain it even if presented with incentives. In short, structural constraints may perpetuate motivational inability.

Moving on to the assessment of viability, recall the previously formulated test:

> **Viability** (binary): *The universal republic is viable if and only if (i) a critical mass of citizens and groups would be reasonably likely to succeed in complying with its rules, provided that they try; and (ii) those citizens and groups are able to try to comply with the rules of the universal republic.*

The focus of the achievability assessment is on citizens and the groups they form, including what would become 'local' governments within the UR. Condition (i) leads us to ask what may prevent citizens from complying with the rules of the UR if they tried. A possible answer is that compliance may require a type of large-scale cooperation that is hampered by the diversity of the world, maybe especially its linguistic diversity. This is a possible interpretation of the idea that 'as the range of government expands laws progressively lose their vigor' (Kant 1795/1996, 336). Condition (ii) prompts us to ask whether citizens and groups are robustly disposed not to try to act in accordance with the rules of the UR. These rules are both procedural (how to make collectively binding decisions in the UR) and substantive (what the collective decisions allow, prescribe, and proscribe in various areas of human activity). Again, the distinction between motivational and structural constraints is relevant. If decisions to act in accordance with UR rules were based only on individual beliefs and preferences, positive or negative incentives could be able to influence them. In that case, citizens and groups may be disposed not to comply, but not robustly so. By contrast, if a disposition not to comply is rooted in deeper patterns of cultural diversity and economic inequality, citizens and groups may persist even if presented with incentives. This could happen, for instance, if citizens refused to comply because of an unshakable belief that people from a different ethnic or religious background can never be trusted to comply in return. Noncompliance can be robust—for instance, if people believe that their own unreciprocated compliance would put them at an existential risk. As in the case of achievability, it is possible that structural constraints create and perpetuate motivational inability.

Whether these conditions are met in the real world is ultimately an empirical question. The issue cannot be settled by means of assumptions, because for each assumption negating the feasibility conditions, such as Waltz's postulate on the primacy of state self-preservation, an opposite assumption can be posited, such as the following: 'To the extent that leaders face a trade-off between preserving state sovereignty and assuaging a particular constituency, shifting the electoral balance in their party's favour, or institutionalizing deep-seated preferences, they may sacrifice state sovereignty' (Marks, Hooghe, and Blank 1996, 350; see also Paul 1999; Howes 2003). But how can the presence or absence of the feasibility conditions be assessed empirically?

Possibility theory, which has been developed as an alternative to probability theory in the analysis of uncertainty (Zadeh 1978), provides a vocabulary for conceptualizing the differences and relationship between two types of possibility judgement. It distinguishes between what is 'not impossible' because it is not ruled out by our beliefs and what is 'guaranteed possible' because it has been observed. Uncertainty about what is possible can be reduced or modelled through 'knowledge', 'data', and their merger (Benferhat et al. 2008; Dubois and Prade 2009). Knowledge is conceived as negative information in the sense that it expresses *constraints* on how the world behaves, such as physical laws or common sense. Data is positive information as it consists of actual observations on the world. The accumulation of negative information restricts the set of possible worlds, whereas the accumulation of positive information expands it.

Given that a universal republic has never been achieved, an empirical assessment of the conditions of its possibility—understood as encompassing both achievability and viability—must rely to a significant extent on background 'knowledge' rather than 'data'. There is broad consensus that the absence of a state of affairs is not sufficient to demonstrate its impossibility. Already in his *Judgement* of the abbé de Saint-Pierre's plan, Rousseau dismissed the criticisms of 'those who do not judge reasons by reason but only by results, and who have nothing to object against this plan other than it has not been executed' (Rousseau 1782/2005, 53). Major societal changes, such as the outlawing of the slave trade and slavery, were 'possible' before they became a reality. For instance, the expansion of the suffrage to women has been described (probably with some exaggeration) as 'inconceivable before 1860 and inevitable after 1948' (Przeworski 2009, 314; see also Barry 1999, 60).

While the assessment of possibility can legitimately rely on 'knowledge' and not only on 'data', determining *what* should count as relevant knowledge in an analysis of global democracy is not straightforward. My answer has two parts. First, I aim for knowledge that can be expressed in terms of the standard causal models that are typical in contemporary political science. This means that the analysis is distinct from and runs parallel to the teleological argument for the inevitability of a world state developed by Wendt (2003).[10] Second, I suggest that what counts as useful knowledge differs depending on whether we are considering motivational, structural, or institutional constraints.

Most relevant knowledge on motivational constraints is provided by evidence on the beliefs and preferences of politically relevant agents. As seen earlier, these agents encompass state agents, social movements, and individual citizens. The evidence can be gathered from a variety of sources, such as opinion surveys, voting choices, campaign material, records of debates, speeches, and other official statements and documents.

For structural and institutional constraints, the relevant evidence has to be more indirect. Authors who express scepticism about the possibility of global democracy often appear to rely on an interpretation of what made democracy successful in some countries and unsuccessful in other contexts, even if they do not articulate this inference explicitly. This line of reasoning can be summarized as follows: (i) democracy was successfully established only in some countries; (ii) this is due to the presence of some favourable conditions in those countries; (iii) these conditions are lacking at the international level, now and in the foreseeable future; and hence (iv) global democracy is either highly unlikely or virtually impossible. In other words, not only optimists but also sceptics about global democracy often rely, implicitly or explicitly, on a 'domestic analogy', which in its broader definition is 'presumptive reasoning ... about international relations based on the assumption that since domestic and international phenomena are similar in a number of respects, a given proposition which holds true domestically, but whose validity is as yet uncertain internationally, will also hold true internationally' (Suganami 1989, 24).

---

[10] A fortiori, the mode of analysis is distinct from approaches emphasizing supranatural forces, such as the vision of global democracy evoked by Philo of Alexandria in the first century CE: 'For the divine Word brings round its operations in a circle, which the common multitude of men call fortune. And then, as it continually flows on among cities, and nations, and countries, it overturns existing arrangements and gives to one person what has previously belonged to another, changing the affairs of individuals only in point of time, in order that the whole world may become, as it were, one city, and enjoy the most excellent of constitutions, a democracy' (Philo 1993, 172).

Diagnostic (as opposed to prescriptive) domestic analogies have been used to affirm as well as to deny the possibility of global democracy.[11] An important recent example of the 'possibilist' use is Robert Goodin's argument that 'Similar things seem to be happening in today's international order as happened centuries ago in the domestic sphere to curtail the arbitrary exercise of power and to make it accountable' (Goodin 2010, 181). Some 'absence-of-conditions' arguments against global democracy often use the same logic in reverse, for they draw on what is known about the successful democratization of states to deny the possibility of democratization at the global level.

The domestic analogy is a plausible basis for assessing arguments about structural and institutional conditions. Despite their numerous differences, both international systems and domestic political systems consist of a multitude of collective actors who engage in a variety of modes of interaction—from coercion and competition to negotiation and cooperation—based on complex power relations, conflicting and compatible interests, and norms of appropriate behaviour. A rigid analytical separation is therefore unwarranted (Milner 1991). Accordingly, the analyses of structural and institutional conditions presented in the next chapters rely primarily on evidence provided by the historical experiences of existing states, in ways that will be detailed in the relevant sections. However, it is important to bear in mind the limitations of such an exercise. It is intended to reflect relevant knowledge gathered through an analogical strategy, and its results are bound to be more uncertain than the findings normally produced by social science research. Hence, the aim of the exercises presented in the following chapters is not to attain the level of confidence normally expected from statistical analyses of events that have already occurred, but to improve on the more informal 'intuitions' and 'judgement' that according to Bull (1966) play an inescapable role in the study of questions of 'significance', including the possibility of leaving international anarchy behind us.

2.6 Concluding remarks

This chapter considered a range of arguments about the feasibility of the universal republic and organized them in relation to three types of constraints: motivational, structural, and institutional. The case for considering motivational constraints is straightforward: major political reforms are highly

---

[11] See Suganami (1989, 136) for the distinction between the diagnostic and the prescriptive use of the domestic analogy.

unlikely if they have little support among politically relevant actors. Establishing empirically how stringent the motivational constraints are is also relatively straightforward, as social science has developed various methods for measuring beliefs and preferences. However, authors who emphasize structural conditions can point out that what actors happen to believe and prefer at any point in time may be less consequential than relatively stable social, economic, and cultural structures, which are the ultimate drivers of human behaviour. While structures may be more fundamental determinants of possibility, it is also more difficult to evaluate the empirical validity of arguments that invoke them. The next chapter tackles this challenge.

3
Would the universal republic be viable?

This chapter will examine the viability of the universal republic. In this context, viability refers to the risk that, once established, a global polity with democratic features would morph into something else over time. In Chapter 2, I argued that three types of constraints could potentially make the universal republic unfeasible: motivational, structural, and institutional. Most of this chapter considers potential structural constraints, with some attention given to institutional constraints in section 3.4. Imagining the universal republic as existing depends on the assumption that any motivational constraints to its establishment have been overcome. Chapter 4 will examine to what extent this assumption can be justified. The assumptions made in this chapter do not directly address whether people would be sufficiently motivated to keep a universal republic viable, but they address the structural and institutional conditions that might shape that motivation, if the arguments considered in Chapter 2 are compelling.

I first discuss the methodological approach used to examine the question of viability and then the data used for the analysis. Subsequently, I present and discuss the findings.

3.1 Method

The analysis presented in this chapter is based on the domestic analogy approach introduced in Chapter 2. The assumption is that the consideration of conditions that may be associated with the survival and end of democracy within countries can provide imperfect but valuable information on the likelihood of survival of an imagined democratic state that extends over the whole planet. The starting point is building a statistical model of democratic survival that estimates the potential contribution of a range of economic, cultural, and social variables to the longevity of democracy in nearly all countries of the world over a period of almost 120 years. Having used machine-learning tools to estimate such a contribution, I then predict the longevity of democracy of a hypothetical state that is assumed to have the values of the current

The Universal Republic. Mathias Koenig-Archibugi, Oxford University Press. © Mathias Koenig-Archibugi (2024).
DOI: 10.1093/9780198921158.003.0003

world on each of those variables. Such a hypothetical state is a 'world state', which can be regarded as fulfilling the universal republican ideal as long as it remains governed democratically.

The analysis of democratic longevity is based on a statistical approach known as survival analysis or event history analysis. Event history procedures model the occurrence of events as potentially influenced by a set of explanatory variables and help researchers establish which variables delay the onset of the event and which ones accelerate it. In our case, the relevant event is a transition from democratic governance to a non-democratic political condition. In this chapter, I present estimates of the longevity of a world state using survival curves based on the model specification discussed in each section.

I use machine learning to select the combination of covariates that has the strongest predictive power for the outcome of interests. Specifically I use the lasso (least absolute shrinkage and selection operator) method with cross-validation (Tibshirani 1996; StataCorp 2023). In cross-validation, a subset of observations (training set) is split into smaller sets, or 'folds'. On each of these folds, the procedure validates models trained using the remaining folds, in a loop. The out-of-sample predictive ability of the selected model can be assessed based on a 'testing' subset. I apply the lasso approach to a semi-parametric survival model, the Cox proportional hazards model.

Applied to the issue at hand, this procedure yields what can be called an 'extreme counterfactual' (King and Zeng 2007). It is a counterfactual because the world state is hypothetical. It is extreme because, first, for some variables the world state has values that are outside the range of values ever observed in nation states. The distance from observed values is greatest for population and territory. Inferring the likely democratic longevity of a world state based on such unobserved values involves extrapolation. The second and more subtle reason why the counterfactual is extreme is that on some variables the world state has values that are within the empirically observed range, but the way it combines them has no direct equivalent among the units of the observed sample. Formally stated, the hypothetical world state falls outside of the convex hull, defined as the smallest convex set that contains all observed data points (King and Zeng 2007).

For our purposes, the main problem with extreme counterfactuals is that predicted values are dependent on model choices. Changing the functional form and adding or removing control variables and interaction terms can affect out-of-sample predictions substantially. If it is not possible to collect more relevant data or select models based on highly specific theoretical predictions, the methodological difficulties posed by extreme counterfactuals are largely insurmountable (King and Zeng 2007).

At least two reactions to this predicament are conceivable. The first is to conclude that statements on the viability of global democratic statehood cannot be empirically evaluated. As noted in Chapter 2, the arguments considered there are concerned with empirical possibility, not with logical or metaphysical possibility. In effect, the first reaction would imply that all those arguments should simply be ignored. Considering the important role played by disagreements about viability in debates about a global democratic polity, this response would entail a drastic limitation of what can and cannot be said on this topic. Even if such a limitation were desirable in principle, it seems unrealistic to expect widespread compliance with the tenet 'Whereof one cannot speak, thereof one must be silent' (Wittgenstein).

The second reaction is to construct a model that can be considered a fair first empirical operationalization of the arguments advanced in the literature, and which can serve as a foundation for further analyses. This approach envisages a dynamic process. The first stage consists of the construction and application of a relatively simple model that incorporates the variables highlighted by the main existing arguments and combines them in a parsimonious way. In a second stage, the arguments are refined and formulated in terms that are specific enough to guide modelling choices. If the refined arguments suggest modelling assumptions that differ from those applied in the first stage, the analysis is repeated based on those assumptions. Further stages are possible if researchers present novel variants of existing arguments or entirely new arguments that can then be reflected in model selection.

The analysis presented in this chapter reflects the latter reaction to the problem of extreme counterfactuals. Given that the arguments in the literature are formulated in fairly generic terms, I develop relatively simple operationalizations of the relevant variables that are in line with how they are used by political scientists to address other questions. I also privilege simpler over more complex functional forms. The important caveat is that, because of the extreme counterfactual nature of the analysis, the results display considerable levels of uncertainty and may change substantially under different modelling choices.

This uncertainty is also reflected in the way I present the results. As noted earlier, the longevity of a world state is displayed using survival curves based on the model specification discussed in each section. In principle, the information conveyed by the graphs could be translated into sentences, such as 'the probability that the world state survives for 50 years without a breakdown of democracy is 70 per cent'. However, I will generally abstain from formulating such sentences, to emphasize that the estimates entail substantial uncertainty and have to be seen as indicators of the order of magnitude of survival probabilities rather than anything more precise.

3.2 Measures of democracy and its correlates

The quantity of interest in this chapter is the likelihood that a democratic regime will survive within a given period. The analysis of democratic survival is based on the Varieties of Democracies (V-Dem) dataset and two datasets that build on it, Regimes of the World (RoW) and Episodes of Regime Transformation (ERT) (Coppedge et al. 2021; Pemstein et al. 2021; Lührmann, Tannenberg, and Lindberg 2018; Maerz et al. 2021). V-Dem is designed and managed by over fifty scholars worldwide and relies on the input of more than 3,000 country experts. These experts provide country-focused information on over 400 fine-grained indicators on various aspects of democracy, which are then aggregated into indices that express five broad understandings of democracy. The resulting aggregation yields the *electoral, liberal, participatory, deliberative*, and *egalitarian* democracy indices. Each country is assigned a score between 0 and 1 in each of the five interval-level indices. Whenever possible the data cover every country in the world since 1789. In other work, I have discussed the limitations of V-Dem in regard to identifying who belongs to the *demos* of democracy, in contrast to its comprehensive measurement of the ways in which it may be said to 'rule' (Koenig-Archibugi 2022). However, this does not detract from its usefulness in identifying the presence and functioning of democratic institutions, which is what is needed here.

For the purposes at hand, it is useful to be able to determine when a polity is no longer part of the set of democratic polities, which requires a dichotomous measure. The RoW dataset is useful in that regard, as it classifies countries as democracies or autocracies based on their scores on several V-Dem indicators. To qualify as a democracy, countries must score above 0.5 on V-Dem's electoral democracy index, which combines indices measuring extent of suffrage, elected officials, clean elections, freedom of association, and freedom of expression; in addition, countries must also score above a minimum level on indicators for free and fair multiparty elections. Among the cross-national empirical indicators of democracy developed by scholars, the RoW democracy index comes closest to the understanding of democracy presented in the introduction to this volume.

The RoW democracy index is an attractive measure for our purposes because it strikes a balance between two desiderata. On the one hand, it is a 'realistic' measure in so far as it does not require polities to meet ideal standards perfectly in order to qualify as democracies. All existing democracies fall short of ideal standards in one way or another, and a democratic world state would be no different. On the other hand, the criteria for democracy used in RoW are relatively stringent—specifically, more stringent than those of most other datasets commonly used in political science and International Relations. The main existing binary democracy measures (Cheibub, Gandhi, and Vreeland 2010; Boix, Miller, and Rosato 2013; Geddes, Wright, and Frantz 2014) classify as democracies several regimes that are considered autocracies by RoW (with fewer cases displaying the opposite pattern). According to the calculations of Kasuya and Mori (2022), to achieve the highest consistency between those binary measures and RoW, RoW's cutpoint on the electoral democracy index would need to be .39, which is substantially lower than the .5 cutpoint chosen by the creators of RoW. Baltz, Vasselai, and Hicken (2022) considered an even wider range of binary democracy measures and found a remarkable level of agreement around a .42 cutpoint on the electoral democracy index. In the following, I will use the more demanding threshold implemented by RoW. The rationale is that the universal republic should be held to demanding but still realistic standards.

The ERT dataset captures over 600 episodes of regime transformation along the democracy–autocracy continuum from 1900 to 2020, including cases when a democracy as defined by RoW turned into an autocracy. The following analysis is based on ERT data on when democratic regimes start, how long they endure, and when they break down. I depart from the ERT classification in one respect: in cases where a democracy collapsed as a direct result of invasion and military occupation by a foreign power, I recode the state as having retained a democratic character throughout the period of foreign invasion and treat the post-occupation regime as a direct continuation of the pre-occupation regime.[1] The reason for this is that I am interested in the internal factors that may be associated with a breakdown of democracy.

The list of democratic regimes that are potentially included in the analyses is in Appendix I. The same state can have more than one democratic spell in the observed period. The actual analyses may be based on a smaller set of

---

[1] I identified the cases to be recoded by determining which autocratic transitions occurred in the wake of a sudden loss of autonomy, operationalized as a change from a positive to a negative score on V-Dem's Domestic Autonomy variable. The recoded cases are Belgium during World War I and Belgium, Czechoslovakia, Denmark, France, Luxembourg, the Netherlands, and Norway during World War II. I assume these countries to have an uninterrupted spell of democracy between the early twentieth century and the present time, with the exception of Czechoslovakia, which is coded as having experienced a breakdown of democracy as a result of the 1948 coup.

democratic spells, depending on the time and geographical coverage of the variables included in the models. It is also worth noting that some very small states are not covered in ERT.

The analysis of democratic survival is based on two groups of variables. The first group is meant to reflect directly the arguments presented in Chapter 2. Most relate to arguments about structural conditions, notably ethnic diversity, religious diversity, linguistic diversity, economic inequality, population size, land area, prior experience of statehood, and the pressure of neighbouring states.

To capture three forms of diversity—ethnic, religious, and linguistic—I follow most of the literature (Alesina et al. 2003; Fearon 2003; Wimmer, Cederman, and Min 2009; Ramos et al. 2019) and for each of the three I calculated a fractionalization index that equals 1 minus the Herfindahl index, which—as Page (2010, 70) noted—is the most commonly used measure of diversity. Specifically,

$$Diversity_j = 1 - \sum_{i=1}^{N} s_{ij}^2$$

where s_{ij} is the share of group i $(i = 1 \ldots N)$ in country j. The Herfindahl index expresses the probability (from 0 to 1) that two randomly chosen people in the same country belong to the same ethnic, religious, or linguistic group. If all individuals were to belonge to the same group, the index would be 1. If each individual constituted a distinct group, the index would be 0. The value of the index is subtracted from 1 in order to express the degree of diversity, with 1 indicating the highest possible degree of diversity.

My main measure of economic equality is the Gini index of income distribution. Of course, it is possible that, if it existed, a world state would modify economic inequalities through global taxation and other measures. For the purposes of the simulation, I will assume that the current level of global economic inequality would remain a structural feature of a democratic world state.

To capture the positive and negative effects of the existence of other states, which might be competitors or security threats, I include the number of land borders each country has with other countries. To capture how long polities had experienced independent statehood prior to transitioning to democracy, I construct a variable consisting of the year in which the democratic regime started (or 1900) minus the year in which the polity acquired the status of independent state according to the States System Membership dataset of the Correlates of War (COW) project (Correlates of War Project 2017b). This dataset treats 1816 as the earliest state tenure date. I retain this start date even if state formation preceded it in some countries, given that they experienced key nation building processes (e.g. education, mass conscription, expansion of state administrations) in the nineteenth century (e.g. Weber 1976). It is also worth noting that States System Membership dataset emphasizes diplomatic recognition in the Europe-dominated international system and is likely to underestimate earlier consolidated statehood in other world regions. Thus, the indicator used to capture the experience of independent statehood prior to democratization should be regarded as a particularly imperfect proxy.

The second group of variables are invoked less often in debates about global democracy, but they are frequently discussed in relation to the durability of democracy within countries and thus should be taken into account. These variables include income per capita, growth of income per capita, level of education of the population, economic dependence on natural resources, and the percentage of residents who belong to each of the globally largest religions (Catholics, Protestants, Christian Orthodox, Muslims, Buddhists, as well as not religious). I also include for the average level of democracy of all states in the world weighted by their share of global material capabilities, as a proxy for the prevalent ideological orientation of the international political environment.

The data sources for those variables and the values assigned to the world are presented in Appendix II.[2]

3.3 Simulating the world state: structural constraints

The following variables were offered to lasso for selection: ethnic diversity, religious diversity, linguistic diversity, economic inequality, population size, land area, prior experience of statehood, the pressure of neighbouring states, income per capita, growth of income per capita, level of education of the population, dependence on natural resources, the percentage of residents who belong to each of the globally largest religious groups, and international political environment. Through cross-validation, lasso identified the best combination of covariates to be included in the Cox survival model. I used this model to simulate the probability that a state with the structural

---

[2] The variables reflect the original data, except population size and land area, which are logged. The rationale is that it would be implausible to assume that, say, the difference between a population of 1 million and one of 100 million counts the same as the difference between a population of 100 million and one of 199 million, and a similar reasoning applies to land area. Footnote 4 in section 3.3 reports results for unlogged population and area.

features of a world polity would break down within a given interval of time.[3] Figure 3.1 shows the survival curves for two hypothetical polities. The continuous line represents the survival curve of a democratic state that has the values of the world on the variables selected by lasso. The dashed line represents the survival curve of a democratic state that has the average value for democracies on each of those selected variables. The graph suggests that democracy has a slightly larger probability of surviving in the world state than in the average democracy since 1900.

In the 'best' model that underlies Figure 3.1, lasso included some but not all the variables capturing the presumed structural constraints discussed in Chapter 2. Specifically, it included prior statehood experience and religious diversity, but it did not include ethnic diversity, linguistic diversity, economic inequality, population size, and land area. Given our purposes, it can be desirable to take into account all these variables even if lasso does not consider

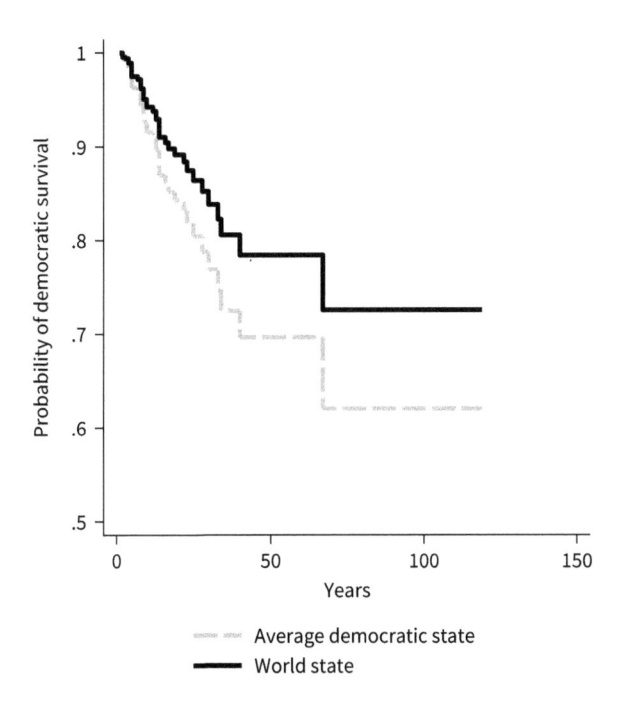

Figure 3.1 Survival of democracy in world state compared to average country.

---

[3] I define the universal republic as a *federal* democratic state. However, in the main analysis I treat all democratic states as providing potentially useful information on the longevity of democracy in a hypothetical world state. The first reason for that is that I do not assume any specific division of competences between the supranational and the other governance levels. The second reason is that this approach enables me to estimate whether federal institutions would make a difference for the longevity of democracy in the hypothetical world state, in an analysis shown later in this chapter.

them useful for predicting democratic longevity. Figure 3.2 shows survival curves based on a model in which lasso was 'forced' to include these seven presumed constraint variables, in addition to other variables that it could select freely. This simulation yields a slightly lower democratic longevity of the world state, bringing it in line with the average democratic state.[4]

Figure 3.1 assumes that a democratic world state will have the values that the world had around the year 2019. However, some of the relevant structural conditions may be subject to considerable change. We can consider the estimated probability of democratic survival of a hypothetical world state that is established a few decades in the future rather than at the time of writing. This exercise will draw on attempts to construct scenarios relating to two of the variables that are most likely to change in the foreseeable future: GDP per capita and population size. Specifically, I use a scenario included in the

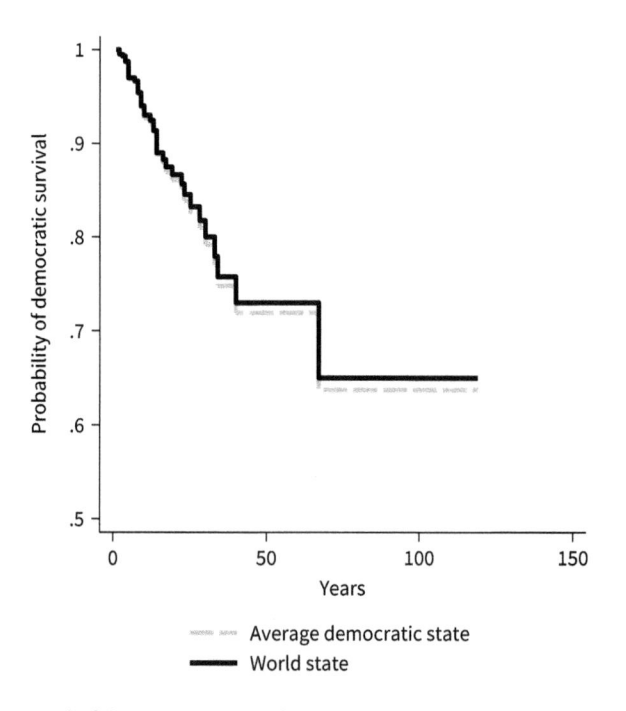

Figure 3.2 Survival of democracy in world state compared to average country, with forced entry of presumed constraint variables.

---

[4] As stated in footnote 2, population and land area are logged for the analyses. When lasso can select variables without constraint (Figure 3.1), population and area are not selected regardless of whether they are logged or not. When lasso is forced to include all seven presumed constraint variables (Figure 3.2), forcing the inclusion of unlogged population and unlogged land area generates an implausibly high survival probability for the world state (graph not shown). Using logged values is the most conservative option as it avoids artificially inflating the world state's prospects of democratic survival.

Shared Socioeconomic Pathways (SSP) database (v.2.0) (Dellink et al. 2017; Fricko et al. 2017; Riahi et al. 2017; Samir and Lutz 2017). By singling out population and per capita income, I do not mean to suggest that the other variables are likely to remain unchanged over the next decades. For instance, it is possible that advances in artificial intelligence may drastically affect the issue of language diversity by making instant translation from and to any language available to anyone with access to simple technical devices (Cabrera 2022). But other variables have not been subject to the same kind of plausible scenario-building as population and income.

Lasso selected GDP per capita but not population. Figure 3.3 shows the probability of survival of a hypothetical democratic world state with the GDP per capita that the world is projected to have in 2050 compared with the probability of survival with the value it had closer to the time of writing, holding all other variables selected by lasso at their present levels. The graph indicates that survival would be more likely with the projected 2050 average income levels.

The models considered so far treat the various sources of societal diversity as separate variables. It is conceivable, however, that diversity becomes risky when multiple types of it accumulate in the same polity. In other words, forms

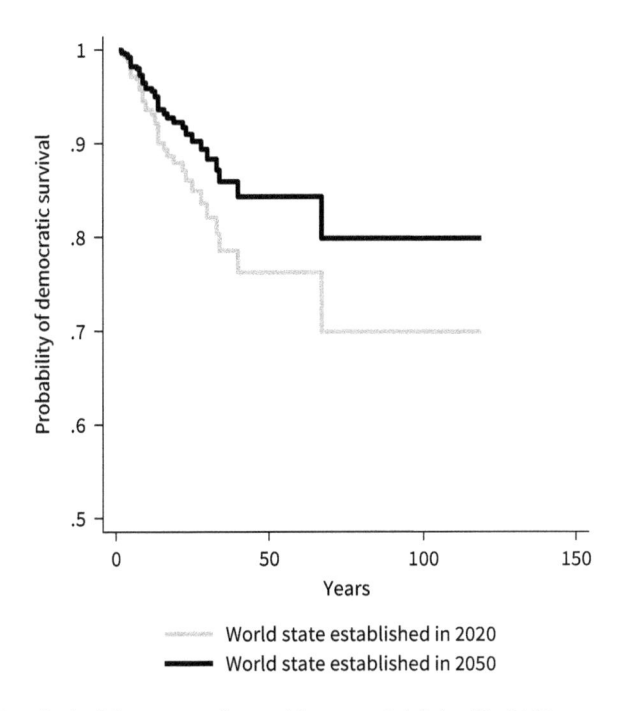

Figure 3.3 Survival of democracy in world state established in 2050.

of diversity that are not problematic for democracy *all else being equal* may become so when they are found in combination with other forms of diversity (Koenig-Archibugi 2012a). To account for this possibility, I constructed a composite variable 'superdiversity', which is the multiplicative product of four variables: ethnic diversity, religious diversity, linguistic diversity, and income inequality. Lasso failed to select superdiversity as part of the best model. However, I 'forced' its selection because of the intrinsic interest of this composite variable. The resulting survival curve for the world state is shown in Figure 3.4.

The emphasis so far has been on economic inequality as measured by the income Gini index, but there are other forms of inequality. Dingwerth (2014), for instance, refers to deficits in human security, health, and education as obstacles to participation in a global democracy. I considered two measures taken from the V-Dem dataset: educational equality and health equality. Educational equality refers to the extent to which high-quality basic education is guaranteed to all and sufficient to enable them to exercise their basic rights as adult citizens. Health equality refers to the extent to which high-quality basic health care is guaranteed to all and sufficient to enable them to exercise their basic political rights as adult citizens. Lasso included

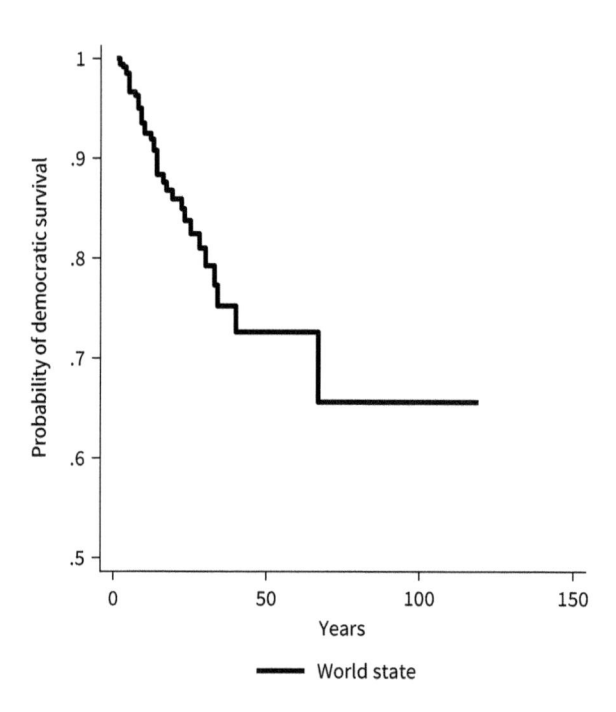

Figure 3.4 Survival of democracy in world state, accounting for superdiversity.

health equality in the preferred model, but not educational equality. Figure 3.5 shows the democratic longevity of a world state under two different scenarios. In the first scenario, health equality is low, at the 10th percentile of all democratic countries. That scenario probably reflects best the state of the world today. In the second scenario, the universal republic manages to improve health equality and raise it to a moderate level, defined here as the average level of all democratic countries since 1900. The graph suggests that such an achievement might boost the survival chances of global democracy.

Inequality is closely related to freedom of movement across borders (Milanovic 2012). The universal republic does not automatically imply such freedom of movement: in principle, a global parliament may authorize the constituent states to restrict immigration (see Chapter 5). But whether individual freedom of movement is guaranteed or not might affect the viability of the democratic world state. Figure 3.6 shows the democratic survival curves for a world state at two levels of V-Dem's freedom of domestic movement variable: a low level corresponding to major restrictions (lowest percentile among democratic states) and a moderate value (average of democratic states). The graph suggests that larger freedom of movement might be associated with more resilient global democracy.

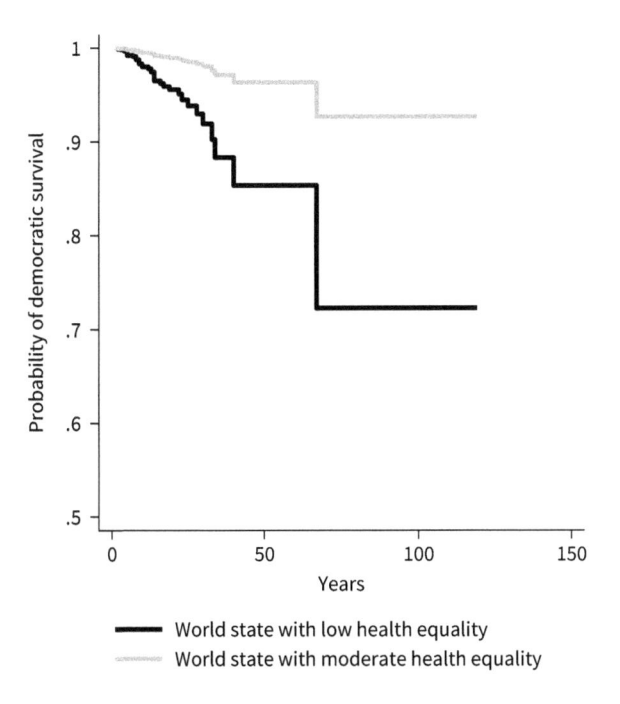

Figure 3.5 Survival of democracy in world state with low or moderate health equality.

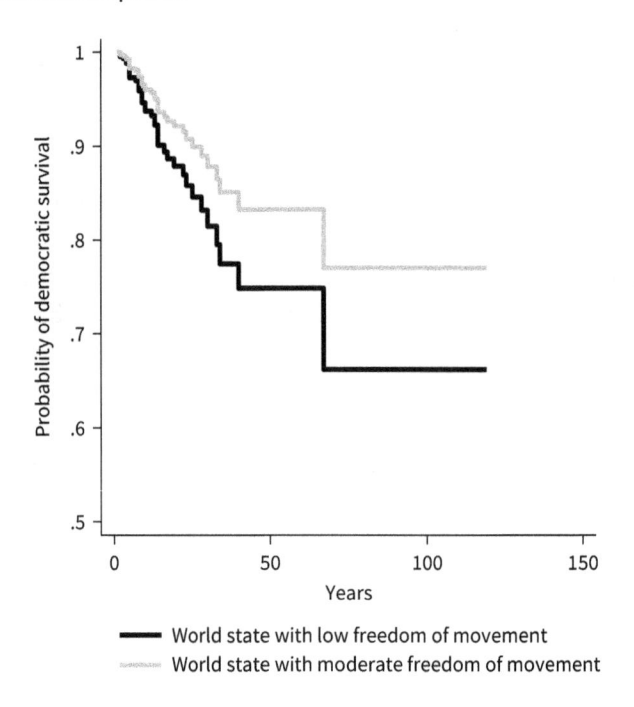

Figure 3.6 Survival of democracy in world state with low or moderate freedom of movement.

We conclude this section by considering the values held by citizens. Even if they are not as slow-changing as, for instance, ethnic identities, values can still be considered a structural feature of global society and could affect the viability of a democratic world state. Unfortunately, data limitations severely constrain the application of the approach used so far. I attempted to address this question by examining 'emancipative values', which is a construct developed by Welzel (2013) and measured through an index that averages responses to twelve items included in the World Values Survey (WVS) (Inglehart and al. 2014), clustered in four sub-themes: autonomy (support for independence and imagination rather than obedience as desired child qualities); equality (support for women's equal access to education, jobs, and power); choice (toleration of homosexuality, abortion, and divorce); and voice (importance attached to freedom of speech and people's say in local, job-related, and national affairs). While not uncontroversial (e.g. Sokolov 2018), the emancipative values index has the advantage of being provided in a time-pooled cross-sectional dataset. Brunkert, Kruse, and Welzel (2019) constructed this dataset by using cohort differences revealed by individual WVS surveys to estimate country-mean scores of the emancipatory values index for previous years in which no survey took place. The justification for creating such simulated values is that emancipative values are acquired early during socialization and cohort differences in such values reproduce themselves over time (Welzel 2013; Ruck et al. 2020; Ruck, Bentley, and Lawson 2020). I used the data provided by Li Donni, Marino, and Welzel (2021), which cover the period from 1970 to 2010 for countries included in the WVS. The sample encompasses a low number of democratic break-downs (16). Lasso did not select the emancipative values index into the preferred model. Forcing lasso to include the index yields a range of survival estimates for a world state depending on modelling choices (the world state was assumed to have an index equal to the 2010 average of all countries in the sample weighted by their population). The survival probability curve plateaus slightly under 60 per cent if the emancipative values index is forced into the model by itself, and at 90 per cent if it is forced into the model together with the variables selected by lasso in the model shown in Figure 3.1. These estimates seem too uneven to draw definite conclusions, even with the caveats that apply to all analyses presented in this chapter.

3.4 Simulating the world state: institutional constraints

So far, I have considered conditions that in Chapter 2 were called 'structural', i.e. difficult to change deliberately. This section extends the analysis to conditions that relate to political institutions. Two of them are, in principle, amenable to deliberate institutional design, i.e. the distribution of authority between levels of governance, and judicial review of constitutional conformity. The third is less malleable: the heterogeneity of the political regimes of the territorial political units that will constitute the universal republic. These three features will be considered in turn.

Virtually all proponents of a world state envisage it as a federal system, with constitutionally protected competences and powers for 'lower' levels of governments, which often are meant to be existing states. This raises the question of whether the adoption of a federal structure would help a world state survive as a democracy. To investigate this question, I use the division of power index provided by V-Dem. The index captures the existence of elected local and regional governments and—if present—the extent to which they operate without interference from unelected bodies at the local or regional level. Countries without elected local or regional governments receive the lowest score, while countries with elected local and regional assemblies and executives that are not restricted by unelected actors (except for judicial bodies) receive the highest score. Figure 3.7 shows that a world state with the highest value on the index, indicating high decentralization, would have somewhat better chances of democratic survival than a world with the lowest value.

Next, I considered a variable that captures whether any court in the judiciary has the formal authority to invalidate governmental policies (e.g. statutes, regulations, decrees, administrative actions) on the grounds that they violate a constitutional provision (*v2jureview* from V-Dem). Lasso did not select this variable for the most predictive model. 'Forcing' the variable into the model yields the survival curves shows in Figure 3.8, for a low judicial review and a high judicial review scenario identified as the 10th and 90th percentile among all democracies, respectively (the division of power index is set at the midpoint .5 in both instances). The curves are virtually indistinguishable.

As noted in Chapter 2, debates about global democracy often touch upon the question of whether a global polity could be democratic when not all its component states are. This issue raises the question of the viability of a world state that meets the criteria of electoral democracy at the global level

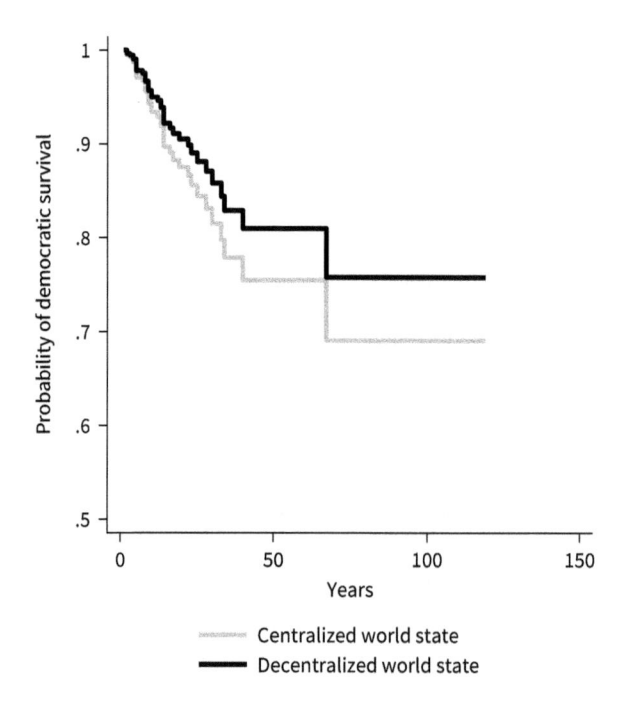

Figure 3.7 Survival of democracy in world state with low or high decentralization.

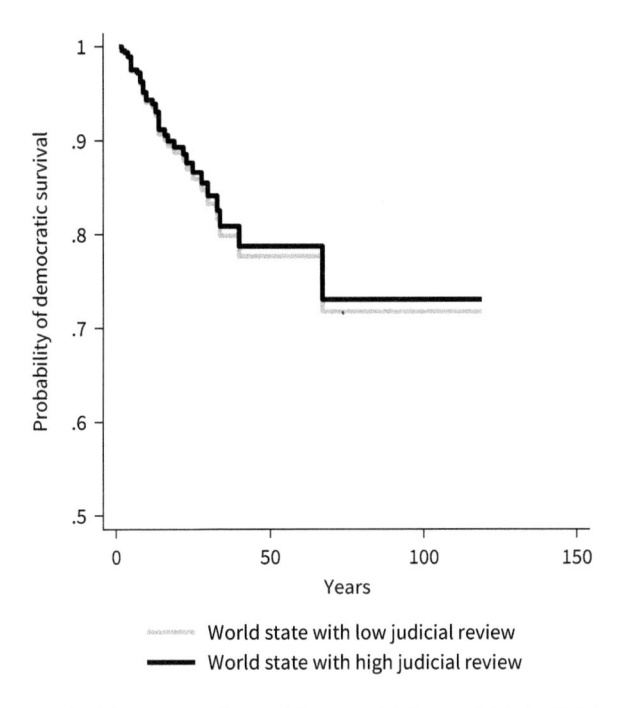

Figure 3.8 Survival of democracy in world state with low or high judicial review.

but where democratic rights are unevenly guaranteed across its territory. In essence: how viable would a world state be if some component states remained governed undemocratically?

We can approach this question empirically by using V-Dem data on subnational election unevenness. The variable *v2elsnlsff* indicates whether and to what extent the freeness and fairness of subnational elections vary across different areas of the country, where subnational elections refer to elections to regional or local offices. There is substantial unevenness in the freeness and fairness of subnational elections in several countries that pass the threshold for being considered an electoral democracy. For instance, democracy was severely restricted in the Southern states of the United States before the Voting Rights Act of 1965 (Rueschemeyer, Stephens, and Stephens 1991, 122). V-Dem reflects changes throughout the history of the USA by assigning to that country a high evenness score until the mid-nineteenth century, then a low score until the 1960s, reflecting civil rights violations in several states, and then a higher score after the 1960s (but still below the average evenness score of all electoral democracies in the V-Dem sample).

We can get some insights into the implications of unevenness in a hypothetical world state by treating the elections to fill offices of the component

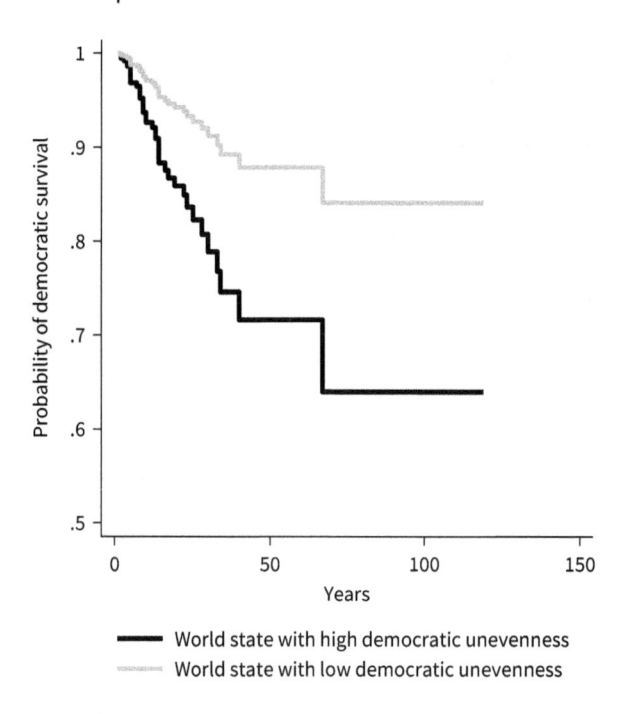

Figure 3.9 Survival of democracy in world state with low or high democratic unevenness.

states as the equivalent of subnational elections captured by the V-Dem variable. Figure 3.9 shows the survival probability of democracy in a world state at two levels of election unevenness: at a low level (90th percentile among democracies, where higher values indicate more evenness) and at a high level (10th percentile among democracies). There is a substantial difference between the two curves, which suggests that the chances of survival of global democracy would be considerably higher if all component states had themselves democratically elected governments.

3.5 Interpretation

Recall the test introduced in the previous chapter: the universal republic is viable if and only if (i) a critical mass of citizens and groups would be reasonably likely to succeed in complying with its rules, provided that they try; and (ii) those citizens and groups are able to try to comply with the rules of the universal republic. The analysis of democratic survival presented in this chapter is designed to be sensitive to the possibility that structural constraints—especially polity size, cultural diversity, and economic inequality—affect the capacity of citizens and groups to try and succeed in complying with democratic rules. But what does 'reasonably likely' mean in this context? We can answer this by adopting threshold or benchmark criteria.

The first approach sets an absolute threshold of likelihood and declares an institutional arrangement to be unviable if it falls short of that threshold. There is a fair amount of subjective judgement involved in deciding what the threshold should be. My assessment of the figures presented in this chapter is that the long-term survival prospects of democracy in a hypothetical world state are reasonably good. Without wanting to give a false impression of precision, it is striking that none of the survival curves shown in this chapter gives the world state less than a 50 per cent chance of surviving as a democracy for at least a hundred years. This suggests that its size, diversity, and inequality would not pose insurmountable obstacles to citizens and groups trying and succeeding in complying with the rules of the universal republic. Hence, it would be viable.

The 'benchmark' approach to what is 'reasonable' consists of comparing the expected viability of democracy in the world state with the viability of democracy in existing states. Democracies sometimes die. Scepticism towards the viability of the universal republic can be phrased as the expectation that it would be at substantially higher risk of death than what we are used to in existing states. Conversely, we could say that citizens and groups would be reasonably likely to succeed in complying with the rules of the UR if that likelihood is not much lower than the compliance seen in existing democratic states. In other words, existing democracies provide the benchmark against which to assess the viability of the UR. I found that the probability of a world state remaining democratic over time is similar to that of an average country, where average is in terms of size, cultural diversity, economic inequality, and other factors that might be associated with regime longevity. The benchmark interpretation of 'reasonableness' converges with the threshold interpretation to suggest that the universal republic would be viable.

Beyond this general finding, the analyses presented in the chapter also offer some more specific insights. Some policies that the universal republic may implement—notably reducing heath inequalities between its citizens and promoting freedom of movement across borders—may increase the long-term resilience of global democracy (apart from any other benefit they may entail). Ensuring that elected governments at subglobal levels retain ample areas of autonomy seems also conducive to democratic stability at the global level. As several authors have pointed out, the persistence of nondemocratic rule at lower governance levels would be a major challenge for a democratic world state and may compromise its ability to survive.

Two related aspects are worth mentioning before concluding this chapter. First, the structural and institutional variables considered in this chapter are quite bad at predicting democratic breakdown. Appendix III displays goodness-of-fit statistics for the models that underlie the survival curves shown in the chapter, specifically a statistic suitable for lasso Cox regression, the deviance ratio. On a range from 0 to 1, most of these models have out-of-sample scores under 0.10. The low predictive ability of the set of variables considered here suggests that, as political processes, democratic survival and breakdown are not subject to strict structural constraints, or at least they are not highly determined by the economic, cultural, and social structures considered in the present analysis.

Second, the focus throughout this chapter has been to gauge the likelihood of democratic breakdown rather than to identify its causes. Prediction and causal inference are separate aims involving different tasks (Shmueli 2010). Hence, I have not discussed the statistical significance of the individual variables included or excluded in the models, given that lasso focuses on comparing the predictive ability of their possible combinations. Nevertheless, the consideration of individual variables can still be interesting. Appendix IV displays the results of regular Cox proportional hazards models including the covariates considered in this chapter. The results suggests that few variables are consistently associated with democratic breakdown at conventionally accepted levels of statistical significance. Income per capita and economic growth are robustly associated with lower risks of breakdown (and lasso usually includes them in models). Religious diversity and land borders are statistically significant in some but not all specifications. Health equality, freedom of movement, and electoral unevenness are statistically significant in the single models that include them. But other variables used to capture the arguments surveyed in Chapter 2 fail to display a significant relationship with democratic survival.

It must be emphasized once more that my aim is not causal inference and the results reported in Tables A.4 and A.5 should not be seen as providing evidence on the causal role of putative drivers of democratic survival. Having said that, these results are not unexpected. Earlier reviews of evidence relevant for global democracy already concluded that several supposedly necessary conditions for democracy did not pass tests of necessity (Koenig-Archibugi 2011b, 2012b). The patterns are also consistent with more recent research. A few examples must suffice. Gerring, Hoffman, and Zarecki (2018) find that religious diversity is associated with lower democracy levels, while ethnic diversity is not. Ansell and Samuels (2014) find that higher income inequality can be conducive to more rather than less democracy. The null result regarding natural resource dependence is consistent with recent literature that cast doubts on the resource curse argument (O'Connor, Blanco, and Nugent 2018; Bergougui and Murshed 2020). The small difference between centralization and decentralization is consistent with the findings of Graham, Miller, and Strøm (2017), who found that what they call dispersive power-sharing arrangements—those based on dividing authority among territorial levels of government—do not have a statistically significant effect on democratic survival (see also Monteux 2006; Elkins and Sides 2007; Roeder 2009). The null result on judicial review is less consistent with their results on the stabilizing effect of constraining arrangements, which entail constitutional protection for individual rights and enable independent judicial institutions to defend such rights, but the measures used differ substantially. On the other hand, the negative and occasionally significant association between the number of land borders and democratic viability is in line with most studies.[5] Overall, the patterns shown in Table A.4 and Table A.5 support the insights produced by the lasso analysis, which is that democratic survival is only weakly determined by structural factors.

3.6 Concluding remarks

This chapter has tackled a difficult intellectual challenge, which is to imagine the likely durability of something that has never yet existed. Faced with such a challenge, the temptation is to retreat into agnosticism. This is not the course of action chosen by many political philosophers, political scientists, and other people who think about global order. As we saw in the Introduction and Chapter 2, statements about the viability of a democratic world state abound—some are optimistic, but most are sceptical and dismissive. This chapter presented a strategy for addressing such issues in a more systematic and evidence-based fashion, although great margins of uncertainty inevitably

---

[5] Most studies suggest that exposure to international threats and conflicts has a negative effect on democracy (Midlarsky 1995; Crescenzi and Enterline 1999; James, Solberg, and Wolfson 1999; Colaresi and Thompson 2003; Rasler and Thompson 2004), but some analyses found no association (Mousseau and Shi 1999; Oneal and Russett 2000; Reiter 2001).

remain. The main conclusion is that it seems far from inevitable that a world state would become 'a forbidding nightmare of tyranny' (Arendt 1970, 81). The chances of its survival as a democratic polity look rather good, and they may be further improved if appropriate institutions and policies are adopted. All this, of course, is based on the assumption that it can be created in the first place. The next chapter tackles this second major challenge for empirical analysis.

4

Is the universal republic achievable?

The analysis in Chapter 3 estimated the likelihood that a world state might be able to retain democratic features over time. This begs the question of whether the universal republic could emerge in the first place. Recall the test proposed in Chapter 2: the universal republic is achievable if and only if (i) a critical mass of states would be reasonably likely to succeed in transferring authority to it if they were to try; and (ii) those states are able to try to transfer authority to the UR. As discussed in Chapter 2, these conditions could be thwarted by motivational and structural constraints, and this chapter examines evidence relating to both of them. In principle, institutional constraints could be relevant too, especially the role of state sovereignty in contemporary global politics. There is little doubt that state sovereignty generates substantial path dependence in historical trajectories (Krasner 1988). In our context, the relevant question is how stringent that constraint is, and the best way to establish that is to consider to what extent it is reflected in motivations. For instance, state sovereignty may affect the achievability of the universal republic by socializing individuals and officials into considering the absence of an overarching political authority in the world as something natural, inevitable, or obviously optimal. This chapter provides some evidence to assess to what extent people and governments hold those kinds of belief.

4.1 Structural constraints

In principle, the structural conditions that might influence the viability of democracy can also affects its achievability. For this reason, the variables used in this section are mostly the same as those introduced in Chapter 3. Specifically, I examine what level of democracy could be expected to be found in a polity given its level of ethnic diversity, religious diversity, linguistic diversity, income inequality, population, and land area, while also taking into account the number of land borders, income per capita, economic growth, education, resource dependence, and the percentage of residents who belong to each of the largest world religions. As a measure of democracy, I will use the electoral

The Universal Republic. Mathias Koenig-Archibugi, Oxford University Press. © Mathias Koenig-Archibugi (2024). DOI: 10.1093/9780198921158.003.0004

democracy index of V-Dem, which varies between 0 and 1. To mitigate the effect of short-term fluctuations, the analysis will examine the association between the independent variables averaged over the 2011–15 period and the dependent variable averaged over the 2016–20 period in a cross-sectional analysis of all countries for which the relevant data are available.

Lasso linear regression is used to predict the level of democracy of a hypothetical polity that encompasses the whole world. The main features of lasso have been summarized in Chapter 3. The observations consist of 152 countries, four fifths of which are randomly assigned to the training set and the remainder to the testing set. Training occurred by cross-validation, with the number of cross-validation folds set at five rather than the standard ten because of the small size of the sample.

Lasso was instructed to estimate two models, one without constraints on which variables the lasso procedure could select, and one with forced selection of six variables corresponding to the presumed structural constraints highlighted in Chapter 2: ethnic diversity, religious diversity, linguistic diversity, income inequality, population, and land area.

The unconstrained model yielded a predicted value of .68 on the electoral democracy index that ranges from 0 to 1. The model with forced inclusion of the presumed constraint variables yielded a predicted value of .63. The predictive power of the models is moderate, as shown by the goodness-of-fit statistics displayed in Appendix III.

I also employed an alternative procedure using Clarify 2.0 (King, Tomz, and Wittenberg 2000). Clarify uses simulations to derive quantities of interests and account for uncertainty. In our case, the quantity of interest is the predicted score of electoral democracy conditional on one chosen value of each explanatory variable. Given that in our application the combination of chosen values corresponds to a hypothetical rather than an observed case, the quantity to be estimated is a simulated counterfactual predicted value—more specifically, the average predicted value and the uncertainty around the average. The predicted values generated by Clarify simulations differ from the expected values in a linear regression in that the former reflect not only the estimation uncertainty caused by not having an infinite number of observations but also the fundamental uncertainty caused by unmodelled random factors. As a result, predicted values have a larger variance than expected values. The values for the world introduced in the previous chapter are used in 1,000 simulations, which yields a mean simulated counterfactual predicted score of .52 for the world state. The 90 per cent confidence interval for the prediction ranges from .21 to .86. The wide range of the interval shows the high level of uncertainty surrounding the estimation, and it encompasses the scores obtained from lasso.

The electoral democracy score for a world state predicted by lasso (.63/.68) and by Clarify (.52) can be compared to the median value of 179 countries averaged over 2016–20, which is .51. To provide a perspective for comparison, Figure 4.1 shows how the values of the electoral democracy index (averaged over 2016–20) are distributed across those 179 countries.

In interpreting this result, it is worth recalling a point made in the previous chapter. The analysis by Baltz, Vasselai, and Hicken (2022) shows that most measures of democracy based on a binary conception (democracy is either present or absent) closely correspond to a .42 cutpoint on the V-Dem electoral democracy index. Hence, the world state's simulated counterfactual predicted score of .52, and a fortiori the higher score predicted by lasso, fall comfortably within the range of values that are associated with a classification as democracy in the most commonly used binary democracy datasets (e.g. Cheibub, Gandhi, and Vreeland 2010; Boix, Miller, and Rosato 2013; Geddes, Wright, and Frantz 2014).

This approach can be extended to include the degree of diversity of political values among the citizens of the polity. This extension is useful as it addresses the argument that democracy requires 'underlying agreement on ethical principles' (Miller 2009, 208; cf. List and Koenig-Archibugi 2010). Some studies use the socio-demographic indicators considered above—religious affiliation, language, ethnicity, and income—as proxies for the distribution of policy preferences across a population (Alesina, Baqir, and Easterly 1999; Gubler and Selway 2012). While such socio-demographic characteristics are likely to influence the formation and distribution of policy values, the correlation between the two is far from perfect (Kriesi 1998; Dion and Birchfield

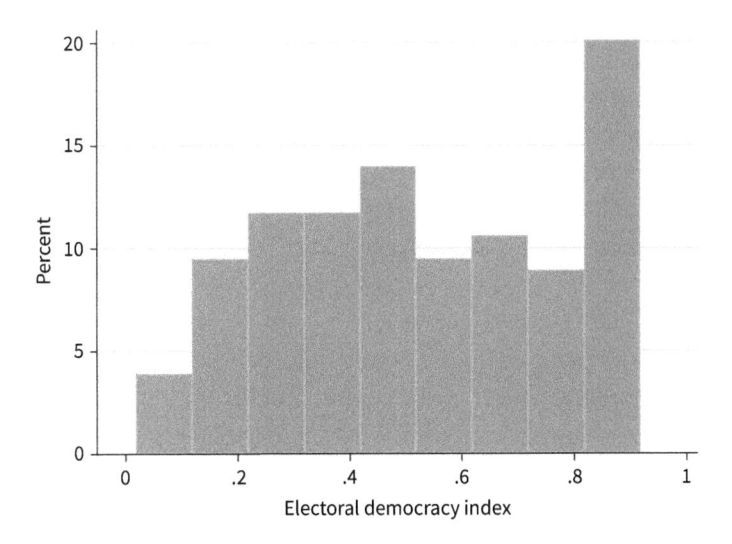

Figure 4.1 Electoral democracy index (averaged over 2016–2020) across 179 countries.

2010; Guillaud 2013). Ideally, an analysis of the association between value diversity and democracy should rely on more direct indicators of such values, notably gathered through surveys that are representative of the general population. The remainder of this section presents a strategy that Thomas Hale and I developed to measure the diversity of policy values at the national and at the global level (Hale and Koenig-Archibugi 2019) and then examines how diversity can be accounted for in the task of generating predictions about the level of democracy of a world state.

A key decision concerns the dimensions that structure value diversity around the world. Research on Western countries seems to have reached the conclusion that public opinion (as opposed to political parties) is divided along at least two distinct dimensions (Kitschelt 1994; Kriesi et al. 2008; Rovny and Marks 2011; Lefkofridi, Wagner, and Willmann 2014; Pan and Xu 2018; Gethin, Martínez-Toledano, and Piketty 2021). First, there is an economic left–right dimension, which concerns issues such as the relationship between governments and markets and the redistribution of income and other resources across economic strata. Second, there is a cultural dimension that pits libertarian against traditionalist–authoritarian value orientations. While these dimensions are compelling and are included in the study, we accepted the argument of Rovny and Marks (2011) for identifying the main dimensions deductively rather than inductively (e.g. via factor analysis). Therefore, we added a third dimension—the importance of protecting the environment even at the expense of economic growth—because theoretically it seems sufficiently independent from the other two dimensions and because of its substantive importance for national and global politics.

Population surveys can be used to estimate two quantities of interest. The first is the diversity of the population along those main dimensions of political contestation. There are various ways in which diversity can be measured (Lindqvist and Östling 2010; Hale and Koenig-Archibugi 2019). A useful measure of diversity is the standard deviation of survey responses, i.e. the extent to which responses are spread away from the average response. This can be interpreted as the level of disagreement among citizens over the principles that should guide public policy. This variable can be called *value polarization.*

The second quantity is *value cross-cuttingness,* i.e. the extent to which views on one policy value (e.g. economic redistribution) are correlated with views on a different policy value (e.g. traditional morality) in a population. Considering cross-cuttingness alongside diversity is useful because an influential tradition in political science argues that diversity poses a risk to democracy only when social cleavages reinforce each other. In an early contribution, E. A. Ross (1920, 164–165), quoted in Coser (1956, 76–77), noted that a society 'which is ridden by a dozen oppositions along lines running in every direction may actually be in less danger of being torn with violence or falling to pieces than one split just along one line. For each new cleavage contributes to narrow the cross clefts, so that one might say that society is sewn together by its inner conflicts.' Seymour Martin Lipset summed up the key insight of this tradition by writing that 'the chances for stable democracy are enhanced to the extent that groups and individuals have a number of crosscutting, politically relevant affiliations' (Lipset 1960, 88–89).[1] Nicholas Miller provided a useful synopsis of four logically distinct, but compatible, arguments supporting the proposition that cross-cutting preferences lead to political stability. For our purposes, the key argument is that cross-cutting preferences distribute political satisfaction. 'In the absence of a majority preference cluster, political outcomes are brought about by shifting coalitions of smaller clusters. Political outcomes probably please and displease nobody all the time; rather they please almost everybody some of the time. Political satisfaction, although probably nowhere total, is widespread' (Miller 1983, 737).

To be useful for the purpose at hand, survey data need to fulfil stringent conditions. First, they should cover as many countries as possible. Second, to measure cross-cuttingness we need to know how the *same* individuals responded to questions on *at least two*, and ideally more, distinct policy dimensions. Third, we need questions that ensure comparability across diverse national contexts. In our study (Hale and Koenig-Archibugi 2019), we relied primarily on the Pew Global Attitudes Survey 2007, which polled around one thousand individuals in each of forty-seven countries.[2] The relevant questions covered values related to traditional cultural and social norms, economic life, and environmental protection. We aggregated individual responses to obtain several variables. The most relevant in this context are an indicator of *value polarization* based on the standard deviation of the response values, for each of the three relevant dimensions: traditionalism, economic values, and environment; and an indicator for *value cross-cuttingness* for each pair of dimensions: traditionalism–economy, economy–environment, and traditionalism–environment. Hale and Koenig-Archibugi (2019) provide these measures for each country in the sample as well as for the 'world', which is made up by the approximately 47,000 respondents in the Pew study, with responses weighted by the population of the respondents' countries. This 'world' includes forty-seven countries,

[1] See also Truman (1951, 514), R. Dahl (1956, 104–105), Dahrendorf (1959, 215), and Hale and Koenig-Archibugi (2016).
[2] The survey respondents are a representative sample of the adult population of the forty-seven countries, except those in seven countries (Bolivia, Brazil, China, India, Ivory Coast, Pakistan, and Venezuela) where the urban population is slightly to moderately overrepresented and one country (South Africa) where the respondents are exclusively urban. See Pew Research Center (2007) for full details.

which together are home to about 60 per cent of the world's population. Thus, it is different from the entity 'world' considered in Chapter 3 and the first part of this section, which included the population of almost all countries. The main finding of Hale and Koenig-Archibugi (2019) is that the distribution of policy values across the 'world' was not significantly different from the distribution of policy values *within* countries. The implications of this finding for the desirability of the universal republic will be discussed in Chapter 6. Here, the usefulness of these measures is in complementing the analyses done earlier in this section.

Regression analyses can be conducted on forty-four countries, given that three countries included in the Pew survey have missing data on key variables. The number is too low for an application of lasso (goodness-of-fit statistics turned negative). But the *value polarization* and *value cross-cuttingness* variables can be added to those already entered into the Clarify simulation reported earlier. The procedure yields a mean simulated counterfactual predicted electoral democracy score of .64 for the 'world' state. The 90 per cent confidence interval for the prediction ranges from .23 to 1.04.

The mean simulated counterfactual predicted score of the forty-seven-country 'world' is larger than the score based on the inclusion of almost all countries in the Clarify simulation reported earlier (.64 vs .52). This is to be expected, considering that the countries included in the 2007 Pew survey were not selected randomly. The average electoral democracy score of the sample including nearly all countries (176) is .53, while the average electoral democracy score of the forty-seven countries in the Pew sample is .61. Moreover, the small number of countries in the regression further increases the confidence interval for the prediction, indicating a very high level of uncertainty. Considering all these caveats, the conclusion we can draw from the inclusion of public opinion in the simulation is mainly negative: the analysis failed to uncover systematic evidence that the level of value diversity across the world would be associated with low levels of democracy.

4.2 Motivational constraints: social movements

Global politics is driven by a myriad of actors, some of which act primarily or exclusively within national political arenas and others whose activities routinely intersect state boundaries in one way or another. In pursuing their interests and values, they intentionally or unintentionally affect the prospects of supranational integration. Zürn and his collaborators analysed nearly

12,000 claims made by a wide variety of actors on several issue-areas across a broad range of political forums, and found that overall cosmopolitan positions are expressed more frequently than communitarian positions (Zürn 2018, 232–233; De Wilde et al. 2019). To make the discussion more manageable, the remainder of this chapter will focus on three sets of actors that, as suggested in Chapter 2, are particularly important for the assessment of motivational constraints: state agents, citizens, and social movements. In some accounts, social movements are expected to be the main drivers of change (Marchetti 2008, 164–166), with state agents and citizens playing the role of veto players who have to be persuaded. I will consider empirical evidence relating to social movements first, followed by citizens and governments.

Organized groups of activists have campaigned for strengthening and deepening international cooperation since the first peace society was created in London in 1816 (Hanschmidt 1977; Cooper 1991). Over the past two centuries, some of those activists supported the establishment of a world state (Mayne and Pinder 1990; Baratta 2004a, b; Threlkeld 2022). However, movements explicitly campaigning for world state formation never developed into mass membership organizations. The question to be considered is whether advocacy for the universal republic could in principle be carried out by a broader set of social movement actors.

In some cases, the activities of world government advocates influenced the outlook of a broader range of groups. For instance, world federalists active during World War II influenced the international stance of anticolonial movements, as reflected in the wording of the 1945 Pan-African Congress resolution quoted in the Introduction: 'We demand for Black Africa autonomy and independence, so far and no further than it is possible in this "One World" for groups and peoples to rule themselves subject to inevitable world unity and federation' (Padmore 1947, 5; see also Bhagavan 2012; Getachew 2019). In the 1990s, the World Federalist Movement coordinated numerous civil society organizations in the campaign to establish an international criminal court (Glasius 2006). The ability of currently active organizations such as Democracy Without Borders to mobilize a broader coalition in a campaign for global government depends on this goal's resonance with the political orientation of a broad spectrum of activists and leaders of civil society organizations. Is it true that 'there is simply no constituency for the visions of' world government advocates (Sørensen 2013, 897)?

Systematic evidence on the views of participants in social movements regarding world government is scarce. Three pieces of evidence are particularly relevant and cover different points on the spectrum from existing leaders of institutionalized NGOs to potential future leaders. First, in 2003 386 NGO leaders from all world regions participated in a survey organized by the Global Stakeholder Panel initiative with the aim of determining 'What NGO leaders want for the Year 2020' (GlobeScan 2004). Of the respondents, 66 per cent declared that an 'evolving world government with global institutions accountable to citizens' described their ideal vision of global governance in 2020, with 19 per cent stating that the sentence did not describe their ideal vision. Conversely, only 20 per cent declared that 'strong national governments with few international controls and weak international institutions' described their ideal vision of global governance in 2020.

Second, a sample of the participants in the 2005 World Social Forum (WSF) was asked whether it was a good or bad idea to have a democratic world government. For 32 per cent it was a bad idea, for 39 per cent it was a good idea but not plausible, and 29 per cent said it was a good idea and plausible (Chase-Dunn et al. 2008).

Third, Webb (2016) surveyed a sample of about 2,000 undergraduate university students in the social sciences, law, management, and education across three countries of the global South in 2013–14: Kenya, Pakistan, and Peru. As social movement leaders are disproportionally likely to evolve from university graduates in such subjects, the survey can provide insights into their future political views. In each of the three countries, respondents in favour of 'expanding the capacities and authority of the United Nations as a democratic world government' outnumbered the opponents by more than two to one.

In sum, these sources show no evidence that present and future leaders and members of civic groups would be fundamentally opposed to the idea of a universal republic.

4.3 Motivational constraints: citizens

The argument that a democratic world state is not attractive to citizens rests on two conjectures (Miller 2009, 2010; see also the discussion by Zürn 2000). The first is that many citizens reject global statehood as a way of ordering the world. The second is about the reasons why they react in that way, or would so react if asked. Among those reasons, a lack of trust, solidarity, and shared identity when it comes to relationships across national borders are often mentioned. More specifically, the conjecture is that most individuals do not trust people of a different nationality enough to accept the risk that they may end up being in the minority in a democratic vote, and/or do not feel enough solidarity towards foreigners to accept a collective decision that may entail sacrifices for themselves or their communities. Examining trust, solidarity, and identity as the supposed drivers of institutional preferences is useful also because many people may not yet have formed a clear view on global government, given that it does not occupy a prominent place on the political agenda (Ghassim 2020). I will consider evidence on trust, solidarity, and identity first, before considering more direct evidence on institutional preferences.

Global surveys provide a major source of information on *trust* in foreigners. The 2017–20 wave of the World Values Survey asked about 140,000 respondents in eighty-eight countries how much they trusted people of another nationality. Excluding 'don't know' and 'no answer', across the whole sample 46.7 per cent completely or somewhat trusted people of another nationality, and 53.3 per cent did not trust them very much or at all. We can also compare levels of trust towards foreigners with levels of trust among members of the respondents' own communities. The most useful question in the WVS asks how much trust respondents have in people in their neighbourhood. In the 2017–20 wave, 72.8 per cent completely or somewhat trusted people in the respondent's neighbourhood and 26.1 per cent did not trust them very much or at all.

To assess whether mistrust across borders is likely to weaken, we can look for trends. In twenty-eight countries, the question about trust in people of another nationality was asked in each of three most recent waves of the WVS. The percentage of respondents completely or somewhat trusting people of another nationality was fairly stable—39.1 per cent in the 2005–09 wave, 40.1 in the 2010–14 wave, and 44.6 in the 2017–20 wave.[3] In almost every country and year, trust in people in the neighbourhood is substantially higher than trust in people of another nationality.[4] But the average difference between trust in foreigners and trust in neighbours across the twenty-eight countries showed some sign of reduction: it was 35.2 percentage points in 2005–09, 33.3 in 2010–14, and 29.8 in 2017–20.

Solidarity beyond borders is somewhat more difficult to measure. There is convincing evidence that the circle of moral concern has expanded over the past two centuries (Buchanan and Powell 2018; Leach, Kitchin, and

---

[3] Own calculation based on data from Haerpfer et al. (2022). The percentages give the average of twenty-eight countries not weighted by population size. The countries are Argentina, Australia, Brazil, Chile, China, Taiwan, Colombia, Cyprus, Georgia, Germany, Jordan, South Korea, Malaysia, Mexico, Morocco, Netherlands, Peru, Poland, Romania, Russia, Slovenia, Spain, Sweden, Thailand, Turkey, Ukraine, Egypt, and the United States.

[4] The main exception is the United States. Excluding 'don't know' and 'no answer', during the 2017–20 wave 10 per cent trusted people in the neighbourhood completely and 61 per cent trusted them somewhat, while 8 per cent trusted people of another nationality completely and 66 per cent trusted them somewhat. The proportions were roughly similar during the 2005–09 and the 2010–14 waves.

Sutton 2023). Based on surveys of nationally representative samples in eight countries (United States, Guatemala, Columbia, Spain, United Kingdom, Germany, China, and Japan), Bai, Gauri, and Fiske (2021) identify two distinct dimensions of moral cosmopolitanism. What they call the 'equitable benefit' dimension concerns the willingness to benefit non-nationals even if the resource reallocation comes at the expense of co-nationals. They find that about half of the respondents across the eight countries (with some national differences) can be classified as moral cosmopolitans in this sense. What they call the 'equitable security' dimension entails the willingness to protect both co-nationals and non-nationals from harm. They find that 95 per cent of respondents show moral cosmopolitan tendencies in this sense. The asymmetry between benefits and harms contributes to explaining why the results of surveys aimed at gauging transnational solidarity are highly sensitive to the specific wording of the questions.

Several surveys help researchers to gauge the prevalence of global *identity* and its relationship with national and other local identities (Bayram 2015; Gorman and Seguin 2018; Reysen and Katzarska-Miller 2018; Reysen 2022). As Bayram (2019) shows, many survey respondents who express identification as world citizens also declare allegiance to their nation and willingness to perform the ultimate patriotic sacrifice of going to war to defend their country. She concludes that world citizens have developed a dual identity that is compatible with patriotic obligations. However, this may not suffice to assuage suspicions directed at 'those supposed Cosmopolites who ... boast of loving everyone in order to have the right to love no one', as Rousseau (*c*.1760/1994, 81) put it. More informative about the prospects of public support for, or opposition to, the transfer of authority to a world government are questions that directly pit national and global identities against each other, forcing respondents to indicate their primary allegiances.[5] The survey company GlobeScan measured agreement with the statement 'I see myself more as a global citizen than a citizen of [survey] country' in multiple countries between 2001 and 2016. Across the eighteen countries included in the 2016 survey, an average of 51 per cent somewhat or strongly agreed with the statement, while 43 per cent somewhat or strongly disagreed (GlobeScan 2016). Based on fourteen countries where the question had been repeatedly asked since 2001, the average proportion of respondents in agreement has increased

---

[5] Montesquieu provided a memorably resounding answer to such a question: 'If I knew something that was useful to me and harmful to my family, I would banish it from my mind. If I knew something useful to my family but not to my Country, I would seek to forget it. If I knew something useful to my Country and harmful to Europe, or else useful to Europe and harmful to the human race, I would regard it as a crime' (Montesquieu 2012, 221).

over the period (see Figure 4.2). The increase is apparent among non-OECD countries, whereas the proportion of respondents who prioritize global citizenship appears to have declined in OECD countries, although these trends need to be treated with caution because the sample of countries was not identical across the waves.

Despite assertions of increasing nationalist attitudes in recent years, no such general trend is detectable (Bieber 2018). There is also some evidence that supranational identities are promoted by institutional integration (Dogan 1994; Luhmann 2017), a dynamic that should be kept in mind when considering the trends in international authority discussed in section 4.4.

I will now consider public attitudes towards institutions of global governance. Some analysts include levels of public support for *existing* international organizations among the evidence on the achievability of cosmopolitan governance (Zürn 2018, 241–243). By contrast, the following discussion will focus on public views about *changing* global governance. Gauging the attitudes of citizens regarding major changes, and specifically world government, faces at least two problems. The first is that relevant representative opinion surveys are scarce. While there are several surveys covering the United States, other countries have none, or at most one or two surveys.

I See Myself More as a Global Citizen than a Citizen of My country
"Agree,"* OECD vs Non-OECD Countries,** Trends, 2001–2016

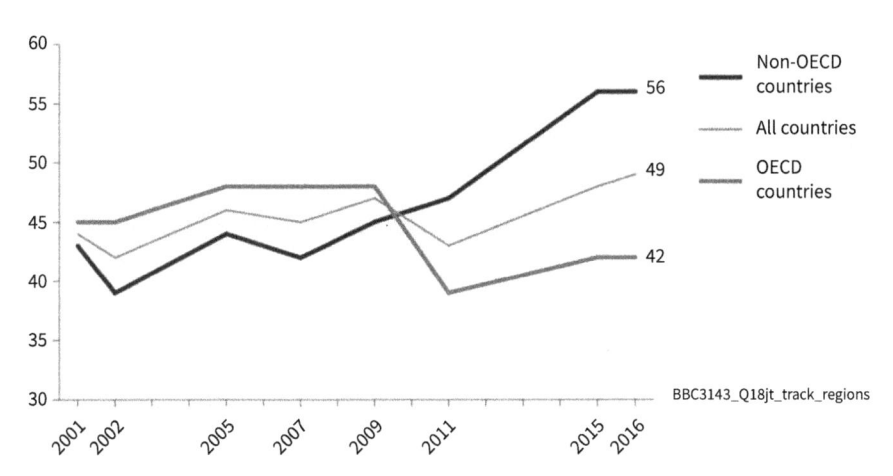

*'Strongly agree' plus 'Somewhat agree'
**OECD countries include Canada, Chile, Germany, Mexico, Spain, UK, and USA; Non-OECD countries include Brazil, China, India, Indonesia, Kenya, Nigeria, and Russia.
Not all countries were asked in all years.

Figure 4.2 Global vs national citizenship over time.

Source: GlobeScan (2016). Copyright © 2005 by GLOBESCAN. Reproduced with permission.

The second problem is that surveys typically gauge support or opposition for broad concepts such as 'world government', while views may depend on specific aspects of institutional design.

A further feature of the relevant surveys is that the distribution of answers is sensitive to the specific wording of the question. For instance, a 1993 survey in the United States found 44 per cent of respondents to be in favour of 'the participation of the United States in a convention where elected delegates from nations work to develop a draft of a constitution that could lead to a democratic world government that would have responsibility in areas where individual nations cannot solve problems alone' (29 per cent were neutral and 22 per cent were opposed) (Americans Talk Issues Foundation 1993).[6] But just two years later, 83 per cent of respondents stated that it would be a 'bad thing' for the United States if it 'did give up its national independence or sovereignty to become part of a world government', with only 9 per cent regarding that as a good thing for the United States (Cable News Network /USA Today 1995). At least part of the large difference between the responses was arguably due to the different framing ('cannot solve problems alone' vs 'give up its national independence or sovereignty'). From the perspective of public opinion research, the sensitivity to survey wording is a 'problem', in so far as it makes it more difficult to identify supposedly 'true' attitudes. From the perspective of those interested in the achievability of a democratic world state, however, that sensitivity is not a problem at all, but a sign that public opinion is relatively malleable and responsive to contrasting political frames and messaging. In other words, it shows that the issue of global political integration can be the subject of 'politics', understood as a contestation between coalitions promoting competing political positions and frames, and whose ability to attract undecided citizens to their side is not fully predictable before intense political campaigning is underway.[7] The malleability of public opinion is in itself an indication that there are no stringent motivational constraints.

With these provisos in mind, we can now review what evidence exists. The years following World War II are often considered a high point for support for world government not only among intellectuals and politicians but

---

[6] Half of the sample of the same survey was, by contrast, asked about the participation of the US in 'a world conference where nations review the charter of the United Nations and propose amendments that would give the U.N. responsibility in areas where individual nations cannot solve problems alone' and favourable responses were higher, at 62 per cent (29 per cent neutral and 22 per cent unfavourable).

[7] Ghassim (2020) used survey experiments across multiple countries to determine whether people's attitudes on global democracy are affected by the positions taken by their preferred political parties on that issue. He found that partisan cues affect the attitudes of supporters of some parties, but not those of others.

also among the public (Baratta 2004b). An international survey carried out for UNESCO in 1948 showed that in six out of nine countries more respondents agreed than disagreed that 'there should be a world government able to control the laws made by each country': Britain (44 vs 40 per cent), France (45 vs 36 per cent), Germany (46 vs 33 per cent), Italy (56 vs 28 per cent), the Netherlands (46 vs 32 per cent), and Norway (48 vs 35 per cent). Substantial minorities were in agreement in the remaining three countries: Australia (35 vs 58 per cent), Mexico (19 vs 72 per cent), and the United States (42 vs 48 per cent) (Buchanan and Cantril 1953, 62).[8]

After a long gap, cross-national opinion surveys on world order preferences were fielded again from 2000. Most surveys tended to focus on support for 'strengthening' the United Nations. For instance, a survey fielded in 2007 found that a relative majority believed that the UN Security Council should have the right to authorize the use of military force to defend a country that has been attacked and to stop a country from supporting terrorist groups in all ten countries where those questions were asked; the right to prevent severe human rights violations such as genocide in all twelve countries surveyed; the right to prevent a country that does not have nuclear weapons from acquiring them in nine out of eleven countries; the right to prevent a country that does not have nuclear weapons from producing nuclear fuel that could be used to produce nuclear weapons in eight out of ten countries; and the right to restore by force a democratic government that has been overthrown in seven out of ten countries (Chicago Council on Global Affairs and WorldPublicOpinion.org 2007). In ten out of sixteen countries, more respondents agreed than disagreed with the statement that, 'When dealing with international problems, [their country] should be more willing to make decisions within the United Nations even if this means that [their country] will sometimes have to go along with a policy that is not its first choice' (Chicago Council on Global Affairs and WorldPublicOpinion.org 2007).

That survey and other similar surveys[9] are useful to gauge public views on how much authority the United Nations and other organizations should have, but they are less useful to understand how citizens would like decisions on

---

[8] The results for the United States are roughly in line with responses to a question repeatedly asked by Gallup in the decade after World War II: 'Do you think the United Nations should or should not be strengthened to make it a world government, with power to control the armed forces of all nations, including the United States?' Respondents in favour of world government outnumbered those against in 1946 (54 vs 28 per cent), 1947 (56 vs 30 per cent), and 1951 (49 vs 36 per cent), and then were slightly outnumbered in 1953 (41 vs 45 per cent) and 1955 (40 vs 42 per cent) (Gallup Organization 1946, 1947, 1951, 1953, 1955).

[9] Notably the World Value Survey before its 2017–20 wave, whose findings are analysed by Ecker-Ehrhardt (2016), and the International Social Survey Programme, whose findings are analysed by Bearce and Scott (2019).

the use of that authority to be made. Preferences on decision-making procedures were captured more directly in a survey conducted in 2007 for the BBC World Service in fifteen countries (Australia, Denmark, Dubai, France, Germany, India, Italy, Norway, Poland, Russia, Singapore, South Africa, South Korea, UK, USA). Respondents were asked 'How likely would you be to support a Global Parliament, where votes are based on country population sizes, and the global parliament is able to make binding policies?' Across the whole sample, 14.4 per cent responded 'Very likely—it is a good idea'; 23.1 per cent responded 'Quite likely—but with reservations'; 14.9 per cent responded 'Quite unlikely—but it might work'; and 19.1 per cent responded 'Very unlikely—it is a bad idea' (responses not averaged by population sizes). Cross-national differences are very significant: an overwhelming majority of Indian respondents supported a global parliament, while US and Danish respondents were the most opposed. It is notable that even the latter countries sizable minorities supported the proposal (24 per cent in USA and 15 per cent in Denmark) (Synovate 2007).[10]

Despite the widespread perception of a backlash against international authority during the past decade, citizens continued to express substantial support for forms of supranational authority in recent cross-national surveys. The Global Challenges Foundation found more people agreeing than disagreeing that 'a new supranational entity should be established to take enforceable global decisions in order to solve global problems such as climate change, environmental pollution, war and poverty' in all nine countries surveyed in 2014 (Brazil, China, Germany, India, Poland, Russia, South Africa, Sweden, USA) and all ten countries surveyed in 2018, and then again in 2020 (Australia, Brazil, China, Germany, India, Russia, South Africa, Sweden, UK, USA) (Global Challenges Foundation 2014; ComRes and Global Challenges Foundation 2018; Novus and Global Challenges Foundation 2020).[11] However, the Global Challenges Foundation surveys did not try to capture preferences on how the new supranational organizations should make

---

[10] The BBC/Synovate survey did not specify that the members of the global parliament would be directly elected by citizens. Other surveys show strong support for this proposal. A 2005 survey covered eighteen countries (Argentina, Australia, Brazil, Canada, Chile, China, Germany, Britain, India, Indonesia, Italy, Mexico, Philippines, Poland, Russia, South Korea, Turkey, USA) and found that in all of them more respondents favoured than opposed the proposal of 'Creating a new UN Parliament, made up of representatives directly elected by citizens, having powers equal to the current UN General Assembly that is controlled by national governments' (Council on Foreign Relations 2009, 211). Majorities in all countries also favoured having their country's official representative to the United Nations General Assembly be elected by the people of their country (Council on Foreign Relations 2009, 211).

[11] Wordings changed slightly across the surveys. The 2018 and 2020 questionnaire had 'supranational organization' and 'to address global risks' instead of, respectively, 'supranational entity', and 'to solve global problems such as climate change, environmental pollution, war and poverty'. The 2020 survey had 'binding' instead of 'enforceable'.

decisions. This aspect is addressed by Ghassim (2020), who conducted an online survey on global democracy in Brazil, Germany, Japan, the United Kingdom, and the United States in 2019. He found that majorities in all five countries supported the creation of a global parliament (average: 67 per cent), the creation of a global government (average: 64 per cent), and a global democracy including both a parliament and a government (average: 65 per cent). A 2023 survey found that the supporters of a new global parliament outnumber the opponents in thirteen out of fifteen countries (average support: 60 per cent) (Bummel 2023). The survey is especially informative because respondents were informed that 'every country would be represented based on how many citizens it has, rather than its own national government representation to the UN', that the global parliament would 'handle global issues like global peace, climate change, and emergency situations like pandemics', and that it would be 'part of a global legislative system that under certain circumstances would pass legally binding laws to govern the world as a whole' (Bummel 2023).[12]

In an important study, Ghassim and Pauli (2023) gauged the level of public support for a democratic world government based on a survey experiment involving over 42,000 citizens in seventeen countries in various regions of the world. When the survey prompt specified that a world government would be democratic, with 'people worldwide ... represented through free and fair elections or other ways of citizen participation', the proposal of a democratic world government was endorsed by 67 per cent of respondents weighted equally, and by 71 per cent with responses weighted by population sizes. Supporters outnumbered opponents in all seventeen countries except the USA and the UK. In the UK, democratic world government attracted majority support when it was further specified that it would have 'the right and the power to deal with global issues like climate change, world poverty, and

[12] The 2017–20 wave of the WVS included a new question on effectiveness and democracy in international organizations should prioritize being effective or being democratic. More specifically, respondents were asked: 'People sometimes say that international organizations should prioritize improving people's lives, even if this may imply that decisions are not made democratically. What do you think international organizations should prioritize, being effective or being democratic?' Across more than 50,000 respondents in forty-four countries, responses have a mean of 5.74 and a median of 6 on a scale where 1 indicates a strong priority for effectiveness and 10 indicates a strong priority for democracy (Lee and Lim 2022). The survey shows a remarkably high level of support for democracy in international organizations, especially considering that respondents were prompted to assume that democracy entails a cost in terms of effectiveness (at least some respondents may firmly believe that democracy is conducive to greater effectiveness). But the interpretation of this finding is not straightforward because the survey offers no direct information on how respondents would define 'democratic' (or 'effective') in the context of international organizations. Lee and Lim (2022) developed a strategy to estimate whether the priority attached to democracy stems from a citizen-centred conception or from a state-centred conception of IO democracy held by the public, finding empirical support for the latter but not for the former. The results are insightful, but they still depend on indirect proxies for citizen-centred and state-centred conceptions.

international peace; while national governments would maintain control over issues that are not global'. The US remained an outlier, as a democratic world government focused on such global issues was opposed by 55 per cent of respondents in that country (Ghassim and Pauli 2023).

The surveys mentioned so far provide valuable insights on the magnitude of citizen support for a democratic world government or key aspects of it, such as a directly elected legislature. Beyond that, it would be useful to know how citizens assess each individual component of the universal republic as it is understood in this book. A study conducted by Farsan Ghassim, Luis Cabrera, and myself provides more evidence on that question (Ghassim, Koenig-Archibugi, and Cabrera 2022). It is based on an online survey completed in 2019 by respondents in six countries: Argentina, China, India, Russia, Spain, and the United States. The respondent samples in each country are nationally representative with regard to age, gender, and region. The survey was designed as a conjoint experiment (Hainmueller, Hopkins, and Yamamoto 2014), a method that enabled us to identify the effect that each of a range of institutional design options has on preferences regarding the UN. Respondents saw on their screen two UN profiles consisting of randomized combinations of reform or status quo options and were asked to indicate which of the two profiles they preferred. Because of the experimental conditions created by random assignment, we can be confident that the patterns revealed by aggregating the responses result only from people's preferences for institutional design.

Table 4.1 summarizes the nine attributes and respective options presented to survey respondents. For each attribute, one of the options reflects the status quo and the other option(s) entail major reforms. The options include several features that can be considered important ingredients of the universal republic. Some relate to the authority of a reformed UN: the possibility of outvoting individual states; the possibility of making decisions that are binding on every country on important security, environmental, and economic matters; the possibility for a strengthened UN organization directly to use force to stop serious violations of UN law by a member country; and the possibility of direct taxation of transnational companies. Other options relate to the democratic quality of decision-making: citizens directly electing their representatives in the highest decision-making body; taking all important decisions in a body that includes all member countries; linking vote shares to relative population size; and avoiding veto rights for any individual country. We also offered an option that has a more ambiguous relationship with the democratic quality of the organization: giving (people in) countries with full press freedom and where political parties compete in free elections more

Table 4.1 Institutional attributes and options presented in the survey on UN reform

---

Authority features

Decision rule: Decisions in the highest UN body would be adopted when they are supported:

(a) by two-thirds of votes for the most important matters, and by a simple majority for other matters
(b) by a simple majority of votes on all matters
(c) only by unanimous agreement of all members.

Bindingness: UN decisions would be binding:

(a) on every country, but only in matters of international peace and security
(b) on those countries that voluntarily accept them
(c) on every country on important security, environmental, and economic matters.

Enforcement: To stop serious violations of UN law by a member country, force could be used:

(a) collectively by other member countries
(b) by no one
(c) directly by a strengthened UN organization.

Budget: The UN would get resources from:

(a) mandatory contributions by member countries, plus voluntary contributions
(b) voluntary contributions by governments
(c) taxes levied on transnational companies directly by the UN.

Representation features

Delegates: The highest decision-making body of the UN would include:

(a) only representatives of national executives
(b) representatives of national executives meeting in one chamber, and representatives elected directly by citizens of member countries specifically to serve in a second chamber
(c) representatives of national executives meeting in one chamber and members of national parliaments or congress meeting in a second chamber.

Important decisions: Important UN decisions would be taken:

(a) by a larger body composed of all member countries, or by a smaller UN body composed of some permanent and some elected member countries, depending on the subject matter
(b) always by a body that includes all member countries.

Vote shares: The share of votes held by each country would be:

(a) equal, regardless of country population sizes
(b) directly proportional to country population sizes
(c) larger for more populous countries, but less than proportional to country population sizes
(d) based on a combination of country population sizes and their contributions to the UN budget.

Veto rights: Special rights to block UN decisions would be held by:

(a) the current permanent members of the Security Council
(b) the current permanent members of the Security Council, plus a few other major countries
(c) no country.

Status of democracies: Countries with full press freedom and where political parties compete in free elections would:

(a) not have more power in the highest UN decision-making body
(b) have more power in the highest UN decision-making body.

Source: Ghassim, Koenig-Archibugi, and Cabrera (2022)

power in the highest decision-making body (Ghassim, Koenig-Archibugi, and Cabrera 2022).

In the cross-country sample, we found support for several of these reforms: respondents were more likely to support a UN model when it can make decisions that are binding on every country on important security, environmental, and economic matters; when citizens directly elect their representatives in the highest decision-making body; when this body includes all member countries; and when democratic countries have more power. By contrast, other potential cosmopolitan reforms reduced preferences for UN models: when a simple majority replaces a qualified majority also for important matters; the possibility of direct taxation of transnational companies; introducing direct and degressive proportionality in voting shares; and abolishing all veto rights. Finally, respondents were indifferent about several reform proposals—in the sense that how they judged a UN model showed to them was not affected by whether it incorporated the proposal or not. Specifically, they were indifferent between entrusting the use of force to stop serious violations of UN law to collective action by member states and entrusting it to a strengthened UN organization; and between equal votes for all countries and weighting them by a combination of population size and budget contribution. Strikingly, *all* proposals to reduce the authority of the UN are rejected by respondents on average—requiring unanimous agreement of all members for decisions; treating them as binding only for those countries that voluntarily accept them (even in matters of peace and security); not allowing anyone to use force to stop law violations; and limiting UN resources to voluntary contributions by governments (Ghassim, Koenig-Archibugi, and Cabrera 2022).

These findings reflect average responses aggregated across the six survey countries. We observed some differences across countries. Most notably, only respondents in the three permanent member states of the UN Security Council oppose the abolition of all veto rights, whereas those in the remaining three states are indifferent. The proposal to grant more power to countries with full press freedom and free elections increases support for UN models among respondents in electoral democracies, while respondents in nondemocracies are indifferent.

As expected, based on the literature on moral value systems (Waytz et al. 2019; Bai, Gauri, and Fiske 2021), we found some differences between subgroups defined by political values, but they are not so extensive to warrant the conclusion that attitudes on United Nations institutional design are affected by political polarization. Opposition to changes that would weaken UN authority is widespread across the political spectrum.

One aspect where political values are associated with somewhat different views on supranational authority concerns the extension of UN authority to areas beyond peace and security. Individuals who hold culturally libertarian values (identified through their views on LGBTQ+ rights) and respondents who prioritize environmental protection over economic growth and jobs are supportive of the proposal to make UN decisions being binding on a range of important security, environmental, and economic matters. By contrast, cultural traditionalists and respondents who do not prioritize the environment are indifferent to it on average (but not opposed). If, as some expect (Welzel 2013, 2021), the share of the world population that holds culturally libertarian and environmentalist values will continue to grow, then the support base for an extension of UN authority is likely to increase as well.

On the whole, the survey shows overall public support for some elements of the universal republic (binding authority for the global organization across more issue-areas, empowerment of directly elected citizenship representatives alongside state delegates), indifference to others (centralizing the enforcement of global law), and opposition to some remaining elements (weighting votes by population sizes, funding the global authority through corporate taxes, and—in P5 countries—abolition of all veto rights).

4.4 Motivational constraints: governments

Instances of state leaders voluntarily ceding core sovereign powers to a new superordinate state are rare. The creation of the USA through the 1777 Articles of Confederation and Perpetual Union and the 1787 Constitution remains the paradigmatic case, and accordingly supporters of world federation frequently point at it as a key precedent (e.g. Pecqueur 1842, 373; K'ang 1902/1958, 97; Tuttle 1919; Van Doren 1948; Zimmern 1953). Griffiths (2010) searched for cases of voluntary political unification between 1816 and 2001 and found that the unification of Italy in 1860 and Germany in 1867–71 account for most cases.[13]

The concentration of cases of political unification to processes of nation-building in the nineteenth century seems to confirm the view that 'there has been no case in postwar history of the citizenry of two or more nation-states voluntarily turning over their sovereignty to a supranational

---

[13] Griffith does not count nineteenth-century Australia as a case of voluntary unification because the formation of the state occurred as part of the independence process from Britain, but it can be plausibly considered a case of voluntary unification nevertheless (Rector 2009). The Kingdom of Serbs, Croats, and Slovenes formed in 1918 arguably also qualifies as voluntary unification.

superstate ... Clearly the historical trend, even and precisely in an era of economic globalization, is toward more rather than less nation-statism, and towards smaller rather than larger units of governance' (Streeck 2018, 41–42). The few exceptions in the twentieth century—the unification of Tanganyika and Zanzibar in 1964 and North and South Yemen in 1990 (Griffiths 2010)— seem to confirm the rule. Furthermore, all cases classified as voluntary unions by Griffiths (2010) occurred between states that shared a language (with the possible exception of Switzerland), which suggests that a common language has been a necessary condition for voluntary political unification. To be sure, language homogeneity is by no means also a sufficient condition. A common external threat, while not strictly necessary, has played a role in some unification processes, typically alongside other material and ideational factors (Cronin 1999; Rector 2009; Parent 2011).

The role of a shared language suggests that the prospects for a world state formation along the lines that are familiar from past experiences of voluntary political unification will remain poor for the foreseeable future. However, this conclusion is only compelling to the extent that the focus is on sovereignty as an attribute that a polity either possesses or not. This was the predominant view in nineteenth-century Europe. By contrast, if authority is conceived as something that in principle can be distributed among multiple governance levels, then the picture becomes more complex.

The complexity emerges from two circumstances. The first is that there are various ways of allocating political authority among governance institutions. When Kenneth Waltz discussed political ordering principles in his *Theory of International Politics*, he maintained that 'two, and only two, types of structure are needed to cover societies of all sorts' (Waltz 1979, 116). These types are anarchy and hierarchy, and for Waltz they correspond to international and domestic politics respectively. But even Waltz acknowledged that many societies fall between the extremes of anarchy and hierarchy and that in reality '[a]ll societies are mixed' (Waltz 1979, 115). As Milner (1991) noted, actual domestic and international political systems are all located on various points along a continuum of centralization of authority. Various authors developed typologies of intermediate forms. For instance, building on Cronin (1999) and others, Donnelly (2006, 154) presents ten systems of 'hierarchy in anarchy': balance of power, protection, concert, collective security, hegemony, dominion, empire, pluralistic security community, common security community, and amalgamated security community. Other authors have also discussed multiple types of international systems (e.g. Wendt and Friedheim 1995; Deudney 2007; Butcher and Griffiths 2017; Griffiths 2018; McConaughey, Musgrave, and Nexon 2018).

The second circumstance is that different distributions of authority are not only conceivable but also actually selected by state agents. Such behaviour runs counter to some basic assumptions of Realist theories of international relations. For instance, Waltz assumed that states are 'unitary actors who, at a minimum, seek their own preservation and, at a maximum, drive for universal domination' (Waltz 1979, 118). While there are some disagreements among Realists over the exact motivations driving states, all of them 'expect states to protect their sovereignty and territorial integrity and to guard their capacity for independent action' (Mastanduno 2014, 28). This assumption is sometimes justified with a 'natural selection' argument: state agents are driven to adopt realpolitik policies by 'the process of selection that takes place in competitive systems' (Waltz 1986, 330). States that fail to conform to structural imperatives are expected to 'fall by the wayside' (Waltz 1979: 117–118). At most, Realists can concede that states voluntarily transfer authority to a superstate entity only when they face an existential threat and maintaining their independence is no longer a feasible option (Riker 1975; Parent 2011).

These assumptions are challenged by several developments that have taken place since the nineteenth century. These can be summarized by saying that (1) states have delegated more authority to international institutions, and (2) they have made such institutions more democratic. These two aspects will be considered in turn.

4.4.1 International authority and resources

The past two centuries have witnesses a dramatic increase in the number of intergovernmental organizations (IGOs). The latest version of the Correlates of War IGO dataset records just three IGOs in existence in 1864, while the number was 335 in 2014 (Pevehouse et al. 2020). The mere existence of IGOs does not indicate by itself a power shift from the national to the international level. Such a shift would require two developments. The first is the conferral to IGOs of the authority to make legally binding decisions on important policy issues. The second is the capacity of IGOs to control the resources needed to implement those decisions. The distinction between authority and resources corresponds to the difference between what Kuhn and Nicoli (2020) refer to as the competence-based dimension and the resource-based dimension of core state powers.

To examine the authority dimension, we can draw on the International Authority Database (IAD) created by Zürn, Tokhi, and Binder (2021). In their understanding of the concept, 'those who recognize authority defer their own judgment or choice without being necessarily forced or persuaded to do so' (Zürn, Tokhi, and Binder 2021, 431). They measure the authority of international organizations as the combination of two features: autonomy and bindingness. On the one hand, to be authoritative IGOs need to be able to make decisions without being under the control of any individual member state. On the other hand, these decisions must reduce the policy discretion of member states. 'Because autonomy and bindingness in our concept jointly constitute authority, an IGO has authority only if it enjoys a minimum level of organizational autonomy *and* if its rules and decisions can bind its member states (at least to some extent)' (Zürn, Tokhi, and Binder 2021, 432). They assign values for autonomy and bindingness to IGOs based on a coding of legal documents, thus what they measure is strictly speaking legal authority. As states have consented to such legal rules, IGO authority is typically the result of international delegation (Bradley and Kelley 2008; Guzman and Landsidle 2008).

The IAD provides combined scores for autonomy and bindingness in relation to seven policy functions potentially performed by IGOs: agenda setting, rulemaking, monitoring, norm interpretation, enforcement, knowledge generation, and evaluation. The data are provided for a sample of thirty-four IGOs that in some ways is representative of the broader population of IGOs in existence now. Figure 4.3 shows the evolution of the authority of this sample of IGOs since 1950, which is based on averaging the authority of each IGO across the seven policy functions then averaging the normalized authority scores of the thirty-four IGOs. The graph shows that, on a scale ranging from 0 to 1, the average authority of IOs has been between .2 and .3 throughout the period since World War II, with a nearly 50 per cent increase since the 1970s. Overall, these data show a moderate degree of willingness of states to delegate authority to international actors.[14]

The measures provided by the IAD do not take into account how much of the world is subject to the authority of an IGO. This is an important aspect, because the degree of political integration in the world does not depend only on the 'intensity' of authority but also on its 'extensity'. I draw on the IAD to capture this aspect more directly, by constructing what can be called a measure of *legal worldstateness*. This measure aims to capture how distant the world as a whole is from a level of legal integration that meets minimal criteria of statehood. I posit such criteria as follows: (1) a world state would

---

[14] Hooghe et al. (2017) and Hooghe, Lenz, and Marks (2019) reach a similar conclusion based on a different operationalization of international authority and a different sample of international organizations.

be fully autonomous and its decisions would be fully binding, in the sense explained by Zürn, Tokhi, and Binder (2021); (2) this level of autonomy and bindingness would be found in five of the policy functions discussed by these authors: agenda setting, rulemaking, monitoring, norm interpretation, and enforcement; (3) the authority of the world state would apply to all policy areas that are nowadays seen as core state responsibilities; (4) the authority of this political entity would extend over the whole world population.

To operationalize these criteria, I combine data on authority and country membership in relation to ten global IGOs that together cover most of the area of responsibility of modern states: security and human rights (United Nations and International Criminal Court), public finance and central banking (International Monetary Fund and Bank for International Settlements), business (World Trade Organization), food and agriculture (Food and Agriculture Organization), social policy (World Bank and International Labour Organization), health (World Health Organization), education, science, and culture (United Nations Educational, Scientific and Cultural Organization). These quantities are aggregated as follows:

$$Legal\ worldstateness_t = \sum_{i=1}^{N} coverage_{it} \times \frac{\sum_{j=1}^{n} \sqrt{autonomy_{ijt} \times bindingness_{ijt}}}{n} \Big/ N$$

where i is an IGO, N is the number of IGOs (ten, in our case), j is the policy function, n is the number of policy functions (five, in our case), t is the year, *autonomy* and *bindingness* are as coded by Zürn, Tokhi, and Binder (2021), and *coverage* indicates the share of the world population that lives in members states of the IGO. Coverage is calculated based on IGO membership data from Pevehouse et al. (2020), country population data from the sources indicated in Appendix II, and global population data from the United Nations (2019).

For the world to attain a full score (i.e. one) on the legal worldstateness scale, every state of the world would need to be member of each of the ten core IGOs, which in turn would need to display the highest possible level of autonomy and bindingness in each of the five policy functions. As shown in Figure 4.3, the world is somewhat over the .5 mark. The graph also shows that legal worldstateness has increased over the decades. But the line arguably underestimates the level it had in the 1950s and 1960s, because colonial populations were affected by IGOs indirectly even though their local governments could not yet become member states.

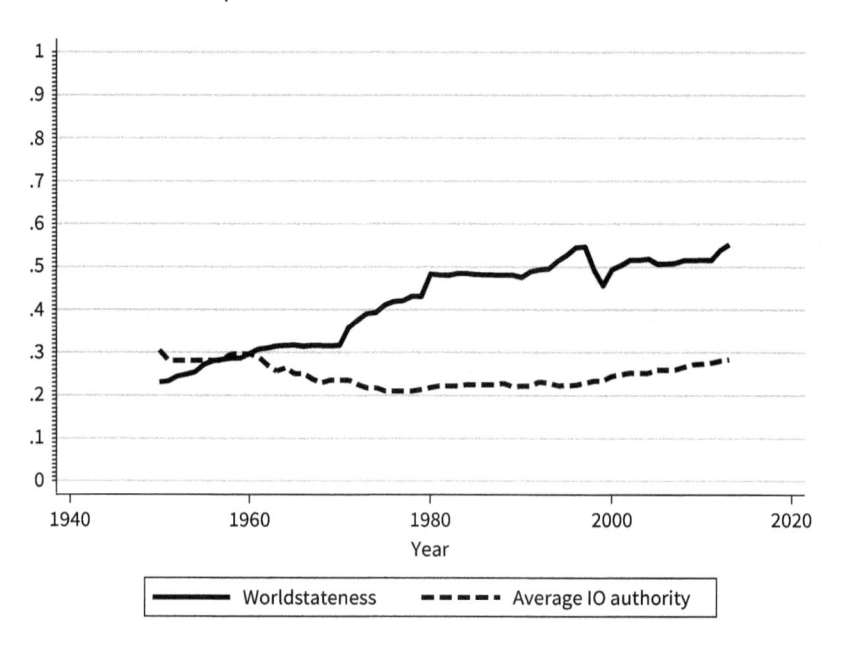

Figure 4.3 Average authority of international organizations, and legal worldstateness.

One relevant dimension that the IAD does not capture is a state's right to end its own membership of IGOs and hence to escape its authority. Withdrawal clauses are common in international agreements—out of the random sample of 234 international agreements collected by Koremenos, 70 per cent contain a withdrawal clause (Koremenos 2016, 143). Most constitutive treaties of IGOs contain a provision on withdrawal from the organization (Brölmann et al. 2018). There are exceptions, with the United Nations, the World Health Organization, and the EU before 2009 being the most prominent IGOs without such withdrawal clauses. In such cases, states can withdraw from an IGO legally only if the stringent criteria for the permissibility of unilateral withdrawal stated in the Vienna Convention on the Law of Treaties are met (Brölmann et al. 2018). While the right of states to withdraw from IGOs is often stated explicitly in the constitutional documents of the latter, the right of territorial entities within countries to secede from the state is much less commonly protected in national constitutions. Ginsburg and Versteeg (2018, 942) find that, among the constitutions of 190 countries in 2014, 67 per cent are silent on secession, 30 per cent ban it either implicitly or explicitly, and only five include a right to secession. The legal impossibility of secession for constituent parts is not a conceptually necessary dimension of statehood. However, the authority exercised by most IGOs differs from the authority exercised by most states in the extent to which they allow territorially defined components to withdraw from their jurisdictions.

A set of international rules deserves special mention: *jus cogens*, or peremptory norms of general international law. International lawyers include in this category prohibitions of aggression, genocide, crimes against humanity, war crimes, piracy, slavery, and torture. The specificity of these norms is that states cannot 'opt out' of them, as they can with regard to their membership in international organizations and treaties. The superiority of those specific norms over national law has been interpreted by Goodin (2012) as evidence that the rudiments of world government already exist.[15] However, as Goodin acknowledges, there is no supranational institutional apparatus wielding both the authority and the capability to enforce those norms systematically. In its absence, 'the authority is institutionally free-floating', being exercised by various groupings or even individual states that claim to be engaging in 'humanitarian interventions' (Goodin 2012, 158). Not surprisingly, this situation leads to interventions being highly selective, as they reflect the priorities of the states that are able to conduct them (Binder 2016).

As indicated earlier, full worldstateness would require not only the delegation of the authority to make legally binding decisions but also the ability to control the resources needed to implement those decisions. The following analysis examines to what extent such resources are currently controlled at the international level. I rely on data on the budget of thirty-two major international organizations between 1985 and 2015 collected by Sommerer et al. (2022). Figure 4.4 shows the ratio between the sum of those IGO budgets and the GDP of the world. It remained low and stable across the three decades, fluctuating between a minimum of 0.19 per cent (2011) and a maximum of 0.3 per cent (2001).

The figure also shows that IGO budgets as a percentage of world GDP are considerably lower than the spending of national governments as a percentage of national GDP.[16] Even countries with relatively low government spending (the 10th percentile is shown in Figure 4.3) vastly outspend IOs relative to their respective economies.

To be sure, the figures on administrative IGO budgets do not provide a complete picture of the resources that IGOs can mobilize (Heldt and Schmidtke 2017). Most notably, in 2021 the IMF had an administrative budget of $1.19 billion but a lending capacity of about $1 trillion (IMF 2021). But even this lending capacity amounted to only about 1 per cent of global GDP.

---

[15] On the idea that a form of world statehood already exists see also Shaw (2000); Chimni (2004); Albert et al. (2012); Albert (2014); Brunkhorst (2014).

[16] Based on data on Expense (% of GDP) [GC.XPN.TOTL.GD.ZS] from World Bank (2021). Missing data between available data were interpolated, and the earliest available value was extended to previous years when missing.

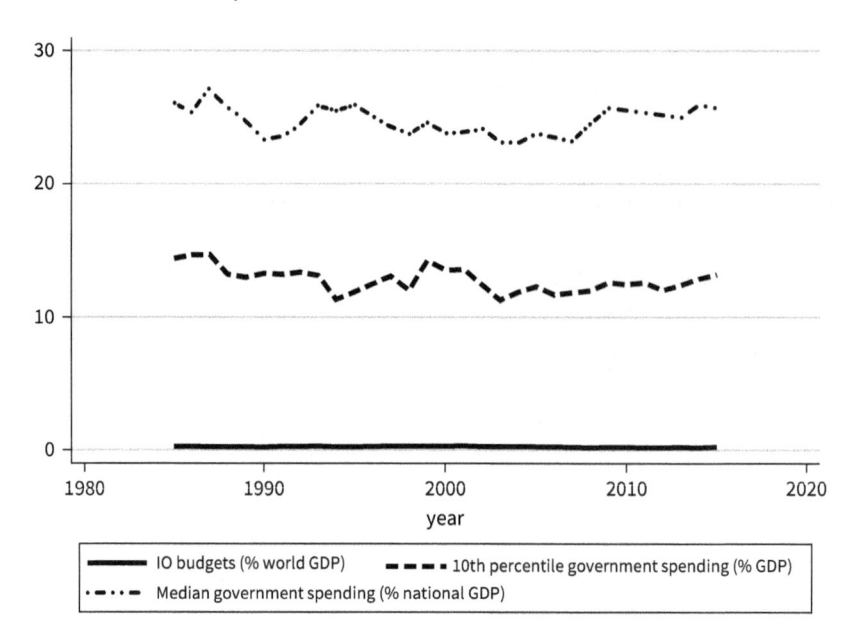

Figure 4.4 Intergovernmental organizations' combined budgets compared to national government spending.

The proportion of resources controlled by today's IGOs is closer to that controlled by pre-industrial states than to the size of the public sector in contemporary states. For instance, fiscal revenue in China in the early twentieth century is estimated to have been in the region of 1–2 per cent of GDP (Ma and Rubin 2019, 287–288). The proportion of resources controlled by IGOs is also much lower than the proportion of resources controlled by the central government relative to all governmental resources in multilevel national systems. In a dataset starting in 1990s, the lowest proportion of revenue collected centrally is 47 per cent and the lowest proportion of central expenditures is 35 per cent (both in Canada) (Dziobek, Gutierrez Mangas, and Kufa 2011).

The lack of direct control over resources is not by itself bound to make the legal authority of international institutions inconsequential. In many states, some public bodies have little direct control over the state apparatus but nevertheless exercise substantial influence over political outcomes. The clearest example is constitutional courts, which typically have no direct control over government personnel, but in some states elicit high compliance with their rulings by virtue of the authority conferred to them by the constitution (Goldsmith and Levinson 2008). However, these figures confirm a point made by Zürn (2018, 239): redistributive policies are largely excluded from the domain of international authority.

4.4.2 Democracy in international organizations

The second major development that puts into question the assumption that states cling to their autonomy and power is the introduction of democratic elements in the way international organizations work. Assuming that international organizations can be democratized is controversial. For instance, Streeck (2018, 42) claims that, 'while many existing states are far from democratic, ... states remain the only political organizations that can in principle be democratized, in the final instance by armed revolution'. However, two things run counter to that view. The first is that governments themselves describe international organizations as entities that can be democratic to a greater or lesser extent. The second is that governments acquiesced to, and sometimes actively promoted, reforms of international organizations that increased those organizations' democratic features. The two aspects will be considered in turn.

Grigorescu (2015) provides a rich account of the invocation of norms of democracy beyond the state by government representatives since the nineteenth century. He shows that analogies with domestic democratic governance have often been made in the context of debates on the creation and reform of major intergovernmental organizations. The words democracy and democratic were uttered dozens of times during the 1945 San Francisco Conference that created the United Nations. For instance, the Cuban delegate argued against the right of veto for the great powers by saying that 'one of the democratic ideas for which the United Nations had been courageously fighting is that of government by the majority. This would be completely destroyed by permitting the will of one nation to dominate the will of the rest of the world' (cited by Grigorescu 2015, 107). While in 1945 the US delegates had been arguing that the veto was not undemocratic if it was linked to the exercise of greater responsibilities, twenty years later Dean Rusk, the US Secretary of State, urged the US Senate to ratify a UN Charter amendment allowing for an increase of non-permanent Security Council seats by saying that 'our world is a better and more democratic world because [the new non-permanent members] have taken their rightful places in the councils of our times ... this is the last nation on the face of the earth to shun diversity, or to reject the open forum, or to fear the growth of democratic practices' (cited by Grigorescu 2015, 68).

The end of the Cold War intensified the use of domestic democratic analogies, which has led some scholars to go as far as claiming that 'democracy is becoming the paramount legitimizing principle of world politics' (Thérien and Bélanger Dumontier 2009, 358). Democratic principles have been invoked both to legitimize as well as delegitimize international institutions. An example of the former use comes from the way in which international organizations present themselves and their decision-making. Dingwerth, Schmidtke, and Weise (2020) coded the official annual reports of twenty global IGOs from 1980 to 2011 and found a substantial increase of democratic legitimation narratives. The share of reports that invoke democratic norms at least once in a given year increased from 14 per cent in the 1980s to 34 per cent in the 1990s and 53 per cent during the 2000s. These figures include both statements on an IGO's role in promoting democracy globally and statements on the democratic quality of the IGO's own internal procedures and decision-making. The latter, which are more relevant for the question at hand, experienced the largest growth, as their share of all democratic legitimation statements increased from 63 per cent during the first half of the period covered in the dataset to 80 per cent during the second half.

A crucial test of the applicability of democracy to international relations is the extent to which it is discursively endorsed by governments. Eisentraut (2020) analysed speeches delivered in the UN General Assembly between 2003 and 2013 by representatives of 159 states, in the context of the debates held each year on reforming the Security Council and the General Assembly. Her conclusions are based on a search for mentions of democracy and democratization in relation to UN organs in the 1,014 country-years for which reform speeches are available. Among her findings is that '41 percent of actors involved in the Council's reform debate—that is a total of 314 country years—invoke the notion of democracy, whereas 456 country years never mention the term. By contrast, in the debate about the GA, only 14 per cent of the actors involved in the debate—namely 34 country years—embrace the term' (Eisentraut 2020, 96). The content of the speeches follows a clear pattern: the Security Council is uniformly denounced as undemocratic, while the Assembly is praised for its democratic character. Importantly for our purposes, Eisentraut (2020, 101) found that 'Not a single country year invokes the concept of democracy to contest its relevance for global rule. Even if states entertained doubt that Council rule was meant to be democratic, they certainly did not express these thoughts.' She also found a high degree of agreement on the meaning of democratic rule in the UN among diplomats who *did* invoke democracy. First, they associated democracy with its traditional aspects of equality, representation, and elections. Second, they overwhelmingly identified 'states' as the subjects of democracy, with 'people' or 'peoples' being mentioned rarely, and then only as passive subjects fully represented by states.

Eisentraut's research reveals a nuanced picture of global democracy understandings among diplomats representing their countries at the UN. Understandings are highly consistent among those who explicitly invoke democracy—i.e. they share a statist representative conception. Interviews with diplomats who did not use the word in their speeches reveals that their reticence is partly due to a disagreement with this statist understanding, including a reluctance to describe as democratic an international body that has several non-democratic governments among its members. This also contributes to explaining another finding, i.e. that representatives of authoritarian states are much more likely to mention democracy in their speeches on UN reform than representatives of democratic states. '[S]ome democracies clearly object to what autocracies have few problems doing: replacing the original subjects of democracy, namely people, with a new type of actor, namely states' (Eisentraut 2020, 223).

Behind the lack of open contestation regarding the applicability of democracy to international governance lurk disagreements about two contrasting conceptions of global democracy: a communitarian model focused on states as the 'citizens' holding democratic rights, and a cosmopolitan model focused on individuals and social groups (Bienen, Rittberger, and Wagner 1998). Supporters of the cosmopolitan model emphasize organs composed of elected parliamentarians (as opposed to government representatives), but also the participation of non-governmental organizations. UN secretaries-general aimed to navigate a path between the two conceptions. Boutros-Ghali was particularly interested in presenting NGOs as part of the global democracy mix, arguing that 'the growth of non-governmental organizations at all levels, from grassroots to global, can be a powerful factor for democratization throughout the international system' (Boutros-Ghali 1995, 15).

So far, this section has been considering the discourse of global democracy. It is however possible that it merely constitutes an example of 'organized hypocrisy' (Krasner 1999). Is there evidence that 'words' are matched by 'deeds' (Thérien and Bélanger Dumontier 2009)? Research done in the past decade has documented a trend towards the adoption of IGO design features that, according to many, improved their democratic character. Grigorescu examined seventy-two attempts to reform six major IGOs in line with five democratic norms: fair representation of states, fair voting, transparency, non-governmental actor participation, and transnational parliamentary oversight. He finds that in more than half of these cases the outcome was either the originally promoted change or at least partial change (Grigorescu 2015, 266). The normative pressure created by the invocation of democratic principles played a role in most cases. Data-collection projects on larger samples of IGOs showed that, over the past decades, there have been major increases in the proportion of IGOs that have parliamentary organs, give access to non-state actors, have rules about public access to information, actively communicate to broader audiences, and implement staffing policies that make their secretariats more representative of the global population (Tallberg et al. 2013; Grigorescu 2015; Ecker-Ehrhardt 2018; Schimmelfennig et al. 2020; Parizek and Stephen 2021). Studies also show that, despite their diplomats' reluctance to use the language of democracy in relation to intergovernmental UN bodies, democratic governments are often key promoters of democratizing reforms. If an IGO has more democratic members, it is more likely to have policies that allow access to information and to put into practice such policies, to actively communicate with a broader audience, and to be more open to non-state actors (Grigorescu 2007; Tallberg, Sommerer, and Squatrito 2016; Ecker-Ehrhardt 2018).

A tentative conclusion of this overview is that, overall, governments affirm the applicability of democracy to international organizations, by using discourses condemning institutional privileges held by a subset of states (voiced disproportionally by non-democratic member states) and by promoting openness and transparency of international organizations vis-à-vis audiences beyond national executives (supported disproportionally by democratic member states).

4.5 Multilevel governance?

The previous sections failed to uncover insurmountable motivational obstacles to the transfer of political authority to supranational levels. Of course, this is just an indication that the universal republic is achievable, not that it is the most likely outcome of global political trends—a question over which this book remains agnostic. Before drawing some conclusions, we need to consider a further argument, which is that the formation of a world state would run counter to what may appear to be a much more powerful trend across the world—i.e. the widespread preference for bringing the sites of governance closer to the citizens and to the smaller communities they are most attached to. This preference can be expressed politically as demands for greater territorial decentralization or even secession from existing states. If such demands for more localized governance were incompatible with demands for stronger global governance, the prospects for the creation of a democratic world state might be poor.

But are they incompatible? Rather than positing a tension between subnational and supranational governance preferences, an alternative perspective is that the main cleavage is between those who want authority to be concentrated at one level, notably the nation-state, and those who prefer it to be diffused across multiple levels, from subnational to supranational, according to their ability to satisfy citizens' needs. From this perspective, as long as enough citizens and political actors consider multilevel governance legitimate and appropriate, there is no inherent contradiction between strengthening subnational sites of governance and transferring authority to higher levels.

While a thorough examination of this question is beyond the scope of this chapter, we can examine some tentative evidence. Specifically, we can look at citizen attitudes, at the political parties that link those attitudes to political decision-making, and at the choices made by national governments in relation to international governance.

Let us consider citizen attitudes first. Ideally, we would be able to rely on representative surveys in many countries that could offer deep insights on what the *same* respondent thinks about both subnational and supranational authority. The International Social Survey Programme (ISSP) national identity modules fielded in 1995 and 2003 may come closest to offering that (ISSP Research Group 1998, 2012). Based on the responses given by approximately 40,000 individuals across twenty-one countries in 1995 and fourteen countries in 2003, I found that, compared to respondents who agree with the statement 'It is essential that [*country*] remains one [nation/state/country]', respondents who believe that 'Parts of [*country*] should be allowed to become fully separate [nations/states/countries] if they choose to' are also more likely to agree with the statement 'For certain problems, like environment pollution, international bodies should have the right to enforce solutions.' The correlation is small but statistically significant at conventional levels. This suggests that, in the mind of a large sample of citizens, supporting the right to secession and supporting supranational authority are seen as compatible.

We can consider political parties next. In European countries, regionalist and secessionist parties are often supportive of European integration (Gómez-Reino 2014). The vigorous opposition of the Scottish National Party to Britain and Scotland leaving the European Union is a prominent example (Bremberg and Gillespie 2022). To assess the question systematically, I analysed 5,089 party manifestos included in the Manifesto Project Dataset, whose 2023a version covers sixty-seven countries between 1945 and 2022 (Budge et al. 2001; Klingemann et al. 2006; Lehmann et al. 2023). Among the parties contesting the 849 parliamentary lower house elections and presidential elections in the dataset, higher support for decentralization or federalism is associated with fewer negative references to the EU and international cooperation (e.g. emphasis on national independence, isolation and/or uni-lateralism as opposed to internationalism). This relationship, captured by regression models with election fixed effects, is statistically significant at conventional levels. By contrast, on average there is no statistically signifi-cant relationship between a party's support for decentralization/federalism and positive mentions of internationalism and the EU in its manifesto. This suggests that political advocacy for (more) subnational governance is associ-ated with lower opposition to supranational authority, but not with stronger support for it.

Finally, let us consider the actions of governments. There is some evi-dence that the governments of decentralized countries are more willing to strengthen supranational integration. In past work, I found that, among member states of the European Union, strong regional governance is associ-ated with more support given by their governments for institutional reforms that would facilitate a supranational foreign and security policy (Koenig-Archibugi 2004a). In a global sample, Tom Ginsburg found that federal states are more likely to sign treaties and join international organizations (Ginsburg 2009). There can be several explanations for such an empirical association. It could reflect familiarity with, and a constitutional culture favourable to, the dispersion of authority across multiple levels, as hypothesized in Koenig-Archibugi (2004a). It could also reflect the desire of domestically constrained government to gain room for manoeuvre by colluding with other gov-ernments, as Ginsburg implies (Ginsburg 2009; see also Koenig-Archibugi 2004b).

Taken together, the findings reported in this section suggest that many cit-izens, parties, and governments around the world regard subnational and supranational governance as potentially compatible within a broader multi-level conception of political authority. Why this may be the case is a question that deserves further research. For our purposes, it is sufficient to conclude that the desire to empower governance institutions that are closer to citizens does not seem to pose an insurmountable constraint to global state formation.

4.6 Concluding remarks

I proposed that the universal republic should be regarded as achievable if and only if (i) a critical mass of states would be reasonably likely to succeed in transferring authority to it if they were to try; and (ii) those states are able to try to transfer authority to the universal republic. What does the evidence offered in this chapter tells us about those conditions? First, the data from the IAD shows that states have already transferred a non-negligible amount of legal authority to international organizations. If we define a world state as an entity that has full autonomy and whose decisions are fully binding across all main policy functions and across all policy areas that are nowadays seen as core state responsibilities, and whose authority extends to the whole world population, then the world seems halfway there already. We also saw that this conclusion needs to be qualified in two ways: states have normally retained the legal right to withdraw from those organizations, and the IGOs have not acquired the authority to impose taxes, which limits considerably their ability to mobilize resources. Another insight provided by the literature is that the democratic character of the UR may not inhibit the transfer of authority to it, given that governments frequently assert the relevance of democratic principles for international governance and have agreed to some democratizing institutional reforms. On the whole, the transfer of authority that occurred can give us enough confidence that states would be reasonably likely to succeed in transferring further authority to the universal republic if they were to try—so condition (i) is met.

The next question to consider is whether governments would be able to try to transfer the required quantity and quality of authority. The Realist assumption that states are intrinsically unable to sacrifice their autonomy fails to convince. If something could prevent states from trying to set up the universal republic, it would be their core constituents. While in principle several groups could try to stop political leaders joining a process of world state formation (e.g. the army, business leaders, religious groups), governments would definitely be prevented from trying only if the mass of citizens were overwhelmingly opposed to it. However, the review of opinion surveys offered in this chapter fails to find such an overwhelming opposition. In most countries with data, people tend to be quite evenly divided over the desirability of a world state. This finding emerges both from surveys that gauge support for a generically described supranational entity able to take enforceable global decisions on global problems and from surveys that capture more fine-grained preferences about institutional design options. The fact than a non-negligible share of citizens in multiple countries is already sympathetic towards a democratic world state suggests that the proportion of supporters would further increase under the right conditions. What could produce that effect? This is where the findings on social movements are particularly relevant. What information is available about them suggests that most people involved in them find the prospect of a global democratic state more attractive than repulsive. They are more likely to support governments willing to try to empower democratically controlled supranational authorities than to thwart them, and their role could be decisive in persuading members of the general public. Overall, then, we can conclude that states are not unable to try to transfer authority to the universal republic—condition (ii) is satisfied as well. As both conditions appear to be met, the available evidence gives us little reason to conclude that the universal republic is unachievable.

PART II

IS THE UNIVERSAL REPUBLIC DESIRABLE?

5
Arguments on desirability

Part I provided some reasons to believe that the universal republic is achievable and viable, and hence worthy of consideration within practical deliberation. Part II considers whether it is worthy of support.

World government has been advocated on many grounds. As noted in the introduction, for Dante it was necessary to ensure the full realization of humanity's potential (Dante Alighieri *c.*1312/1996). In his view, all human generations were together engaged in a process of collective development of cognitive capacities, but this process was hindered by conflict and violence. For mid-twentieth century proponents of world government, its essential rationale was to increase the chances of survival of a humankind threatened by nuclear annihilation. Many agreed with Albert Einstein's reasoning: 'I advocate world government because I am convinced that there is no other possible way of eliminating the most terrible danger in which man has ever found himself. The objective of avoiding total destruction must have priority over any other objective' (Einstein 1948/2007a, 397).

In this chapter, I will consider the question of global political order not simply in terms of ensuring people's bare survival, but in terms of the broader goal of promoting their personal autonomy while ensuring equal respect for all.

5.1. Normative postulates

5.1.1 Foundations

I posit that global political orders are desirable to the extent that they promote and protect four principles:

(1) Political orders are desirable when they treat human beings with equal respect, regardless of characteristics such as race, colour, ethnic origin, age, gender, sexual orientation, disability, language, and religious and philosophical beliefs.

The Universal Republic. Mathias Koenig-Archibugi, Oxford University Press. © Mathias Koenig-Archibugi (2024). DOI: 10.1093/9780198921158.003.0005

(2) Political orders are desirable when they protect and promote the personal autonomy of people, i.e. their ability to develop and pursue authentic personal goals, compatibly with protecting the same abilities in other people.

(3) Political orders protect and promote personal autonomy when:

a they establish and enforce laws aimed at regulating behaviour that can affect personal autonomy, and

b the institutions and agencies empowered to create and enforce those laws are controlled, directly or indirectly, by all those affected by them.

The importance of (1) will be assumed rather than justified, except to note that the principle of equal respect is shared by many contemporary moral philosophies (Stuurman 2017). The importance of (2) is perhaps less straightforward, as autonomy is not emphasized to the same degree by all ethical traditions. However, the desire for autonomy is deeply felt across a range of social contexts (Sen 1999, 2009). Having autonomy is associated with higher subjective well-being across the world, although not necessarily to the same extent in all regions (Tay and Diener 2011; Yu, Levesque-Bristol, and Maeda 2018; Li et al. 2022). When the desire for autonomy is frustrated, people protest, resist, and rebel (e.g. Fick 1990; White and Rastogi 2009; Lim 2016; Nafafé 2022; Panda and Pandey 2022). In the words of Raz (1986, 369), 'The ideal of personal autonomy is the vision of people controlling, to some degree, their own destiny, fashioning it through successive decisions throughout their lives.' Raz identifies three basic conditions for autonomy. First, the capacity to form intentions of a sufficiently complex kind and plan their execution. Second, there must be adequate options available to choose from. Third, the person must be independent, i.e. free from coercion as well as manipulation exercised by others (i.e. perversions of how a person reaches decisions, forms preferences, or adopts goals) (Raz 1986, 372–378). Raz notes that all three conditions come in degrees. The capacity for autonomy of an actor is susceptible to being limited and compromised by other agents, notably when they significantly limit the quantity and quality of the options available to the actor (Valentini 2011, 164–168). For the purposes of this discussion, autonomy is treated as an important value, but not the only important value or one that necessarily trumps any other in all circumstances.

Proposition (3a) entails that a desirable political order should promote autonomy not only by attempting to educate and persuade, but also by constraining what people can do to other people. This requires both the making of laws and mechanisms for the enforcement of those laws. The laws must contain substantive rules that define what actions are mandatory, permitted, and prohibited given the circumstances, and application rules that prescribe how disputes are to be resolved and decisions enforced. Typically, this involves the creation and empowerment of institutions and agencies with legislative, judicial, and executive tasks.

Proposition (3b) requires those institutions and agencies to be under the control of all those affected by their actions. The rationale for this requirement is two-fold. First, such empowered institutions and agencies could themselves become a threat to personal autonomy. The protection of autonomy promoted by a system of law could be outweighed by a loss of autonomy if those rules and/or their application are oppressive. This risk can be minimized by subjecting them to the control of those who are so threatened (Pettit 2012). Second, people disagree both on the best way of promoting autonomy and on how to balance this goal with other goals they want public bodies to promote. Consequently, they should have an equal opportunity to shape the content of the laws that affect them (Caney 2006; Valentini 2012, 2013).

Propositions (3a) and (3b) together imply that the desirability of political orders should be assessed based on the extent to which all affected persons have a fair opportunity to participate in a system of control over the rules that govern their interaction—more specifically, to participate on an equal basis in formulating the content of the rules and to hold accountable the agencies in charge of applying them. The problem, as Rousseau put it, is 'to find a form of association which will defend and protect the person and goods of each associate with the full common force, and by means of which each, uniting with all, nevertheless obey only himself and remain as free as before' (Rousseau 1762/1997, 49–50).[1] Popular control over the making of laws, and popular accountability of the actors that monitor and enforce compliance with those laws, confers democratic legitimacy to the political order.

It is not an aim of this chapter to justify the normative postulates stated above, but it is useful to remark briefly on their genealogy. They are inspired by several strands of political thinking stretching back several centuries. The versions of classical liberalism and republicanism formulated by Locke, Rousseau, Kant, Cloots, and the authors of *The Federalist* papers play a crucial role in them, but also thinkers and activists who have sought to overcome the sexist, classist, racist, ethnocentric, and other biases permeating traditional liberalism and republicanism (Wollstonecraft 1792/1995; Marx 1875/1989; Rosselli 1930/1994; Ambedkar 1936/2016; Du Bois 1945; King, Jr 1967; Mills 1997; Woodhull 2010; L'Ouverture 2019; A. Dahl 2020, 2021;

---

[1] For a recent defence of democracy in terms of the value of autonomy see Lovett and Zuehl (2022).

DuBois 2022). Among contemporary political theory, this framework for thinking about political orders is indebted to both liberal and republican traditions (Held 1995; Pettit 1997, 2012; Caney 2006). I will briefly elaborate on the link with the latter. Classical republican theory held that freedom 'is not a matter of having a just master, but of having none at all' (Cicero 51 BCE/1998, 48–49 [II.43]). While contemporary republican theory is fairly diverse, the common premise is that a political order should minimize domination, understood as the power to interfere in other people's choices in a way that is not controlled by those on the receiving end. The version of republicanism developed by Pettit has a close fit with propositions (3a) and (3b), as it has two main components: 'The republican theory of social justice would argue that the state should establish equal non-domination for its citizens in relation to one another. The republican theory of political legitimacy would argue that that in the course of providing for them in this way the state ought not to dominate its citizens' (Pettit 2012, 18–19). The first step is necessary to protect individuals against *dominium*, i.e. domination potentially exercised by private actors. The second step is necessary to protect them from *imperium*, i.e. domination potentially exercised by public authorities. For Pettit (2012, 24), the latter is relatively more important than the former in so far as an illegitimate (i.e. undemocratic) state dominates its citizens and at the same time cannot be relied on to protect citizens from domination by other citizens. In what follows, both conditions will be considered jointly necessary to legitimize political orders.

The four postulates are formulated in terms that are general enough to be compatible with multiple interpretations. These interpretations differ with respect to the concrete implications of the abstract concepts evoked in the postulates. For our purposes, two dimensions of disagreement are especially relevant. The first dimension concerns the types of behaviour that are seen as having a problematic impact on autonomy and thus require regulation through democratically approved laws and accountable agencies. I call this the question of *regulatory scope*. The second dimension concerns the question of whether autonomy-affecting behaviour requires regulation only when it occurs in reality or also if it could occur potentially. This can be called the question of *modal robustness*.

5.1.2 The question of regulatory scope

When considering the types of autonomy-affecting behaviour that are in need of regulation through democratically approved laws and accountable agencies, some theories emphasize *coercion*, while other theories enlarge the scope to include non-coercive behaviour that inflicts a *harm*. Some extend the scope further and include any behaviour that has a *profound impact* on people's interests, regardless of whether it is harmful or beneficial (Koenig-Archibugi 2022). The three types will be considered in turn.

Coercion can take the form of a coercive act or of a coercive threat. Abizadeh explains the distinction as follows:

> A *coercive act* directly and preemptively deprives a person of some options that she would otherwise have had. The most obvious kind of coercive act is physical force, where the person's body and physical environment are acted on by an agent. ... A *coercive threat*, by contrast, simply communicates the intention to undertake an action in the future whose (anticipated) effect is to prevent a person from choosing an option that she otherwise might choose. So beyond directly thwarting the pursuit of some options, states also threaten persons with sanctions should they carry out proscribed actions. (Abizadeh 2008, 40)

Approaches that emphasize the role of coercion as a trigger for legal regulation and participatory entitlements point at the especially damaging effect of coercion on autonomy, which affects people irrespective of the quantity and quality of options that coercive acts and threats actually remove from the choice set. Part of what is seen as problematic in coercion is that the removal of options is deliberate rather than merely the side effect of actions undertaken for other reasons. Raz (1986, 378) notes that 'The natural fact that coercion and manipulation reduce options or distort normal processes of decision and the formation of preferences has become the basis of a social convention loading them with meaning regardless of their actual consequences. They have acquired a symbolic meaning expressing disregard or even contempt for the coerced or manipulated people.'

While coercion plays a particularly prominent role in discussions about political justice, numerous accounts envisage a broader regulatory scope. Personal autonomy can be limited also by non-coercive interventions, such as modifying the material environment of individuals in ways that endanger their health, safety, and life (Valentini 2014, 792–793). The near ubiquity of legal rules punishing harmful negligence shows that interventions causing significant *harm* are widely seen as requiring regulation even if they cannot be described as intentional and coercive (Bussani and Sebok 2015). Accordingly, several authors advocate a broader regulatory scope that includes coercion but is not restricted to it. An example is the principle formulated by Cavallero (2009, 58). He posits that: 'An individual, Q, is relevantly affected by the exercise of a sovereign competence C and has a right of democratic participation in the processes by which C is exercised if (a) Q is a member of a polity P and there is a significant chance that policy decisions that will be made repeatedly or sustained on an ongoing basis under C will otherwise impose significant external costs on members of P . . . '. Note that Cavallero's statement refers specifically to 'costs' and not also to 'benefits'. Like other authors, he assumes that participatory entitlements derive from what economists call 'negative externalities', but not necessarily from 'positive externalities'. Whether only the former or both kinds of externalities should give rise to participatory entitlements has been labelled the 'question of asymmetry' by Bengtson (2021).

A third group of authors extends the scope of participatory regulation even further. Based on a distinction between vital needs, life chances, and lifestyle needs, Held (2004, 374) formulates the principle that 'those whose life expectancy and life chances are significantly affected by social forces and processes ought to have a stake in the determination of the conditions and regulation of these, either directly or indirectly through political representatives'. In other words, any behaviour that has a *profound impact* on people should be regulated by laws adopted with their direct or indirect participation. Similarly, Goodin (2007, 2022) develops a justification of democratic entitlements that focuses on interests, without positing an asymmetry between actions that are harmful and those that are beneficial.

One way of justifying the democratic regulation of potentially beneficial behaviours is to posit a collective responsibility for ensuring that individuals can lead autonomous lives. Autonomy requires not only freedom from interference but also reliable access to resources. Within many domestic political systems, it is widely accepted that decisions to help other citizens to access such resources should not be confined to individual acts of charity but governed by laws about taxation, social insurance, and the provision of government services and transfers. In democratically governed welfare states, citizens have a say in the formulation of those laws that determine how they should help each other secure essential resources and not only of those laws that address the harms that they could inflict on each other. In normative terms, this can be justified by positing that political orders should rest not only on freedom and equality but also on solidarity.

There is disagreement on the best criterion for determining regulatory scope—coercion, harm, or profound impact—not only among theorists but also among the public. Cicero anticipated subsequent debates by positing that people had obligations towards the whole human race, but also that these duties were largely negative in nature—for example, the obligation not to prevent strangers from accessing common resources such as running water. Cicero argued that resource scarcity should lead positive duties of assistance and benevolence to be reserved to those sharing closer bonds of fellowship, especially common citizenship in the same polity (*civitas*) (Cicero 44 BCE/2001, 19–22 [§ 50–59]). Such views are widespread today. As noted in Chapter 4, cross-national surveys show widespread agreement with the principle that foreigners should be protected from harm as much as co-nationals. By contrast, only about half of the public in each country believes that non-nationals should be provided with benefits even if the resource reallocation comes at the expense of co-nationals (Bai, Gauri, and Fiske 2021). The distribution of views on these questions arguably affects the possibility of different international political orders. However, it does not settle the question of normative desirability, which is the focus on this chapter (Baderin et al. 2018).

It is not my aim here to take a definite position on which one of the three criteria for the question of regulatory scope is the most compelling. Rather, it is to highlight that they offer three partly overlapping but sufficiently distinct vantage points for assessing actual and hypothetical global political orders. However, it is important to note that the 'profound impact' criterion is more plausible than some critics believe, especially in the light of the normative postulates introduced earlier in this chapter. Consider the reasons why Abizadeh rejects the profound impact criterion as a basis for democratic participation entitlements. He argues that being subjected to coercion creates an intrinsic right to having a democratic say, but having one's fundamental interests affected by a decision does not; depending on the circumstances, due consideration of those interests 'might also be secured through fiduciary institutions, binding arbitration, or contestatory judicial institutions' (Abizadeh 2012, 878). This position neglects an important distinction, which was clearly formulated by Abizadeh himself in a different context: 'democratic legitimacy does not normally require that individuals "democratically justify" to others their *application* of laws in particular instances; it requires that the *formulation* of laws result from democratic processes of justification involving those subject to the laws' (Abizadeh 2010, 127, emphases in original). Accordingly, fiduciary institutions, binding arbitration, or contestatory judicial institutions may well be tasked with adjudicating between competing claims in particular instances, in cases of non-coercive impact but plausibly also cases of coercion. But normative postulate (3a) implies that such institutions should perform that function in the context of general rules that authorize them to do so and provide general parameters for making decisions in specific cases. And normative postulate (3b) implies that such general rules need to be formulated democratically, either because they have the potential of affecting the fundamental interests of all, or because they take the form of coercively enforced laws, or both. The postulates require democratic participation in making laws, as opposed to democratic participation in every decision that the laws aim to regulate. Hence, a rejection of profound impact as a criterion to determine participatory entitlements would need to be based on an argument that laws should be limited to regulating potentially coercive behaviour and remain silent on any other behaviour, regardless of how deeply it affects the interests of other people. While some authors may be willing to endorse such a position (e.g. Nozick 1974), it is not a commonly held position among democratic theorists.

This subsection has offered three criteria for determining the scope of regulation and participation, and an argument against rejecting the most expansive criterion. Before we can apply the three criteria to existing global relationships, we need to address the second dimension mentioned at the beginning of the chapter: modal robustness.

5.1.3 The question of modal robustness

The previous section has distinguished between three types of behaviour that may trigger the need for mechanisms of common regulation and for the democratic control of those mechanisms: coercion, behaviour that produces harm (which normally includes coercion), and behaviour that has a profound impact (which normally includes both coercion and harm). An important aspect to consider is the 'reality status' of the behaviour in question. A clear and concise statement that *potential*, not *actual* harm, is sufficient to trigger the requirement of subjection to common laws comes from Kant:

> It is usually assumed that one may not behave with hostility toward another unless he has actively *wronged me*; and that is also quite correct if both are in a condition of *being under civil laws*. For by having entered into such a condition one affords the other the requisite assurance (by means of a superior having power over both). But a human being (or a nation) in a mere state of nature denies me this assurance and already wrongs me just by being near me in this condition, even if not actively (*facto*) yet by the lawlessness of his condition (*statu iniusto*), by which he constantly threatens me; and I can coerce him either to enter with me into a condition of being under civil laws or to leave my neighborhood. Hence the postulate on which all the following articles are based is that all men who can mutually affect one another must belong to some civil constitution. (Kant 1795/1996, 322)

Among contemporary political theories, republican theory has placed particular emphasis on protection against potential encroachments. It insists that nondomination should be *modally robust*, i.e. absent or minimized not only in relation to the choices that the relevant agents actually want to make but also in relation to choices that they could potentially want to make. To count as nondomination, the absence of interference has to be robust across the range of options that the potentially *interfered* actor could choose, because otherwise this actor could achieve freedom simply by adapting her preferences and desiring to do only what the interfering actor allows her to do (Berlin 1969). Crucially, to count as nondomination the absence of interference must additionally be robust across the range of preferences that the potentially *interfering* actor could have regarding the actions that the interfered might perform. In other words, '[i]t is not enough to enjoy non-interference across a range of worlds in which your preference or will changes … For full or ideal freedom of choice, you also have to enjoy non-interference across a range of worlds in which there are also changes in the preference or will of agents as to what you should do' (Pettit 2012, 67). In the canonical example, a slave whose master is benevolent and unwilling to interfere remains unfree.

The conception of modally robust nondomination raises the important question of *how robust* it should be, i.e. in what range of possible worlds potentially interfering actors must be constrained from actually interfering. At one extreme, nondomination could be seen as requiring the absence of uncontrolled interference in *any* non-actual but possible circumstance. Nondomination would then be not just a modally demanding value but what Southwood (2015, 509–510) calls an 'infinitely modally demanding value'. At the other extreme, nondomination could be seen as requiring the absence of uncontrolled interference only in the closest possible worlds, where closeness describes a non-actual world that differs only minimally from the actual world.

The most plausible understandings of freedom embody 'a modal robustness requirement, according to which freedom requires the absence of the constraints in a *sufficiently large* class of possible worlds (relevant hypothetical scenarios) over and above the actual world' (List and Valentini 2016, 1046, emphasis added). However, there is no settled answer to the question of what counts as 'sufficiently large'. List and Valentini (2016, 1071) themselves suggest that freedom should be regarded as a matter of degree because '[t]he set of possible worlds across which constraints on the agent's doing X are absent can be smaller or larger'.

The same applies to related values such as democracy. Southwood (2015) argues that democracy should be regarded as a value that is modally demanding but not infinitely so. In his account, a polity is governed democratically if the will of its people would continue to determine the decisions of the polity across a range of non-actual situations. When this condition is fulfilled, there is what he calls collective 'self-rule' (which is modally demanding) rather than mere 'self-governance' (which is not modally demanding). Southwood proposes that self-rule should involve at least two counterfactual requirements. These are that 'the polity must be such that the will of the people would continue to determine the decisions of the polity across certain changes in *the content of the will of the person or persons who occupy the position of highest authority in the polity*' and 'across certain changes in *the content of the will of the people*' (Southwood 2015, 512, 514, emphases in the original text).

While for Southwood democracy requires 'at least' those two counterfactual requirements, more requirements can be plausibly added. Under the two requirements he proposes, a polity would continue to count as democratically governed even if the will of the people ceased to determine the decisions of the polity because a foreign power decided to coercively impose its will on it—as long as that foreign power does not have the *formal* authority to do so. An alternative and arguably more plausible approach would not privilege formal authority over actual power and instead posit that democracy is reduced when outside powers have the capacity—whether connected to formal authority or not—to impose a decision on a people without that people having given their consent. Putting it the other way round: if an outside power can form a will and has the (material) capacity to impose that will on the people of another polity, then those people must have the right to participate in formulating general laws that regulate the exercise of that capacity. Democratic principles are violated if that right is not put into practice.

Positing that the mere capacity to perform autonomy-affecting behaviour requires subjection to a democratically formulated system of law may strike some as overly demanding. One possible way of weakening this requirement is to posit that autonomy-affecting behaviour calls for democratic regulation when it is probable, not merely possible. In other words, actors capable of affecting the autonomy of others need to be subject to a democratic system of coercive laws only when it is sufficiently probable that they will exercise that capability. A properly specified probabilistic understanding of robustness may not be fundamentally distinct from a modal approach (List 2006; List and Valentini 2016, 1052–1055). It is not necessary to settle the question here. In the remainder of my argument, I will take into account the position that the probability (as opposed to mere possibility) of autonomy-affecting behaviour is a relevant criterion when assessing the desirability of a coercive legal order that regulates that behaviour.

5.1.4 Democracy and human rights

I posited that political orders need to enable individuals to participate as free and equal in crafting laws to regulate the actual/potential behaviour of individuals, social groups, and state actors, in so far as such behaviour affects people's autonomy by virtue of its coercive/harmful/impactful nature. From this perspective, democracy is instrumentally valuable as a mechanism to protect personal autonomy as well as intrinsically valuable as a procedure to pool autonomy when collective decisions are needed.[2] But this normative requirement raises an important question. Being empowered in participating freely and equally in a democratic process does not guarantee that the outcome of the decisions will match one's preferences and/or interests. For instance, the profound impact that the distribution of material resources can have on individuals' interests generates a need for democratically decided regulation, but it does not by itself determine what the content of that regulation should be. One dimension of this issue is the problem of persistent minorities, which will be discussed in Chapter 6. An even more fundamental problem arises in relation to the relationship between democracy and human rights. There are good reasons to expect democratic institutions to be associated with better protection of physical integrity rights, social rights, and economic rights, and there is indeed empirical evidence of such an association (Cabrera 2020, 83–90; Gerring, Knutsen, and Berge 2022). Nevertheless, democratic collective decisions may fail to promote, or even actively violate, what can be plausibly considered to be human rights of some individuals. For the purposes of this chapter, two points are worth noting.

First, and from a normative point of view, the postulates formulated in this chapter are compatible with seeing democracy and human rights as 'co-original', to use the expression proposed by Habermas (Habermas 1996, 2001; cf. Schaffer 2015). Whether or not one accepts that democracy and human rights ultimately rest on the same normative foundation (such as the discourse principle formulated by Habermas), most contemporary political theories agree that democratic decision-making should be limited by human rights. But the question of which rights should be considered human

---

[2] The relationship between intrinsic and instrumental approaches to (global) democracy is discussed by Caney (2006), Weinstock (2006), and Cabrera (2020).

rights, and how general principles should be interpreted in specific contexts, is controversial (Ibhawoh 2001; Caney 2006; Valentini 2012, 2013; Tobin 2014; Cabrera 2020; von Arnauld, von der Decken, and Susi 2020; An-Naim 2021; Freeman 2022; Escobar 2023). The arguments advanced for and against specific rights in the context of state policies would also apply to the safeguards included in the constitution of a universal republic. Its deliberative-democratic mechanisms would mitigate some of the tensions that exist today between international human rights law and domestic democratic institutions (Schaffer 2015).

Second, and from an empirical point of view, we can ask whether a world state would be more likely to protect human rights than to flout them. Imagining what the human rights practices of a hypothetical polity might be is, of course, very challenging. Chapter 6 offers some tentative insights on the question. It presents estimates of the expected score of the world state on several democracy indices that are associated with different clusters of human rights. Specifically, it presents the predicted score of the world state on the V-Dem's liberal democracy index, which incorporates respect for various civil and freedom rights, and on the egalitarian democracy index, which incorporates protection of economic and social rights. Moreover, it estimates the expected score of the world state on the deliberative democracy index, which can be interpreted as reflecting process-oriented (as opposed to outcome-oriented) constraints on democracy. A prominent example of a process-oriented constraint on democratic decision-making is 'public reason', which requires justifying positions on matters of public policy by providing arguments that people holding different moral or social beliefs could in principle accept (Rawls 1996, 1999b; Afnan 2023). Chapter 6 examines to what extent the structural diversity of the world would be an obstacle to public reason-giving in a universal republic.

5.2 The state of the world

The previous section has considered the conditions under which the relationship between actors requires the establishment of a coercive legal order that is controlled by those subjected to it. This section presents an assessment of whether and to what extent those conditions are empirically present today at the global level. The question has been answered already by Kant, who pointed at 'the earth's surface on which, as a sphere, [human beings] cannot disperse infinitely but must finally put up with being near another' (Kant 1795/1996, 329). In his argument, the sphericity of the Earth makes mutual affectedness inescapable, hence the relationship between all human beings must be regulated by law (Kant 1795/1996, 322). This section fleshes out the empirical dimensions of Kant's argument.

A general premise is important. Theoretical justifications for systems of law often refer to the relationship between 'citizens' (e.g. Pettit 2012), which tends to direct the attention towards individuals. Of course, this is a simplification even in domestic contexts, as threats to individual freedom are as likely to originate from group agents as from individuals (List and Pettit 2011). In the global context, it is even more important to focus on the impact of group agents, since often only group agents have the capacity to deeply affect lives over long distances. Multinational companies and international organizations can affect the livelihoods, working conditions, and natural environment of millions of people. But, above all, it is *states* that possess the resources to produce deep impacts on people well beyond their borders. This is important because the capacity to affect autonomy is the key variable in the normative framework presented in the previous section. To keep things simple, most of the following discussion will refer to states as the agents with the largest capacity.[3] Later in the chapter, I will touch upon the question of private power, and specifically corporate power.

As discussed earlier, autonomy-affecting behaviour can be conceptualized more stringently or more expansively along two dimensions: the type of impact that they have (coercion, harm, and profound impact) and in terms of the modal demandingness (behaviour in the actual world, in probable worlds, or in all possible worlds). Figure 5.1 mentions some examples corresponding to various combinations. The remainder of this section considers the examples in some depth.

5.2.1 Coercion beyond borders

A particularly visible instance of actual coercion directed against outsiders is border control. Many states of the world aim to stop outsiders from accessing their territory by issuing coercive laws that prohibit unauthorized access, threatening potential violators and authorizing state agents to use force to prevent access and punish violators (Abizadeh 2008). A database of inbound travel restrictions imposed by 214 reporting countries and territories on citizens of specific countries shows that, in 2013, around three-quarters of all

---

[3] This argument is distinct from the assumption that powerful extra-state actors affect individuals only through their impact on the individuals' states, rather than directly. As the examples in this section show, this assumption is implausible.

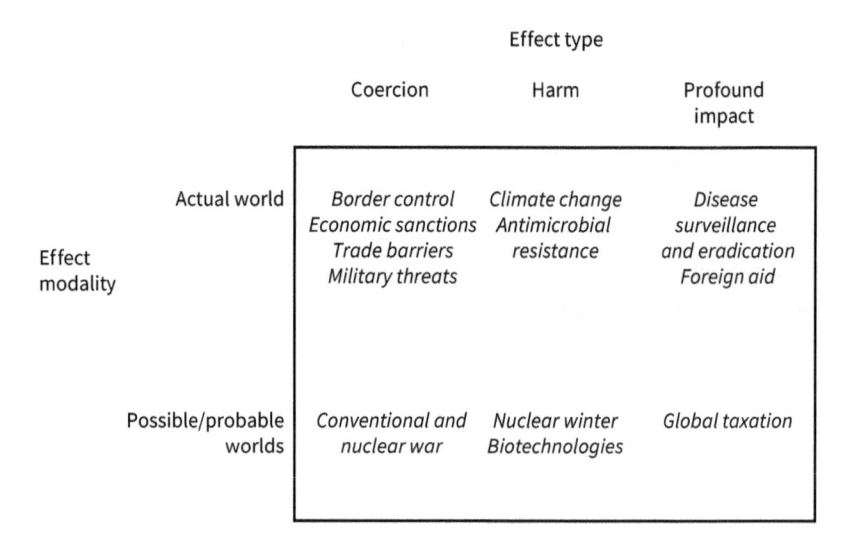

Figure 5.1 Autonomy-affecting outcomes distinguished by effect type and effect modality.

country dyads in the world had such restrictions in the form of visa require-ments. The proportion of country dyads with restrictions increases to nearly 90 per cent when population sizes are taken into account (Czaika, de Haas, and Villares-Varela 2018). States also invest significant resources into coercive capabilities aimed at deterring and stopping unauthorized movements into their territory. Gülzau and Mau (2021) classify land borders architectures into five categories on a spectrum from relatively open to relatively close: 'no man's land' borders, landmark borders, checkpoint borders, barrier borders, and fortified borders. They find that checkpoint borders are the most com-mon form of land border, but barriers and fortified borders are common as well (see also Simmons and Kenwick 2022). The restrictive nature of contem-porary territorial boundaries becomes even more pronounced if sea borders and airport borders are considered as well.

Of course, the absence of a barrier or fortified border does not indicate ease of international mobility, given that state coercion is not exercised only in the proximity of borders but also deep into the territory of states, and unauthorized travellers are constantly vulnerable to seizure, imprisonment, and deportation. Data collected by Peters show that almost all states have adopted stricter deportation policies and other enforcement policies over the last half-century (Peters 2015, 129–130).

Being coercively prevented to move across international borders has very deep impacts on the options available to individuals. More than two-thirds of the variability of incomes of people across the world is determined by where they live (Milanovic 2016, 133). This means that 'people from poor countries have the opportunity to double or triple or increase ten-fold their real incomes by moving to a rich country' (Milanovic 2016, 134). Importantly, the impact on people's life opportunities is not only economic. For instance, attitudes to same-sex relationships differ across the world (Roberts 2019) and restricting the ability of people to move where acceptance is higher can make a big difference for personal safety, respect, and quality of life. Whatever their motivation, a substantial proportion of the world's population would migrate if they could, and thus it is directly and actually affected by the coercive threats and acts aimed at restricting transnational mobility (Esipova, Pugliese, and Ray 2018).

A second example of actual coercion consists of barriers to economic transactions across borders. One type of such barrier consists of economic sanctions. Sanctions are 'actions that one or more sender states or an international institution take to limit economic relations with a single target state in an effort to persuade the latter to change its policies' (Morgan, Bapat, and Kobayashi 2021). Sanctions are common. The Global Sanctions Database lists a total of 1,101 publicly traceable, multilateral, plurilateral, and unilateral sanction cases between 1950 and 2019 (Kirikakha et al. 2021). Over this period, about a third of all sanction cases originated from the United States. More than 200 sanction cases were active in 2019. Sanctions have a major impact on key dimensions of well-being, such as poverty, health, discrimination, and political repression (Peksen 2011; Drury and Peksen 2014; Neuenkirch and Neumeier 2015; Lucena Carneiro and Apolinário, Jr 2016; Neuenkirch and Neumeier 2016; Liou, Murdie, and Peksen 2021; Early and Peksen 2022).

A different type of restriction to economic transactions across borders are imposed for economic rather than political reasons. They are still coercive measures, because they use the tools of state authority to prevent economic actors based in different countries from completing voluntary transactions that those actors may find to be in their mutual interest. Governments make extensive use of their authority to limit trade. To gauge the extent of such behaviour in recent years, we can consider the trade freedom indicator developed by the Heritage Foundation (2022), which combines data on tariffs and non-tariff barriers. Figure 5.2 shows the level of trade freedom since 1995 as the average score of 184 countries (not weighted by population) on a scale from 0 to 100, where a score of 100 would indicate the complete absence of trade barriers. While this form of coercion has decreased since the 1990s, it is still very common. It also a substantial impact on living standards around the world (Choi, Kim, and Ma 2021).

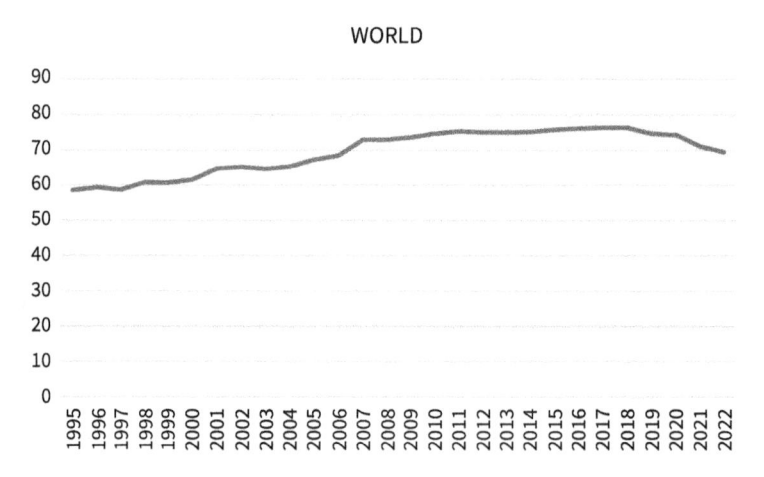

Figure 5.2 Trade freedom indicator, 1995-2022.

Source: Own elaboration based on data from Heritage Foundation (2022).

A third notable instance of actual coercion across borders is the threat to use military force against the armed personnel, populations, and infrastructure of other states. The capacity to use weapons to inflict damage beyond borders is very substantial. The vast majority of states in the world possess armed forces and are in principle able to initiate a militarized action against other states and their residents (Barbey 2013; International Institute for Strategic Studies 2022). In 2021, active-duty military and paramilitary personnel amounted to more than 27 million people and military spending amounted to nearly 2 trillion US dollars (International Institute for Strategic Studies 2022, 526). The history of warfare during the twentieth and early twenty-first century shows that wars fought with conventional weapons can be extremely destructive, but the threat to use nuclear weapons deserves a special mention. Nine states currently possess them. While the number of nuclear warheads has decreased considerably since the early 1980s, there were still around 12,700 warheads in 2022 (Federation of American Scientists 2022).

In the current international system, coercive threats are real, and coercive acts are clearly *possible*. But are such acts *probable*? Nowadays, coercive threats are nearly always justified in terms of an apparently narrow goal: to ensure the 'security' and 'defence' of the home state. However, states typically reserve the right to interpret what that goal entails. This extends to the threat to use nuclear weapons. Officially, this threat is directed at preventing attacks against the state possessing the weapons or other states that are under its protection. For instance, the US Nuclear Posture Review of 2018 declares: 'The United States would only consider the employment of nuclear weapons in extreme circumstances to defend the vital interests of the United States, its allies, and partners. Extreme circumstances could include significant non-nuclear strategic attacks.' What constitutes a vital interest, who are the 'partners' (as distinct from allies), and what actions would be perceived as an 'attack' are deliberately left ambiguous. The same document states: 'It remains the policy of the United States to retain some ambiguity regarding the precise circumstances that might lead to a U.S. nuclear response.' In sum, the coercive threat clearly identifies one type of action that would trigger a nuclear response—a nuclear attack against the United States and/or its allies—but is also meant to counter a more ambiguous set of behaviours that may threaten US 'vital interests'. Russia also maintains substantial ambiguity. During its war against Ukraine, Russian officials emphasized that Russia might use nuclear weapons in response to 'an act of aggression' committed against Russia and its allies, even if conducted with the use of conventional weapons (Boffey 2022). In both cases, the 'threat' of nuclear use aims at deterring other actors from actions that seriously interfere with the interest of the country as the governments understand them.

According to many analysts, the rhetorical emphasis placed on defensive goals by most states today reflect a real change in the orientation of states towards war. Sørensen (2013, 897) expressed a widely held opinion in stating that 'the problem of war between states lacks the centrality it once had. Processes of democratization, economic and political integration, and increasing respect for common rules about territorial integrity have all but eradicated the occurrence of interstate war.' He explicitly related this assessment to the arguments of global government advocates: 'The threat of interstate war no longer warrants a world state' (Sørensen 2013, 897).

There is wide agreement that wars between any two states in the international system is a low-probability event, but also that the relatively low risk is counterbalanced by their destructive impact and potential for escalation. Much of the recent debate concerned the question of whether the risk and the intensity of international war is substantially lower today than it was in the past and, if so, whether this is likely to remain so for the foreseeable future.

The starting point of many analyses is the idea of a 'long peace' among major powers since 1945 (Gaddis 1986). For some authors, the relative rarity of war today is the culmination of a long-term trend towards the reduction of violence among and within states. Several of the analysts supporting this interpretation also maintain that war is likely to remain rare for the foreseeable future, because the trend is driven by factors that are unlikely to be reversed. Sørensen (2013) mentioned those that are most often invoked:

democratization, economic and political integration, and respect for territorial integrity norms. Goertz, Diehl, and Balas (2016) are among the proponents of this view. To assess broad trends, they first identified pairs of countries that have some form of meaningful 'relationship' among all pairs of states existing in the world at a given point in time. Then, they classified all relevant pairs as belonging to one of these types: rivalry, 'cold' peace, and what (following Johan Galtung) they call 'positive peace', i.e. friendly interaction. Finally, they calculate the proportion of states in any kind of relationship that experience a war in any given year. Figure 5.3 summarizes their findings. It shows that the percentage of state pairs involved in a war has declined since 1946 and reached a low of 0.1 per cent in the last year of their dataset (2008).[4]

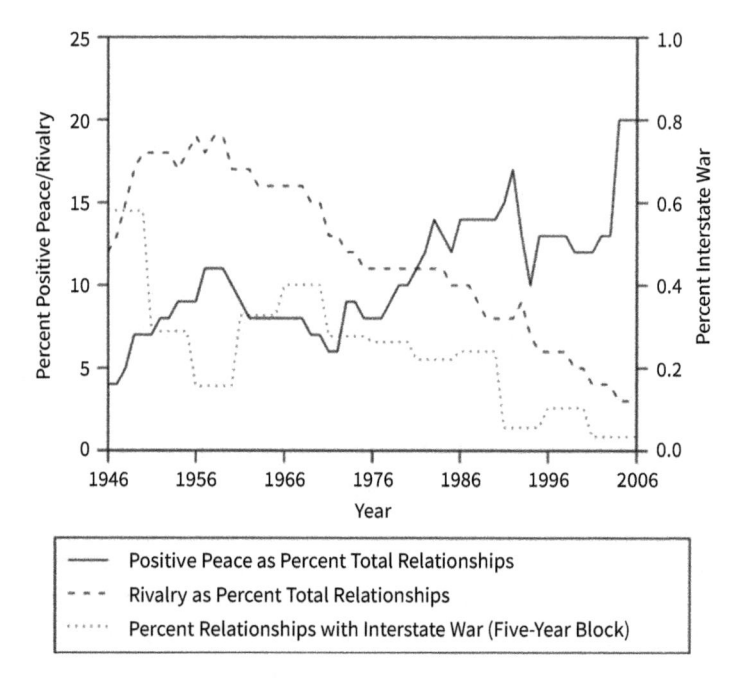

Figure 5.3 The evolution of interstate war compared with positive peace and rivalry over time.

Source: Gary Goertz, Paul F. Diehl, and Alexandru Balas. 2016. *The Puzzle of Peace: The Evolution of Peace in the International System.* © Oxford University Press 2016. Reproduced with permission of the Licensor through PLSclear.

---

[4] Diehl, Goertz, and Gallegos (2021) update their analysis to 2015. Of course, these global averages do not capture more specific trends. For instance, according to the Military Intervention Project the US has undertaken almost 400 military interventions since 1776. Half of these interventions were undertaken between 1950 and 2019 and over a quarter between the end of the Cold War and 2019 (Kushi and Toft 2023).

Over the same period, rivalries have declined to less than 5 per cent of all relationships and pairs experiencing 'positive peace' have increased to nearly 20 per cent.

The 'optimists' have been countered by other authors who deny that the probability of armed conflict in the current period is fundamentally different from that of previous periods. Braumoeller (2019) considered the frequency of cases where force was used or threatened in the relationship between formally recognized states, relative to the number of opportunities for conflict (as measured by the number of 'politically relevant' pairs of states in the international system). He found no long-term trend towards less war: the Cold War period was more conflictual than the sixty years preceding World War I, and the post-Cold War period was slightly more conflictual than the first third of the century following the Napoleonic Wars. Braumoeller extended the analysis to wars other than conflicts between formally recognized states, i.e. to 'extra-state wars' (imperial conquest and independence wars) and 'nonstate wars' (between or among nonstate actors taking place outside of states). He found no general upward or downward trend throughout the period (see Figure 5.4).

In the same vein, other authors have reached the conclusion that statistically it is too soon to say whether the probability of war has declined compared to previous periods in history—the scarcity of war between major powers during the past seventy years is not a sufficiently unusual pattern from a long-term perspective (Cirillo and Taleb 2016; Clauset 2018). In

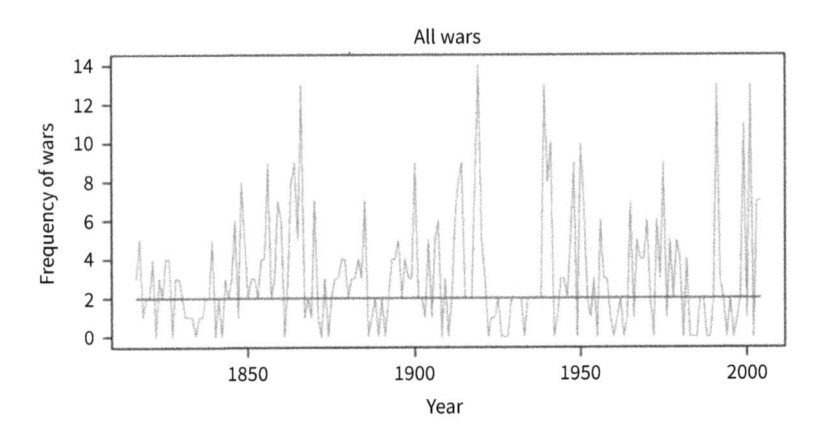

Figure 5.4 The number of international, extra-state or nonstate wars started in each year, 1815–2007. The horizontal straight line indicates the median.

Source: Bear F. Braumoeller, *Only the Dead: The Persistence of War in the Modern Age.* © Oxford University Press 2019. Reproduced with permission of the Licensor through PLSclear.

this view, the long period of relative peace since World War II is consistent with the absence of change in the underlying risk of war and its severity. The debate on the statistical patterns is still ongoing (Clauset and Gleditsch 2018; Cunen, Hjort, and Nygård 2020; Fagan et al. 2020; Spagat and van Weezel 2020).

Proponents of the decline of war thesis retort that the relative peace of the post-1945 world cannot be accounted for simply in terms of normal variation long-term patterns but should be interpreted as the result of fundamental changes in the major determinants of conflict (Pinker n.d.). As noted above, the development of norms against conquest and violence, the decline of nationalism, the spread of democracy and gender equality, international economic integration, and the growth of international institutions are all invoked as responsible for the decline of war (Goldstein 2011; Pinker 2012; Mueller 2013). There is indeed evidence that these factors influence the likelihood of war (Boehmer, Gartzke, and Nordstrom 2004; Kinne 2012; Schrock-Jacobson 2012; Cranmer, Menninga, and Mucha 2015; Gruffydd-Jones 2017; Bakaki 2018; Barnhart et al. 2020; Altman, Rojas-de-Galarreta, and Urdinez 2021; Gill-Tiney 2022). Consequently, we might conclude that the actual probability of war is lower than it was in the past. However, the expectation that the probability will remain low, or even decrease further, in the foreseeable future would depend on the persistence of those peace-inducing factors. As recent developments affecting democracy, international institutions, economic interdependence, and territorial integrity norms suggest, those drivers of peace cannot be assumed to be irreversible (Jenne 2018; Lührmann and Lindberg 2019; Norris and Inglehart 2019; Von Borzyskowski and Vabulas 2019; Diamond 2021; Bieber 2022; Boese et al. 2022; Bown 2022; Fazal 2022).

Within the broader debate on the likelihood and severity of war, some authors have addressed specifically the risk of nuclear weapons use. Views diverge sharply. According to Waltz, the logic of deterrence makes the probability extremely low, whereas Sagan regards the probability as substantial, considering that it is affected also by accidents, false alarms, and uncontrolled escalation (Sagan and Waltz 1995). There has been only one nuclear war in history—World War II—but the empirical frequency of this kind of event is a poor guide to the underlying risk (Baum, de Neufville, and Barrett 2018). Baum, de Neufville, and Barrett (2018) identify fourteen different scenarios that could lead to nuclear war: six scenarios involve a nuclear-armed state intentionally initiating a first-strike nuclear attack and eight scenarios involve a nuclear-armed state falsely believing that it has been attacked with nuclear weapons and launching what it believes to be a retaliatory nuclear attack. While none of the scenarios was fully realized after 1945, Baum, de Neufville, and Barrett (2018) describe sixty historical incidents that might have plausibly led to a nuclear war. Only a handful of studies have attempted to provide actual numerical estimates of the probability of a nuclear war. Barrett, Baum, and Hostetler (2013) develop an approach to estimate the annual probability of an *inadvertent* war between Russia and the United States, i.e. a nuclear attack initiated by a state because of the mistaken belief that it is under attack itself. Their mean estimate is an annual probability of 2 per cent, but with a large margin of uncertainty: the 90 per cent credible interval ranges from 0.02 per cent to 7 per cent. This estimate has an order of magnitude similar to the estimates presented by Hellman (2008), for whom the annual probability of nuclear war is 1 per cent, and by Lundgren (2013), for whom the average chance of a nuclear exchange during the Cold War was 2.1 per cent per year (with a very wide credible interval). While these estimates are subject to very high uncertainty, they suggest that under reasonable assumptions the chances of nuclear weapons use cannot be regarded as negligible.

Some authors regarded the probability of the use of nuclear weapons after 1945 to be very low because of a 'nuclear taboo' (Tannenwald 2007). However, recent survey research suggests that the aversion to nuclear weapons felt by the American public does not reach the level of a taboo: many Americans support the use nuclear weapons when they are better than conventional weapons in destroying critical targets (Press, Sagan, and Valentino 2013; Haworth, Sagan, and Valentino 2019). Publics in other countries seem more averse to the use of nuclear weapons, but not everywhere or always (Sukin 2020; Egel and Hines 2021; Dill, Sagan, and Valentino 2022; Smetana and Onderco 2022; Onderco, Smetana, and Etienne 2023). The main proponent of the nuclear taboo thesis has warned that 'the global nuclear normative order is unravelling' (Tannenwald 2018, 90–91).

5.2.2 Harm beyond borders

A significant proportion of the world population is harmed by the emissions of greenhouse gasses originating from other countries. The damage is already considerable and will increase in the coming decades. Lives are and will be lost directly because of heatwaves, the spread of tropical diseases to new areas, and extreme weather events such as droughts, storms, and floods (Romanello et al. 2021). Attempts to quantify the expected death toll build on the 'representative concentration pathways' (RCPs) developed by the Intergovernmental Panel on Climate Change. Carleton et al. (2020) estimate that under a high-emissions scenario (RCP 8.5), which is sometimes described as a 'business as usual' scenario, higher temperatures will cause 73 deaths per year per 100,000 population by 2100, taking into account future income growth and adaptation. Assuming a global population of 10 billion, this translates to over 7 million deaths per year. The authors note that the impact is similar in size to the current global mortality burden of all cancers or all infectious diseases. Assuming moderately intense efforts to mitigate climate change (RCP 4.5), there will be an estimated 11 deaths per year per 100,000 population by 2100, equivalent to over one million deaths per year. Almost all of the total increase in mortality rates will be experienced in the bottom third of countries by income (Carleton et al. 2020; for similar estimates see Bressler et al. 2021).

Burke, Hsiang, and Miguel (2015) estimate that unmitigated warming (RCP 8.5) will reduce average global incomes by roughly 23 per cent by 2100, compared to scenarios without climate change. The damage will be concentrated in countries with high average temperatures, which also tend to be poorer. They estimate that 'average income in the poorest 40 per cent of countries declines 75 per cent by 2100 relative to a world without climate change, while the richest 20 per cent experience slight gains, since they are generally cooler' (Burke, Hsiang, and Miguel 2015, 238). Climate change can therefore be expected to increase global economic inequality. These estimates are conservative as they are limited to the effects of higher temperatures, without taking into account other losses associated with global warming, such as rising sea levels and cyclones. Emissions have already caused very large economic losses through their effect on extreme weather events, notably storms, droughts, and wildfires (OECD 2021). Loss and damage can also affect intangible values and lived experiences (Tschakert et al. 2017). Climate change can also cause harm by increasing violent conflict, although the evidence that this has already happened is ambiguous (Koubi 2019).

A second example of actual harm is antimicrobial resistance (AMR), which happens when micro-organisms such as bacteria, viruses, and fungi evolve to become resistant to antimicrobial medicines. Drug-resistant bacteria spread across borders (Barlam and Gupta 2015; Frost et al. 2019; Bokhary et al. 2021). The overuse and misuse of antibiotics in health care and farming exacerbate AMR. Hence, governments that permit excessive and inappropriate use of antibiotics and/or fail to effectively enforce regulations cause harm beyond their own jurisdictions (Heinzel and Koenig-Archibugi 2023). Such harm is substantial, as AMR is one of the most severe dangers to human health. Murray et al. (2022) estimate that at least 1.27 million people died in 2019 as a direct result of AMR. The threat is growing, and experts warn that AMR could lead to a future without effective antibiotics. A 2015 report commissioned by the UK Prime Minister estimated that, in the absence of remedial action, the loss of life due to AMR will accelerate to an estimated 10 million annual deaths by 2050 (Review on Antimicrobial Resistance 2016). World Bank economists projected a global cumulative GDP loss of US$85 trillion during 2015–50 and an additional 24 million people to live in extreme poverty (Ahmed et al. 2018). Roope et al. (2019) point out that the expected economic costs are similar to those of a 2°C rise in global average temperature above preindustrial levels. Even analysts who point at the considerable uncertainty of such estimates and projections agree that AMR causes a large and growing health burden and that urgent action is required (de Kraker, Stewardson, and Harbarth 2016).

While emissions and antibiotics policies are causing *actual* harm across borders, the use of nuclear weapons is a key instance of *possible* harm. Populations of states that are the direct targets of such weapons are subject to coercion, as discussed above. But their use can harm populations well beyond the target states. One pathway to widespread harm involves the so-called 'nuclear winter': fires caused by nuclear explosions would cause a large quantity of smoke to rise into the stratosphere, where it would spread globally and cause a reduction in surface temperatures and precipitation and an increase in ultraviolet radiation (Mills et al. 2014). The effect on the global climate could last for a decade or longer. Climate model simulations indicate that a limited regional nuclear war (equivalent to India and Pakistan each detonating fifty 15 kiloton weapons) would reduce global mean temperature by 1.8 °C and precipitation by 8 per cent for at least five years. Jägermeyr et al. (2020) calculate that these changes would have severe effects on global food production: global caloric production from soya beans, maize, wheat, and rice would fall by 17, 13, 11, and 3 per cent respectively over five years. The shock would reverberate through the food trade network. Because the main exporting countries of the northern hemisphere would experience the highest reductions and reserves would decline rapidly, it may not be possible to mitigate the impact of crop losses in countries with high levels of food insecurity by using trade or food aid. Jägermeyr et al. (2020, 7071) estimate that, 'By year 5, maize and wheat availability would decrease by 13 per cent globally and by more than 20 per cent in 71 countries with a cumulative population of 1.3 billion people.' These estimates are based on a scenario of a hundred nuclear explosions: a conflict involving parties with larger stockpiles, notably Russia and the USA, might escalate and produce global harm of much greater magnitude.

Another domain where significant harm is possible is the development and regulation of biotechnologies. Such technologies have the potential of contributing to major advances in health care, but they also involve very substantial risks. Such risks are not necessarily the result of malicious intent, they can also stem from well-intentioned research. Two types of risk are especially notable. The first is the spread of dangerous *biological material*, such as viruses and other pathogens escaping laboratories. Manheim and Lewis (2022) list seventy-one publicly known incidents between 1975 and 2016 involving accidental or purposeful exposure to a highly infectious pathogenic agent because of human activities rather than natural sources. Several of these incidents had pandemic potential, and one—H1N1 influenza in 1977–78—actually developed into a pandemic that infected millions, although the mortality impact was modest (Rozo and Gronvall 2015). The fact that some of these incidents occurred in high-safety laboratories suggests that the accidental release of pathogens is likely to remain not just possible but also 'fairly likely' (Klotz 2019). Klotz (2019) assesses specifically the risks of a lab-created, mammalian-airborne-transmissible, highly pathogenic avian influenza virus. That author estimates at 20 per cent the probability that such a virus would be accidentally released into the community from at least one of ten laboratories over a decade of developing and researching this type of pathogen. The probability that any such release would trigger a pandemic would be in the region of 15 per cent (Merler et al. 2013). For the purposes of this discussion, biotechnologies are classified as possible rather actual harm, but at the time of writing it has not been conclusively ruled out that the pathogen-causing Covid-19 originated in a high-safety laboratory (Maxmen 2022).

The second type of risk posed by biotechnology involves the spread of *biological information* (as opposed to biological material). Information on potentially pandemic pathogens can be 'dual use': useful not only to scientists and agencies aiming to increase health security but also to malicious actors interested in using disease as a weapon (Lewis et al. 2019; Sandberg and Nelson 2020). This dual use creates major challenges for regulation, as there is no consensus on the balance of costs and benefits of different regulatory options. Lewis et al. (2019) describe several real-world examples of biological research that raise such challenges in stark terms, such as the question of whether the purposeful mutation of the H5N1 avian influenza virus into a variant that is easily transmissible between mammals should be reported in scientific journals, and indeed whether it should have been conducted in the first place. The large research efforts targeting Covid-19 also involves the significant risk that findings are used for malicious purposes (Musunuri et al. 2021).

Finally, the rapid development of artificial intelligence (AI) is likely to magnify all these risks of harm beyond borders in ways that are still difficult to gauge and quantify, but which may be devastating for humanity as a whole (Ord 2020).

Most examples provided so far involve direct externalities across borders. Harms can also be more indirect, such as situations where states find it difficult to implement the policies preferred by their citizens because of the pressures of international competition (short of coercion). This type of harmful impact is examined in section 6.4.

5.2.3 Profound impact beyond borders

Decisions taken in one country can have a profound impact on the autonomy of individuals in other countries in ways that are difficult to describe as coercion or non-coercive harm. Within this broader category, we can further distinguish between decisions that involve a transfer of resources across state borders and those that do not.

An example of the latter type is the surveillance of outbreaks of known or new diseases. Each government must decide whether to devote scarce domestic resources to create the infrastructure and personnel needed to detect the emergence and re-emergence of dangerous pathogens within their territories. This decision does not only affect the population of that state but also outsiders—potentially everyone on Earth. Early detection of, and depth of information about, outbreaks is a major determinant of the effectiveness of response (Moon et al. 2015). Based on obligations stated in the International Health Regulations of 2005, the WHO monitors the ability of member states to detect, analyse, and respond to outbreaks through an assessment framework encompassing thirteen 'core capacities', namely policy and legal instruments, coordination, financing, laboratory, surveillance, human resources, health emergency management, health services provision, infection prevention and control, risk communication and community engagement, points of entry and border health, zoonotic diseases, and food safety (plus chemical events and radiation emergencies) (World Health Organization 2021). Based on this framework, WHO reported in 2019 that 'The vast majority of countries currently have low or moderate levels of national preparedness' (World Health Organization 2019, 11). Government decisions to invest in capacity building, at home and abroad, have profound impacts on the interests of people worldwide. In some cases, delays in reporting outbreaks are not primarily due to capacity deficits but to political factors (Lencucha and Bandara 2021). Such decisions have major impacts beyond borders.

Another example of profound impact beyond borders concerns the eradication of diseases. Eradication, as opposed to control, requires reducing the presence of a pathogen to zero everywhere in the world. If a pathogen remains present in one single country, policy-makers in all other countries must assume that the pathogen will eventually be re-imported and take this fact into account in health policy decisions—for instance, they may decide to keep vaccinating their whole population until the disease is eliminated from the very last country. The only example of the successful eradication of a human disease is smallpox. By investing in the elimination of smallpox from their territories under the coordination of the WHO's Smallpox Eradication Programme, each country contributed to total eradication, which was declared in 1980 (Barrett 2007). By providing this contribution, each country provided benefits to the others: these benefits consisted of the elimination of death and disability due to smallpox, but also of major financial savings generated by discontinuing vaccination across the world.

Smallpox eradication also provides an example of decisions that benefit outside actors because of resource transfers, since richer countries contributed to part of the cost of vaccination in poorer countries (Barrett 2007). Regarding the immunization of children more generally, donors provided US$34.5 billion for vaccination in less developed countries between 1990 and 2016. Of this, US$12.4 billion was channelled through the Global Alliance for Vaccines and Immunization (Gavi) since it was created in 2000 (Ikilezi et al. 2020). Ikilezi et al. (2020) estimate that the number of children vaccinated through 2016 attributable to Gavi support was 46.6 million, 75.2 million, and 12.3 million for pneumococcal conjugate, pentavalent, and rotavirus vaccines respectively. There are various other examples of states with larger resources sometimes transferring some of them to the populations of states with fewer resources. For instance, in 2021 the World Food Programme received contributions amounting to US$9.6 billion, mostly from high-income countries, and used them to provide food support to 128 million people in over 120 countries (World Food Programme 2022).

The examples given so far relate to actual behaviours having beneficial impacts, but of course many more are possible. For instance, there are several diseases that could in principle be the target of global eradication initiatives. Efforts to eradicate polio are underway, and governments continue to face the decision of how many resources to devote to that goal. Other potential candidates for elimination or eradication include measles, rubella, malaria, yaws, and lymphatic filariasis (Thompson and Cochi 2016; Thompson 2017).

Governments' decisions on whether to invest in elimination in their territory has a profound impact on the population in other countries.

Regarding resource transfers across borders, governments could increase them and/or direct them towards different purposes. There have been various proposals in this respect. For instance, the Sustainable Development Solutions Network (2014) examines what investment in health would be required to attain 'universal health coverage'—defined as a situation where all people receive the quality health services they need without suffering financial hardship—and make the following proposal: all countries should make progress towards allocating at least 5 per cent of national GDP as public financing for health, and high-income countries should allocate at least 0.1 per cent of gross national income to supporting the efforts of low- and middle-income countries (Sustainable Development Solutions Network 2014). According to Ooms et al. (2014), such an arrangement should be considered an equalization scheme analogous to the transfer mechanisms that are common within federal states. This is only one of the proposals aimed at making international resource transfers more similar to a taxation-funded welfare system as they are found within countries (Basu, Stuckler, and McKee 2014).

5.2.4 The problem of private power

The discussion has so far focused on coercion, harm, and profound impact caused by states. To some extent, this reflects the extraordinary power wielded by today's states, or at least some of them. But there is no question that private actors have the capacity to coerce, harm, and have profound impacts as well. In many normative theories of political authority, this capacity is precisely what justifies the existence of states in the first place. In principle, states should be able to constrain and regulate the exercise of private power within their territory. For instance, they should be able to hold companies accountable for violations of laws that protect the environment, consumers, workers, taxpayers, and other groups. If citizens are involved in creating such laws, they can be said to exercise indirect democratic control over companies. In practice, however, indirect forms of control can fail because of at least four reasons: state weakness, collusion between state officials and companies, subversive activities by companies, and regulatory competition (Koenig-Archibugi 2004c). The unwillingness or inability of a state to regulate private actors that operate within its territory can have effects well beyond its borders. For instance, if a government fails (for whatever reason) to regulate corporate biotechnology programmes that could potentially generate dangerous pathogens through AI-powered gain-of-function research, the populations of other countries would be exposed to severe risks without the opportunity to participate democratically in regulatory decision-making. While this problem is by no means limited to large companies, corporate size can exacerbate it because it increases opportunities to pressurize decision-makers and shift regulation away from deliberative citizen preferences.

State weakness, collusion between state officials and companies, and subversive activities by companies can undermine effective democratic control regardless of the level at which governance is exercised. A world state may be exposed to such risks as much as an average state. By contrast, the negative effects of regulatory competition are exacerbated by the existence of a plurality of governments, where each of them retains the authority to regulate unilaterally and/or to veto collective intergovernmental decisions. Hence, the absence of an overarching authority whose jurisdiction matches the global reach of many companies raises additional hurdles for the democratic control of private power. Chapter 6 will consider in more detail whether 'anarchy' hinders the implementation of popular preferences in the domain of taxation, environmental standards, and labour standards, where governments may be tempted to lower demands on companies in order to attract them into their jurisdictions or to keep them there. For now, the upshot of this discussion is that private actors have the capacity to coerce, harm, and profoundly affect people across borders in ways that cannot be adequately counteracted by national regulation. For some scholars, curbing the transnational power of nonstate actors requires the creation of novel nonstate control mechanisms (T. Macdonald 2008). By contrast, the remainder of this chapter develops what some may consider a more 'conventional' solution: nonstate power should be limited and regulated mainly through democratically controlled state power. But that state power should extend over the whole globe.

5.3 The universal republic as a solution

The previous section offered an overview of problems that deeply affect a person's life, even though they originate beyond the borders of the person's country. The aim was not to make suggestions on how each of those problems should be solved, but to highlight that they trigger the need for supranational governance, if certain normative criteria are to be met. As sketched in the Introduction, the idea of the universal republic is based on the transposition of the main institutions of constitutional democracy to the global level.

This section examines how this approach addresses the normative postulates introduced in section 5.1 in the light of the empirical circumstances described in section 5.2.

An important first step is to consider the implications of modal robustness for the question of global governance. Many agree that there is a tension between national democracy and international interdependence, because of the discrepancy between those who are affected in some relevant way by political decisions and those who participate in making it (Hobson 1934, 113–152; Reves 1945, 105–116; R. Dahl 1970, 88–98; Held 1995). Dani Rodrik (2000, 2011) expresses the problem in terms of a trilemma, with international interdependence, the nation-state, and democracy as the nodes (similarly Reves 1945, 261). The argument is that only two of them (any two) can be realized at the same time. Sovereign statehood and democratic responsiveness to popular preferences can occur together only when interdependence is low. If interdependence is high and states remain the primary site of policy-making, democratic responsiveness is heavily constrained. Preserving democracy under conditions of high interdependence would require abandoning state sovereignty and transferring authority to a world federation. Rodrik focused on economic interdependence, but the argument can be extended to other policy areas. The question of modal robustness is important here because the answer determines whether the first scenario—opting for sovereign statehood and democracy by keeping interdependence low— would be compatible with the normative postulates introduced earlier in this chapter. Under a modally undemanding approach, which simply considers which external impacts *actually* result from behaviour at any given time, the need to subject a state to a supranational legal order would be lower if that state made and implemented a *unilateral* decision to minimize its impact on people beyond its borders. Under a modally more demanding approach, however, that would not be sufficient. For that approach, what triggers the requirement of participation in a democratically legitimate legal order is the mere *possibility* of (the right kind of) external impact, so the essential question is whether a state has the capacity to have that impact, not whether and how it uses that capacity at any particular time. To the extent that states ultimately 'cannot avoid living side by side with all others' (Kant 1797/1996, 451), a modally demanding approach leaves only two alternatives: to give up democracy, or to give up state sovereignty to achieve some form of transnational democracy. The remainder of this section discusses the latter route.

Recall the postulates stated in the first section: political orders protect and promote personal autonomy to the extent that (3a) they establish and enforce laws aimed at regulating behaviour that can affect personal autonomy, and (3b) the institutions and agencies empowered to develop and enforce those laws are controlled, directly or indirectly, by all those affected by them. The universal republic would address (3a) by enabling the creation and application of laws for the regulation of social behaviours that can affect the personal autonomy of others across borders. The universal republic would address (3b) by placing the institutions and agencies empowered to create and apply those laws under the direct or indirect control of all those affected by them. The control mechanisms are those familiar from constitutional democracies, above all representatives elected by universal and equal suffrage in free and fair elections, with citizens enjoying the full range of freedoms that needed to exercise democratic control over power-holders. Given that the normative postulates are compatible with the tenets of contemporary republican theory, in terms of institutional design the argument in this section is most closely aligned with the republican case for a global republic developed by Martí (2010), but its deeper roots are in the historical tradition of radical cosmopolitan republicanism (Cloots 1792/1979, 1793/1979; L'Aurora 1796/1956; Görres 1798/1979; Barlow 1801; Woodhull 1871).[5]

5.3.1 Legislative, judicial, and executive functions

To perform (3a), the universal republic would exercise legislative, judicial, and executive functions based on a constitutional framework guiding exercise, limits, and interactions of those functions. The classical triad of legislative, judicial, and executive functions is somewhat ambiguous and possibly incomplete (Przeworski 2010, 129). However, there is sufficient agreement on its meaning to provide a useful heuristic for the discussion that follows. Most constitutions of the world describe the basic functions of the state in a way that explicitly or explicitly evokes the classical triad.

Distinguishing between functions does not per se establish how their performance should be distributed among state organs (Przeworski 2010, 129–131). Contemporary democratic states do not organize the exercise of

---

[5] My preference for a modally demanding approach is the main reason for the affinity with the republican tradition in political theory. Pettit notes that Rome-inspired 'Italian-Atlantic' republicanism is based on three ideas: freedom as nondomination (the modal conception of freedom discussed earlier), the mixed constitution, and a contestatory citizenry. He further points out that, '[a]mong the three ideas associated with the republican tradition, the conception of freedom as nondomination is the most distinctive' (Pettit 2013, 172). Moreover, Pettit considers freedom as domination to be the only one of the three ideas that the Italian-Atlantic version shares with what he calls the 'Franco-German' version of republican theory, i.e. the thought of Rousseau and Kant.

those three basic functions in the same way. Specifically, in some states the distinction between legislative and executive functions is reflected in a separation of powers whereby the functions are performed by clearly demarcated and largely independent branches, whereas in other states there can be substantial overlap between the holders of legislative and executive power (Lijphart 1999; Krotoszynski 2011). There is also substantial variation with regard to judicial independence and authority (Hayo and Voigt 2014; Melton and Ginsburg 2014). The universal republican model presented here assumes that the three functions of government are distinct, but it remains agnostic on how their performance should be organized and specifically how independent the legislative, executive, and judicial powers should be from each other. As Cabrera notes, the risk that a world government may experience an authoritarian turn may justify 'greater separation of powers than is standard in the nation-state, as well as a wider range of checks on and balances at the various levels' (Cabrera 2004, 115; cf. also Deudney 2007).

The universal republic entails a body that represents the global population and is authorized to deliberate on and adopt binding law—in brief, a global parliament.[6] A global parliament is a deliberative forum, in which representatives of diverse populations discuss solutions to common problems. But it is also a decision-making body where, after thorough discussion, those representatives vote on policy solutions and create binding law. As deliberation may or may not lead to consensus, it complements but does not replace the aggregation of preferences (Zürn 2000, 201–202; Fishkin 2009, 85–88; Mackie 2018).

Most constitutions of the world place some limits on what the ordinary legislative process can legitimately decide, most commonly in the form of inviolable rights that even democratic majorities cannot override (Law and Versteeg 2011). Given that the normative postulates discussed in this chapter refer to instances of coercion, harm, and profound impact, we could ask whether decisions about them should be subject to a legislative procedure at all, rather than be protected through constitutional rights whose application in specific cases is decided by judicial authorities (Miller 2010). It is certainly the case that the impacts described in the previous section have human rights implications. However, the regulation of coercion, harmful behaviour, and behaviour with profound impacts should still be largely within the competence of a deliberative and decision-making legislative body. The content of regulation can take a variety of forms and alternative solutions should be

---

[6] It may be argued that there is now a world legislature—the UN Security Council (Talmon 2005). Of course, it is not a democratic legislature, as stressed by many authors (e.g. Kelsen 1946, 1121).

subject to deliberation and democratic decision-making (Caney 2006).[7] This applies to most of the policy issues mentioned in the previous section. In the following, I will provide some examples, but the argument applies to a broader range of issues.

At the deliberation stage, representatives may want to argue that states should be entitled to use coercion to restrict immigration, for instance for the sake of limiting the level of cultural diversity within each territorial unit; or they could propose that states should be able to erect trade barriers, for instance by arguing that livelihoods should be shielded from disruptions caused by volatile global markets. At the decision-making stage, such proposals could gain majority support among representatives and become binding law. As long as such global law does not violate basic human rights, for instance by depriving the most vulnerable people of essential protection, it can be a legitimate response to the problem of border coercion. Similarly, in principle a global parliament could also decide that each state should be free to maintain armed forces, even if they can be used coercively against other states. This may even extend to the possession of nuclear weapons. Some believe that nuclear weapons are effective in preventing destructive conventional wars between great powers (e.g. Schelling 2009; Kroenig 2020) and thus can prevent great harm—proponents of this view should be entitled to make their case in a democratic debate. Addressing climate change raises a wide range of issues, ranging from the balance between mitigation and adaptation to the preferred speed of emission reduction, the advantages and risks of geoengineering, and different understandings of equity in the distribution of the cost of various policy approaches (Mattoo and Subramanian 2012; Markandya et al. 2015; Underdal and Wei 2015; Weitzman 2017b, 2017a; Markkanen and Anger-Kraavi 2019; Dooley et al. 2021). In the field of health, there is a lively debate on the advantages and risks of permitting and funding various kinds of biotechnology research and publishing the findings, on the cost and benefits of devoting attention and resources to eradicating individual diseases, and other important health policy decisions (Sathyamala et al. 2005; Koenig-Archibugi 2011a; Brown 2012; Razum et al. 2019; Smith and Sandbrink 2022; Tanasoca and Dryzek 2022).

On each of those issues there is a variety of positions that can be legitimately defended, criticised, and ultimately voted upon in a collective legislative process. In the universal republic, this process takes the form of parliamentary politics resting on electoral mechanisms of authorization

---

[7] As noted in section 5.1.4, there are divergent views on the extent to which democratic majority decisions need to be constrained by social justice requirements (Cabrera 2020, 180–199), but the disagreement is not specific to the question of *global* institutional design.

and accountability. Candidates for the role of delegates stand for competitive elections, the elected are authorized to represent their constituents in the global legislative assembly, and they (or their parties) are accountable to those constituents through the mechanism of regular elections. It is difficult to predict what concrete policies will emerge from this political process.[8]

In the universal republic, the exercise of legislative functions (the formulation of general laws) would be distinguished from judicial functions (the application of those laws to specific cases). A global judiciary would also ensure that the acts of the legislature do not violate basic rights guaranteed in a global constitution—both individual rights and the rights of the constituent states of the global federation. In the model of world state formation promoted by Kelsen (1944a), the development of global judicial authority precedes temporally the development of global legislative authority. Kelsen justified this sequence by analogy with the historical development of existing (domestic) legal systems, which he interpreted as entailing a 'primitive' phase where judges applied customary legal principles and a later phase that saw the development of legislative institutions and procedures. Kelsen's argument aimed at identifying a feasible pathway to a world state, and it is not incompatible with positing the universal republic as the outcome of that process. However, given the scope for legitimate disagreement over global public policies highlighted earlier, an extension of judicial authority that would not build on democratic processes of will-formation would suffer from serious deficits of political legitimacy.

Finally, the universal republic would perform executive functions, including exercising effective control over means of coercion to enforce compliance with legislative and judicial decisions. The essential rationale for this requirement has been summarized, in relation to democracy in general, by Linz and Stepan (1996, 10–11): 'Democracy is a form of governance of life in a polis in which citizens have rights that are guaranteed and protected. To protect the rights of its citizens and to deliver the other basic services that citizens demand, a democratic government needs to be able to exercise effectively its claim to the monopoly of the legitimate use of force in the territory.' They

---

[8] De Wilde, Junk, and Palmtag (2016) analysed around two thousand claims made by delegates in the UN General Assembly and the European Parliament, showing that expressed support for cosmopolitan policies on climate change, human rights, migration, and trade was more widespread in the former than in the latter. They relate this to the different nature of representation in the two bodies (delegates of executives in the General Assembly vs directly elected by citizens in the European Parliament). The authors warn that 'advocates of a global democratic parliament may find that an empowered democratic World Parliament would support less cosmopolitan policies than the current United Nations General Assembly' (De Wilde, Junk, and Palmtag 2016, 823).

go as far as arguing that '[d]emocracy is a form of governance of a modern state. Thus, without a state, no modern democracy is possible' (Linz and Stepan 1996, 10–11). Similarly, O'Donnell (1993, 1361) argues that a polity without the capacity to enforce its laws can at most support a 'democracy of low-intensity citizenship', which denies the rights of poor and otherwise deprived citizens. In this view, the monopoly of violence and an administrative infrastructure is necessary to restrict the capacity of a myriad of more or less organized groups to ignore and challenge the decisions taken by democratic institutions.

The historical experience of the United States can be instructive. Some analysts deny that the United States can be considered a 'state' before the war of 1861–65. Daniel Deudney instead argues that it constituted a 'Philadelphian System', that is, a distinctive states-union consisting of semi-autonomous republics in which power was more concentrated than it would be in a confederation, but less than in a Westphalian state. 'With the armed citizenry institutionalized, the central government of the Union explicitly lacked a monopoly of violence capability and of legitimate violence authority' (Deudney 2007, 178). Moreover, policing and criminal law enforcement were almost completely in the hands of the states until the twentieth century. The impact on democracy was ambiguous. On the one hand, this low level of stateness may have facilitated the expansion of political rights to a substantial share of the population before that process started in other countries. On the other hand, it arguably enabled first slavery and then the disenfranchisement of the Black minority, most intensely in the South before the Voting Rights Act of 1965. González and King (2004) detail how the limited presence of the federal government in the Southern states before the New Deal permitted local violations of the rights of citizenship and undermined democracy.

The delegation of authority to international organizations discussed in the previous chapter also offers insights. The EU puts into question the generalization that legal rules produced by a political unit can be enforced *only* when the unit possesses the key attributes of statehood, notably a monopoly of the legitimate use of force and bureaucratic control over a territorial jurisdiction. Weiler (2003, 10) interprets the EU as a combination of a 'confederal' institutional arrangement and a 'federal' legal arrangement. On the one hand, EU law is widely accepted as having direct effect in the jurisdictions of member states and supremacy over national law. On the other hand, EU institutions lack both the means of coercion and the bureaucratic apparatus to enforce EU law. 'There is a hierarchy of norms: Community norms trump conflicting Member State norms. But this hierarchy is not rooted in a hierarchy of normative authority or in a hierarchy of real power. Indeed, European federalism is constructed with a top-to-bottom hierarchy of norms, but with a bottom-to-top hierarchy of authority and real power' (Weiler 2003, 9). Zürn and Joerges (2005) showed empirically that legal systems without a central monopoly of force can be as effective in securing compliance than legal systems backed up by such a monopoly. However, the EU example also shows that a legal system that depends entirely on lower governance levels for the enforcement of its rule is vulnerable to disruptive political changes in those lower levels. The problems with getting the governments of some EU member states to respect commitments on the rule of law show the limits of the hybrid model highlighted by Weiler (Kelemen and Pech 2019). Perhaps it is excessive to conclude, as Caney (2005, 167) does, that 'making compliance optional rarely results in compliance', but the lack of formalized enforcement mechanisms certainly makes compliance more partial, uncertain, and unreliable (Ulaş 2016; Lu 2018). Hence, the universal republic would possess the resources to perform executive functions. However, multiple checks and balances, both among global bodies and in the relationship between different levels of government, would alleviate the concern that '[t]rue world government would be not only universal but also total' (Mangone 1951, 225).

5.3.2 Institutional design for autonomy and equality

The previous subsection has discussed some basic institutional features that a universal republic must have to address the normative postulates presented at the beginning of this chapter and the empirical facts presented in the middle section. Beyond those basic features, political institutions differ in a wide range of ways, and there is no consensus on which institutional design is best suited to promoting autonomy and equality of all those subject to their authority. Variation can occur along many dimensions, with the following arguably being among the most important: (a) the relationship between voters and their representatives, and specifically the procedures for electing delegates to the assembly; (b) the relationship between the assembly and executive agencies; (c) the relationship between the assembly and judicial bodies; and (d) the relationship between different levels of government.

Concerning (a), delegates can be directly elected by citizens or through the mediation of other bodies. Bicameral assemblies sometimes combine a directly elected chamber and a chamber composed of delegates appointed by regional assemblies. Both direct and indirect elections are compatible with a variety of methods for allocating seats. Gallagher and Mitchell (2005) identify six dimensions on which electoral systems vary: the number of seats per constituency, the number of votes that a voter can cast, the ballot structure, how much choice the voter has regarding individual candidates, the number of levels of seat allocation, and measures to limit the degree of proportionality.

There are long-standing debates about which design possibilities and combinations are best suited to promoting core democratic principles (Beitz 1989; Christiano 1996; Powell 2000; McGann 2006; Van der Hout and McGann 2009; Ward and Weale 2010; Carey and Hix 2011; McGann 2013; Ganghof 2016; Wilson 2019; Abizadeh 2021b, 2021a; Wintein and Heilmann 2022). One promising idea is to combine an elected chamber with a second chamber composed of randomly selected citizens (Abizadeh 2021b). While this design deserves much attention and discussion, for the time being I assume that the legislative branch of the universal republic will consist only of elected delegates, since this is a tried and tested method for translating citizen preferences into public policies (see section 7.5), and the popular legitimacy of randomly selected citizen assemblies needs further study (Goldberg and Bächtiger 2023). Even in the context of traditional mechanisms of electoral representation, many authors discuss institutional design as involving trade-offs between different principles, especially between the principle of equal representation of all voters, the principle that minorities need to be protected, and the principle that voters should be able to clearly identify alternative proposals before the election and who is responsible for policy decisions in order to hold them accountable at the next election (Powell 2000; Ganghof 2015). Electoral and voting rules can be seen as placed in a space between three vertexes that maximize one goal at the expense of another. At the 'plurality' vertex, the population is divided into a number of electoral districts that matches the number of seats in the assembly, and the plurality rule determines who is elected. Identifiability and clarity of responsibility is often seen as higher in such settings, but at the cost of making some voters more influential than others. At the 'proportionality' vertex, the whole population in a single electoral district allocate seats to party lists in proportion to the overall share of votes they obtain. Within the legislature, decisions are then taken by simple majority vote. These features are often regarded as favourable to equality of representation, but also as making it more difficult for voters to hold representatives accountable, as responsibilities can be blurred. At the 'consensus' vertex, proportional electoral systems are combined with formal or informal rules that require supermajorities for legislative decisions, to ensure that any major policy change is supported by a broad coalition. Qualified majority requirements, bicameralism, and federalism are formal mechanisms to limit pure majority rule. The consensus vertex can embody a specific understanding of proportionality, which holds that 'all the representative groups in the assembly should have influence on policy making in proportion to their size, which itself reflects the proportion of voters who supported them' (Powell 2000, 92). As Ganghof (2015) notes, this is a different interpretation of proportionality than that embedded in the second vertex, where citizens elect parties through proportional mechanisms but then legislative majorities decide without having to secure approval from minority representatives. Institutions at the consensus vertex protect minorities, but at the expense of blocking some policy changes desired by the median voter (Powell 2000, 92). Given the trade-offs involved, some authors advocate mixed systems (Carey and Hix 2011; Ganghof 2019).

From the point of the normative postulates stated in section 5.1, promoting the political equality of all citizens is a particularly important yardstick for the assessment of political orders. Hence, both plurality and consensus institutions can be seen as problematic, as they tend to give some citizens more weight compared to others. Procedures closer to the plurality vertex enable policy changes opposed by a majority of citizens, while procedures closer to the consensus vertex allows the possibility of changes to be blocked even if they are desired by a majority of citizens.

In debates about global governance, however, some authors advocate institutional arrangements at or close to the consensus vertex. A strong version of this position rejects the idea of a world state altogether and advocates a confederal arrangement—this position will be considered in Chapter 6. Weaker versions support consociational designs (Moore 2006) and other countermajoritarian devices for global institutions. The most prominent mechanism to limit majoritarianism in global governance debates is federal division of authority between global and national levels. Another approach consists of designing electoral systems based on constituencies that correspond to the boundaries of existing states. Most discussions about establishing a directly elected global parliament—whether as a second chamber of the UN or an independent body—assume that its electoral districts will match existing countries (Penrose 1946; Newcombe 1983; Bummel 2010; Schwartzberg 2013; Colomer 2014; Leinen and Bummel 2018).[9] The problem then becomes identifying a suitable formula for assigning seats to countries. Among the most popular options is the degressive proportionality approach proposed by Penrose (1946, 57): 'the voting power of each nation in a world assembly should be proportional to the square root of the

---

[9] For alternative approaches see for instance Sartorius (1837, 251), K'ang (1902/1958, 111), and Monbiot (2003, 87). Of course, there also authors who think that, as a way of promoting global democracy, 'direct elections are a non-starter' (Dryzek 2011, 224).

number of people in millions on each nation's voting list'. Penrose argued that the square root method is egalitarian as it would equalize the probability that an individual vote is decisive for the outcome. There is an ongoing debate on whether this argument in favour of degressive proportionality should guide institutional design (Felsenthal and Machover 1998; Gelman, Katz, and Bafumi 2004; Koriyama et al. 2013; Kurz, Maaser, and Napel 2017; Weber 2020; Kirsch and Toth 2022). As Bummel has noted, the square root method remains desirable if the goal is to avoid that decision-making is dominated by delegates from larger nations, as it would be under simple proportionality (Bummel 2010, 28). Bummel (2010, 25) also argued that, 'if a UNPA is to reflect the political plurality of the population of the UN member states in this sense, there should be a minimum of two delegates allocated to every country—one to be selected by the legislative majority and the other by the minority or opposition party in parliament'. This would result in approximately half of the delegates of a global assembly to be selected based on a 'one country, two votes' principle, with the remainder being allocated based on degressive proportionality or another formula.

The question of whether electoral districts for a global parliament should match existing countries deserves further study. In section 7.5, I argue that it would be democratically desirable to have transnational programmatic political parties offer voters across the world a choice between policy packages to be pursued in a world parliament. The literature on institutional design mentioned in this section suggests that this outcome may have a better chance of emerging with alternatives to country-based electoral districts (see also Bright et al. 2016).

Regarding (b), we should ask which relationship between the legislative assembly (which could include more than one chamber) and executive agencies is more likely to satisfy the normative postulates. One common way of conceptualizing the relationship is distinguishing between 'separation' systems, where the two branches are mostly autonomous, and 'fused' systems, where they are closely connected (Kreppel 2014). However, for our purposes a related but distinct dimension of variation relates to the relative strength of the two organs. Given the risk that empowering an unchecked executive could result in a loss rather than a gain of autonomy for citizens, the global executive should remain subordinate to the representative assembly in most respects. There have been various efforts to identify the elements that make legislative assemblies strong vis-à-vis executives (Fish and Kroenig 2009; Chernykh, Doyle, and Power 2017; Wilson and Woldense 2019; Tusalem 2021; Chaisty and Power 2022; Ishiyama 2022). A survey of experts has highlighted the following as the most important features that a legislative assembly should have to be powerful (Chernykh, Doyle, and Power 2017): it must be able to appoint and replace the main officials of the executive, to conduct independent investigation of executive actors, to exercise effective oversight over the agencies of coercion (the military, organs of law enforcement, intelligence services), to initiate bills in all policy domains, and to control the resources that finance its own internal operation. Furthermore, the executive must not be able to dissolve the assembly, to veto laws passed by it, and to appoint any members of the legislature, which should be all elected. The relationships between the executive and legislative branches of the universal republic should be organized along these lines to minimize the risk that its office-holders dominate the citizenry.

Regarding (c), the relationship between the assembly and judicial bodies, the key question is whether a constitutional court should have the mandate to determine whether the output of the assembly is compatible with the constitution. Across the world, there has been a trend towards the adoption of constitutional review in recent decades. According to Ginsburg and Versteeg (2014), in 2011 83 per cent of the world's constitutions had given courts the authority to invalidate legislation for constitutional incompatibility, up from 38 per cent in 1951. However, judicial review remains controversial. One debate concerns its effectiveness in protecting individual and collective rights. Empirical research indicates that formal authority assigned in constitutional texts translates into actual power and influence only under specific conditions (Stephenson 2003; Ginsburg and Versteeg 2014; Vanberg 2015; Chilton and Versteeg 2018; Krehbiel 2021). This resonates with the findings presented in Chapter 3, which suggest that having judicial review would not make a noticeable difference to the chances of a world state remaining democratic. The controversy over judicial review also questions its normative legitimacy (Ely 1980; Dworkin 1995; Habermas 1995; Waldron 2006; Bellamy 2007; Lever 2009; Watkins and Lemieux 2015; Follesdal 2017; Gebeye 2021). While these important questions cannot be fully addressed here, the position most compatible with the normative postulates is that judicial review should focus on the important function of protecting and expanding the democratic process (Ely 1980; Follesdal 2017).

Regarding (d), the relationship between different levels of government, the universal republic is defined as a *federal* state. This means that authority over some issues is *constitutionally* reserved for layers of government that encompass a more limited circle of citizens and are closer to them, and that authority cannot be appropriated unilaterally by the higher level of government. The rationale for this definitional move is that a global state is justified only in so far as there must be laws aimed at regulating behaviour that can affect personal autonomy and that some of these behaviours have effects beyond national borders. Any behaviour that does not have such transnational effects, or where such effects are minor, should not be placed under the authority of the universal republic, with the exception of the protection of essential human rights. While this reasoning suggests that *in principle* supranational institutions should be prevented from legislating on some issues, it does not specify what those issues should be concretely. I assume that the division of competences would emerge from a constitutional deliberative process and that it can be revised through special procedures that protect minority rights.

5.4 Concluding remarks

In this chapter I postulated that political orders are desirable when they treat human beings with equal respect and protect and promote their personal autonomy, i.e. their ability to develop and pursue authentic personal goals, compatibly with protecting the same abilities in other people. I also postulated that political orders protect and promote personal autonomy when they establish and enforce laws aimed at regulating behaviour that can affect it and when the institutions and agencies empowered to create and enforce those laws are controlled, directly or indirectly, by all those affected by them. The institutional implications of these postulates vary depending on whether the behaviour that may trigger the need for democratic mechanisms of common regulation is taken to include only coercion or also harm and profound impact, and on whether the relevant behaviour needs to be actual or probable or just possible. The survey of empirical facts about the world has highlighted instances of all relevant types of impact having a transnational, and often global, scope, which leads to the conclusion that global democratic governance is desirable. An extension of the argument would be to point at the asymmetric nature of such impacts, which would lend support to the argument by Tim Murithi (2012, 139): 'the potential beneficiaries of global democratic transformation would remain the societies in the so-called developing regions of the world—Africa, Asia, the Middle East and Latin America'. But asymmetry does not seem strictly necessary to show the desirability of global democracy. The last part of the chapter discussed how the universal republic would instantiate global democracy. However, the UR may not be the only institutional model that could promote the normative postulates in a highly interdependent world. Chapters 6 and 7 provide a comparative analysis of advantages and disadvantages.

6

Universal republic or confederation of democracies?

It is not enough to show how the universal republic would put into practice the normative postulates given the state of the world: other institutional arrangements may do so equally well, and perhaps better. What is required is a comparative assessment. This chapter and Chapter 7 offer some building blocks for such an assessment.

6.1 Institutional models

The focus is on institutional blueprints that have been proposed to reconcile international interdependence and democracy. Elitist (technocratic or meritocratic) approaches to global governance are therefore not considered (e.g. Wells 1933; Bai 2019). This still leaves a variety of institutional models. Following Archibugi, Koenig-Archibugi, and Marchetti (2012), I suggest that most models can be identified by their location in a conceptual space delimited by three *ideal* types, as shown in Figure 6.1.

As elaborated in the general introduction, the universal republic is a particular kind of world state. Historically, the main alternative ideal has been a confederation of sovereign (democratic) states. More recently, both of these 'statist' approaches have been rejected in favour of a more pluralist model of

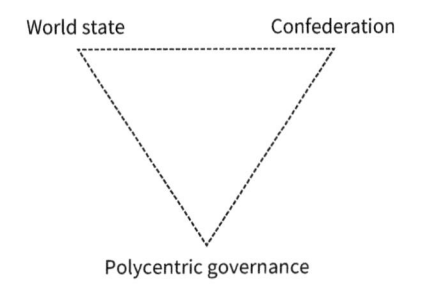

Figure 6.1 Models of democracy in global governance.

The Universal Republic. Mathias Koenig-Archibugi, Oxford University Press. © Mathias Koenig-Archibugi (2024).
DOI: 10.1093/9780198921158.003.0006

global governance, where democratic practices are instituted in a large variety of transnational settings, both governmental and non-governmental, without an overarching and unified institutional structure. The latter approach will be considered in Chapter 7, while this chapter compares the normative attractiveness of the UR with models that are closer to the confederal ideal type.

The debate between supporters of world statehood and those favouring confederalism has a long history, as the fourteenth-century disagreement between Dante and Dubois mentioned in the Introduction attests. Most famously, the tension between the two models is reflected in Kant's thinking. Until 1793, Kant unambiguously hoped for the establishment of a *Völkerstaat*. After that year, he shifted his support to a voluntary and looser *Völkerbund*. He still maintained that a world state was demanded by reason, but settled for what he called a 'negative surrogate'. There is an intense scholarly debate over the interpretation of the reasons he gave for this shift and over whether those reasons are cogent and consistent with Kant's overall moral and political philosophy.[1] The aim here is not to contribute to the debate about what Kant meant, or 'should have said' (Carson 1988), but to highlight that the alternatives presented by Kant—*Völkerstaat* or *Völkerbund*—still structure a significant proportion of the debate about a just global political order.

There is no uniform understanding of what the looser counterpart of the world state would be. The variety of labels attached to it by supporters and critics reflects the variety of conceptions: it has been called the confederal model (Archibugi 2008, 102–107), intergovernmental multilateralism (Marchetti 2012), fair voluntary association among democratic states (Christiano 2012), republican association of sovereign states (Bellamy 2019), international democracy based on the communitarian principle (Bienen, Rittberger, and Wagner 1998), *demoi*cracy (Nicolaïdis 2012), among other labels. Each of those concepts has specific nuances, but from the literature on unions of states (Sartorius 1837, 251; Kelsen 1942, 123–144; Aurobindo 1950; Lauterpacht 1950, 456–463; Forsyth 1981; Archibugi 2008; Ulaş 2016) it is possible to derive four features of confederal models that are common to most theorizations. First, a confederation is a voluntary union of states, where each is free to join or not and maintains a unilateral right of exit. This differs from unitary and federal states, where secession may or may not be legally permissible, but when it is it must happen consensually rather than

---

[1] The substantial literature includes, for instance, Archibugi (1995); Brandt (1996); Habermas (1998); Cavallar (1999); Höffe (2006); Mori (2008); Brown (2009); Flikschuh (2010); Eberl and Niesen (2011); Kleingeld (2011); Valdez (2019); Ulaş (2021).

unilaterally. Second, each member state has a veto on important decisions, either because they can only be adopted by unanimity and/or because decisions are only binding on states that have accepted them through a domestic ratification process. Third, the institutions of the confederation do not control means of coercion directly but are entirely reliant on the member states for the enforcement of joint decisions. In federal and unitary states, the central government does not always hold a monopoly of legitimate violence, because subnational governments can control armed forces such as militias and police, but it is entitled to maintain armed forces and use it to enforce federal law. Fourth, in a confederation there is no direct legal relationship between the confederal institutions and individual citizens: both rights and obligations are mediated by the institutions of their respective states. In contrast, citizens of federal states are direct addressees of federal laws and, at least in democratic federations, participate in the selection of office holders at the federal level.

Kant added an important ingredient to a normatively desirable confederation, i.e. the republican constitution of all member states. Domestic democracy is a component of major confederal blueprints that have been advocated as alternatives to a world state (Miller 2010; Pettit 2010b, 2010a; Christiano 2012; Bellamy 2019). This chapter will compare a democratic world state with a confederation composed by democratically governed states.

The comparison will focus on the ideal types and ignore otherwise important distinctions between blueprints. Several authors advocate what Ulaş (2016) calls 'intermediary models', which combine elements of statism and confederalism. One example is 'cosmopolitan democracy', at least in the version developed by Archibugi (2008). Another example is the distinction made by Bellamy (2019, 48–49) between his favoured republican association of sovereign states and the 'thinner' version of cosmopolitan statism preferred by Miller (2007). Moreover, institutional models can also be found between the confederal and the polycentric pole. For instance, Erman and Kuyper (2020) conclude that a confederation of democracies and polycentric democracy can, in combination, generate the conditions for realizing the principle that all agents who are subjected to a system of laws have an equal say in the decision-making about its basic form and the overarching societal goals and aims. Without downplaying the importance of such nuanced positions, this chapter will focus on the general arguments endorsed by those criticizing world statehood from a confederalist standpoint.

Among the arguments pertaining to the comparative advantages attributed to the universal republic or to the confederation of democracies, some are primarily conceptual or normative while others rest on factual assumptions that are more amenable to empirical falsification. The former type of arguments have been thoroughly examined by Tamir (2000), Cabrera (2004, 2020), Caney (2005, 2006), Kokaz (2005), Höffe (2007), Marchetti (2008, 2012), Martí (2010), Tinnevelt (2011), Ulaş (2013, 2016), Lu (2018), and other authors. Hence, I will focus on the latter, more empirical, type of argument.

However, one important conceptual issue deserves to be at least mentioned here. It has its roots in Kant's argument that, when states are internally constituted in a legal manner, it would be illegitimate to *compel* them to join a supranational state or to prevent them from leaving it (Flikschuh 2010; Kleingeld 2011, 52–58).[2] Note that this is distinct from the argument that forcing any state to join a world state would involve unacceptable moral costs, for instance because it may trigger a 'world civil war' (Waltz 1979, 112). The argument in question is that the *legal constitution* of a state would make an involuntary union with other states intrinsically, and not just prudentially, illegitimate. However, it is not clear why the condition of internal legality should be sufficient to override Kant's more general argument about juridical state formation. To recall, it is that 'a human being (or a nation) in a mere state of nature ... already wrongs me just by being near me in this condition, even if not actively (*facto*) yet by the lawlessness of his condition (*statu iniusto*), by which he constantly threatens me; and I can coerce him either to enter with me into a condition of being under civil laws or to leave my neighborhood' (Kant 1795/1996, 322). The basic problem with treating legitimately organized states differently from individuals had already been highlighted by Rousseau:

> It is important to note that this rule of justice [the will of the body politic], dependable with respect to all citizens, can be false with respect to strangers; and the reason for this is clear: that in that case the will of the state, although general with respect to its members, is no longer so with respect to the other states and their members, but becomes for them a particular and individual will ... Thus it is not impossible that a well-governed republic might wage an unjust war. (Rousseau 1755/1997, 7, 8)[3]

Kant's argument is conceptual (Flikschuh 2010), but it might have been influenced by his belief that republics would abstain from aggressive wars. This was a reasonable hypothesis in the eighteenth century, but a glance at the historical record tends to confirm Rousseau's caveat: domestic democracy offers no guarantee that a state will abstain from unjustly threatening or using

---

[2] A modern version of the argument is presented by Bellamy (2019, 86).
[3] Kumm (2013) develops a similar point with reference to contemporary debates about constitutionalism.

coercion against foreigners, let alone harming them in other ways (Archibugi 1997, 2008, 2012; Henderson 2002; Ravlo, Gleditsch, and Dorussen 2003; Ferejohn and McCall Rosenbluth 2008; Johnston et al. 2011; Lebow 2011; Stein 2015; Koenig-Archibugi 2022). This experience supports Kant's more abstract position on the legitimacy of coercion as a means of bringing and keeping states into a condition of being under civil laws, rather than his reservations in the specific case of legally constituted states. But, of course, this does not settle the separate question of whether the moral costs of coercion would be excessive. Partly because it is safe to assume that a coercive pathway to a world state would cause unacceptable harm even if it were possible, in Chapter 2 I expressly presented the feasibility question in terms of voluntary transfers of authority to the universal republic.

The remaining sections of these chapter examine four questions. First, whether transferring authority to a global state would promote a geographical extension of democracy at the expense of its quality. Second, whether that transfer would lead to political decisions that fail to respect the diversity of values around the world and increase the risk of condemning some people to a status of persistent minority. Third, whether keeping international collective action essentially voluntary undermines the ability of states to satisfy the democratically expressed policy preferences of their citizens. And fourth, whether the institutions of a UR would have the potential of creating a democratic forum for the expression of political cleavages that are suppressed in intergovernmental institutions.

6.2 Quality of democracy

The first argument to be considered is that political decision-making within states has, or has the potential of attaining, a higher democratic quality than political decision-making beyond states. Even if the universal republic could attain some minimalist level of democracy, the argument goes, transferring political authority from states to such a supranational entity would entail a loss of democratic quality (Kymlicka 2001). As Miller put it, 'those who advocate highly inclusive forms of democracy—democracy at the global level, for example—should be ready to concede that this may come at the price of a relatively thin form of democracy' (Miller 2009, 226; similarly Miller 2010). If there is a trade-off between the spatial extension of democracy and its strength, people committed to democratic principles may prefer to keep authority at the national level even if that reduces the opportunities for people to shape decisions that coerce, harm, or otherwise affect them.

Of course, an assessment of how the democratic quality of a hypothetical universal republic would compare to the democratic quality of states is inherently challenging, given that we can directly observe instances of the latter but not of the former, which never existed. Attempts to address the issue speculatively runs into legitimate criticisms, as they have been expressed for instance by Bull (1979, 115): 'What is not acceptable—but what critics of the states-system commonly do—is to compare a Utopian vision of a world central authority, or of whatever other alternative universal political order they favor, with the states-system, not in a Utopian form but as it exists now.'

I approach the difficult task of assessing a hypothetical situation while, as much as possible, comparing 'like for like' by adapting for this purpose the strategy already used in Chapter 4. There, I examined what level of democracy can be expected to be found in a global polity that would have important demographic, economic, and cultural similarities with today's world, based on what we know about the association between those features and democracy in existing countries. I use a similar procedure to predict various indicators of democratic quality of a hypothetical world state, and to compare it to the levels displayed by existing countries. The indicators of democratic quality come from the V-Dem database and will be explained in due course.

Similar to the analysis conducted in section 4.1, I use two different simulation procedures: lasso and Clarify (King, Tomz, and Wittenberg 2000; StataCorp 2023; Tibshirani 1996). Both rely on regression analysis applied to a sample of countries to estimate the association between indicators of democratic quality and a set of background variables. These variables are those introduced in Chapter 3 and 4: the level of ethnic diversity, religious diversity, linguistic diversity, income inequality, population, and land area, the number of land borders, income per capita, economic growth, education, resource dependence, and the percentage of residents who belong to the globally largest religious groups. As before, to address possible distortions due to short-term fluctuations, the analysis is based on associations between the background variables averaged over the 2011–15 period and the quality variables averaged over the 2016–20 period in a cross-section of all countries with data. The next step consists in lasso and Clarify predicting the democracy quality of a hypothetical polity that encompasses the world. Lasso uses cross-validation to identify the combination of variables with the largest predictive power; Clarify uses simulations to derive quantities of interest and account for uncertainty. In our case, the quantity of interest is the predicted score of the democratic quality indicator conditional on a particular value of each explanatory variable. Given that in our application the combination of chosen values corresponds to a hypothetical rather than an observed case, the quantity to be estimated by Clarify is a simulated counterfactual predicted value—more specifically, the average predicted value and the uncertainty around the average. It is important to bear in mind the caveat mentioned in Chapter 4: the predicted values generated by Clarify simulations differ from the expected values in a linear regression in that the latter reflect not only the estimation uncertainty caused by not having an infinite number of observations but also the fundamental uncertainty caused by unmodelled random factors. Hence, predicted values have a larger variance than expected values.

In what follows, I discuss each dimension of democratic quality in turn, by first discussing the relevant argument in relation to a world state, then introducing the empirical indicator for that dimension, and finally presenting the predicted values for the world state and comparing it to the distribution of values among existing states.

The first dimension of quality is *participatory quality*. In recent decades, the trade-off between the size of the polity and the ability of citizens to actively participate in its governance has been emphasized especially by Robert Dahl. In his earlier work on the relationship between size and democracy, Dahl was clear that democracy requires not only 'citizen effectiveness' but also 'system capacity', i.e. the polity's ability to respond to the collective preferences of its citizens (R. Dahl 1970; Dahl and Tufte 1973). Hence, a 'rational or reasonable democrat who wished to maximize the chances of attaining certain of his goals might well trade some loss of personal effectiveness for some gain in the capacity of the system to attain them' (Dahl and Tufte 1973, 23). Accordingly, he expressed some sympathy for the idea of 'world democracy' (R. Dahl 1970, 92). In later years, he interpreted the trade-off more pessimistically, arguing that international political systems are bound to remain below any reasonable threshold of democracy because 'the opportunities available to the ordinary citizen to participate effectively in the decisions of a world government would diminish to the vanishing point' (R. Dahl 1999a, 22).

For some authors, the participation deficit of governance beyond the state is to a significant extent driven by language barriers. Kymlicka (2001, 213), for instance, argues that 'democratic politics is politics in the vernacular. The average citizen only feels comfortable debating political issues in their own tongue.' It is not clear to what extent language diversity will continue to be an obstacle to political participation beyond national borders. Advances in artificial intelligence may soon make instant translation from and to multiple languages affordable to anyone with access to simple technical devices (Cabrera 2022). At the time of writing, the implications of these developments are still unclear.

Another facet of the broader argument is that typically citizen participation in governance is aided and structured by their participation in civil society organizations, but that is commonly regarded as more challenging across national borders (Grimm 2015, 126). Christiano (2006, 105), for instance, argues that 'it is hard to see how nongovernmental institutions of global reach such as political parties can establish the kind of trust that is necessary for citizens to be able to rely on them in the process of participation'. The obstacles that large polities may put in the way of citizens organizing in civic groups can be especially troubling to republicans, given the emphasis this tradition of thought places on the notion of an active and vigilant citizenry. Hence, they worry that, 'within a *cosmopolis*, active citizenship and the ongoing exercise of civic virtues and institutional monitoring would be very hard indeed to achieve' (Ronzoni 2017, 204).

To address such arguments, I assess to what extent a polity encompassing our diverse world would allow for participatory forms of government. As an indicator of the participatory quality of democratic regimes, I rely on the participatory democracy index provided by the V-Dem dataset (Coppedge et al. 2019). The index combines two components. The first is the electoral democracy index already used in previous chapters. The second is a 'participatory component index', which is constructed by averaging several lower-level indices: popular vote in referendums and other direct democracy initiatives, elected local government power or elected regional government power (whichever has higher score), and civil society participation. In turn, the latter index captures the extent to which there are many diverse civil society organizations and it is considered normal for people to be active in them, the extent to which women are prevented from participating in them, the extent to which major civil society organizations are routinely consulted by policy-makers on policies relevant to their members, and the extent to which party members and other constituency groups are involved in the selection of candidates for political office (as opposed to top-down selection).

Figure 6.2 shows how the values of the participatory democracy index are distributed among 179 countries in the world, with the values consisting of country averages over 2016–20. The median value is .32 on a scale from 0 to 1.

The lasso procedure yields a predicted participatory democracy score of .41 for a world state. When lasso is 'forced' to include all six presumed constraint variables (ethnic diversity, religious diversity, linguistic diversity, income

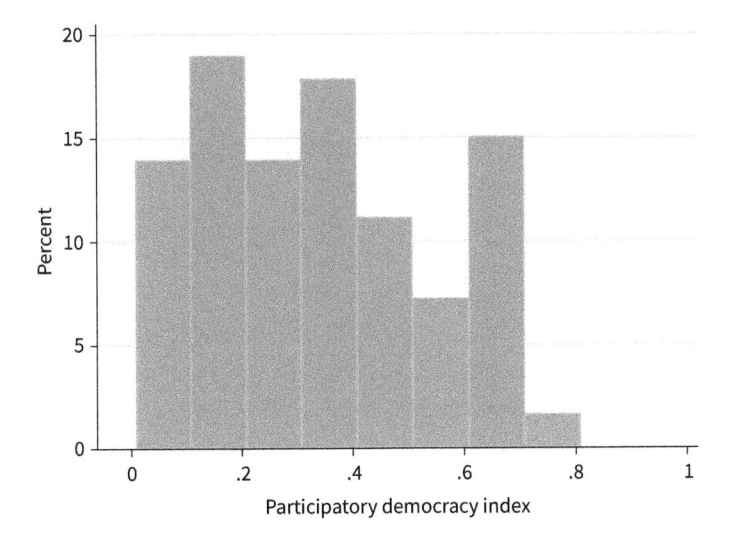

Figure 6.2 Participatory democracy index (averaged over 2016–20) across 179 countries.

inequality, population, and land area), the predicted score is .38.[4] The Clarify procedure yields a simulated counterfactual predicted value of .32 for a world state, with a 90 per cent confidence interval ranging from .04 to .58. The average value predicted by Clarify happens to be identical to the median value of today's countries. In other words, the analysis suggests that a world state would behave like a 'regular' country in relation to participatory democracy, rather than being an outlier displaying exceptionally low values.

The second dimension of quality I considered is *deliberative democracy*. An influential strand of recent democratic theory maintains that the task of the democratic process should not be merely the aggregation of existing preferences, but (also) to shape those preferences though a rational and respectful dialogue between participants who are open to persuasion and present arguments that could in principle be accepted by others (Elster 1986; Cohen 1989; Habermas 1996; Bächtiger et al. 2018). According to some proponents of deliberative democracy, 'territorialized linguistic/national political units provide the best and perhaps the only sort of forum for genuinely participatory and deliberative politics' (Kymlicka 2001, 324). Part of the reason is that deliberation involving citizens, rather than only elites, requires a shared language (Bellamy 2019, 79, 111). But some authors add that, unless there is underlying agreement on ethical principles, 'no democratic deliberation

---

[4] Goodness-of-fit statistics for these and the other estimates in this section are reported in Appendix III.

will be possible, because the idea of making arguments that other people are bound to take on board, either accepting them or responding to them, will have no purchase' (Miller 2009, 208). Such agreement is thought to be thinner across countries than within countries. The validity of this assumption will be examined directly in section 6.3, while here I limit myself to examining an implication: a world state would display low levels of deliberative democracy compared to existing states.

For the empirical assessment of this implication, I rely on the deliberative democracy index provided by the V-Dem dataset (Coppedge et al. 2019). The index combines two components: the electoral democracy index and a 'deliberative component index' that itself is calculated by averaging several indicators. These indicators capture the behaviour of elites when important policy changes are being considered, and specifically whether they give public and reasoned justifications for their positions, whether they justify their positions in terms of the common good, whether they acknowledge and respect counterarguments, and whether there is wide consultation at elite levels. An additional indicator captures the extent to which large numbers of non-elite groups as well as ordinary people tend to discuss major policies among themselves, in the media, associations, neighbourhoods, and the streets, in an unconstrained way.

The deliberative democracy index ranges from 0 to 1. Figure 6.3 shows how the values of it are distributed among 179 states in the world, with the values consisting of country averages over 2016–20.

Lasso provides a deliberative democracy score for the world of .52, or .50 when all six presumed constraint variables are forced into the model. Clarify yields a simulated counterfactual predicted value for a world state of .42. The latter is slightly higher than the value of the median country, which is .39. The confidence interval of the prediction ranges from .06 to .78.

The third dimension of quality is *liberal democracy*. The liberal conception focuses on the protection of individual and minority rights, advocating *limits* on the power of government even when it acts with the approval of a majority of citizens. John Stuart Mill presented a case against supranational government from a liberal perspective, which led him to conclude that 'it is in general a necessary condition of free institutions, that the boundaries should coincide in the main with those of nationalities' (Mill 1861/1991, 430). He advanced two arguments. First, without 'common sympathies' created by a shared language and exposure to the same 'books, newspapers, pamphlets, speeches', different sections of society perceive their interests as antagonistic and they are either indifferent or supportive of the government

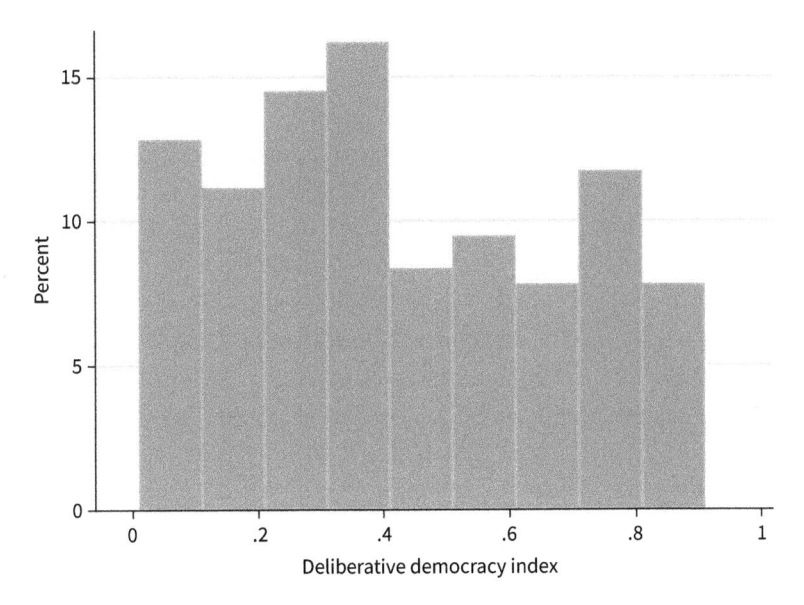

Figure 6.3 Deliberative democracy index (averaged over 2016–20) across 179 countries.

when it oppresses other groups. Even when they share grievances against the government, the groups do not trust one another sufficiently to coordinate a successful resistance to oppression. Second, Mill argued that the government finds it easier to persuade the members of the armed forces to suppress liberty when those members have little in common with the oppressed group (Mill 1861/1991, 428–429).

To assess the extent to which a world state can be expected to reflect liberal democratic principles, I use the liberal democracy index provided by the V-Dem dataset (Coppedge et al. 2019). This index is formed by the electoral democracy index plus a 'liberal component index', which is obtained by averaging three sub-indices that capture judicial constraints on the executive, legislative constraints on the executive, and the effective protection of equality before the law and individual liberties. In turn, the latter index is constructed by taking the point estimates from a Bayesian factor analysis model of country expert assessments of the extent to which a country has rigorous and impartial public administration, transparent laws with predictable enforcement, access to justice for men and women, property rights for men and women, freedom from torture, freedom from political killings, freedom from forced labour for men and women, freedom of religion, freedom of foreign movement, and freedom of domestic movement for men and women.

Figure 6.4 shows how the values of the liberal democracy index were distributed among the 179 countries in the world, in 2016–20.

The liberal democracy score generated for the world by lasso is .53 (or .51 with the forced inclusion of the six presumed constraint variables). Clarify's simulated counterfactual predicted value for a world state is .41 (90 per cent confidence interval runs from .06 to .77), which is very close to the median country value (.39).

The last dimension of quality to be considered in this section concerns *egalitarian democracy*. The argument to be assessed is that, if the world state managed to promote the equality of its citizens, this equality would be formal rather than substantive. The reason would be two-fold. First, without a sense of commonness provided by national identities, societies do not have sufficient levels of social solidarity to support egalitarian redistribution (Bellamy 2019, 46). Second, there might be a self-reinforcing cycle: pre-existing material inequalities confer disproportionate influence on global government decision-making to the wealthiest citizens, and in turn this influence leads to global government policies that further entrench economic and social inequalities (Mangone 1951, 92–113).

For the empirical assessment of this implication, I rely on the egalitarian democracy index included in the V-Dem dataset (Coppedge et al. 2019). The index combines two components: the electoral democracy index and

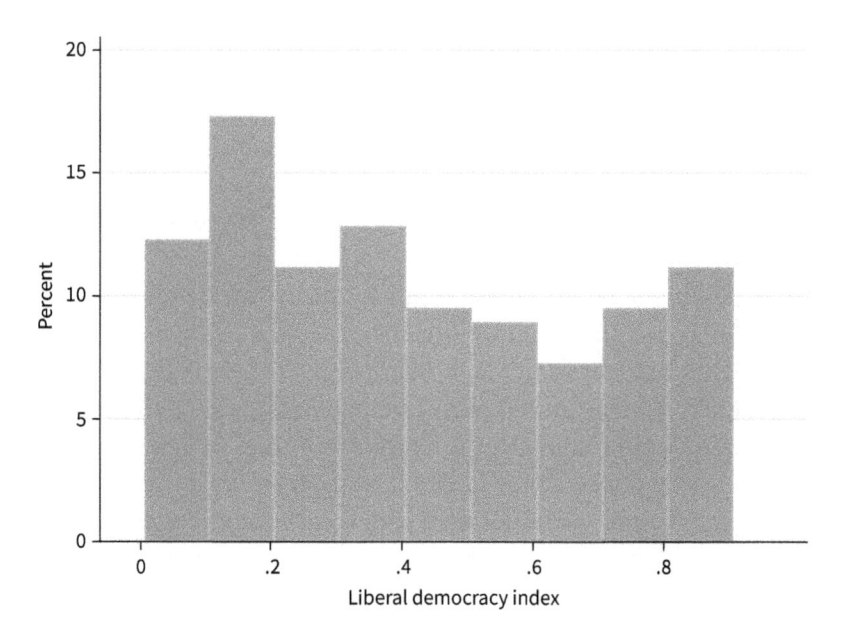

Figure 6.4 Liberal democracy index (averaged over 2016–20) across 179 countries.

an 'egalitarian component index' that itself is calculated by averaging three lower-level indices. The first is the equal access index, which combines indicators for the distribution of power according to socioeconomic position, by social group, and by gender. The second is the equal protection index, which combines indicators for social class equality in respect for civil liberties, social group equality in respect for civil liberties, and per cent of population with weaker civil liberties. The third is the equal distribution of resources index, which combines indicators for particularistic or public goods, means-tested vs universalistic welfare policies, educational equality, and health equality.

Figure 6.5 shows how the values of the egalitarian democracy index are distributed among the 179 countries in the world, over 2016–20. The median value is .33 on a scale from 0 to 1.

The lasso procedure assigns to the world an egalitarian democracy score of .32 (.35 with the forced inclusion of the constraint variables). The simulated counterfactual predicted value for a world state obtained from Clarify is .27 (90 per cent confidence interval runs from -.05 to .59). Both estimates are slightly lower than the median country value.

Overall, these findings do not support the argument that the quality of democracy would be markedly lower in a world state compared to what it is in a typical country. Of course, the simulations suggest that democratic quality is likely to be lower in the UR than it is in some democratic countries,

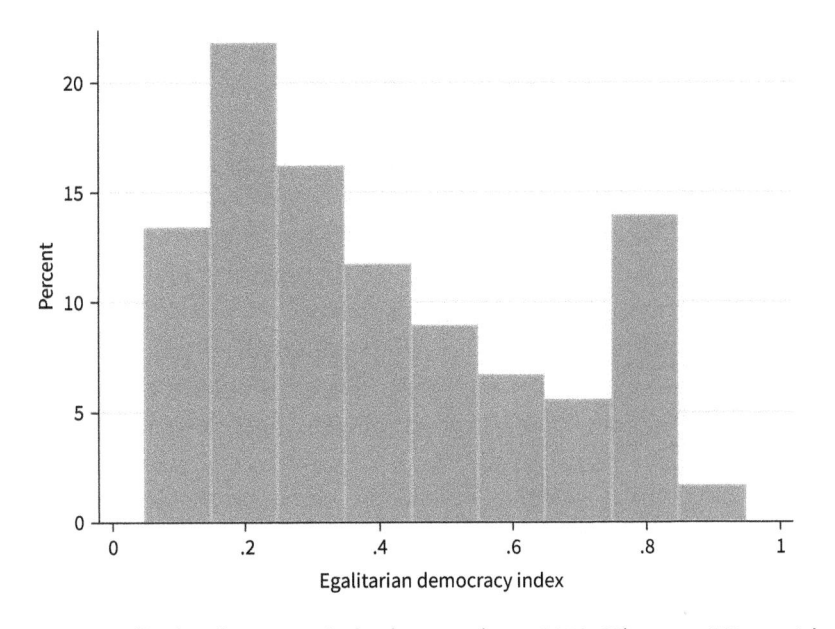

Figure 6.5 Egalitarian democracy index (averaged over 2016–20) across 179 countries.

but at the same time also that it could be expected to be higher than it is in other countries, and the two gaps seem to balance each other out. A partial exception to these conclusions is egalitarian democracy, where the counterfactual predicted value for a world state is lower than the median country value, but not by a large amount. All these estimates are necessarily highly approximate, also because there may be drivers of democratic quality that are not captured by the variables that entered the model. But they suggest that advocates of confederal models based on the allegedly higher democratic quality of national politics should consider whether there is enough evidence to support their preference.

6.3 Majority rule, diversity, and persistent minorities

The idea of global democracy endorsed in Chapter 5 entails not only the existence of mechanisms aimed at reducing political inequality among people around the world but also the expectation that, when extensive and inclusive deliberative processes are unable to generate consensus, policy decisions should reflect the preferences of the largest number. This expectation holds even though all known blueprints for a world state contain devices for protecting the rights and interests of individuals and minorities, notably the judicial review of legislative and executive decisions by a constitutional court, a federal distribution of authority across governance levels, and sometimes 'consociational' arrangements that include all major groups in decision-making. Notwithstanding such devices, the possibility that certain groups are outvoted—even if they form a majority within a component state—remains a key difference between the a democratic world state and a confederation of democracies based on consensus (Marchetti 2008, 64–65; see also Follesdal 2012, 99). The universal republic would not grant veto rights to any constituent unit, while a confederation would typically require unanimous support at least for the most important decisions.

In terms of democratic principles, simple or qualified majoritarianism is easier to justify than the unanimity rule. The unanimity rule compromises political equality because it privileges people who happen to prefer the status quo (Kelsen 1929, 1955; May 1952; R. Dahl 1956; Rae 1975; Christiano 1996; McGann 2004, 2006). Attempts to defend the unanimity rule (e.g. Munger and Vanberg 2023) ultimately fail to address this problematic implication.

This section examines two reasons why introducing democratic-majoritarian procedures at the global level may be normatively undesirable: the first reason is that such a move would fail to respect and accommodate the legitimate diversity of policy values among the people of the world, which is better served by protecting national democracies from being outvoted in international forums. The second reason is that the global diversity of policy values is distributed in such a way that democratic-majoritarian procedures at the global level would generate a serious problem of persistent minorities. I examined both reasons in an article written with Thomas Hale (Hale and Koenig-Archibugi 2019), and this section summarizes our arguments, methods, and findings.

At the root of much criticism of the idea of global democracy is the view that, as Andrew Hurrell (2007, 47) summarizes a central aspect of the pluralist interpretation of global politics, 'diversity is a fundamental feature of humanity and that the clash of moral, national, and religious loyalties is not the result of ignorance or irrationality but rather reflects the plurality of values by which all political arrangements and notions of the good life are to be judged'. Robert Jackson (2000, 178–179) distinguishes two ways in which the current world order is pluralist: it displays jurisdictional pluralism, i.e. the recognition of the equal sovereignty and territorial integrity of states; and it displays value pluralism, i.e. a strong diversity of values held by people in different states. 'There is almost unlimited heterogeneity in the history, politics, ideology, religion, language, ethnicity, culture, customs, traditions, of the member states of global international society' (Jackson 2000, 403). In Jackson's account, the key function and achievement of jurisdictional pluralism is the protection of value pluralism. 'People want to do their own thing in their own way in their own place' and thus 'the most important thing is to have a local sovereign jurisdiction within which different groups of people can endeavour to build their own political life according to their own enlightenment and free of foreign interference' (Jackson 2000, 403–404). The conclusion reached by pluralists is that, '[i]f diversity and value conflicts are such important features of international life, then we should seek to organize global politics in such a way as to give groups scope for collective self-government and cultural autonomy in their own affairs and to reduce the degree to which they will clash over how the world should be ordered' (Hurrell 2007, 47). From this perspective, schemes such as the universal republic are undesirable because '[r]educing the number and diversity of civic regimes comes at a cost in terms of diminishing the plurality of forms of social life that can flourish' (Bellamy 2019, 147; similarly Aurobindo 1950; Zolo 1997, 154; Walzer 2000; Pavel 2015, 137; Unger 2022, 3).[5]

---

[5] A related but distinct argument against world government is that it may lead to 'value lock-in', i.e. a condition where a single value system persists for an extremely long time. In this interpretation, value

Authors who stress the role of national sovereignty in protecting the pursuit of a diverse range of values do not necessarily have the same views on why such diversity deserves to be protected. Martha Nussbaum (2006, 314) notes that '[t]o protect national sovereignty in a world of pluralism is an important part of protecting human freedom. In that sense, any world state is *ipso facto* tyrannical' (cf. also Nussbaum 2019, 136–137). In Miller's analysis of where the boundaries of *demoi* should be drawn, the importance attached to value diversity derives from a specific understanding of the conditions in which democracy can flourish. Miller argues that a group must possess several qualities in order to be able to function properly as a *demos*, including underlying agreement on ethical principles. The latter is especially important in our context. Miller maintains that agreement on ethical principles is weaker beyond nation-states than within them, and as a consequence we should be cautious about expanding the *demos* transnationally, especially when there are alternative ways of dealing with the detrimental external effects of the decisions of national democracies (Miller 2009; 2010, 145–146).[6]

Significantly, these authors tend to assume a high correspondence between people's views on public policy and their membership in societies delimited by state boundaries. These arguments do not simply stress that the world population is diverse with regard to policy values and preferences, but they maintain that patterns of diversity and commonality track the division of the world into states. Simply put, they contrast relatively homogeneous state citizenries with a relatively heterogeneous world population.

The second line of argument that leads from the distribution of policy preferences in the world to a rejection of global democracy has been developed mainly by Thomas Christiano, who expects that global democracy would greatly exacerbate the problem of persistent minorities compared to national democracies. A persistent minority consists of members of a population who are systematically outvoted across all policy issues, rather than being sometimes on the winning side and sometimes on the losing side. Christiano distinguishes this problem from the problem of tyranny of the majority, which results from a majority knowingly exploiting and violating the basic rights of minorities. Christiano (2008) argues that the existence of persistent minorities weakens the legitimacy of democracy even if the majority decision

---

uniformity is undesirable not because existing value systems have an intrinsic right to be protected, but because cultural and intellectual diversity ensures that, 'over time, the norms and institutions that are morally better are more likely to win out, leading us, over time, to converge on the best possible society' (MacAskill 2022, 99).

[6] From a different perspective, Kukathas (2006, 20) objects to the establishment of global political institutions by, among other things, positing that 'the likelihood of agreement on justice diminishes with the increasing size of the polity'. See also Lovett and Zuehl (2022, 24).

does not violate basic rights, and other authors have advanced similar arguments (Barry 1979; Dworkin 1987; Guinier 1994; Saunders 2010; Cabrera 2014, 2020; Bellamy 2019; Lovett and Zuehl 2022). The existence of a group that almost never gets the policies that it wants is normatively problematic, Christiano argues, because it clashes with several important features of a just democratic process:

> Clearly, if a group never or almost never has its way in the process of collective decision-making then it will not be able to provide a corrective to the cognitive bias of the majority in making the laws. They will not be able to make the larger world it lives in a home for themselves. And since other citizens will experience no need to listen to their ideas about justice and well-being, they will not learn much from the democratic process. Finally, since they can see that these interests are being neglected by the democratic process, they will have reason to think that they are not being treated as equals by the society at large. So they will not have their equal status recognized and affirmed. (Christiano 2008, 296)

Christiano posits that the problem of persistent minorities would be more severe in a global democracy than in national democracies. 'This is a significant problem in modern states as they are. But it would appear to be an even greater problem in global and transnational institutions if they were fully democratized. The larger the constituency, the larger the chances are that particular minorities would simply get lost in the democratic decision-making' (Christiano 2012, 76).[7]

The two related issues—the diversity of forms of cultural, social, and economic life, and the risk of persistent minorities—are the foundation of the rejection of supranational governance and the preference accorded to a confederation of democracies by authors such as Christiano (2010, 2012) and Bellamy (2019, 79, 119–122). One response to such concerns is to emphasize the federal and subsidiary nature of a democratic world state, which would not interfere in primarily 'local' matters, such as cultural traditions and education (Tamir 2000).[8] Given that my definition of the universal republic

---

[7] Isensee (2003) expressed similar concerns. Cabrera (2014, 231) agrees that the problem of persistent minorities 'could again be magnified with a global extension of participatory institutions', but thinks that this problem is soluble with the appropriate approach to defining the boundaries of the demos.

[8] It must be acknowledged that some cosmopolitans hold diversity in little regard. Condorcet (1811, 274) articulated this attitude particularly clearly, commenting on Montesquieu: '[a]s truth, reason, justice, the rights of man, the interests of property, of liberty, of security, are in all places the same; we cannot discover why all the provinces of a state, or even all states, should not have the same civil and criminal laws, and the same laws relative to commerce. A good law should be good for all men.' Contemporary cosmopolitans tend to be more respectful of the diversity of human experiences and practices.

includes federalism but does not specify which issues fall under the competence of which level of government, in the remainder I pursue a different response that does not depend on such a prior specification.

Neither the diversity argument nor the persistent minority argument is purely normative: they rest on specific empirical assumptions. The former assumes that policy values are significantly more diverse at the global than at the national level, and the latter assumes that persistent minorities are more likely at the global than at the national level. How accurate are these empirical assumptions? To answer this question, Thomas Hale and I used survey data that enabled us to compare the distribution of policy values in the world with the distribution of values within countries (Hale and Koenig-Archibugi 2019). Two of the measures we created have already been explained in section 4.1: *value polarization*, measured as the standard deviation of survey responses, and *value cross-cuttingness*, measured as the correlation between survey responses across the three dimensions of culture, economy, and environment. These two measures are useful in capturing the risk that persistent minorities emerge. When value diversity is high, high cross-cuttingness ensures that individuals who are likely to be on the losing side on one issue are also likely to be on the winning side on other, unrelated issues. By contrast, low cross-cuttingness means that some risk being on the losing side on all issues that they care about.

Hale and Koenig-Archibugi (2019) present three further measures that help us understand the potential deficit of satisfaction with the outcome of majority decisions. The first is *heterogeneity*, which refers to the extent to which the members of the population are evenly divided between all possible views on a policy value. The second is the *overall policy dissatisfaction* in a population. We created this indicator to measure the distance of all individuals' policy values from the 'central' individual in each policy dimension, averaged across policy dimensions. Because of our interest in majoritarian decision-making, we measured each individual's distance from the median value, which in a perfect voting environment can be expected to be the policy adopted. We measured overall dissatisfaction using the following formula:

$$D = \frac{\sum_{k=1}^{P} \left(\sum_{n=1}^{N} \hat{x}_k - x_{i,k} \right)}{NP}$$

Where $x_{i,k}$ is individual i's policy value on dimension k, $\hat{x}_k$ is the median policy value on dimension k, N is the total number of individuals in the society, and P is the total number of policy dimensions. The third measure is *inequality of policy dissatisfaction* across all issues among the members of a polity, which captures the extent to which dissatisfaction is concentrated in certain parts of the population. We adopted the standard deviation as a measure of inequality. High inequality of policy satisfaction is an indicator that there are persistent minorities in the polity.

In addition to the Pew Global Attitudes Survey described in section 4.1, we applied these five measures also to the fifth wave of the World Values Survey (WVS), which was conducted between 2005 and 2007 and polled nationally representative samples of the adult population in each of ninety countries. Because not every question was asked in every country in the fifth wave of the WVS, in practice we included only fifty-two countries from that survey, which covered about 70 per cent of the world population. Estimates for the 'world' refer either to all the approximately 47,000 participants in the Pew study or to the 50,000 individuals surveyed for the questions we selected in the WVS fifth wave. Together they cover around 100,000 individuals in seventy-two unique countries representing 86 per cent of the world population.

Table 6.1 provides an overview of our findings, showing how a world polity would compare to existing countries in relation to the various measures presented above. In relation to each measure and policy dimension, the table indicates the place of the world in a ranking where the first-ranked country displays the highest level of heterogeneity, value polarization, overall dissatisfaction, and inequality of dissatisfaction.

Our analysis revealed that the distribution of policy values across countries was not significantly different from the distribution of policy values within countries. In terms of heterogeneity and polarization, the world was about as diverse as the average country in most respects, and in any case it cannot be described as an outlier. At the same time, policy values across countries tended to cross-cut one another slightly more than policy values within countries. Overall dissatisfaction with the median position was similar in the world as a whole and in the average country, and this dissatisfaction was spread somewhat more equally among individuals. The most striking finding is how 'normal' a hypothetical global polity would be in terms of diversity of citizen's policy values (Hale and Koenig-Archibugi 2019).[9]

We then extended our analysis in two ways. First, we examined whether and how our findings change when considering disagreements about

---

[9] Our analysis moves beyond the focus on global diversity by highlighting value diversity between individuals in the same country, but a further step consists of considering how individuals themselves are conflicted about which values to endorse. Chris Brown evokes this issue by pointing out that 'the "clash of civilizations" quite frequently takes places within particular individuals' (Brown 2010, 102).

Table 6.1 Rank of the world in relation to heterogeneity, polarization, cross-cuttingness, overall dissatisfaction, and inequality of dissatisfaction

Measure	Dimension(s)	Pew Survey			WVS		
		Average of countries	World	Rank of World	Average of countries	World	Rank of World
Heterogeneity	Economy	0.59	0.59	28th of 48	0.82	0.84	9th of 53
	Traditionalism	0.58	0.59	19th of 48	0.63	0.68	14th of 46
	Environment	0.65	0.67	18th of 48	0.59	0.62	16th of 53
Polarization	Economy	0.68	0.65	37th of 48	1.68	1.90	11th of 53
	Traditionalism	0.66	0.63	33rd of 48	0.78	0.91	5th of 46
	Environment	0.85	0.85	25th of 48	0.69	0.73	17th of 53
Cross-cuttingness	Economy-Traditionalism	0.73	0.69	31st of 48	0.91	0.96	13th of 46
	Economy-Environment	0.88	0.96	12th of 48	0.90	0.93	28th of 52
	Environment-Traditionalism	0.92	0.99	4th of 48	0.90	0.96	9th of 46
Overall dissatisfaction	All dimensions	0.94	0.93	30th of 48	0.88	0.88	19th of 46
Inequality of dissatisfaction	All dimensions	0.19	0.21	16th of 48	0.26	0.30	37th of 46

Source: Thomas Hale and Mathias Koenig-Archibugi. 'Could global democracy satisfy diverse policy values? An empirical analysis'. *Journal of Politics* 81 (1):112–126. © 2018 by the Southern Political Science Association. https://doi.org/10.1086/700106.

transnational solidarity (Hale and Koenig-Archibugi 2019). This increases the world polity's heterogeneity and polarization. Significantly, however, the effect is modest, shifting the world from the middle of the distribution to the top quartile, still comfortably within the range of countries. The effect on cross-cuttingness and overall dissatisfaction is instead largely neutral or even slightly positive. Specifically, we found no empirical reason to believe that citizens in rich countries would be constantly outvoted by citizens of poor countries over issues of transnational redistribution under a regime of global democracy. Transnational solidarity is a contentious issue, but not more so *across* countries than *within* them.

In a second extension, we considered alternative assumptions about citizen representation in global institutions (Hale and Koenig-Archibugi 2019). The measures for the 'world' reported in Table 6.1 assume that public policies will reflect median policy values and that each individual counts the same, irrespective of the size of her country of residence or other factors. However, in principle there are various ways in which individual responses can be combined into a global measure, reflecting alternative assumptions on how citizen preferences may be represented and aggregated in a global decision-making process (Segall 1990; Held 1995; Archibugi 2008; Bummel 2010; Schwartzberg 2012; Colomer 2014). We considered measures based on a further three aggregation principles: a world where individual votes are weighted by the square root of the country's population (the 'Penrose' formula discussed in section 5.3.2); a world where they are weighed by the GDP of their country (understood as proxy for financial contributions to providing global public goods); and a world where votes are distributed in a way that ensures equality of countries (irrespective of population) rather than equality of individuals. We found that the other worlds differ only marginally from the 'one person, one vote' world.

In sum, our analyses suggest that concerns about the greater risks of value conflicts and persistent minorities in a universal republic do not have strong empirical support.

6.4 International competition and democracy

The discussion in the previous section was based on an implicit assumption: both a global democracy and national democracies would implement the policy preferences of the median voter. Based on these assumptions, some existing states produce more policy dissatisfaction than a hypothetical global state and some less. However, the assumption that national democracies implement the policy preferences of the median voter is problematic. Departures from the assumption can occur for several reasons. A vast literature examines how government policies are biased towards the preferences of certain categories of citizens, notably those with higher incomes or education (Rosset and Stecker 2019; Elsässer, Hense, and Schäfer 2021; Schakel and Van Der Pas 2021; Traber et al. 2022; Elsässer and Schäfer 2023). Without denying the importance of such biases, my concern in this section is different. I am interested in deviations from the policy preferences of median voters that derive specifically from the fact that countries are not obliged to decide on policies collectively. This situation occurs in pure 'anarchy' but would also apply to a confederation of democracies in which each government can veto any major decision and/or retains the unilateral right to exit. In a system where cooperation is strictly voluntary and revocable, governments may end up making policy decisions on a specific issue that do not reflect only the distribution of preferences of their voters on that issue (such as the preference of the median voter) but also factors over which those voters have no control. This outcome is possible in the presence of 'negative policy externalities', which 'occur where the policies of one nation imposes costs on the domestic nationals of another, thereby undermining the goals of the second government's policies' (Moravcsik 1993, 485). In such cases, policies adopted by other governments alter the cost and benefits of different courses of action for the government in question. I am especially interested in cases where most or all governments experience negative policy externalities that lead them to adopt policies that they would not have otherwise adopted. Choosing policies under the influence of negative externalities means that those policy do not reflect only citizen preferences—more specifically, it is a sufficient condition for policy deviation from median voter preferences.

The influence that negative policy externalities may have on government decisions is a problem for democracy over and above the possibility that such externalities might affect the personal autonomy of citizens, through the mechanisms of coercion, harm, and profound impact discussed in Chapter 5. The reasons for this have been summarized by David Charny:

> The jurisdiction that relaxes its standards in response to relaxed standards set by other jurisdictions finds, from the viewpoint of democratic theory, that its exercise of democratic will has been tainted by the external impacts of the decision of other polities. Into the decisions of these other polities, the citizens of home jurisdiction have no direct input. In that sense, not only the home jurisdiction's welfare, but also its own democratic autonomy, are affected by the decision of other jurisdictions. (Charny 2000, 297–298; see also Zürn 2000, 184)

By allowing policy decisions of a state to be 'tainted' by the external impact of policy decisions taken elsewhere, a confederation of democracies would be vulnerable to a form of democratic deficit that is less likely in the universal republic. While the mere possibility of this happening should matter, a comparative assessment of the two models of global political order requires some information on the magnitude of this effect. Considering that institutional selection is usually a matter of trade-offs, can we say that the democratic cost of purely voluntary cooperation is substantial? This is primarily an empirical question, which I try to assess in this section.

Empirically, externalities-affected policy-making can be detected by determining whether the policies adopted by one country are influenced by the policies adopted by other countries. However, not all cases of policy interdependence entail deviations from median preferences. The literature on policy interdependence has identified at least five mechanisms of diffusion: emulation, learning, cooperation, competition, and coercion (Simmons, Dobbin, and Garrett 2008; Baccini and Koenig-Archibugi 2014). Emulation means that governments imitate policies adopted by high-prestige actors and/or regarded as normatively appropriate by the members of a social peer group. States adopt these policies because they want to be seen as 'good' (legitimate, 'modern', etc.) states. Learning means that governments adopt policies that are perceived as having been successful in other countries. Governments are interested in policy success, not in international recognition. Cooperation means that a government agrees to change its policies in exchange for a similar promise made by other governments. Competition means that governments feel compelled to certain policies that have been or may be adopted by competitors because non-adoption may put them at a disadvantage. Competition can be over economic goods, such as export opportunities for domestic industries, and/or over the military balance of power. Finally, coercion occurs when governments are exposed to the threat of sanctions if they do not adopt the policies requested by others. Of these five mechanisms, only competition and coercion generate forms of transnational influence that are problematic deviations from the median preference: the other three are in principle compatible with it (although they may not be in practice).

To what extent are the policies of states driven by competitive pressures? The fact that competition is only one potential driver of diffusion raises a challenge for empirical analysis: finding evidence that policies in one state are influenced by policies adopted by other states, for instance states that are close in terms of territorial contiguity and/or communication links (e.g. Schmitt et al. 2015), is not sufficient to prove the effect of competition. What is needed is a research design that can plausibly identify the effect of competition as distinct from other mechanisms of diffusion. In the following, I will discuss the state of knowledge about the effect of competition in various domains.

The first domain is military expenditure. International Relations scholars have studied extensively the implications of the security dilemma for arms races (Jervis 1978; Fearon 2018; Coe and Vaynman 2020; cf. also Tinbergen and Fischer 1987, 57). Several econometric studies found that military expenditure in one country is affected by the military expenditure of neighbouring countries (Goldsmith 2007; Skogstad 2016; Yesilyurt and Elhorst 2017; George, Hou, and Sandler 2019). There is strong empirical support for concluding that decisions about military spending in one state are influenced by decisions taken abroad over which citizens of that state have no democratic say.

Another area where policy interdependence is thought to be pervasive is corporate taxation (Cao 2010; Dietsch and Rixen 2015; Baker and Murphy 2021). Corporate income tax rates have declined globally over the last decades. Heimberger (2021) conducts a meta-analysis of data from thirty-three studies of corporate tax competition and finds a statistically significant and substantially important effect: 'a one percentage point decline in corporate tax rates in competitor jurisdictions is, on average, associated with a fall in the corporate tax rate at home by about 0.8 per cent—with the 95 per cent confidence interval ranging from 0.7 per cent to 0.9 per cent'. However, most of the studies included in the meta-analysis operationalize interdependence between jurisdictions in ways that do not allow the effect of economic competition to be isolated from the effect of learning or emulation (e.g. Overesch and Rincke 2011). Naitram (2022) presents a strategy that is particularly well suited to capture competitive mechanisms. In determining the weight that a country i should be assumed to have in influencing the tax rates of country j, Naitram (2022) uses three types of capital stock: capital instock from j to i, capital outstock from i to j, and the competition between j and i for capital stock from a third country m. Using this approach, Naitram (2022) finds that a one percentage point reduction in the foreign tax rate is associated with a 0.23 percentage point tax rate cut in response by the home country.[10]

---

[10] Arel-Bundock (2017) emphasizes a second form of form of policy interdependence in taxation that is different from the competitive logic just considered. Two countries can influence each other's corporate tax rates also by concluding a bilateral tax agreement with a third country. Bilateral tax agreements were created to limit double taxation, but now they are often exploited by multinational companies to avoid taxes (Arel-Bundock 2017). When two governments sign a bilateral agreement to reduce withholding taxes, they create a path through which companies can route funds. Multinational corporations can engage in treaty-shopping, shifting funds across jurisdictions in a way that minimizes taxes paid or avoid any taxes at all. If alternative indirect routes involving low taxation become available to companies, governments

The domain of environmental policy also displays policy interdependence. Based on an analysis of virtually all countries of the world, Steinebach, Fernández-i-Marín, and Aschenbrenner (2021) found that governments are more likely to opt for carbon pricing policies when competitor countries (those that export goods to the same market) do so. Governments also adopt more ambitious carbon pricing policies when their closest trade competitors do so as well. The results suggest that '[c]oncerns over potential competitive disadvantages thus seem to constitute a major obstacle to policy diffusion and the strengthening of carbon pricing policies' (Steinebach, Fernández-i-Marín, and Aschenbrenner 2021, 277).

While the hypothesis of competition-driven policy interdependence is now supported by a substantial number of empirical studies, some caveats are necessary. Studying competition-driven interdependence raises significant methodological challenges. These can be illustrated with reference to the debate on labour standards. The possibility that international economic competition puts working and employment conditions under pressure has worried policy reformers and labour-friendly scholars for over two centuries. Governments concerned about the competitive position of their industries in world markets are widely expected to be reluctant to help workers obtain better conditions and even to actively thwart their efforts. If certain governments start promoting or tolerating a deterioration of labour protections in their jurisdictions, the argument goes, their closest competitors will be under pressure to do the same, and the result will be a 'race to the bottom' (RTB) in labour standards. As a theory, the RTB argument is over two hundred years old, with French statesman and financier Jacques Necker already outlining the basic logic in 1788 (Bairoch 1999, 161). Social reformers, labour activists, and government officials have debated the issue extensively since the nineteenth century, and it contributed to the creation of the International Labour Organization (ILO) (Follows 1951). Since then, concerns about an RTB have often been voiced by organized labour and prompted numerous attempts to include 'social clauses' in multilateral and bilateral trade agreements, as well as unilateral trade measures. Notwithstanding all the attention it received, empirical knowledge regarding the RTB hypothesis was very rudimentary until the mid-2000s. A decisive breakthrough was the systematic collection of data on levels of actual respect for workers' rights in many countries over time, especially in relation to freedom of association

---

are under pressure to lower taxes on direct routes. The pressure affects tax policies considerably: Arel-Bundock finds that a 1 per cent decrease in the indirect withholding tax is associated with a cut of about 0.3 in bilateral rates. He concludes that 'the harmonization of policies through multilateral agreement or under the aegis of an international organization seems highly desirable' (Arel-Bundock 2017, 367–368).

and collective bargaining rights (Kucera 2002; Mosley and Uno 2007; Mosley 2011; Barry, Cingranelli, and Clay 2022). These data enabled researchers to systematically assess the effect of economic globalization and specifically the observable implications of the RTB argument. Some of this research has found evidence for competitive deregulation in the field of labour standards (Mosley and Uno 2007; Mosley 2011; Davies and Vadlamannati 2013; Olney 2013; Wang 2017, 2018). However, Alessandro Guasti and I have shown that these conclusions are not supported when the RTB hypothesis is subjected to particularly rigorous testing (Guasti and Koenig-Archibugi 2022). In that study, we highlighted four problems that researchers have to solve in order to credibly measure the competitive pressure on states. The *directionality* problem arises because, as in any race, the direction of movement matters. The RTB logic posits that a movement in the direction of worse labour conditions will be followed by movements in the same downward direction, while it is agnostic about the impact of improvements. However, previous studies did not isolate the effects of deterioration of labour rights protections among competitors from the effects of their improvement. In our analysis, we applied an approach designed to do that. The *specificity* problem arises because accurate measures of competition should reflect actual competition between firms offering similar products, rather than export similarity in relation to a few very broad product categories. The *proportionality* problem arises because it matters not only *what* competitor countries export but also how *much* of it they export, since larger volumes give countries more weight in the determination of world market prices for specific products. However, previous studies did not take volume of exports into account when identifying key competitors. The *exposure heterogeneity* problem arises because states may be exposed to export competition to different degrees. We also highlighted a further issue insufficiently addressed by previous studies, i.e. the *endogeneity* problem that stems from the fact that the working conditions in a country may not only be influenced by the conditions in its competitors but also affect them in turn.

To overcome the limitations of previous studies, we developed an approach to measuring export competition between countries that fulfils several criteria: it reflects actual competition between firms offering similar products, rather than export similarity in relation to a few very broad product categories; it captures not only what competitor countries export but also how much; it takes into account that states are exposed to export competition to different degrees; and it focuses on the downward pressure stemming from a deterioration of labour rights protections among close competitors. To address endogeneity, we implemented a two-stage least-squares (2SLS) instrumental variable approach and a difference two-stage generalized method of moments (GMM) approach. We found no evidence that export competition has triggered a race to the bottom in two samples covering most states in the world over nearly three decades (Guasti and Koenig-Archibugi 2022).

Guasti and I also assessed the related but separate argument about a 'regulatory chill', which posits that competitive pressures cause a *lack of improvement* (rather than a deterioration) of standards (Esty and Geradin 1998). If researchers found that states improve their labour practices when the practices of their main competitors have improved, they could infer that those instances where practices do not improve can at least partly be explained by the absence of improvement among the country's main competitors. This counterfactual argument assumes that pro-worker organizations exert a pressure to raise standards, but this pressure is counterbalanced by competitiveness concerns; if and when improvements among the main competitors lessen such concerns, policy-makers and firms are more willing to make concessions to pro-worker interests and allow standards to rise. We considered this possibility but found no empirical evidence of a regulatory chill (Guasti and Koenig-Archibugi 2022).

The upshot of this section is somewhat mixed. Regarding some policy areas, notably corporate taxation, we can be reasonably confident that leaving decision-making in the hands of each individual government has led to policy outcomes that deviate from domestic (democratic) preferences. A confederation of democracies may mitigate the problem by promoting coordination, but the content of an international agreement may reflect the lowest common denominator, and its voluntary nature would prevent it from eliminating the problem completely and durably. On the other hand, the case of labour standards suggests that the democratic costs of the multiplicity of decision-making units should not be taken for granted even in sectors where it is traditionally assumed to be substantial. Over the past decade, there has been substantial progress in devising methodological tools for the study of policy interdependence, and further studies in the coming years may give us a clearer picture of the extent to which it interferes with democratic decision-making.

6.5 Transnational political cleavages

This section addresses a key criticism that cosmopolitans raise against intergovernmental designs for global institutions, which is that they fail to reflect and respect the diversity of policy preferences and interests *within* countries. This kind of criticism of what has been called 'executive multilateralism'

(Zürn 2005) also targets intergovernmental designs that assume the democratic character of member states. The argument is that, by giving governments elected by domestic majorities a monopoly over the representation of the country at the international level, a confederation of democracies would give domestic minorities no constitutionally protected opportunities to participate in international governance.[11]

This criticism is shared by proponents of polycentric forms of global democracy and by authors who prefer a more centralized design. Accordingly, a wide range of alternatives to intergovernmentalism have been proposed, short of creating a full-fledged democratic world state. These include letting members of the opposition participate in national delegations to international institutions (Archibugi 1993), creating and strengthening networks of national parliamentarians overseeing existing multilateral organizations (Charnovitz 2002; Shaffer 2004; Slaughter 2004; Cabrera 2007), establishing a popularly elected global assembly (Segall 1991; Falk and Strauss 2001; Cabrera 2018; Leinen and Bummel 2018) or a mixed global assembly of territorial and non-territorial actors (Kuper 2004), and involving randomly selected citizens in the formulation of international law and the scrutiny of specific international organizations (Frey and Stutzer 2006; Goodin and Ratner 2011) or as part of a global citizens' jury or assembly (Wells 1942, 88–92; Dryzek, Bächtiger, and Milewicz 2011).

This section addresses an empirical implication of this debate. The objection to intergovernmentalism would be particularly compelling if it could be shown that, when minorities participate in international governance, they advocate policies that depart from those preferred by their own governments. If, by contrast, the positions (and votes) of non-governmental representatives essentially duplicated those of governmental representatives from the same country, the case for inclusion of non-governmental representatives in the formal decision-making process of international institutions would be weaker.

The expectation that shared national priorities trump domestic differences when it comes to international governance is rarely voiced in explicit terms, but it is often implicit in the possible assessment of the consequences of

---

[11] Intergovernmental models are prone to a further problem, which is that it gives executives an informational and agenda-setting advantage in relation to international negotiations, which they can exploit to agree on international policies that are closer to the executives' own preferences than to the preferences of their constituents (Moravcsik 1994; Wolf 1999; Zürn 2000; Koenig-Archibugi 2004b). In principle, this problem could be mitigated without abandoning the intergovernmental model, for instance by strengthening the capacity of national parliaments to influence international negotiations (Bellamy 2019). As the informational and agenda-setting asymmetry seems a contingent rather than intrinsic feature of the intergovernmental model, it will not be considered further here.

non-governmental participation in international intergovernmental organizations (IGOs). For instance, Kahler (2005, 29–30) noted that incorporating NGOs into the decision-making of the World Trade Organization might give to industrialized countries, where most major NGOs are based, a form of 'double counting' in their representation in that organization. Similarly, the assumption that representatives would normally vote along national lines is implicit in Joseph Nye's criticism of proposals for a UN parliamentary assembly, as he notes that 'treating the world as one global constituency implies the existence of a political community in which citizens of around 200 states would be willing to be continually outvoted by more than a billion Chinese and a billion Indians' (Nye 2002, 17; see also Ewing 1947, 289; Morgenthau 1954, 480; Tullock 2006). The expectation that delegates chosen in constituencies located in the same country (or neighbouring countries) would tend to vote in the same way 'continually' reflects the belief that territoriality and/or nationality plays a crucial role in structuring interest cleavages. According to Terry Macdonald (2008, 128), 'many significant conflicting interests within global society are concentrated in territorial areas (commonly states), such that the populations of different states often have widely divergent and strongly conflicting interests'. If delegates representing domestic minorities were to 'vote' primarily along national lines, as Nye and others assume, many putative benefits of overcoming the governmental monopoly on international representation might fail to materialize.

Supporters of global institutions such as a world parliament reject such assumptions. In their plan for world government, Lloyd and Schwimmer (1942, 5) proposed that each country should have ten representatives, and claimed that '[e]very important group in a nation can be represented among its ten delegates, and will find like-minded groups from other nations in the World Parliament, where divisions will consequently occur along lines of opinion, not lines of geography'.[12] The ability of global democratic institutions to reflect the internal ideological diversity of each country better than intergovernmental institutions is often cited as a major advantage (Broda 1920, 308–309; Ewing 1947). But which of the two assumptions is closer to reality?

Research shows that it matters whether international policy-making is entirely in the hands of governments or whether nonstate actors participate in some form. For instance, Böhmelt and Betzold (2013) analyse information on twenty-three environmental treaty regimes in the International Regimes

---

[12] While some authors expected ideological divisions in federal institutions to run along a conservative-progressive dimension, Jacques Novicow (1901, 730) expected them to pit a 'party of centralizers' against a 'party of decentralizers', similar to the Swiss politics of his time.

Database (Breitmeier et al. 2006) and find that a higher degree of access for environmental NGOs to the negotiations and a higher number of NGOs participating in the negotiations led to treaties demanding deeper behavioural changes from the member states. The trend in organizing interests along sectoral lines through non-state associations is undermining the idea that governments are the only legitimate representatives of citizen's interests on the international stage (Zürn 2018, 240).[13] However, most existing research addresses the consequences of access in relation to IOs that maintain a strong differentiation between the rights and prerogatives of state members and those of non-state actors and that do not actively strive to ensure a balanced participation of non-governmental actors across member states or participating regions. This reflects the relative rarity of IGOs in which non-governmental actors are given roles comparable to those of states. Less than 10 per cent of the IGO bodies analysed by Tallberg et al. (2013) offer non-state actors the same rights and opportunities for participation as member states' representatives.[14] It may be risky to generalize from such experiences to what would happen under the scenario preferred by many cosmopolitans, which is that access of domestic minorities to international decision-making is not simply granted subject to major limitations, but institutionalized and formally guaranteed.

To assess the domestic diversity objection to intergovernmentalism more conclusively, we would need to consider whether the positions (and votes) of non-governmental representatives tend to duplicate those of governmental representatives from the same country in the context of international organizations that give them *deep and balanced access*. Balanced access means that IGOs do not simply wait for non-governmental actors to demand access, but formally state and try to implement the principle that participating non-governmental actors should be somehow representative of constituencies in each member state or country group. Deep access means that non-governmental actors have formal rights to participate in policy decisions within organizational bodies. Among the international bodies that offer this kind of balanced and deep access, the European Parliament (EP) is particularly notable. Research by Simon Hix and other scholars has shown that, since they started to be directly elected, members of the EP have voted increasingly along party lines and decreasingly along national lines (Hix, Noury, and Roland 2007; Hix and Noury 2009). The European Parliament's

---

[13] But see also Agné, Dellmuth, and Tallberg (2015).

[14] The percentage was 0 in 1950, 8.1 in 1970, 8.7 in 1990, and 9.2 in 2010 (Tallberg et al. 2013, 84). Most of the bodies that offer 'full and autonomous access' to non-state actors applied demanding selection criteria (Tallberg et al. 2013, 86).

political groupings (such as the socialists and the European people's party) have become increasingly cohesive in their voting behaviour, and now the European Parliament is dominated by the classic left–right dimension that is characteristic of many national parliaments. The fact that the voting behaviour of members of the world's most powerful multinational assembly, the European Parliament, is more strongly influenced by ideological/partisan positions than national positions provides reasons to conjecture that, if given representation in global institutions, domestic minorities would not simply align with their governments. But sceptics can still retort that 'it is doubtful that the analogy [with the EU] makes sense under the conditions of diversity that prevail on the global scale' (Nye 2002, 17).

To determine whether the pattern seen in the European Parliament might hold at the interregional level, it would be useful to analyse voting behaviour in international assemblies that share four features: (a) the inclusion of *non-governmental* delegates as full members, who are (b) drawn from (nearly) *all countries* of the world and (c) *vote* competitively (d) on decisions that have some kind of impact on *international law*. The International Labour Organization (ILO) fulfils these criteria. As already noted by Ernst Haas in 1962, it provides a good context for examining the question of whether non-governmental delegates in international organizations tend to vote along national lines or according to non-national cleavages (Haas 1962). The ILO is based on the principle of tripartism, which entails that 'the representatives of workers and employers, enjoying *equal status* with those of governments, join with them in *free discussion* and *democratic decision* with a view to the promotion of the common welfare' (ILO 1944, emphases added). The ILO is important for debates about the democratization of international governance because (1) it has global membership, rather than merely regional scope; (2) it has worked under roughly the same procedural rules for over a century; (3) the delegates drawn from two kinds of non-state actors (trade unions and employers' associations) have the same voting and speaking rights as government delegates; (4) the delegates have extensive opportunities to debate issues in plenary meetings, committees, and other forums; (5) the delegates vote on the adoption of international legislation and non-government delegates can choose to side with their government or with the majority of their functional group (or neither).

Between 1919 and 2014, the ILO created and adopted 190 conventions on international labour standards, which are binding international law for those states that have chosen to ratify them. It also adopted 199 recommendations, which usually consist of non-binding guidelines on how the standards mandated in the conventions can be applied. My analysis focuses on these outputs of the ILO and related decisions of a legislative nature. The text of proposed conventions and recommendations is drafted and discussed by ad hoc committees of the International Labour Conference (ILC), which usually meets once a year. The proposed conventions and recommendations are then presented to the plenary ILC for further discussion and adoption. In order to be adopted, conventions and recommendations must obtain a two-thirds majority in a final record vote of the delegates. The quorum rule is important: adoption is only possible if the sum of votes in favour and against equals or exceeds half of the number of delegates entitled to vote because they have been accredited to the ILC session during which the vote takes place.

The ILO is distinctive among international organizations in that national delegations include representatives not only of governments, but also of workers and employers. Governments nominate non-government delegates to the ILC, but they are required by the ILO constitution to select them from the most representative workers' or employers' organizations in the country (the ILC Credentials Committee has some ability to enforce this provision). In the committees, the three functional groups (governments, employers, and workers) have equal voting power. In the plenary of the ILC, two government delegates, one worker delegate, and one employer delegate are entitled to vote.

The ILO is an interesting case because there are reasons to expect functional groups in the ILO (workers, employers, and governments) to be more cohesive than national delegations, but also reasons for expecting the opposite. Among the former, we can consider that (1) labour standards might be designed to redistribute resources domestically between capital and labour and their representatives can be expected to vote against each other, with governments supporting one or other group depending on the circumstances; (2) the institutional context and procedural rules of the ILO favour functional group-based voting, and the Bureau for Workers' Activities and the Bureau for Employers' Activities perform information, coordination, and support tasks on the issues discussed in ILO bodies; (3) beyond the economic interests of their constituencies, ILO delegates may be socialized into attaching priority to their 'class' identity over their national identity. However, also the opposite expectation that national delegations will be more cohesive than functional groups can be based on a number of plausible assumptions: (1) governments nominate non-government delegates to the ILC and this gives to the former some influence over the latter, despite the constraints on selection mandated by the ILO Constitution; (2) the nation-state may be the main focus of loyalty and affective attachment, especially in the context of international interactions; (3) delegates may consider international economic competition more important than domestic redistribution and, at least in developing countries, trade unions may join governments and employers in opposing international labour standards that may reduce the country's comparative advantage and hinder exports and inflows of foreign direct investment; (4) delegates from the same country are more suitable partners for issue linkages and logrolling than foreign delegates belonging to the same functional group, because in the domestic context there are more issues that can be traded and more opportunities to retaliate against defectors, which increases the credibility of commitments.

Considering that both sets of assumptions can be derived from coherent theoretical premises, it is mainly an empirical question to determine which one is more persuasive on balance. To assess that, I conducted a quantitative analysis of roll-call voting in the plenary ILC. The focus is on the position of delegates on the final text of the proposed conventions and recommendations, at a stage when the negotiation on individual provisions has already been completed. The first question I examined is whether national delegations—i.e. the representatives of the government ('Governments'), the trade unions ('Workers'), and the employers' associations ('Employers') from each country—tend to be more cohesive in their voting behaviour than functional groups—i.e. the set of Worker, Employer, and Government representatives from all countries. The following analysis is based on 159 roll-call votes taken in the ILC between 1966 and 2006 on legislative acts, i.e. conventions, recommendations, and a small number of other decisions of a legislative nature. Roll-call votes are obligatory for these categories of votes. The voting choices were coded manually from the printed records of proceedings of the ILC (a research assistant collated the data for me in 2007). Figure 6.6 summarizes the voting choices of all accredited delegates, broken down by functional group.

Figure 6.6 shows that, when they participate in votes in the plenary body of the ILO, Workers almost always vote in favour of proposals and very rarely vote against or abstain. Employers vote in favour most of the time, but often abstain or, more rarely, vote against. Governments occupy an intermediate position: normally they support proposals, but sometimes abstain, usually in roll-call votes where a substantial proportion of Employers abstains as well.[15]

---

[15] Conventions and recommendations that pass through the committee deliberations are usually supported by majorities in all three groups at the plenary sittings, but there are exceptions. For instance, the vast majority of employers and many government delegates opposed the Convention on Home Work during the 1996 plenary session and the Work in Fishing Convention during the 2006 plenary session.

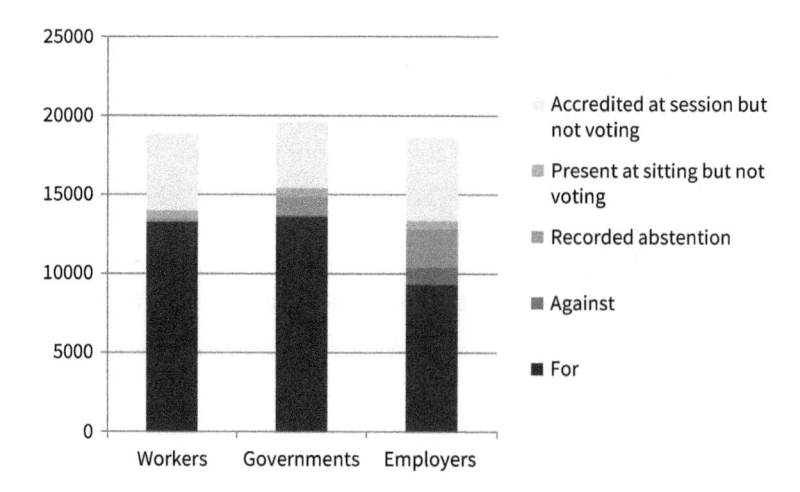

Figure 6.6 Distribution of voting choices across 159 roll-call votes, 1966–2006.
Note: Government votes have been divided by two to ease comparison with the other groups.

We can compare the voting cohesion of the Workers and Employers functional groups with the average cohesion of tripartite national delegations, i.e. the Government, Employer, and Worker delegates from each country. Cohesion scores have been calculated according to the following criteria: (1) The scores are based on Yes, No, and recorded Abstentions. (2) Cohesion scores for tripartite national delegations are considered only when the Worker, the Employer and at least one Government delegate voted Y, N or A, and, if both Government delegates voted, they made the same choice. When both Government delegates voted, they were treated as one single delegate for the purpose of calculating the score. (3) No and Abstain votes have been both interpreted as expressing opposition to the proposed legislation, and combined to form an 'Opposed' vote. While in other assemblies recorded abstentions can be interpreted as an option that is intermediate between 'Yes' and 'No',[16] this is not the case in the International Labour Conference. The reason is the quorum rule: proposals cannot pass if the sum of Yes and No votes is not at least equal to half of the number of accredited delegates. As a result of this rule, 'abstentions became a real weapon, more effective than negative votes for blocking a decision considered politically inexpedient' (Ghébali, Ago, and Valticos 1989, 184). (4) Since cohesion scores should reflect two options (support or opposition) rather than three, it is possible

---

[16] For instance, in the European Parliament (Hix, Noury, and Roland 2007, 91). Authors make different coding choices even in relation to the same assembly. For instance, in analyses of roll-call votes in the UN General Assembly, Voeten (2000) treated both No votes and abstentions as signs that states reject resolutions, while Thacker (1999) coded a vote in favour as 1, a vote against as 0, and an abstention as 0.5.

to use the Rice index of cohesion (Rice 1925), which equals the absolute difference between the number of Yes and Oppose votes of the members of a group (national delegation or functional group) divided by the sum of Yes and Oppose votes.

Figure 6.7 shows the cohesion of the Employers group, the Workers group, and the mean cohesion of all tripartite national delegations for each individual roll-call vote, with cohesion scores averaged over each of four decades to increase readability.

Figure 6.7 shows that the Workers have been very cohesive throughout the forty years under consideration. The Employers have been less cohesive, with substantial minorities sometimes voting against majorities. *On average*, national delegations have been less cohesive than the workers, and more cohesive than the employers in most votes, with the average national cohesion index occasionally falling below that of the employers, notably since the end of the Communist regimes in Central and Eastern Europe.

Thus, the answer to the question asked above—whether national delegations tend to be more cohesive in their voting behaviour than functional groups, specifically Workers and Employers—is mostly negative. Non-governmental delegates are not simply replicating the voting behaviour of governmental representatives. It is often the case that either the workers delegate or the employers delegate from a country (virtually never both) votes differently from the government delegate(s) of that country. This is an indication that the voting choices of non-governmental delegates are guided

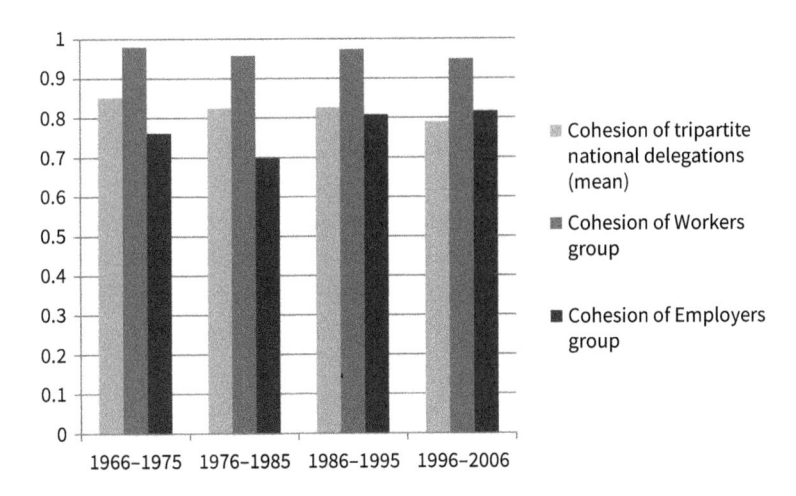

Figure 6.7 Cohesion of national delegations, Workers and Employers, individual roll-call votes. Average cohesion across roll-call votes for each decade.

by interests, values, and beliefs that are not merely a reflection of 'national positions'. The cleavages between functional groups is especially evident on some controversial issues, such as the long-standing conflict between Workers and Employers over whether ILO conventions protect the right to strike, which erupted in 2012 and paralysed the ILO's machinery for supervising compliance with its labour standards (La Hovary 2015).

There are reasons to believe that the discrepancy between government and non-governmental delegates would be larger in a confederation *of democracies*. A democratic domestic environment may play a role in allowing non-governmental delegates to vote against government delegates. The word 'allowing' must be emphasized, since it is most plausible as a *permissive* condition for voting choices that deviate from the preferences of governments. We can assess this through the data on ILO voting patterns. In democratic countries, all else being equal, trade unions and employers' associations should be more independent of governments, governments are more likely to appoint non-governmental delegates proposed by the most representative unions and associations (as opposed to delegates close to state officials), and those delegates are more free to vote without fear of government retaliation.

To test this hypothesis, I analysed the association between democracy and voting cohesion of national tripartite delegations. Cohesion scores are calculated following the criteria stated above, but having replaced the Rice index of 0.33 (indicating a 2 to 1 split) with 0 for the statistical procedure. The outcome is dichotomous (Government, Worker, and Employer delegates are either united in supporting the tabled proposal, or they are not) and the method used is logistic regression. I estimated four models, two using country fixed effects and two using random effects with robust standard errors. For each of those procedures, I estimated a reduced model that includes only the V-Dem index of electoral democracy, and a model that includes several control variables, which are mostly available for a shorter period and hence yield a smaller sample. These control variables are income per capita; whether the country has a chief executive professing a left-wing ideology, who might not only instruct Government delegates to vote in favour of a convention but also pressurize the Employer representative to do the same; the extent to which core workers' rights are recognized and respected in a country, including freedom to form and join trade unions; the occurrence of general strikes as a proxy for the militancy of organized labour; and the degree of economic globalization in a country, since higher sensitivity to international economic competition might lead to greater commonality of interests between Employers, Workers, and the Government (the data sources are provided in Appendix II).

The results presented in Appendix IV (Table A.6) confirm the expectation that electoral democracy leads to lower levels of cohesion. When representatives of trade unions and business associations operate in a national political environment that gives them autonomy, they are more likely to vote in ways that do not align with government preferences. Taken together, these findings support the critics of intergovernmentalism, who assert that it weakens the international representation of social groups that are not aligned with government positions. Conversely, these results reinforce the view that, in a freely elected world parliament, divisions will occur 'along lines of opinion, not lines of geography' (Lloyd and Schwimmer 1942, 5).

6.6 Concluding remarks

The relative advantages of the universal republic and a confederation of democracies depend on a number of factors, some of which are to some extent amenable to empirical testing. The evidence presented in this chapter strengthens the claim that the UR constitutes the better response to the problem of promoting democracy globally, because the assumptions of its supporters survive the impact with the data in better shape than the assumptions underlying confederal solutions. The assumption that a world state could have at best a 'low-quality' democracy—defined in terms of participation, deliberation, liberalism, and egalitarianism—is not supported, if we use existing countries as reasonable benchmarks. Similarly, the assumptions that the world as a whole is much more diverse in terms of policy values than the typical countries, and that the risk of persistent minorities would be substantially larger, are not supported by the data I have presented. By contrast, the assumption that governments do not enact the policies preferred by their citizens if they retain sovereign decision-making under conditions of interdependence receives some support, strengthening the case for collective decisions that do not depend on universal agreements among governments. Finally, the assumption that domestic interest or advocacy groups would often align with their foreign counterparts rather than with their own government representatives is supported by the experience of the ILO.

The message that consistently emerges across these analyses is that participants in debates about world order should not overestimate the flaws of global democracy and the virtues of national democracy.

7

Universal republic or polycentric democracy?

7.1 Polycentric perspectives

This chapter considers a second alternative to the universal republic, which is supported by scholars and analysts who share the ultimate goal of democratizing global politics but see more promise in a pluralist approach that emphasizes a multiplicity of centres of governance and participation. The rejection of centralist approaches to global democratization is based on arguments about feasibility as well as desirability. As the feasibility of the UR has been considered in the first part of this book, this chapter focuses on whether polycentric democracy provides a model that is normatively more attractive.

David Mitrany was a prominent critic of global federalism and parliamentarism, advocating the alternative of a plurality of functional governance agencies at the transnational level, for which he envisaged forms of citizen representation through non-governmental organizations (Mitrany 1975; Steffek 2015). Recent proponents of polycentrism regard the idea of a democratic world state as a reflection of an obsolete and narrow conception of democracy, which is excessively dependent on statist, territorialist, electoralist, aggregative (as opposed to deliberative), and/or Western-centric intellectual frameworks and assumptions. Proponents of polycentric democracy have developed a wide range of arguments that draw from various philosophical, sociological, anthropological, and legal traditions as well as historical and contemporary debates on international relations (e.g. Bohman 2005; Dryzek 2006; T. Macdonald and K. Macdonald 2006, 2020; T. Macdonald 2008, 2012; Krisch 2010; Dryzek, Bächtiger, and Milewicz 2011; K. Macdonald 2012; Little and Macdonald 2013; Scholte 2014, 2020; Pavel 2015; Holthaus 2018; Theiler 2022; see also Gadinger and Scholte 2023). For instance, Scholte (2014, 2020) regards a pluralist institutional structure as better suited to democratize diffuse power relationships in a highly diverse world and, while recognizing a possible role for suprastate parliaments, notes that 'a more transformative vision of global democracy would

The Universal Republic. Mathias Koenig-Archibugi, Oxford University Press. © Mathias Koenig-Archibugi (2024).
DOI: 10.1093/9780198921158.003.0007

not regard modern representative assemblies to be a necessary condition for, let alone the total extent of, people's rule in global politics' (Scholte 2014, 12). Terry and Kate Macdonald (2020) link polycentric democracy with the theoretical tradition of pragmatism (Dewey 1946), which privileges creativity, innovation, and flexible adjustment to social difference over standard models of rationality. Pavel (2015, 141–170) argues that a pluralist system is less prone to the pathologies that plague centralized institutional schemes, because it encourages experimentation, innovation, and processes of self-correction and spontaneous coordination that facilitate institutional learning and effective problem-solving.

Krisch approaches the question from the perspective of legal theory and contrasts constitutionalism and pluralism as two opposed ways of thinking about the rule of law in a global context. Constitutionalists consider democratic values to be best promoted by high degrees of international integration and legal hierarchy, whereas pluralists stress the democratic benefits of polycentrism and coexistence of a plurality of rule systems with no agreed hierarchy between them. Krisch (2010, 68) argues that constitutionalism 'will be less suited for the radical diversity that marks the global populace ... The greater the distance between different groups in a population, the easier a constitutional settlement may appear as imposed by one group on the other, as an imperial tool rather than an expression of common self-government.' He points out that proponents of pluralism tend to stress three virtues: it is more adaptable to changing social and political circumstances; it provides greater contestatory space for weaker actors and hinders powerful actors from locking in their privileges; and it builds checks and balances into the postnational order more effectively than constitutionalism can do. Krisch stresses a key virtue: pluralism is more respectful to people's actual preferences regarding the political associations in which they are members and the political structures that govern their lives. Since citizens have a multiplicity of identities and allegiances, and various degrees of acceptance of different governance structures 'depending on the issue and situation at hand' (Krisch 2010, 98), a pluralist constellation of authority is likely to be more acceptable to them than the imposition of a constitutional framework that requires an ultimate authority to be identified. A pluralist system will also be morally legitimate, if individual institutions can provide a convincing account of how they strike a balance between the claims of insiders to pursue their particular goals and the claims of outsiders to be included in decisions that affect them.

The diversity of arguments in favour of polycentric democracy and the different levels (epistemological, pragmatic, etc.) they address makes it challenging to compare their assumptions to those supporting institutionally integrated models—at least more challenging than the comparison with confederal approaches. The aims of this chapter are therefore relatively modest. I will first offer some brief comments on something that is common to many understandings of polycentric democracy, i.e. its acceptance of non-electoral forms of democratic representation. This is a *contingent* feature of polycentric democracy because, at least in principle, electoral mechanisms could be built into structures of polycentric representation, even though some supporters consider that undesirable. The remainder of the chapter is devoted to examining and evaluating the consequences of a *defining* feature of polycentric democracy, i.e. the absence of an overarching governance framework that adjudicates between competing demands and manages the relationship between multiple policy issues. The systematic assessment of this common feature can enrich the dialogue with all polycentric perspectives, regardless of the diversity in their epistemological, theoretical, and empirical underpinnings.

7.2 Democratic representation

One of the differences between most statist and most polycentric models of global democracy consist in the institutional mechanisms through which constituencies authorize representatives to make decisions on their behalf and hold those representatives to account. The question is whether and to what extent one can argue that non-electoral accountability can be an appropriate way of ensuring democratic control of decision-making (T. Macdonald and K. Macdonald 2006). Representatives are often self-appointed. Montanaro argues that self-appointed representatives can be democratically legitimate under certain conditions—that is when they both provide political presence for an affected constituency and are authorized and held by them (Montanaro 2012). As an example of non-electoral but democratic authorization and accountability mechanisms, Montanaro refers to the relationship between Rwandan women and the umbrella organization Pro-Femmes. The women 'organizationally authorize Pro-Femmes, if indirectly, through their participation in its member organizations', while exit and voice accountability are exercised 'by exiting its organizations and by expressing dissatisfaction in its consultations' (Montanaro 2012, 1104).

Such non-electoral forms may be the best available mechanisms in certain circumstances, but they suffer from a major drawback compared to elections. If members of a constituency fail to authorize a self-appointed representative to speak on their behalf, or revokes that authorization by 'exiting' the relationship, they have no guarantee that a different actor will represent them, or that an alternative representative would have access to the same resources. For instance, Pro-Femmes offers services funded by foreign donors, and refusing to participate in its programmes may lead to exclusion from empowerment opportunities. The electoral logic is different. Elections are held for offices that give access to legal authority and control of material resources, a plurality of candidates compete to fill those offices by proposing ways of using the authority and the resources, and the elected power-holders are then held accountable for that use at the next election. Under an electoral system it can happen that some voters may find themselves excluded from benefits, but in principle this would be the result of a democratic decision rather than of exit from an unsatisfactory relationship.

In principle, polycentric democracy could be realized by making each of the governance units subject to electoral control (e.g. Frey and Eichenberger 1999). They could even be internally organized so as to replicate the relationship between legislative, executive, and judicial authority that we considered in the previous chapter in relation to the universal republic. For this reason, the question of electoral vs non-electoral representation and accountability will not be pursued further. The rest of this chapter will address a defining, as opposed to optional, aspect of polycentric democracy, which is that governance is exercised in a multiplicity of forums and settings, without a clear hierarchy of authority or even formal 'interface' rules between them. From a democratic standpoint, this feature raises two major problems.

The first problem is that polycentric models offer no clear mechanism to adjudicate between competing claims for exclusion and inclusion. As noted above, Krisch argues that pluralism can be morally legitimate when individual institutions can provide a convincing account of how they strike a balance between the claims of insiders to pursue their particular goals and the claims of outsiders to be included in decisions that affect them. But the absence of a constitutional framework means that there is neither a forum in charge of assessing whether an account is convincing when people disagree about that, nor a previously agreed set of criteria that would guide that assessment. As a result, polycentric democracy offers no robust safeguard against unjustified exclusion (Follesdal 2012, 110). The alternative approach, as formulated by Marchetti (2008, 81), is more compelling: 'It is … only through an all-inclusive world system that the drawing of jurisdictional boundaries can be implemented democratically and the problem of political exclusion avoided. Exclusion is considered legitimate only when its boundaries are collectively decided through an all-inclusive procedure. Only self-exclusion is legitimate.' From this perspective, a global constitution is required to codify transparent and participative procedures for drawing jurisdictional boundaries and for enabling any group to appeal against unjustified exclusion in the context of a judicial process (Marchetti 2008, 161–164). Agné applies a similar approach specifically to the problem of contested political boundaries and argues that 'a state is founded in accordance with democracy if the foundational decision is made by people who will live within as well as beyond the boundaries once founded (ultimately involving humanity as a whole) and if each individual has the same opportunity to influence such politics of foundation' (Agné 2010, 405). Given that this aspect has received sustained attention already, I will not consider it further and move on to presenting and examining in depth a second problem in the remainder of the chapter.

7.3 Nonseparable preferences and democracy

The second problem inherent to polycentric democracy derives from the circumstance that it 'represents individuals by issue-area' (T. Macdonald 2008, 158). The focus on specific issue-areas can restrict considerably the ability of people to exercise democratic control over decisions that affect their autonomy (Koenig-Archibugi 2012a, 476). In brief, the argument is as follows. Decisions on a specific issue are likely to have effects on other issue-areas—for instance, decisions on trade have an impact on climate change, decisions on financial flows have an impact on workers' rights, decisions on health policy have an impact on gender equality, and so on. Sometimes these policy externalities are positive, but often they are negative, which means that policies aimed at attaining one goal can be an obstacle in the promotion of other goals. As McGann (2006, 66–67) notes, 'many policy choices are intrinsically multidimensional and interconnected' and a 'great deal of policy-making is about the relative weight we give to different objectives'. In the domestic context, executive, judicial, and especially legislative institutions have general competences that enable them—and to some extent compel them—to address trade-offs between different issue-specific goals within deliberative and decision-making processes. The fragmentation of global governance into issue-specific institutions greatly limits the ability of affected populations to provide inputs into deliberation and decisions on trade-offs. The problem is distinct from the problem of exclusion of groups from decision-making processes that affect them: even if all issue-specific institutions fulfilled normative requirements for inclusion, groups would be pursuing different goals in different forums, without the opportunity to indicate priorities between them in cases where they conflict. To the extent that making choices is a key aspect of democracy, the absence of international institutions for the comprehensive balancing of multiple social goals is bound to generate a democratic deficit.

This line of reasoning leads to a prima facie argument for the normative superiority of the universal republic over polycentric democracy. However, it is only valid prima facie, because its weight in a comparative assessment depends on the extent to which the empirical premise—decisions are interdependent across issue-areas—accurately describes the state of the world. The mere theoretical possibility of interdependence would not support a strong case for a central coordinating authority such as the universal republic.

Before the empirical situation is considered in the next section, the remainder of this section discusses why the problem of interdependence is challenging from a *democratic* perspective, i.e. one that assumes that decisions should reflect people's own assessment of the advantages and disadvantages of various options, as opposed to technocratic solutions. By focusing on the aggregation preferences, I do not wish to deny the importance of deliberation. While institutional design should promote democratic deliberation, it should also take into account that deliberation may not lead to consensus and disagreement may have to be resolved through aggregation procedures (Fishkin 2009, 85–88; Mackie 2018).

The argument focuses on the concept of separability. When a person has separable preferences, she can form a preference between two (or more) options regardless of which decisions are made on other issues. Somewhat more formally: 'Suppose that a and b are alternatives pertaining one single issue, and X and Y are sets of outcomes of decisions made in some other issue (or issues). A voter's preference a>b is said to be separable if the following holds for that voter: (a, X)>(b, X) if and only if (a, Y)>(b, Y) for all X and Y' (Lagerspetz 2016, 365). The following argument is sufficiently general that 'voters' can be either individual citizens or representatives of large groups. If preferences over issue-dimensions are separable, and if additionally they are single-peaked, then issue-by-issue majority voting identifies the Condorcet winner in relation to each issue (Ward and Weale 2010). Preferences over a set of possible outcomes are said to be single-peaked when they can be ordered in such a way that, for each person, outcomes that are more distant from her best outcome are preferred less. A Condorcet winner is the option that is preferred by the majority in every pairwise vote against each of the other options. This attractive feature leads some scholars to conclude that 'the issue-by-issue median is the best approximation we shall have to a popular will' (Weale 2007, 179).

Conversely, preferences are non-separable across two issue-dimensions when an individual's preferences for outcomes regarding an issue-dimension vary depending on which outcome occurs (or is expected) in the other issue-dimension. For instance, an individual may believe that two policy interventions are complementary: if one is not implemented, implementing the other will only waste resources. Alternatively, an individual may believe that both interventions would be beneficial and independent but nevertheless support only one (either of the two) because funding both would leave insufficient resources for other purposes.

When preferences are non-separable, issue-by-issue voting can lead to situations where a Condorcet winner may not be chosen when one exists, where a Condorcet loser may be the social choice, and where the chosen outcome may be Pareto-dominated by all other potential outcomes (Lacy and Niou 2000). An outcome is Pareto-dominated when there is an alternative outcome that at least some people prefer and no one prefers less. The following highly stylized examples illustrate these outcomes. Suppose a situation in which three voters can vote Yes or No on each of two issues. Table 7.1 shows the possible outcomes of those votes, with YN denoting the approval of the Issue 1 proposal and failure of the Issue 2 proposal, YY denoting the approval of both proposals, and so on. The table shows how each voter ranks the combined outcomes on the two issues.

The outcome of the decision depends on how votes are taken. If the issues are decided *together* (as a package) by pairwise majority voting, combination YY beats all others (it is the Condorcet winner). If voters first decide on the Issue 1 and then on Issue 2, their separate votes will yield outcome NY. If they vote on Issue 2 first and then on the other issue, the result would be YN. If the issues are decided simultaneously *but separately*, the outcome will be NN (voters 2 and 3 vote N on issue 1 and voters 1 and 3 vote N on issue 2). Lacy

Table 7.1 Issue-by-issue voting produces an outcome ranked last by a majority

Rank	Voter 1	Voter 2	Voter 3
1	YN	NY	NN
2	YY	YY	YY
3	NY	YN	NY
4	NN	NN	YN

Source: Dean Lacy and Emerson M. S. Niou. 2000. 'A problem with referendums'. *Journal of Theoretical Politics* 12 (1). https://doi.org/10.1177/0951692800012001001.

and Niou (2000, 12) describe why that is a problem in stark terms: 'YY is the Condorcet winner, NN is the Condorcet loser. For majority voting to select a Condorcet loser over a Condorcet winner is certainly perverse.'

An even more problematic outcome is possible. If preferences are non-separable, issue-by-issue voting may lead to a result that *all* voters regard as the *worst* outcome (an outcome that is Pareto-dominated by all other out-comes). Table 7.2 shows this with an example. The situation can be thought of as a vote on which ones of three policy interventions to approve. No voter wants all three interventions to be approved—for instance, because this outcome would violate a budget constraint agreed by all. All voters want to approve one or two interventions but disagree on what deserves most support.

In this example, separate majority decisions produce the combination YYY, even though this is everybody's least preferred outcome. Combina-tions YYN, YNY, and NYY form a cycle, thus there is no Condorcet winner, but any of those three combinations would be unanimously preferred to the combination that emerges from issue-by-issue voting.

These outcomes would frustrate the will of citizens who participate in the democratic process. Moreover, it is worth bearing in mind Christiano's point that they may also undermine political equality. Egalitarians should require equality of persons in terms of their total life prospects, and '[any] egalitarian scheme that neglects the complementarity of their preferences and differ-ences of intensity, especially to the point that it will defeat Condorcet choices, is unable to give individuals equality over their whole life prospects' (Chris-tiano 1990, 177). According to Christiano, an egalitarian procedure should

Table 7.2 Issue-by-issue voting produces an outcome ranked last by everyone

Rank	Voter 1	Voter 2	Voter 3
1	YYN	YNY	NYY
2	YNY	NYY	YYN
3	NYY	YYN	YNY
4	NNY	NYN	YNN
5	YNN	YNN	NYN
6	NYN	NNY	NNY
7	NNN	NNN	NNN
8	YYY	YYY	YYY

Source: Dean Lacy and Emerson M. S. Niou. 2000. 'A problem with referendums.' *Journal of Theoretical Politics* 12 (1). https://doi.org/10.1177/0951692800012001001.

not only take into account how issues are inseparably connected in individuals' preferences ordering, but ideally combine all issues that will come up in their lives (Christiano 1990, 161–163). Such a global procedure would be practically unworkable, given the informational requirements it entails, but from an egalitarian perspective procedures that combine issues are an improvement over issue-by-issue procedures because they allow us to address complementarity of preferences and differences of intensity through vote trading (Christiano 1990, 183).

7.4 Nonseparability and trade-offs in global policy

Nonseparability means that preferences on one issue depend on how one or more other issue is addressed. If preferences on issues are nonseparable, issue-by-issue voting may not yield outcomes that are democratically legitimate. This poses a problem for models of polycentric democracy, which 'represents individuals by issue-area' (T. Macdonald 2008, 158).

How serious the problem is depends on how common nonseparable preferences are in practice. In abstract terms, they should be more common than separable preferences and the difference should increase dramatically as more issues are added. For two issues, eight preference orderings are separable and sixteen are non-separable. For three issues, less than 0.01 per cent of all possible preference orderings are separable (Lacy and Niou 2000, 10–11). These numbers suggest that choosing a governance architecture based on an *assumption* that issues can be separated is likely to be highly problematic. On the other hand, it is difficult to estimate the *empirical* prevalence of nonseparable preferences among citizens, given that voting systems and surveys are rarely designed to capture them (Lacy 2001). Empirical evidence shows that the preferences of some citizens on some issues are indeed nonseparable.[1] However, existing survey-based studies cover only few of the issue-dimensions that would be likely to be on the agenda of global democratic institutions. In this section, I develop an alternative approach.

To gauge how serious nonseparability is for governance arrangements that cover one issue-area at a time, this section considers the findings of research on the interdependencies among global policy issues. As Lagerspetz

---

[1] See the studies by Lacy and Niou (2013); Stoetzer and Zittlau (2015); Green et al. (2020); Stoetzer and Zittlau (2020); Helbling, Maxwell, and Traunmüller (2024).

(2016, 372) notes, 'Like "dimension" and "issue", "dependence" or "interdependence" of issues are agent-relative and situation-relative properties.' This means that it is difficult to predict in advance which issues citizens and their representatives will consider interdependent, and how they will interpret that interdependence. However, we can use the current state of scientific knowledge as an indication of which issues well-informed citizens of global democratic arrangements are likely to consider as interdependent when they have the opportunity to express what they want.

For this exercise we can examine the literature on the Sustainable Development Goals (SDG). The SDG framework encompasses 17 goals and 169 targets. Researchers have recognized that, 'With such a plethora of goals and targets, interaction is inevitable. Possible interactions range from cancellation (achievement of an SDG makes progress on another impossible) to indivisibility (success in an SDG is contingent on success of another)' (Scherer et al. 2018, 65). However, the SDGs emerged from a negotiation process that at least nominally was based on the assumption that reaching the individual goals constitutes progress towards an overarching goal: 'sustainable development'. This means that focusing on the SDG gives a conservative picture of the nonseparability of global issues: because of how the goals have been selected, interactions are more likely to be synergies (where progress in one goal favours progress in another) than trade-offs (where progress in one goal hinders progress in another). Considering goals and issues not included in the SDGs may well show a larger number of trade-offs, although this analysis is not pursued here.

Both perceived synergies and trade-offs can lead to nonseparability. If a voter believes that goal A and B are synergistic, she may prioritize goal A over C if B is likely to be achieved and prioritize goal C over A if B is unlikely to be achieved. Conversely, if a voter believes that there is a trade-off between goal A and B, she may prioritize goal C over A if B is likely to be pursued and goal A over C if B is unlikely to be pursued.

Using SDG indicator data for every country in the world, Pradhan et al. (2017) and Anderson et al. (2022) calculated correlation coefficients between all pairs of indicators. A statistically significant positive correlation between a pair of indicators is interpreted as showing a *synergy* between them when it equals or exceeds a relatively high threshold (a Spearman's ρ value that is greater than 0.6 on a scale from -1 to 1). A statistically significant negative correlation between a pair of indicators is interpreted as showing a *trade-off* between them when it is sufficiently strong (a Spearman's ρ value of less than -0.6). Pairs of indicators with weak or no correlation (ρ values between -0.6 and 0.6) are considered 'non-classified', i.e. non-interacting.

Figure 7.1 shows the shares of positive and negative correlations between SDG indicators. The left panel of the figure shows correlations between indicators pertaining to the *same* SDG. For most countries, positive correlations between indicator pairs outnumber both negative ones and nonclassifieds, but the figure shows that trade-offs exist as well. For instance, in the context of SDG 8 (*Decent work and economic growth*), shifting employment from the informal to the formal sector appears to hamper the improvement of resource efficiency in consumption and production (Anderson et al. 2022).

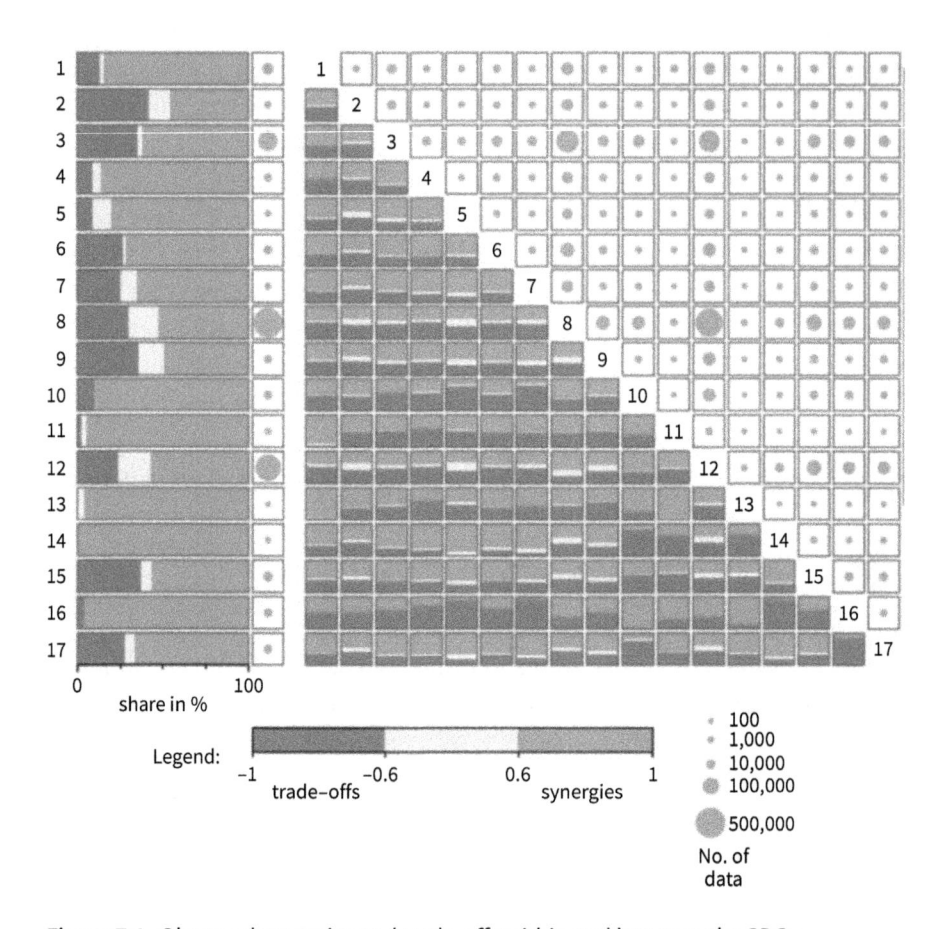

Figure 7.1   Observed synergies and trade-offs within and between the SDGs.

Note: The SDGs are represented by the numbers from 1 to 17. The bars represent the share of synergies (blue/dark grey), trade-offs (orange/medium grey), and nonclassifieds (yellow/light grey) observed within each SDG (left panel) and between each pair of SDGs (right panel). The area of the circle in the boxes indicates the number of data pairs used to calculate the correlation.

Source: Carl C. Anderson, Manfred Denich, Anne Warchold, Jürgen P. Kropp, and Prajal Pradhan. 2022. 'A systems model of SDG target influence on the 2030 Agenda for Sustainable Development'. *Sustainability Science* 17 (4). https://doi.org/10.1007/s11625-021-01040-8. Creative Commons CC BY licence. Image has been modified for greyscale printing.

The right panel of Figure 7.1 shows correlations between indicators pertaining to *different* SDGs. Positive correlations outnumber nonclassifieds by a wide margin and negative correlations by a smaller margin. SDG 1 (*No poverty*) has a mostly synergetic relationship with most other goals. By contrast, the figure shows that SDGs 4 (*Quality education*), 10 (*Reduced inequalities*), 11 (*Sustainable cities and communities*), 12 (*Responsible consumption and production*), and 16 (*Peace, justice, and strong institutions*) are involved in a high number of trade-offs with other SDGs. It is worth noting that many but not all the within-SDG and between-SDG trade-offs reflect the tension between economic growth and the associated human welfare benefits on the one hand and environmental sustainability on the other.

These findings capture correlations and do not demonstrate causality.[2] Negative correlations could be due to a direct effect of changes in one indicator on other indicators, or to external factors driving both indicators in divergent directions. Whatever the causal relationship, the findings provide a strong indication that the ability to achieve most goals is not independent from progress in the achievement of most other goals, for better or for worse.[3]

To illustrate the implications of these findings for the problem of issue-by-issue voting in the presence of nonseparability, consider the following example. The starting point is the simplifying assumption that, in a polycentric governance system, decisions on whether to pursue targets within the same SDG are made within the same governance unit, whereas decisions pertaining to different SDGs are made by separate governance units. Hence, the governance unit focused on SDG 2 (*End hunger and promote sustainable agriculture*) makes decisions on how to pursue and allocate resources among

---

[2] The study by Scherer et al. (2018) is more clearly focused on causal effects. Specifically, they estimate the environmental impacts of ending poverty (related to SDG 1: *No poverty*) and reducing inequality (related to SDG 10: *Reduced inequalities*). The impact is assessed in relation to three environmental footprint categories, corresponding to carbon (CO_2-equivalents, related to SDG 13: *Climate action*), land (land stress, related to SDG 15: *Life on land*), and water (freshwater scarcity, related to SDG 6: *Clean water and sanitation*). They find that achieving a minimum income level of US$1.25 per capita per day (SDG 1) for the extremely poor leads to relatively small environmental impacts: carbon, land, and water footprints increase by 0.8, 1.4, and 2.1 per cent respectively. A minimum income level of US$1.90 a day would increase carbon, land, and water footprints by 1.9, 3.3, and 5.6 per cent. Reducing intranational inequality (SDG 10) by limiting the Gini index of income to a maximum of 0.3 increases carbon, land, and water footprints by 0.8, 0.9, and 1.3 per cent. Reducing intranational inequality more by halving the Gini index of all countries increases carbon, land, and water footprints globally by 1.7, 1.8, and 5.7 per cent. Scherer et al. (2018) also estimate that achieving simultaneously an elimination of extreme poverty and a reduction of the water, land, and carbon footprints of households at the global level by 50, 15, and 50 per cent, respectively, would require a 77 per cent reduction of the carbon footprint of the higher income group (out of four groups).

[3] Other studies that identify both synergies and trade-offs between SDG targets include Fuso Nerini et al. (2018); Barbier and Burgess (2019); Kroll, Warchold, and Pradhan (2019); Lusseau and Mancini (2019).

the SDG 2 targets, while the governance unit focused on SDG 6 (*Water and sanitation*) makes decisions on how to pursue and allocate resources among the SDG 6 targets. Let us also assume that the members of the SDG 2 governance unit are guided by the belief that, in line with the systematic expert assessment of Fader et al. (2018), two targets that both relate to SDG 2— 2.a (on investment) and 2.b (on trade)—interact negatively, in the sense that pursuing one target limits options regarding the other.[4] Given that pursuing both targets simultaneously could be counterproductive, they decide to prioritize one of the two, possibly hoping that a way of turning the trade-off into a synergy will be discovered in the future. Which one will be supported by a majority? Let us assume that they also believe that both targets have positive as well as negative interactions with targets relating to different SDGs. Specifically, they believe—again, in line with the expert assessment of Fader et al. (2018)—that target 2.a has a synergy with target 6.a (International capacity building) but a trade-off with target 6.b (Local water management), whereas the opposite is the case for target 2.b: it interacts negatively with 6.a and positively with 6.b. Given these interdependencies, the choice between 2.a and 2.b may depend on whether 6.a or 6.b is pursued. But we assumed that the latter decision is taken by a separate governance unit responsible for the *Water and sanitation* SDG. Thus, a majority of voters in the SDG 2 governance unit may prefer to prioritize target 2.a provided that the SDG 6 governance unit prioritizes target 6.a, and it may prefer to prioritize target 2.b if the SDG 6 governance unit prioritizes target 6.b.

Moreover, as Figure 7.1 shows, synergies and trade-offs typically extend across multiple SDGs. For instance, the same experts who posited the above relationship between food and water targets also maintain that target 7.b (on sustainable energy) displays a synergy with 2.a and a trade-off with 2.b (Fader et al. 2018). Thus, the choice between 2.a and 2.b is likely to be affected not only by the choice between 6.a or 6.b but also by whether a third governance unit decides to prioritize 7.b or not. Given the synergies and trade-offs identified in the literature on SDG interactions, the choice is likely to be affected by decisions on a wide range of other SDG targets.

In these examples, the governance unit that happens to decide first will affect the choices of the other governance units. For the reasons explained in the previous section, the resulting combination of policies may not be the one that majority of voters would have chosen if the policies had been decided together as a package.

---

[4] Both 2.a. and 2.b are 'means of implementation' targets. On the difference between outcome targets and means of implementation targets see Bartram et al. (2018).

7.5 Institutional design for nonseparability

The project of polycentric democracy envisages participatory mechanisms that match the dispersed nature of power in the contemporary global system. However, this strategy transfers into the practices of democratic control the absence of an overarching authority that coordinates action across policy domains. Leebron explains how that differs from domestic governance within most countries:

> [I]n the domestic context, there is virtually always some coordinating mechanism and superior authority … to coordinate both the allocation of tasks and the substantive resolution of issues. To this extent, all issues are potentially linked in political units where a governmental organ (such as a national parliament or chief executive) enjoys plenary authority. Although various international organizations have mechanisms for cooperating with each other, these relationships are generally neither hierarchical nor comprehensive. (Leebron 2002, 8)

The universal republic would address the implications of nonseparability by adopting institutional devices that are well known in domestic political systems, and specifically the combination of parliamentary institutions and political parties. Parliaments provide a forum for decision-making across issue boundaries, and political parties give a structure to the relationship between citizens and that forum. Each of those two components contributes an important element to the solution, and they do so by performing both aggregative and deliberative functions.

Parliamentary institutions ensure that all issues of public concern are deliberated upon and decided in one forum, by representatives who are held accountable for public policy as a whole, rather than for the attainment of specific goals. In parliamentary debates and legislation, issues can be considered separately or bundled in 'packages'. The bundling can be based on functional interdependencies or be purely strategic, in the sense that they reflect exchanges of concessions on distinct issues. Typically, issues that are closely connected—such as taxation and public spending levels, and the distribution of public expenditure among sectoral departments—are bundled together, for instance in an annual budget law.

Given that the parliamentary forum allows for decisions on trade-offs across issues, voters can take such trade-offs into account when electing their representatives. '[R]epresentative elections result in aggregation or bundling across the entire range of issues or potential issues. Each voter casts his or her vote (that is, allocates his or her equal but limited allotment of political power) according to whatever issue or set of issues he or she considers most important' (Clark 1998, 469). In principle, each individual candidate for office can propose to voters a distinctive bundle of policies. In practice, political parties play an essential role in making the choice understandable and meaningful to citizens. Historically, at least some parties emerged to solve a social choice problem in policy-making affecting members of legislatures: organizing for the long term helps them avoid voting cycles and achieve stable collective outcomes (Aldrich 2011). With the expansion of mass electoral politics, the structuring function of political parties helps voters to exercise their democratic rights. Individual voters typically do not have strong incentives to collect large quantities of information relating to potential interdependencies between a broad range of issues.

> [T]o offer the electorate a choice, [political parties] have to package seemingly disparate claims into more or less coherent bundles. In effect, they create predetermined bargains. When multiple parties present the voters with different bundles of issues and solutions, voters have a choice. They choose from within a more or less crystallized, active policy agenda.' (Klingemann et al. 1994, 8)

Parties address the social choice problem

> by working out a joint preference ranking supported by multiple politicians (program). Voters, in turn, may then more clearly anticipate how their choice between programmatic teams will affect binding, collective democratic outcomes of the policy-making process. ... If parties develop even a modicum of programmatic coherence, also relatively uninformed voters can infer a party's position on a range of issues from basic programmatic cues and then choose between the alternatives in an intelligent fashion. (Kitschelt 2000, 848)

Political parties help voters identify trade-offs and choose between a manageable set of bundles, providing a structure to an otherwise confusing constellation of policy issues (Hinich and Munger 1994; Clark 1998; Kitschelt 2000; Noel 2014). As noted by Rosenblum (2010, 307):

> Parties draw politically relevant lines of division, reject elements of the others' account of projects and promises, and articulate positions, and their antagonism is the engine of 'trial by discussion'. Party antagonism focuses attention on problems, information and interpretations are brought out, stakes are delineated, points of conflict and commonality are located, the range of possibilities winnowed.

This function is performed most effectively when parties bundle issues not just according to a strategic logic of vote-maximization but based on a coherent overarching conception of social justice. Given the multidimensional complexity of political issues in modern societies, *programmatic* political parties perform the important epistemic function of helping citizens to reflect and deliberate about justice by shaping a collection of disparate values into a coherent and specific conception of what a just society would look like.

> [Party] members work together in a collective process to produce party programs that reflect and give shape to the core normative commitments of their supporters. Party programs furthermore represent an attempt to produce a consistent ordering of these core commitments and a corresponding moral conception of society which is *sufficiently coherent* to count as a conception of justice and not just an assemblage of moral commitments. Given the normative complexity of advancing the justice of modern societies, political parties are necessary institutions of collective moral deliberation with the aim of arriving at a sufficiently coherent conception of justice. (Ebeling 2016, 635; see also Weinstock 2015)

The benefits of political parties are not limited to the aggregation of existing views but extend to deliberative processes aimed at rational understanding among citizens (Follesdal 2012, 101). They contribute to a normatively attractive form of political justification when they justify policy proposals with reference to conceptions of the common good and to reasons that could in principle be acceptable to all citizens (White and Ypi 2016). To perform this desirable function,

> parties should display a form of *cohesiveness* in their claims to represent citizens, and thus campaign on the basis of a discourse that aggregates dispersed issues of political relevance into a normatively grounded, coherent program of government. [... C]ohesiveness also requires partisans to establish the relative importance of [political] objectives according to their particular conception of the common good. (Herman 2017, 743–744)

Parties are often criticized for disempowering citizens and calls are made for shrinking their influence compared to forms of participatory and direct democracy. As Budge (2006) observes, however, representative and direct democracy are not necessarily opposites. By presenting alternative policy platforms to voters, modern political parties transformed oligarchic representation mechanisms into a form of 'direct policy voting—but in contrast to "direct democracy" as classically and currently conceived, this is voting on a

package of policies rather than on each individual policy within the package'
(Budge 2006, 8; similarly Clark 1998).

In the universal republic, political parties would perform the role they
perform in existing parliamentary democracies. For the reasons that have
been briefly summarized, it would be desirable for such transnational political parties to be programmatic parties organized around conceptions of the
common good, as opposed to highly contingent coalitions driven purely by
compromises reached in the pursuit of particularistic interests. However, ultimately it would be up to citizens to determine, via their votes and political
engagement, which kind of parties would be prevalent in global political institutions. Based on the experience of existing party systems, we can expect
a global party system to reflect a complex mix of interests, identities, and
ideals of justice, but the precise nature of the mix would be the outcome of
contingent political processes.

What are the prospects for the formation of a global party system? The
role of actual and potential transnational parties in international governance has received a substantial amount of attention (Roth 1977; Fraser
and Salzberg 1979; Goldman 1983; Taylor 1986; Chase-Dunn et al. 2006;
Sehm-Patomaki and Ulvila 2007; Archibugi and Held 2011; Patomäki 2011;
White and Ypi 2016; Lefkofridi and Katsanidou 2018; Chase-Dunn and
Almeida 2020; Bonotti and Stojanović 2022; Kinski 2022; Norman and Wolfs
2022; Senninger, Bischof, and Ezrow 2022). According to Zürn (2018, 240),
'there is no sign that party-like groupings are developing at the international level or that any such groupings are able to aggregate and bundle
societal interests across issues in coherent ideological positions, or have
the power to even out representational imbalances'. This assessment may
too negative. It is true that transnational party formation faces additional
challenges compared to domestic parties (White and Ypi 2016, 185–208).
However, there are two reasons for regarding a global party system as feasible. The first is that relatively cohesive parties or party-like groupings tend to
form when the institutional context offers opportunities and incentives. The
examples of the European Parliament and the International Labour Organization discussed in section 6.5 are particularly relevant. Second, in the
contemporary global system there are already social movements defined by
ideology and generalized interests that could function as aggregation points
for transnational party formation under the right political opportunity structure (Cabrera 2004, 99–100). These transnational movements are to be found
across the ideological spectrum, from progressive (Chase-Dunn et al. 2006;
Bronfenbrenner 2007; Chase-Dunn and Reese 2007; Della Porta 2007; Bieler
et al. 2015; Valdez 2019, 153–175; Gardner, Carvalho, and Valenstain 2022;

Della Porta and Portos 2023) to conservative (Bob 2012; Stewart 2020; Kalm and Meeuwisse 2023; Wojczewski 2024) and even authoritarian (Albanese and Del Hierro 2016; Hackenesch and Bader 2020). The development of transnational party structure is by no means guaranteed, but there seems to be no compelling reason to regard it as unfeasible.

7.6 Concluding remarks

As pointed out in the chapter introduction, polycentric perspectives pose a range of challenges to the transposition of classical democratic institutions from the national to the global level. I have addressed only two contested dimensions: the democratic quality of non-electoral representation and, in more depth, the implications of a non-hierarchical multiplicity of governance sites for democratic decision-making. The analysis has attempted to provide a systematic and abstract framework for thinking of the democratic costs of issue-specific governance, followed by an evidence-driven estimate of how serious such costs are in relation to concrete global policy goals that governments and other agents have committed themselves to pursue. My assessment is that (1) the democratic costs of polycentricity are substantial, and (2) well-known mechanisms of parliamentary and partisan contestation, deliberation, and aggregation would mitigate them considerably, if they could be transported beyond the national level. As we saw in Part I, we have reasons to be optimistic that they can.

8
Conclusions

In 1964, a year after making his 'I have a dream' speech at the March on Washington, Martin Luther King, Jr. wrote down his thoughts on world peace: 'As we grow and come to see the oneness of mankind and the geographical oneness of the world, made possible by man's scientific and technological ingenuity, more and more we are going to have to try to see our oneness in terms of brotherhood. This does not mean that everyone has to agree at every point. There can be a world government where diversity can exist and this would lessen many tensions that we face today, and it would also enable everybody to understand that we are clothed in a single garment of destiny, and whatever affects one nation directly in the world, indirectly affects all' (King, Jr. 1964/2012, 149). Dr King's statement is a stirring call for action, but it can also be read as containing an empirical hypothesis that demands systematic scrutiny and falsification. This book is an attempt to make some progress towards that extraordinarily challenging task. In planning and writing it, I have been mindful of a warning given by Thomas Weiss: 'The surest way to secure classification as a crackpot is to mention a world government as either a hypothetical or, worse yet, desirable outcome' (Weiss 2009, 261). But I also heeded another warning he gave on the same occasion: 'By not even struggling to imagine a fundamentally different system, we make the continuation of the current lackluster one inevitable' (Weiss 2009, 263).

These remarks were part of the address that Professor Weiss delivered as newly elected President of the International Studies Association, and I suspect that they were targeted mainly at the association's many members who see themselves primarily as empirical researchers of international relations. An audience of political philosophers might reasonably be thought to be more forgiving towards colleagues seriously debating the desirability of a world state. But such difference highlights the conundrum discussed in the Introduction. Political theorists, like IR scholars during the heyday of the 'classical' approach, are willing to talk about world government, but they usually do so in a way that does not reflect systematic engagement with the empirical assumptions that underlie their stances. By contrast, empirically oriented political scientists and IR scholars have easier access to the methods,

The Universal Republic. Mathias Koenig-Archibugi, Oxford University Press. © Mathias Koenig-Archibugi (2024).
DOI: 10.1093/9780198921158.003.0008

tools, and data needed to subject such assumptions to systematic scrutiny, but they typically avoid talking about world government, possibly for fear of the consequences mentioned by Weiss. Building a bridge between these two scholarly communities means relinquishing the safety of the solid ground on which each of them dwells. The risk is to offer analyses that are deficient in both philosophical and empirical rigour. It is of course up to the reader to decide whether this book has fallen into that void.

Substantively, the analyses presented in the preceding chapters failed to find solid empirical support for several of the legitimate worries associated with the prospect of a world state. We saw that, if a world state were established and endowed with democratic institutions, the longevity of its democracy might be quite respectable and comparable to those of a typical existing state, taking into account various cultural, economic, and social factors that might undermine it. Furthermore, simulations suggest that the level of democracy of a world state might be reasonably high. It would be less successful in meeting more stringent participatory, deliberative, liberal, and egalitarian criteria, but not more so than the average state that exists today. The analysis summarized in this book also suggests that the population of a world state would not be substantially more diverse in terms of policy-relevant values than the average state, and that it would not entail a higher risk of producing persistent minorities. Levels of dissatisfaction with the outcome of majoritarian decision-making would be similar in the world as a whole and in the average country, and there are even reasons to think that in a global democracy satisfaction would be spread somewhat more equally among individuals.

The analysis also provided some evidence about the disadvantages of alternative models. Intergovernmental decision-making suppresses the representation of some important domestic groups that would rather align with foreign like-minded groups than with their own government. A plurality of issue-specific sites of governance creates major obstacles to the aggregation of democratic preferences across issues and may perversely lead to policy outcomes that few desire. Given the substantial drawbacks of alternative models, my conclusion is that the universal republic seems to offer a quite attractive solution to the problem of promoting democratic self-government in a diverse and yet interdependent world.

The evidence considered in the book provided some insights also into whether the universal republic would be achievable. States have already delegated a remarkable degree of authority to international institutions and provided them with some democratic features, while insisting that 'democracy' *should* apply to international relations—this suggests that further reforms are feasible, although not necessarily likely. Some expect that publics across the world would stop their politicians if the latter attempted to give away too much sovereignty, but international survey data does not reveal widespread public opposition to strengthening international institutions, especially when democratic accountability mechanisms are added to them. Participants in social movements show sympathy to the idea of democratic world government when asked, but this has not yet generated sustained, large-scale transnational campaigns.[1] Would they succeed in gaining the support of sufficiently large sections of the public if they tried? The evidence presented here does not offer any guarantee of success, but nor has it uncovered reasons why they would be destined to fail.

The message of the book is ultimately anti-determinist. By arguing that a democratic world state is neither inevitable nor infeasible, and that regarding it as the best solution to the global democratic deficit is neither obvious nor obsolete, it may help open spaces for political deliberation and contestation that risk being foreclosed by insufficiently examined assumptions and inhibitions. I hope that this message feels liberating for scholars, students, and—perhaps, one day—politically engaged citizens. It's up to us.

---

[1] The closest is the Campaign for a UN Parliamentary Assembly (Vallinoto 2014; Bummel 2019).

APPENDICES

List of democratic regimes

Table A.1 Democratic spells included in the survival analyses

Country	Start of democratic spell	End of democratic spell or last observed year
Albania	2005	2020
Argentina	1918	1929
Argentina	1964	1965
Argentina	1984	2020
Armenia	1990	1994
Australia	1900	2020
Austria	1921	1932
Austria	1945	2020
Bangladesh	1992	2001
Barbados	1960	2020
Belarus	1992	1995
Belgium	1900	2020
Benin	1992	2018
Bhutan	2009	2020
Bolivia	1986	2018
Bosnia and Herzegovina	1997	2020
Botswana	1967	2020
Brazil	1987	2020
Bulgaria	1991	2020
Burkina Faso	1999	2014
Burkina Faso	2016	2020
Canada	1921	2020
Cape Verde	1991	2020
Chile	1959	1972
Chile	1990	2020
Colombia	1991	2020
Comoros	2006	2014
Costa Rica	1950	2020
Croatia	2000	2020
Cyprus	1974	2020
Czechoslovakia	1920	1948
Czechoslovakia/Czechia	1990	2020

Continued

Table A.1 *Continued*

Country	Start of democratic spell	End of democratic spell or last observed year
Denmark	1902	2020
Dominican Republic	1982	1989
Dominican Republic	1996	2020
Ecuador	1980	2020
El Salvador	1999	2020
Estonia	1920	1933
Estonia	1990	1991
Estonia	1993	2020
Fiji	1970	1986
Fiji	1993	1999
Finland	1918	2020
France	1900	2020
Georgia	2004	2020
Germany	1919	1932
Germany	1949	2020
Ghana	1996	2020
Greece	1975	2020
Guatemala	1997	2020
Guinea-Bissau	2015	2020
Guyana	1998	2020
Honduras	1991	2008
Hungary	1990	2017
Iceland	1904	2020
India	1952	2018
Indonesia	1999	2020
Ireland	1922	2020
Israel	1949	2020
Italy	1947	2020
Ivory Coast	2016	2019
Jamaica	1955	1976
Jamaica	1984	2020
Japan	1952	2020
Kosovo	2002	2004
Kosovo	2010	2020
Latvia	1923	1933
Latvia	1990	2020
Lesotho	2002	2020
Liberia	2006	2020
Lithuania	1921	1926
Lithuania	1990	2020
Luxembourg	1920	2020
Madagascar	1994	2000
Malawi	1995	1999
Malawi	2010	2018
Malawi	2020	2020
Maldives	2009	2012

Country	Start of democratic spell	End of democratic spell or last observed year
Maldives	2019	2020
Mali	1993	2011
Mali	2014	2018
Malta	1948	1957
Malta	1963	2020
Mauritius	1968	2020
Mexico	1996	2020
Moldova	1992	2004
Moldova	2010	2020
Mongolia	1991	2020
Montenegro	2010	2012
Namibia	1995	2020
Nepal	2014	2020
Netherlands	1918	2020
New Zealand	1900	2020
Nicaragua	1990	2006
Niger	1993	1995
Niger	2000	2008
Niger	2011	2020
Nigeria	2012	2020
North Macedonia	1999	2011
North Macedonia	2017	2020
Norway	1906	2020
Palestine/West Bank	2003	2006
Panama	1991	2020
Papua New Guinea	1974	1996
Papua New Guinea	2002	2003
Paraguay	1993	2020
Peru	1981	1991
Peru	2001	2020
Philippines	1988	2003
Philippines	2010	2017
Poland	1920	1925
Poland	1990	2020
Portugal	1976	2020
Romania	1991	2020
Sao Tome and Principe	1991	2020
Senegal	1988	2020
Serbia	2001	2012
Seychelles	2016	2020
Sierra Leone	2003	2020
Slovakia	1994	2020
Slovenia	1990	2020
Solomon Islands	1979	1999

Continued

Table A.1 *Continued*

Country	Start of democratic spell	End of democratic spell or last observed year
Solomon Islands	2007	2020
South Africa	1995	2020
South Korea	1988	2020
Spain	1932	1936
Spain	1978	2020
Sri Lanka	1947	1981
Sri Lanka	1995	2004
Sri Lanka	2015	2020
Suriname	1950	1979
Suriname	1992	2020
Sweden	1922	2020
Switzerland	1900	2020
Taiwan	1996	2020
Tanzania	1996	2000
Tanzania	2010	2014
Thailand	1998	2005
Timor-Leste	2002	2020
Trinidad and Tobago	1962	2020
Tunisia	2012	2020
Turkey	1966	1979
Turkey	1988	2012
Ukraine	1994	1997
Ukraine	2006	2010
United Kingdom	1919	2020
United States of America	1921	2020
Uruguay	1919	1932
Uruguay	1939	1972
Uruguay	1985	2020
Vanuatu	1980	2020
Venezuela	1963	2002
Zambia	2000	2013

Sources of data

Sources for Chapters 3 and 4

Ethnic diversity: To measure levels of ethnic diversity, I mostly rely on the Composition of Religious and Ethnic Groups Project (CREG) dataset (v.1.02) (Nardulli et al. 2012). CREG provides data on the sizes of ethnic and religious groups in most countries of the world between 1945 and 2013. To capture the degree of ethnic diversity, I followed most of the literature (Alesina et al. 2003; Fearon 2003; Wimmer, Cederman, and Min 2009) and calculated an ethnic fractionalization/diversity index that equals 1 minus the Herfindahl index (after dropping duplicates present in the original CREG dataset). Specifically

$$(1) \; \textit{Ethnic diversity}_j = 1 - \sum_{i=1}^{N} S_{ij}^2$$

where s_{ij} is the share of group i ($i = 1 \dots N$) in country j. The Herfindahl index expresses the probability (from 0 to 1) that two randomly chosen people in the same country belong to the same ethnic group. If all individuals were to belong to the same group, the index would be 1. If each individual constituted a distinct ethnic group, the index would be 0. The value of the index is subtracted from 1 in order to express the degree of diversity, with 1 indicating the highest possible degree of diversity.

Compared to other datasets of ethnic heterogeneity, CREG has the advantage of capturing changes over time, providing yearly observations between 1945 (or year of independence) and 2013. Since no time-varying data for the period before 1945 exist, I assign the value for the earliest year available for each country to all preceding years (for instance, for the United States all years between 1900 and 1945 have the value that the country had in 1945). However, given territorial changes and population movements in Eastern Europe as a result of World War II, I used the Herfindahl score provided by Kosinski (1969, 396) for Albania, Bulgaria, Czechoslovakia, Hungary, Poland, Romania, and Yugoslavia in the years prior to 1945. I also extend the value of 2013 to subsequent years for all countries. Ethnic group estimates for certain countries (Cameroon, France, India, Kosovo, Montenegro, Mozambique, and Papua New Guinea) are missing in the CREG. For those countries, I use the time-invariant ethnic fractionalization data provided by Alesina et al. (2003).

To calculate the level of ethnic diversity of the world as a whole, I identified the size of all ethnic groups as reported in the CREG for the most recent year with data (2013), determined their share of the total world population, then calculated a global fractionalization index by applying formula (1). As detailed above, I used Alesina et al. (2003) for a few countries not included in the CREG. Ethnic groups are not merged across countries but are treated as separate groups even when they have the same name. For instance, the Fulani of Mali are treated as a separate ethnic group from the Fulani in Cameroon and those of several other countries.

Religious diversity: To measure the level of religious diversity, I use the Religious Characteristics of States (RCS) dataset (v.2.0) (Brown and James 2018). This provides annual data on religious demographics for ninety-seven denominations and nearly all states in the world, starting as early as 1800. I calculated a religious fractionalization index based on the Herfindahl index. The categories used for the calculation are the tier-2 categories in the RCS codebook, i.e. neither 1,000 (Christians) nor 1,410 (Lutherans), but 1,400 (Protestants).[1] I used data on absolute sizes of these groups to determine their relative shares in a country, to which formula (1) is then applied. The value for the last year in the dataset, 2015, is extended to subsequent years.

To calculate the level of religious fractionalization of the world as a whole, I calculated the sum of adherents of each religious denomination across all countries in the RCS dataset and their share of the world population in the most recent year with data (2015), and used these shares to calculate the one-minus-Herfindahl index. Adherents of a religion are treated as members of the same group irrespective of which country they live in.

Linguistic diversity: To measure linguistic diversity, I rely on the data on linguistic fractionalization provided by Alesina et al. (2003), which captures the language demographics of countries around the year 2000. Contrary to ethnic and religious groups, to my knowledge there is no time-varying dataset on linguistic groups. A linguistic fractionalization index based on formula (1) applied to the Alesina et al. (2003) data will therefore be used for all years covered in my analysis. The measure captures *native* speakers and does not consider whether individuals speak a lingua franca and/or a foreign language.

The calculation of the linguistic fractionalization of the world as a whole followed the same procedure as for religious fractionalization, using the data on language groups provided by Alesina et al. (2003). Native speakers of a language living in different countries are treated as one single language group—for instance, English speakers in Canada and Australia, or Spanish speakers in various Latin American countries.

Income inequality: The measurement of income inequality relies on two sources. I use the mean estimated Gini index of disposable income for all countries and years that are available in the Standardized World Income Inequality Database (SWIID v.9.0) (Solt 2020). The value for the last year in the dataset (2017) is extended to 2018–20. For country-years that are not available in SWIID, I use the dataset from Clio Infra (Van Zanden et al. 2014) and, for Germany between 1907–44, from Gómez León and De Jong (2019). Clio Infra data on Gini are available at twenty-year intervals between 1890 and 1950 and at ten-year intervals afterwards. The years in between are obtained via linear interpolation. The correlation between the mean SWIID disposable-income Gini and the interpolated Clio Infra Gini is high (0.87), which makes me confident that the latter measure is suitable to cover the country-years for which SWIID data are not available. For the world as a whole, I use the global inequality estimate from Milanovic (2021a) of a Gini coefficient of .63 in 2021.

Population: The 2020 version of the Maddison Project provided the data on total population (Bolt and van Zanden 2020). The National Material Capabilities (NMC) data set (v.5.0) provides data for some countries missing in the Maddison Project: Papua New Guinea, Fiji, and the Maldives; Estonia, Lithuania, and Latvia before World War II; and separate data for West Germany and East Germany (Singer, Bremer, and Stuckey 1972; Greig and Enterline 2017). Data on the population of the world are from United Nations (2019) and refer to 2019.

Land area: Data are provided by the CShapes (v.2.0) dataset (Schvitz et al. 2022). The value for the world is the sum of the land area in 2019 of all countries in the dataset.

Prior statehood: This variable is constructed by subtracting the year in which the polity acquired the status of independent state from the start year of the country's democratic spell. The year of state tenure is provided by the States System Membership dataset of the COW project (Correlates of War Project 2017b) and democratic spells are those identified in the ERT

---

[1] There are two exceptions: (1) categories ending in 001 (unspecified members of tier 1) are included (e.g. 1,001 unspecified Christians); (2) 1,100 and 7,900 are not included because, despite their tier-2 code, they are aggregation of other tier-2 categories.

dataset (Maerz et al. 2021), with the exceptions noted in Chapter 3. Based on the assumption that the universal republic would be created simultaneously as a state and as a democracy, the value for the world state is set at 0.

Land borders: Data on the number of land borders a country has with other countries in a given year comes from the COW Direct Contiguity Data (v.3.20) (Stinnett et al. 2002; Correlates of War Project 2017a). The value for the last year (2016) is extended to subsequent years. As the simulation assumes universal membership in the world state, the number of its borders is set to be zero.[2]

Income per capita and *growth of income per capita*: Data are from the 2020 version of the Maddison Project dataset (Bolt and van Zanden 2020). For a few countries with no data in the Maddison Project dataset, I used the following datasets. Data for Poland between 1918 and 1947, Fiji, Papua New Guinea, Ethiopia, Eritrea, West Germany, and East Germany come from Miller (2015); data for Estonia, Latvia, and Lithuania between the world wars come from Norkus and Markevičiūtė (2021) (missing values interpolated); and data for Guyana and Suriname come from the World Bank, as recorded in Graham and Tucker (2019). The variable measuring growth of GDP per capita expresses the percentage change compared to the previous year. Data for World as a whole in 2019 are as reported in World Bank (2021).

Education: Data on education comes mostly from a variable in the V-Dem (v.11.1) dataset that gives the average years of education in the total population aged 15 years and older, which in turn is based on the Clio Infra database (Coppedge et al. 2021). For missing countries, I used a variable indicating total years of schooling, population aged 15–64, from the Barro and Lee (2013) and Lee and Lee (2016) datasets. Missing years in the Barro and Lee datasets were filled in by linear interpolation and the value of the last year (2010) was extended to the subsequent years. The value for the world refers to the year 2018 and equals the average years of education across the sample of countries weighted by country population.

Resource dependence: The measure is based on the value of petroleum, coal, natural gas, and metals production per capita assembled by Haber and Menaldo (2011) and included in the V-Dem dataset (v.11.1). These data are divided by GDP per capita to obtain a measure of the economic dependence of a country's income on the production of natural resources. The value for the last year (2006) is extended to subsequent years. The value for the world refers to the year 2006 and equals the average natural resource dependence of countries weighted by country population.

Religious composition: The lasso selection procedure is provided with the percentage of population belonging to major religious groups to be found in substantial numbers across several countries: Catholics, extended Protestants, Orthodox, Muslim, Buddhist, and non-religious people. Data are from the RCS dataset (v.2.0) (Brown and James 2018). The value of the last year with data (2015) is extended to later years. The value for the world refers to the year 2015 and equals the average percentage for each religion across countries weighted by country population.

Democratic environment: The overall level of democracy in the international environment is measured by taking the average level of the V-Dem electoral democracy index of all countries in a given year, weighted by the Composite Index of National Capability (CINC) index of each country, from the NMC dataset (v.5.0) (Singer, Bremer, and Stuckey 1972; Greig and Enterline 2017). The CINC consists of six indicators: total population, urban population, energy consumption, iron and steel production, military expenditure, and military personnel. The last

---

[2] Readers are advised to change that number before using the dataset if contact with extraterrestrial civilizations is established after this book is published, if they wish to test the hypothesis formulated by US President Ronald Reagan (1987) that 'some alien threat from outside this world' may be needed for humanity to overcome its internal antagonisms (quoted by Bummel 2021, 328).

value in the NMC v.5.0 (2012) is extended to subsequent years. The democratic environment variable for the world is the 2020 score of this variable.

Sources for Chapter 6

The ILO voting data used in section 6.5 have been coded manually from the printed *Records of Proceedings* of each session of the International Labour Conference between 1996 and 2006. The *Records of Proceedings* are published by the International Labour Office. The remaining variables used in the estimation of the models shown in Table A.6 are from the following sources.

Electoral democracy index, from Coppedge et al. (2021); Pemstein et al. (2021).
Income per capita (logged), from Bolt and van Zanden (2020) as provided by Coppedge et al. (2021).
Labour rights respected, from Cingranelli and Richards (2010).
Left-wing government, from Cruz, Keefer, and Scartascini (2021).
General strikes, from Banks and Wilson (2023).
Economic globalization, from Dreher (2006) and Gygli et al. (2019).

Goodness-of-fit statistics

Table A.2 Goodness-of-fit measures for lasso Cox models (sections 3.3 and 3.4)

Model	Deviance	Deviance ratio	Number of observations
Main model (Figure 3.1)			
Training set	0.082	0.095	3,429
Testing set	0.084	0.074	864
Main model with forced entry of constraint variables (Figure 3.2)			
Training set	0.077	0.121	3,171
Testing set	0.087	0.073	811
Start in 2050 (Figure 3.3)			
Training set	0.082	0.095	3,429
Testing set	0.084	0.074	864
Superdiversity (Figure 3.4)			
Training set	0.081	0.101	3,087
Testing set	0.084	0.081	797
Health equality (Figure 3.5)			
Training set	0.072	0.190	3,116
Testing set	0.082	0.100	802
Freedom of movement (Figure 3.6)			
Training set	0.080	0.121	3,060
Testing set	0.083	0.086	794
Decentralization (Figure 3.7)			
Training set	0.082	0.095	3,429
Testing set	0.083	0.080	864
Judicial review (Figure 3.8)			
Training set	0.082	0.095	3,429
Testing set	0.083	0.078	864
Democratic unevenness (Figure 3.9)			
Training set	0.082	0.120	3,159
Testing set	0.082	0.129	812

Table A.3 Goodness-of-fit measures for lasso linear models (sections 4.1 and 6.2)

Outcome variable	MSE	R^2	Number of observations
Electoral democracy			
Training set	0.029	0.571	114
Testing set	0.041	0.261	38
Electoral democracy (forced)			
Training set	0.025	0.631	110
Testing set	0.042	0.250	37
Participatory democracy			
Training set	0.014	0.668	110
Testing set	0.024	0.251	38
Participatory democracy (forced)			
Training set	0.014	0.671	110
Testing set	0.024	0.254	37
Deliberative democracy			
Training set	0.029	0.553	114
Testing set	0.039	0.317	38
Deliberative democracy (forced)			
Training set	0.025	0.609	110
Testing set	0.042	0.287	37
Liberal democracy			
Training set	0.027	0.613	114
Testing set	0.038	0.376	38
Liberal democracy (forced)			
Training set	0.024	0.666	110
Testing set	0.041	0.348	37
Egalitarian democracy			
Training set	0.021	0.632	114
Testing set	0.028	0.465	38
Egalitarian democracy (forced)			
Training set	0.019	0.678	110
Testing set	0.029	0.450	37

Note: The analysis of electoral democracy is discussed in section 4.1, the other varieties of democracy are discussed in section 6.2. The reported statistics are based on post-selection coefficients from lasso with cross-validation. 'Forced' refers to models where lasso was forced to include six presumed constraints variables: ethnic diversity, religious diversity, linguistic diversity, income inequality, population, and land area.

Regression tables

Table A.4 Cox regression results on risk of democratic breakdown

	(1)	(2)	(3)	(4)
Prior statehood	−0.002	−0.002	−0.006	−0.003
	(0.003)	(0.003)	(0.004)	(0.003)
Ethnic diversity	−0.379		0.273	−0.004
	(0.998)		(1.099)	(1.070)
Religious diversity	2.385*		2.282	2.573**
	(0.980)		(1.204)	(0.992)
Linguistic diversity	−0.416		−1.054	−0.695
	(1.021)		(1.152)	(1.071)
Income inequality	−0.021			−0.028
	(0.019)			(0.019)
Population (ln)	0.068	0.125	0.092	0.035
	(0.154)	(0.145)	(0.134)	(0.159)
Land area (ln)	0.047	−0.057	−0.078	0.058
	(0.130)	(0.126)	(0.150)	(0.129)
Number of land borders	0.120	0.139*	0.239**	0.129
	(0.076)	(0.064)	(0.087)	(0.077)
Income per capita	−0.000***	−0.000***	−0.000**	−0.000***
	(0.000)	(0.000)	(0.000)	(0.000)
Economic growth	−7.526***	−7.508***	−7.850**	−7.142**
	(2.182)	(2.166)	(2.468)	(2.232)
Education	0.043	0.046	0.090	0.043
	(0.107)	(0.093)	(0.104)	(0.108)
Resource dependence	0.835	2.853	−0.812	1.056
	(3.825)	(3.261)	(3.827)	(3.753)
Catholics (%)	0.014	0.011	0.021	0.015
	(0.015)	(0.012)	(0.015)	(0.015)
Protestants (%)	−0.008	0.003	−0.001	−0.011
	(0.015)	(0.014)	(0.013)	(0.015)
Christian Orthodox (%)	0.024	0.018	0.038*	0.024
	(0.016)	(0.014)	(0.015)	(0.017)

Continued

Table A.4 *Continued*

	(1)	(2)	(3)	(4)
Muslims (%)	0.017	0.011	0.026*	0.015
	(0.013)	(0.012)	(0.013)	(0.013)
Buddhists (%)	0.018	0.020	0.049**	0.016
	(0.016)	(0.015)	(0.016)	(0.017)
Not religious (%)	0.017	0.037	0.048	0.017
	(0.023)	(0.022)	(0.025)	(0.023)
Democratic international environment	2.854	3.417	1.053	3.805
	(2.270)	(2.206)	(2.230)	(2.276)
Superdiversity		1.147		
		(2.174)		
Educational equality			0.303	
			(0.305)	
Health equality			−1.048**	
			(0.323)	
Freedom of movement				−2.079*
				(0.949)
Observations	3832	3832	3918	3832

Standard errors in parentheses. * $p < 0.05$, ** $p < 0.01$, *** $p < 0.001$

Table A.5 Cox regression results on risk of democratic breakdown (continued)

	(1)	(2)	(3)
Prior statehood	0.003	−0.002	−0.004
	(0.009)	(0.003)	(0.003)
Ethnic diversity	−4.413	−0.682	−0.276
	(3.734)	(1.034)	(0.921)
Religious diversity	5.003	2.161*	2.478*
	(3.532)	(0.985)	(1.073)
Linguistic diversity	2.719	−0.103	−0.789
	(3.312)	(1.057)	(0.791)
Income inequality	0.015	−0.018	−0.027
	(0.055)	(0.019)	(0.016)
Population (ln)	0.231	0.059	0.108
	(0.577)	(0.159)	(0.122)
Land area (ln)	0.041	0.095	−0.156
	(0.651)	(0.132)	(0.127)
Number of land borders	−0.047	0.121	0.201***
	(0.153)	(0.079)	(0.057)
Income per capita	−0.000*	−0.000***	−0.000***
	(0.000)	(0.000)	(0.000)
Economic growth	−2.739	−7.304**	−7.788***
	(5.060)	(2.223)	(2.322)
Education	0.075	0.089	−0.017
	(0.176)	(0.111)	(0.088)
Resource dependence	24.232**	0.553	−0.968
	(8.472)	(4.062)	(3.927)
Catholics (%)	0.063	0.015	0.017
	(0.035)	(0.015)	(0.012)
Protestants (%)	−0.014	−0.009	−0.005
	(0.032)	(0.015)	(0.013)
Christian Orthodox (%)	0.069	0.021	0.023
	(0.038)	(0.016)	(0.015)
Muslims (%)	0.054*	0.016	0.016
	(0.027)	(0.013)	(0.011)
Buddhists (%)	0.070	0.016	0.010
	(0.042)	(0.015)	(0.015)
Not religious (%)	0.089	0.015	0.042*
	(0.052)	(0.023)	(0.021)
Democratic international environment	1.304	3.280	0.431
	(11.324)	(2.461)	(2.549)
Emancipatory Values Index	−2.080		
	(9.058)		
Judicial review		−0.130	
		(0.184)	
Decentralization		−0.680	
		(0.656)	
Election unevenness			−0.602***
			(0.123)
Observations	1926	3832	3795

Standard errors in parentheses. * $p < 0.05$, ** $p < 0.01$, *** $p < 0.001$

Table A.6 Correlates of voting cohesion of tripartite national delegations in ILO

	(1)	(2)	(3)	(4)
Electoral democracy	−1.569***	−1.635***	−1.324***	−1.396***
	(0.171)	(0.310)	(0.200)	(0.258)
Income per capita		−0.000		−0.000
		(0.000)		(0.000)
Government ideology		0.172***		0.170***
		(0.044)		(0.048)
General strikes		0.146*		0.098
		(0.068)		(0.077)
Labour rights protected		0.148*		0.142
		(0.073)		(0.073)
Economic globalization		−0.007		−0.003
		(0.006)		(0.004)
Constant			1.591***	1.289***
			(0.126)	(0.177)
N	10,306	4941	10,345	5057

Independent variable: cohesion of national tripartite delegations in individual ILO votes between 1966 and 2006. Models 1 and 2 include country fixed effects; models 3 and 4 include random effects with robust standard errors. Standard errors in parentheses. * $p < 0.05$, ** $p < 0.01$, *** $p < 0.001$

References

Abizadeh, Arash. 2005. 'Does collective identity presuppose an other? On the alleged incoherence of global solidarity'. *American Political Science Review* 99 (1):45–60.

Abizadeh, Arash. 2008. 'Democratic theory and border coercion: No right to unilaterally control your own borders'. *Political Theory* 36 (1):37–65.

Abizadeh, Arash. 2010. 'Democratic legitimacy and state coercion: A reply to David Miller'. *Political Theory* 38 (1):121–130.

Abizadeh, Arash. 2012. 'On the demos and its kin: Nationalism, democracy, and the boundary problem'. *American Political Science Review* 106 (4):867–882.

Abizadeh, Arash. 2021a. 'Counter-majoritarian democracy: Persistent minorities, federalism, and the power of numbers'. *American Political Science Review* 115 (3):742–756.

Abizadeh, Arash. 2021b. 'Representation, bicameralism, political equality, and sortition: Reconstituting the second chamber as a randomly selected assembly'. *Perspectives on Politics* 19 (3):791–806.

Acton, John E. E. D. 1877/2007. 'The history of freedom in antiquity'. In *The Spirit of the Age: Victorian Essays*, edited by Gertrude Himmelfarb, 227–247. New Haven: Yale University Press.

Afnan, Maximillian. 2023. 'Global public reason: Too thick or too thin'. *Critical Review of International Social and Political Philosophy*. Published online 24 March. doi: 10.1080/13698230.2023.2193930.

Agné, Hans. 2010. 'Why democracy must be global: Self-founding and democratic intervention'. *International Theory* 2 (3):381–409.

Agné, Hans. 2022. *Democratism: Explaining International Politics with Democracy Beyond the State*. Cheltenham: Edward Elgar.

Agné, Hans, Lisa Maria Dellmuth, and Jonas Tallberg. 2015. 'Does stakeholder involvement foster democratic legitimacy in international organizations? An empirical assessment of a normative theory'. *Review of International Organizations* 10 (4):465–488.

Ahmed, Syud Amer, Enis Barış, Delfin S. Go, Hans Lofgren, Israel Osorio-Rodarte, and Karen Thierfelder. 2018. 'Assessing the global poverty effects of antimicrobial resistance'. *World Development* 111 (November):148–160.

Albanese, Matteo, and Pablo Del Hierro. 2016. *Transnational Fascism in the Twentieth Century: Spain, Italy and the Global Neo-fascist Network*. London: Bloomsbury Publishing.

Albert, Mathias. 2014. 'World state: Brunkhorst's "cosmopolitan state" and varieties of differentiation'. *Social & Legal Studies* 23 (4):517–531.

Albert, Mathias, Gorm Harste, Heikki Patomäki, and Knud Erik Jørgensen. 2012. 'Introduction: World state futures'. *Cooperation and Conflict* 47 (2):145–156.

Albert, Mathias, and Rudolf Stichweh, eds. 2007. *Weltstaat und Weltstaatlichkeit: Beobachtungen globaler politischer Strukturbildung*. Wiesbaden: VS Verlag für Sozialwissenschaften.

Aldington, Richard, ed. 1927. *Letters of Voltaire and Frederick the Great*. New York: Brentano's.

Aldrich, John H. 2011. *Why Parties? A Second Look*. Chicago: University of Chicago Press.

Alesina, Alberto, Reza Baqir, and William Easterly. 1999. 'Public goods and ethnic divisions'. *Quarterly Journal of Economics* 114 (4):1243–1284.

Alesina, Alberto, Arnaud Devleeschauwer, William Easterly, Sergio Kurlat, and Romain Wacziarg. 2003. 'Fractionalization'. *Journal of Economic Growth* 8 (2):155–194.

Altman, David, Federico Rojas-de-Galarreta, and Francisco Urdinez. 2021. 'An interactive model of democratic peace'. *Journal of Peace Research* 58 (3):384–398.

Ambedkar, B. R. 1936/2016. *Annihilation of Caste*. London: Verso.

Americans Talk Issues Foundation. 1993. Americans Talk Issues Foundation Poll: March 1993. Survey conducted by The Telephone Center. Ithaca: Roper Center for Public Opinion Research, Cornell University. doi:10.25940/ROPER-31106103.

Anderson, Carl C., Manfred Denich, Anne Warchold, Jürgen P. Kropp, and Prajal Pradhan. 2022. 'A systems model of SDG target influence on the 2030 Agenda for Sustainable Development'. *Sustainability Science* 17 (4):1459–1472.

An-Naim, Abdullahi Ahmed. 2021. *Decolonizing Human Rights*. Cambridge: Cambridge University Press.

Ansell, Ben W., and David J. Samuels. 2014. *Inequality and Democratization*. Cambridge: Cambridge University Press.

Appiah, Kwame Anthony. 2007. *Cosmopolitanism: Ethics in a World of Strangers*. London: Penguin Books.

Archibugi, Daniele. 1993. 'The reform of the UN and cosmopolitan democracy: A critical review'. *Journal of Peace Research* 30 (3):301.

Archibugi, Daniele. 1995. 'Immanuel Kant, cosmopolitan law and peace'. *European Journal of International Relations* 1 (4):429–456.

Archibugi, Daniele. 1997. 'So what if democracies don't fight each other?' *Peace Review* 9 (3):379–384.

Archibugi, Daniele. 2008. *A Global Commonwealth of Citizens: Toward Cosmopolitan Democracy*. Princeton: Princeton University Press.

Archibugi, Daniele. 2012. 'From peace between democracies to global democracy'. In *Global Democracy: Normative and Empirical Perspectives*, edited by Daniele Archibugi, Mathias Koenig-Archibugi, and Raffaele Marchetti, 254–273. Cambridge: Cambridge University Press.

Archibugi, Daniele, and Marco Cellini. 2017. 'The internal and external levers to achieve global democracy'. *Global Policy* 8 (S6):65–77.

Archibugi, Daniele, and David Held. 2011. 'Cosmopolitan democracy: Paths and agents'. *Ethics & International Affairs* 25 (4):433–461.

Archibugi, Daniele, Mathias Koenig-Archibugi, and Raffaele Marchetti. 2012. 'Introduction: Mapping global democracy'. In *Global Democracy: Normative and Empirical Perspectives*, edited by Daniele Archibugi, Mathias Koenig-Archibugi, and Raffaele Marchetti, 1–21. Cambridge: Cambridge University Press.

Arel-Bundock, Vincent. 2017. 'The unintended consequences of bilateralism: Treaty shopping and international tax policy'. *International Organization* 71 (2):349–371.

Arendt, Hannah. 1970. 'Karl Jaspers: Citizen of the world?' In *Men in Dark Times*, 81–94. San Diego: Harcourt Brace.

Aristotle. 1995. 'Politics'. In *Complete Works of Aristotle*, Volume 2. The Revised Oxford Translation, edited by Jonathan Barnes, 1986–2129. Princeton: Princeton University Press.

Aron, Raymond. 1961/2002. 'The dawn of universal history'. In *The Dawn Of Universal History: Selected Essays from a Witness to the Twentieth Century*, 463–486. New York: Basic Books.

Aron, Raymond. 1966. *Peace and War: A Theory of International Relations*. London: Weidenfels and Nicholson.

Aron, Raymond. 1972. *Progress and Disillusion: The Dialectics of Modern Society*. Harmondsworth: Penguin.

Arrow, Kenneth Joseph. 1951. *Social Choice and Individual Values*. New York: Wiley.

Aurobindo, Sri. 1950. *The Ideal of Human Unity*. New York: Dutton.

Axelsen, David V. 2013. 'The state made me do it: How anti-cosmopolitanism is created by the state'. *Journal of Political Philosophy* 21 (4):451–472.

Baccini, Leonardo, and Mathias Koenig-Archibugi. 2014. 'Why do states commit to international labor standards? Interdependent ratification of core ILO conventions, 1948–2009'. *World Politics* 66 (3):446–490.

Bächtiger, André, John S. Dryzek, Jane Mansbridge, and Mark E. Warren, eds. 2018. *The Oxford Handbook of Deliberative Democracy*. Oxford: Oxford University Press.

Bäckstrand, Karin. 2006. 'Democratizing global environmental governance? Stakeholder democracy after the World Summit on Sustainable Development'. *European Journal of International Relations* 12 (4):467–498.

Baderin, Alice, Andreas Busen, Thomas Schramme, Luke Ulaş, and David Miller. 2018. 'Who cares what the people think? Revisiting David Miller's approach to theorising about justice'. *Contemporary Political Theory* 17 (1):69–104.

Bai, Tongdong. 2019. *Against Political Equality: The Confucian Case*. Princeton: Princeton University Press.

Bai, Xuechunzi, Varun Gauri, and Susan T. Fiske. 2021. 'Cosmopolitan morality trades off in-group for the world, separating benefits and protection'. *Proceedings of the National Academy of Sciences* 118 (40):e2100991118.

Bairoch, Paul. 1999. 'Brief history of the social clause in trade policy'. In *Trade and Jobs in Europe: Much Ado About Nothing?*, edited by Mathias Dewatripont, André Sapir, and Khalid Sekkat, 161–171. Oxford: Oxford University Press.

Bakaki, Zorzeta. 2018. 'Do international organizations reduce the risk of crisis recurrence?' *Journal of Global Security Studies* 3 (3):358–370.

Baker, Andrew, and Richard Murphy. 2021. 'Creating a race to the top in global tax governance: The political case for tax spillover assessments'. *Globalizations* 18 (1):22–38.

Baltz, Samuel, Fabricio Vasselai, and Allen Hicken. 2022. 'An unexpected consensus among diverse ways to measure democracy'. *Democratization* 29 (5):814–837.

Banks, Arthur S., and Kenneth A. Wilson. 2023. *Cross-National Time-Series Data (CNTS)*. Jerusalem: Databanks International.

Baratta, Joseph Preston. 2004a. *The Politics of World Federation*, Volume 1: *United Nations, UN Reform, Atomic Control*. Westport: Praeger.

Baratta, Joseph Preston. 2004b. *The Politics of World Federation*, Volume 2: *From World Federalism to Global Governance*. Westport: Praeger.

Barbey, Christophe. 2013. 'Nonmilitarisation and countries without armies: A necessary step toward nonkilling security institutions'. In *Nonkilling Security and the State*, edited by Joám Evans Pim, 153–176. Honolulu and Omaha: Center for Global Nonkilling and Creighton University.

Barbier, Edward B., and Joanne C. Burgess. 2019. 'Sustainable Development Goal indicators: Analyzing trade-offs and complementarities'. *World Development* 122 (October):295–305.

Barlam, Tamar F., and Kalpana Gupta. 2015. 'Antibiotic resistance spreads internationally across borders'. *Journal of Law, Medicine & Ethics* 43 (S3):12–16.

Barlow, Joel. 1801. *Joel Barlow to His Fellow Citizens of the United States. Letter II. On Certain Political Measures Proposed to their Consideration*. Philadelphia: W. Duane.

Barnhart, Joslyn N., Robert F. Trager, Elizabeth N. Saunders, and Allan Dafoe. 2020. 'The suffragist peace'. *International Organization* 74 (4):633–670.

Barrett, Anthony M., Seth D. Baum, and Kelly Hostetler. 2013. 'Analyzing and reducing the risks of inadvertent nuclear war between the United States and Russia'. *Science & Global Security* 21 (2):106–133.

Barrett, Scott. 2007. 'The smallpox eradication game'. *Public Choice* 130 (1):179–207.

Barro, Robert J., and Jong Wha Lee. 2013. 'A new data set of educational attainment in the world, 1950–2010'. *Journal of Development Economics* 104 (September):184–198.

Barry, Brian. 1979. 'Is democracy special?' In *Philosophy, Politics and Society*, 5th series, edited by Peter Laslett and James Fishkin, 155–196. New Haven: Yale University Press.

Barry, Brian. 1999. 'Statism and nationalism: A cosmopolitan critique'. *Nomos* 41:12–66.

Barry, Colin M., David L. Cingranelli, and K. Chad Clay. 2022. 'Labor rights in comparative perspective: The WorkR dataset'. *International Interactions* 48 (2):327–344.

Bartelson, Jens. 2008. 'Globalizing the democratic community'. *Ethics & Global Politics* 1 (4):159–174.

Bartelson, Jens. 2009. *Visions of World Community*. Cambridge: Cambridge University Press.

Bartram, Jamie, Clarissa Brocklehurst, David Bradley, Mike Muller, and Barbara Evans. 2018. 'Policy review of the means of implementation targets and indicators for the Sustainable Development Goal for water and sanitation'. *NPJ Clean Water* 1 (1):1–5.

Basu, Sanjay, David Stuckler, and Martin McKee. 2014. 'An alternative mechanism for international health aid: Evaluating a Global Social Protection Fund'. *Health Policy and Planning* 29 (1):127–136.

Baum, Seth, Robert de Neufville, and Anthony Barrett. 2018. *A Model for the Probability of Nuclear War*. Global Catastrophic Risk Institute Working Paper.

Bayram, A. Burcu. 2015. 'What drives modern Diogenes? Individual values and cosmopolitan allegiance'. *European Journal of International Relations* 21 (2):451–479.

Bayram, A. Burcu. 2019. 'Nationalist cosmopolitanism: The psychology of cosmopolitanism, national identity, and going to war for the country'. *Nations and Nationalism* 25 (3):757–781.

Bearce, David H., and Brandy J. Jolliff Scott. 2019. 'Popular non-support for international organizations: How extensive and what does this represent?' *Review of International Organizations* 14 (2):187–216.

Beitz, Charles R. 1989. *Political Equality: An Essay in Democratic Theory*. Princeton: Princeton University Press.

Beitz, Charles. 1998. 'International relations, philosophy of'. In *Routledge Encyclopaedia of Philosophy*, Volume 4, edited by Edward Craig, 826–833. London: Routledge.

Belic, Jelena, and Zoltan Miklosi. 2023. 'Cosmopolitanism and unipolarity: The theory of hegemonic transition'. *Critical Review of International Social and Political Philosophy* 26 (2):181–203.

Bellamy, Richard. 2007. *Political Constitutionalism: A Republican Defence of the Constitutionality of Democracy*. Cambridge: Cambridge University Press.

Bellamy, Richard. 2019. *A Republican Europe of States: Cosmopolitanism, Intergovernmentalism and Democracy in the EU*. Cambridge: Cambridge University Press.

Benferhat, Salem, Didier Dubois, Souhila Kaci, and Henri Prade. 2008. 'Modeling positive and negative information in possibility theory'. *International Journal of Intelligent Systems* 23 (10):1094–1118.

Bengtson, Andreas. 2021. 'The all-affected principle and the question of asymmetry'. *Political Research Quarterly* 74 (3):718–728.

Benhabib, Seyla. 2004. *The Rights of Others: Aliens, Residents, and Citizens*. Cambridge: Cambridge University Press.

Benhabib, Seyla. 2007. 'Democratic exclusions and democratic iterations: Dilemmas of just membership and prospects of cosmopolitan federalism'. *European Journal of Political Theory* 6 (4):445–462.

Bergougui, Brahim, and Syed Mansoob Murshed. 2020. 'New evidence on the oil-democracy nexus utilising the Varieties of Democracy data'. *Resources Policy* 69 (December):101905.

Berlin, Isaiah. 1969. *Four Essays on Liberty*. Oxford: Oxford University Press.

Bevilacqua, Alexander. 2012. 'Conceiving the Republic of Mankind: The political thought of Anacharsis Cloots'. *History of European Ideas* 38 (4):550–569.

Bhagavan, Manu. 2012. *The Peacemakers: India and the Quest for One World*. Noida: HarperCollins Publishers India.

Bieber, Florian. 2018. 'Is nationalism on the rise? Assessing global trends'. *Ethnopolitics* 17 (5):519–540.

Bieber, Florian. 2022. 'Global nationalism in times of the COVID-19 pandemic'. *Nationalities Papers* 50 (1):13–25.

Bieler, Andreas, Roland Erne, Darragh Golden, Idar Helle, Knut Kjeldstadli, Tiago Matos, and Sabina Stan, eds. 2015. *Labour and Transnational Action in Times of Crisis*. Lanham: Rowman & Littlefield.

Bienen, Dirk, Volker Rittberger, and Wolfgang Wagner. 1998. 'Democracy in the United Nations system: Cosmopolitan and communitarian principles'. In *Re-imagining Political Community: Studies in Cosmopolitan Democracy*, edited by Daniele Archibugi, David Held, and Martin Köhler, 287–308. Cambridge: Polity Press.

Billion, Jean-Francis. 2021. 'Pan-Africanism, Federalism and Decolonization in Sub-Saharan Africa and the West Indies'. *The Federalist Debate*, 34 (2). https://www.federalist-debate. org/archive/year-xxxiv-number-2-july.

Binder, Martin. 2016. *The United Nations and the Politics of Selective Humanitarian Intervention*. Basingstoke: Palgrave Macmillan.

Bob, Clifford. 2012. *The Global Right Wing and the Clash of World Politics*. Cambridge: Cambridge University Press.

Boehmer, Charles, Erik Gartzke, and Timothy Nordstrom. 2004. 'Do intergovernmental organizations promote peace?' *World Politics* 57 (1):1–38.

Boese, Vanessa A., Martin Lundstedt, Kelly Morrison, Yuko Sato, and Staffan I. Lindberg. 2022. 'State of the world 2021: Autocratization changing its nature?' *Democratization* 29 (6):983–1013.

Boffey, Daniel. 2022. 'Russia reasserts right to use nuclear weapons in Ukraine'. *The Guardian*, 26 March.

Bohman, James. 2005. 'From demos to demoi: Democracy across borders'. *Ratio Juris* 18 (3):293–314.

Böhmelt, Tobias, and Carola Betzold. 2013. 'The impact of environmental interest groups in international negotiations: Do ENGOs induce stronger environmental commitments?' *International Environmental Agreements: Politics, Law and Economics* 13 (2):127–151.

Boix, Carles, Michael Miller, and Sebastian Rosato. 2013. 'A complete data set of political regimes, 1800–2007'. *Comparative Political Studies* 46 (12):1523–1554.

Bokhary, Hamid, Krisna N. A. Pangesti, Harunor Rashid, Moataz Abd El Ghany, and Grant A. Hill-Cawthorne. 2021. 'Travel-related antimicrobial resistance: A systematic review'. *Tropical Medicine and Infectious Disease* 6 (1):11.

Bolt, Jutta, and Jan Luiten van Zanden. 2020. *Maddison Style Estimates of the Evolution of the World Economy: A New 2020 Update*. Maddison Project Working Paper 15.

Bonotti, Matteo, and Nenad Stojanović. 2022. 'Multilingual parties and the ethics of partisanship'. *Journal of Politics* 84 (1):470–482.

Bostrom, Nick. 2006. 'What is a singleton?' *Linguistic and Philosophical Investigations* 5 (2):48–54.

Botero, Giovanni. 1584. *Del Dispregio del Mondo Libri Cinque*. Milano: Francesco & Simon Tini.

Boutros-Ghali, Boutros. 1995. 'United Nations and democratization'. *African Yearbook of International Law* 3:11–16.

Bown, Chad P. 2022. 'Four years into the trade war, are the US and China decoupling?' Peterson Institute for International Economics. https://www.piie.com/blogs/realtime-economics/four-years-trade-war-are-us-and-china-decoupling (accessed 17 February 2024).

Bradley, Curtis A., and Judith G. Kelley. 2008. 'The concept of international delegation'. *Law and Contemporary Problems* 71 (1):1–36.

Brandt, R. 1996. 'Quem fata non ducunt, trahunt: Der Staat, die Staaten und der friedliche Handel'. In *Der Vernunftfrieden: Kants Entwurf im Widerstreit*, edited by Klaus-Michael Kodalle, 61–86. Würzburg: Königshausen & Neumann.

Braumoeller, Bear F. 2019. *Only the Dead: The Persistence of War in the Modern Age*. Oxford: Oxford University Press.

Breitmeier, Helmut, Oran R. Young, and Michael Zürn. 2006. *Analyzing International Environmental Regimes: From Case Study to Database*. Cambridge, MA: MIT Press.

Bremberg, Niklas, and Richard Gillespie. 2022. *Catalonia, Scotland and the EU: Visions of Independence and Integration*. Abingdon and New York: Routledge.

Brennan, Geoffrey, and Nicholas Southwood. 2007. 'Feasibility in action and attitude'. In *Hommage à Wlodek: Philosophical Papers Dedicated to Wlodek Rabinowicz*, edited by T. Rønnow-Rasmussen, B. Petersson, J. Jonefsson, and D. Egonsson. Lund: Department of Philosophy, Lund University. https://www.fil.lu.se/hommageawlodek/index.htm (accessed 7 March 2024).

Bressler, R. Daniel, Frances C. Moore, Kevin Rennert, and David Anthoff. 2021. 'Estimates of country level temperature-related mortality damage functions'. *Scientific Reports* 11 (1):1–10.

Bright, Jonathan, Diego Garzia, Joseph Lacey, and Alexander Trechsel. 2016. 'Europe's voting space and the problem of second-order elections: A transnational proposal'. *European Union Politics* 17 (1):184–198.

Broda, Rudolf. 1920. 'Das kommende Weltparlament'. *Der Völkerbund* 2020:347–358.

Brölmann, Catherine M., Richard Collins, Sufyan Droubi, and Ramses A. Wessel. 2018. 'Exiting international organizations: A brief introduction'. *International Organizations Law Review* 15 (2):243–263.

Bronfenbrenner, Kate, ed. 2007. *Global Unions: Challenging Transnational Capital through Cross-border Campaigns*. Ithaca: Cornell University Press.

Brown, Chris. 2002. *Sovereignty, Rights, and Justice: International Political Theory Today*. Cambridge: Polity Press.

Brown, Chris. 2010. *Practical Judgement in International Political Theory: Selected Essays*. London and New York: Routledge.

Brown, Davis, and Patrick James. 2018. 'The religious characteristics of states: Classic themes and new evidence for international relations and comparative politics'. *Journal of Conflict Resolution* 62 (6):1340–1376.

Brown, Garrett Wallace. 2009. *Grounding Cosmopolitanism: From Kant to the Idea of a Cosmopolitan Constitution*. Edinburgh: Edinburgh University Press.

Brown, Garrett Wallace. 2012. 'Distributing who gets what and why: Four normative approaches to global health'. *Global Policy* 3 (3):292–302.

Brunkert, Lennart, Stefan Kruse, and Christian Welzel. 2019. 'A tale of culture-bound regime evolution: The centennial democratic trend and its recent reversal'. *Democratization* 26 (3):422–443.

Brunkhorst, Hauke. 2014. *Critical Theory of Legal Revolutions: Evolutionary Perspectives*. London: Bloomsbury.

Brutus. 1787/1981. 'Brutus Essay No. 1'. In *The Complete Anti-Federalist*, Volume 2, edited by Herbert J. Storing, 363–372. Chicago: University of Chicago Press.

Buchanan, Allen. 2004. *Justice, Legitimacy, and Self-Determination: Moral Foundations for International Law*. Oxford: Oxford University Press.

Buchanan, Allen, and Robert O. Keohane. 2006. 'The legitimacy of global governance institutions'. *Ethics & International Affairs* 20 (4):405–437.

Buchanan, Allen, and Russell Powell. 2018. *The Evolution of Moral Progress: A Biocultural Theory*. Oxford: Oxford University Press.

Buchanan, William, and Hadley Cantril. 1953. *How Nations See Each Other*. Urbana: University of Illinois Press.

Budge, Ian. 2006. 'Direct and representative democracy: Are they necessarily opposed?' *Representation* 42 (1):1–12.

Budge, Ian, Hans-Dieter Klingemann, Andrea Volkens, Judith Bara, Eric Tanenbaum, with Richard C. Fording, Derek J. Hearl, Hee Min Kim, Michael McDonald, and Silvia Mendez. 2001. *Mapping Policy Preferences: Estimates for Parties, Electors, and Governments, 1945–1998*, Volume 1. Oxford: Oxford University Press.

Bull, Hedley. 1966. 'International theory: The case for a classical approach'. *World Politics* 18 (3):361–377.

Bull, Hedley. 1977. *The Anarchical Society: A Study of Order in World Politics*. London: Macmillan.

Bull, Hedley. 1979. 'The state's positive role in world affairs'. *Daedalus* 108 (4):111–123.

Bummel, Andreas. 2010. *The Composition of a Parliamentary Assembly at the United Nations*. Berlin: Committee for a Democratic UN.

Bummel, Andreas. 2019. 'Three important advancements in the campaign for a UNPA'. *Federalist Debate* 32 (1):56–58.

Bummel, Andreas. 2021. 'Towards a planetary polity: The formation of global identity and state structures'. In *Expanding Worldviews: Astrobiology, Big History and Cosmic Perspectives*, edited by Ian Crawford, 325–340. Cham: Springer.

Bummel, Andreas. 2023. 'International poll: Public supports a world parliament and world law'. *Federalist Debate* 36 (3). https://www.federalist-debate.org/current-issue/comments/international-poll-public-supports-a-world-parliament-and-world-law (Accessed 7 March 2024).

Burke, Marshall, Solomon M. Hsiang, and Edward Miguel. 2015. 'Global non-linear effect of temperature on economic production'. *Nature* 527 (7577):235–239.

Bussani, Mauro, and Anthony J. Sebok, eds. 2015. *Comparative Tort Law: Global Perspectives*. Cheltenham: Edward Elgar.

Butcher, Charles R., and Ryan D. Griffiths. 2017. 'Between Eurocentrism and Babel: A framework for the analysis of states, state systems, and international orders'. *International Studies Quarterly* 61 (2):328–336.

Cable News Network/USA Today. 1995. Gallup/CNN/USA Today Poll: News media. Survey conducted by Gallup Organization. Ithaca: Roper Center for Public Opinion Research, Cornell University.

Cabrera, Luis. 2004. *Political Theory of Global Justice: A Cosmopolitan Case for the World State*. London and New York: Routledge.

Cabrera, Luis. 2007. 'The inconveniences of transnational democracy'. *Ethics & International Affairs* 21 (2):219–238.

Cabrera, Luis. 2010a. *The Practice of Global Citizenship*. Cambridge: Cambridge University Press.

Cabrera, Luis. 2010b. 'World government: Renewed debate, persistent challenges'. *European Journal of International Relations* 16 (3):511–530.

Cabrera, Luis. 2014. 'Individual rights and the democratic boundary problem'. *International Theory* 6 (2):224–254.

Cabrera, Luis. 2018. 'The case for a United Nations Parliamentary Assembly as a means of promoting just security'. In *Just Security in an Undergoverned World*, edited by William Durch, Joris Larik, and Richard Ponzio, 413–439. Oxford: Oxford University Press.

Cabrera, Luis. 2020. *The Humble Cosmopolitan: Rights, Diversity, and Trans-state Democracy*. Oxford: Oxford University Press.

Cabrera, Luis. 2022. 'Babel Fish democracy? Prospects for addressing democratic language barriers through machine translation and interpretation'. *American Journal of Political Science*. Published online 18 July. doi:10.1111/ajps.12728.

Caney, Simon. 2005. *Justice Beyond Borders: A Global Political Theory*. Oxford: Oxford University Press.

Caney, Simon. 2006. 'Cosmopolitan justice and institutional design: An egalitarian liberal conception of global governance'. *Social Theory and Practice* 32 (4):725–756.

Cao, Xun. 2010. 'Networks as channels of policy diffusion: Explaining worldwide changes in capital taxation, 1998–2006'. *International Studies Quarterly* 54 (3):823–854.

Carey, John M., and Simon Hix. 2011. 'The electoral sweet spot: Low-magnitude proportional electoral systems'. *American Journal of Political Science* 55 (2):383–397.

Carleton, Tamma A., Amir Jina, Michael T. Delgado, Michael Greenstone, Trevor Houser, Solomon M. Hsiang, Andrew Hultgren, Robert E. Kopp, Kelly E. McCusker, and Ishan B. Nath. 2020. *Valuing the Global Mortality Consequences of Climate Change Accounting for Adaptation Costs and Benefits*. Cambridge, MA: National Bureau of Economic Research.

Carr, Edward Hallett. 1945. *Nationalism and After*. London: Macmillan.

Carson, Thomas L. 1988. 'Perpetual peace: What Kant should have said'. *Social Theory and Practice* 14 (2):173–214.

Cavallar, Georg. 1999. *Kant and the Theory and Practice of International Right*. Cardiff: University of Wales Press.

Cavallero, Eric. 2009. 'Federative global democracy'. *Metaphilosophy* 40 (1):42–64.

Chaisty, Paul, and Timothy Power. 2022. 'Does power always flow to the executive? Inter-branch oscillations in legislative authority, 1976–2014'. *Government and Opposition* 58 (1):61–83.

Chancel, Lucas, and Thomas Piketty. 2021. 'Global income inequality, 1820–2020: The persistence and mutation of extreme inequality'. *Journal of the European Economic Association* 19 (6):3025–3062.

Charnovitz, Steve. 2002. 'Trans-parliamentary associations in global functional agencies'. *Transnational Associations* 31 (2):88–91.

Charny, David. 2000. 'Regulatory competition and the global coordination of labor standards'. *Journal of International Economic Law* 3 (2):281–302.

Chase-Dunn, Christopher, and Paul Almeida. 2020. *Global Struggles and Social Change: From Prehistory to World Revolution in the Twenty-First Century*. Baltimore: Johns Hopkins University Press.

Chase-Dunn, Christopher, and Ellen Reese. 2007. 'The World Social Forum—a global party'. In *Global Political Parties*, edited by Katarina Sehm-Patomaki and Marko Ulvila, 53–91. London and New York: Zed Books.

Chase-Dunn, Christopher, Ellen Reese, Erika Gutierrez, Rebecca Giem, Christine Petit, and Linda Kim. 2006. *Global Party Formation in World Historical Perspective*. IROWS Working Paper.

Chase-Dunn, Christopher, Ellen Reese, Mark Herkenrath, Rebecca Giem, Erika Gutierrez, Linda Kim, and Christine Petit. 2008. 'North–South contradictions and bridges at the World Social Forum'. In *North and South in the World Political Economy*, edited by Rafael Reuveny and William R. Thompson, 341–366. Oxford: Blackwell.

Cheibub, José Antonio, Jennifer Gandhi, and James Raymond Vreeland. 2010. 'Democracy and dictatorship revisited'. *Public Choice* 143 (1):67–101.

Chernykh, Svitlana, David Doyle, and Timothy J. Power. 2017. 'Measuring legislative power: An expert reweighting of the Fish-Kroenig Parliamentary Powers Index'. *Legislative Studies Quarterly* 42 (2):295–320.

Chicago Council on Global Affairs and WorldPublicOpinion.org. 2007. *Public Opinion on the Future of the UN*. Survey. Chicago Council on Global Affairs and WorldPublicOpinion.org.

Chilton, Adam S., and Mila Versteeg. 2018. 'Courts' limited ability to protect constitutional rights'. *University of Chicago Law Review* 85 (2):293–336.

Chimni, Bhupinder S. 2004. 'International institutions today: An imperial global state in the making'. *European Journal of International Law* 15 (1):1–37.

Choi, Seung Mo, Hwagyun Kim, and Xiaohan Ma. 2021. 'Trade policies and growth in emerging economies: Policy experiments'. *Review of World Economics* 157 (3):603–629.

Christiano, Thomas. 1990. 'Political equality'. *Nomos* 32:151–183.

Christiano, Thomas. 1996. *The Rule of the Many: Fundamental Issues in Democratic Theory*. Boulder: Westview Press.

Christiano, Thomas. 2006. 'A democratic theory of territory and some puzzles about global democracy'. *Journal of Social Philosophy* 37 (1):81–107.

Christiano, Thomas. 2008. *The Constitution of Equality: Democratic Authority and its Limits*. Oxford: Oxford University Press.

Christiano, Thomas. 2010. 'Democratic legitimacy and international institutions'. In *The Philosophy of International Law*, edited by Samantha Besson and John Tasioulas, 119–137. Oxford: Oxford University Press.

Christiano, Thomas. 2012. 'Is democratic legitimacy possible for international institutions?' In *Global Democracy: Normative and Empirical Perspectives*, edited by Daniele Archibugi, Mathias Koenig-Archibugi, and Raffaele Marchetti, 69–95. Cambridge: Cambridge University Press.

Churchill, Winston. 1946/2003. 'A "United States of Europe"'. In *Never Give In! The Best of Winston Churchill's Speeches*, edited by Winston S. Churchill, 427–430. London: Pimlico.

Churchill, Winston. 1947/2003. 'United Europe'. In *Never Give In! The Best of Winston Churchill's Speeches*, edited by Winston S. Churchill, 436–444. London: Pimlico.

Cicero. 44BCE/2001. *On Obligations*. Oxford: Oxford University Press.

Cicero. 51BCE/1998. 'The Republic'. In *The Republic and The Laws*. Oxford: Oxford University Press.

Cingranelli, David L., and David L. Richards. 2010. 'The Cingranelli and Richards (CIRI) human rights data project'. *Human Rights Quarterly* 32 (2):401–424.

Cirillo, Pasquale, and Nassim Nicholas Taleb. 2016. 'On the statistical properties and tail risk of violent conflicts'. *Physica A: Statistical Mechanics and Its Applications* 452:29–45.

Clark, Sherman J. 1998. 'A populist critique of direct democracy'. *Harvard Law Review* 112 (2):434–482.

Claude, Inis L. 1956. *Swords into Plow Shares: The Problems and Progress of International Organization*. New York: Random House.

Clauset, Aaron. 2018. 'Trends and fluctuations in the severity of interstate wars'. *Science Advances* 4 (2):eaao3580.

Clauset, Aaron, and Kristian Skrede Gleditsch. 2018. 'Trends in conflict: What do we know and what can we know?' In *The Oxford Handbook of International Security*, edited by Alexandra Gheciu and William C. Wohlforth, 227–245. Oxford: Oxford University Press.

Cloots, Anacharsis. 1792/1979. 'La république universelle ou Adresse au Tyrannicides'. In *Anacharsis Cloots, Écrits révolutionnaires, 1790–1794*, edited by Michèle Duval, 243–318. Paris: Editions Champ libre.

Cloots, Anacharsis. 1793/1979. 'Bases constitutionnelles de la république du genre humain'. In *Anacharsis Cloots, Écrits révolutionnaires, 1790–1794*, edited by Michèle Duval, 473–502. Paris: Editions Champ libre.

Coe, Andrew J., and Jane Vaynman. 2020. 'Why arms control is so rare'. *American Political Science Review* 114 (2):342–355.

Cohen, G. A. 2009. *Why Not Socialism?* Princeton: Princeton University Press.

Cohen, Joshua. 1989. 'Deliberation and democratic legitimacy'. In *The Good Polity: Normative Analysis of the State*, edited by Alan Hamlin and Philip Pettit, 17–34. Oxford: Blackwell.

Colaresi, Michael, and William R. Thompson. 2003. 'The economic development–democratization relationship: Does the outside world matter?' *Comparative Political Studies* 36 (4):381–403.

Colomer, Josep M. 2014. 'What a world assembly could look like'. *Research & Politics* 1 (1): https://doi.org/10.1177/2053168014528684

Comenius, John Amos. 1990. *Panegersia, or, Universal Awakening*. Shipston-on-Stour: Drinkwater.

Comenius, John Amos. 1993. *Panorthosia or Universal Reform: Chapters 19 to 26*. Sheffield: Sheffield Academic Press.

Comenius, John Amos. 1995. *Panorthosia or Universal Reform: Chapters 1–18 and 27*. Sheffield: Sheffield Academic Press.

ComRes and Global Challenges Foundation. 2018. *Attitudes to Global Risks and Governance Survey 2018*. Stockholm: Global Challenges Foundation.

Condorcet, Marie Jean Antoine Nicolas de Caritat Marquis de. 1793/1976. 'Fragment on the New Atlantis, or Combined efforts of the human species for the advancement of science'. In *Selected Writings*, 283–300. Indianapolis: Bobbs-Merrill.

Condorcet, Marie Jean Antoine Nicolas de Caritat Marquis de. 1811. 'Observations on the twenty-ninth book of the Spirit of Laws'. In [Antoine Louis Claude Destutt de Tracy], *A Commentary and Review of Montesquieu's Spirit of Laws*, 261–282. Philadelphia: William Duane.

Cooper, Sandi E. 1991. *Patriotic Pacifism: Waging War on War in Europe, 1815–1914*. Oxford: Oxford University Press.

Coppedge, Michael, John Gerring, Carl Henrik Knutsen, Staffan I. Lindberg, Jan Teorell, David Altman, Michael Bernhard, M. Steven Fish, Adam Glynn, Allen Hicken, Anna Lührmann, Kyle L. Marquardt, Kelly McMann, Pamela Paxton, Daniel Pemstein, Brigitte Seim, Rachel Sigman, Svend-Erik Skaaning, Jeffrey Staton, Agnes Cornell, Lisa Gastaldi, Haakon Gjerløw, Valeriya Mechkova, Johannes von Römer, Aksel Sundtröm, Eitan Tzelgov, Luca Uberti, Yi-ting Wang, Tore Wig, and Daniel Ziblatt. 2019. V-Dem Codebook v9. Varieties of Democracy (V-Dem) Project. Gothenburg: V-Dem Institute.

Coppedge, Michael, John Gerring, Carl Henrik Knutsen, Staffan I. Lindberg, Jan Teorell, David Altman, Michael Bernhard, M. Steven Fish, Adam Glynn, Allen Hicken, Anna Luhrmann, Kyle L. Marquardt, Kelly McMann, Pamela Paxton, Daniel Pemstein, Brigitte Seim, Rachel Sigman, Svend-Erik Skaaning, Jeffrey Staton, Steven Wilson, Agnes Cornell, Nazifa Alizada, Lisa Gastaldi, Haakon Gjerløw, Garry Hindle, Nina Ilchenko, Laura Maxwell, Valeriya Mechkova, Juraj Medzihorsky, Johannes von Römer, Aksel Sundström, Eitan Tzelgov, Yi-ting Wang, Tore Wig, and Daniel Ziblatt. 2021. V-Dem [Country-Year/Country–Date] Dataset v11.1. Varieties of Democracy (V-Dem) Project. https://doi.org/10.23696/vdemds21. Gothenburg: V-Dem Institute.

Correlates of War Project. 2017a. Direct Contiguity Data, 1816–2016. Version 3.2. Data set. https://correlatesofwar.org/ (accessed 17 February 2024).

Correlates of War Project. 2017b. State System Membership List, v2016. https://correlatesofwar.org/ (accessed 17 February 2024).

Coser, Lewis A. 1956. *The Functions of Social Conflict*. Glencoe: Free Press.

Council on Foreign Relations. 2009. *Public Opinion on Global Issues: A Web-based Digest of Polling from Around the World*. New York: Council on Foreign Relations.

Craig, Campbell. 2008. 'The resurgent idea of world government'. *Ethics & International Affairs* 22 (2):133–142.

Cranmer, Skyler J., Elizabeth J. Menninga, and Peter J. Mucha. 2015. 'Kantian fractionalization predicts the conflict propensity of the international system'. *Proceedings of the National Academy of Sciences* 112 (38):11812–11816.

Crescenzi, Mark J. C., and Andrew J. Enterline. 1999. 'Ripples from the waves? A systemic, time-series analysis of democracy, democratization, and interstate war'. *Journal of Peace Research* 36 (1):75–94.

Cronin, Bruce. 1999. *Community under Anarchy: Transnational Identity and the Evolution of Cooperation*. New York: Columbia University Press.

Cruz, Cesi, Philip Keefer, and Carlos Scartascini. 2021. Database of Political Institutions 2020. Data set. Inter-American Development Bank Research Department. https://www.iadb.org/en/sharing-knowledge/research-idb/research-datasets/database-political-institutions (accessed 17 February 2024).

Cunen, Céline, Nils Lid Hjort, and Håvard Mokleiv Nygård. 2020. 'Statistical sightings of better angels: Analysing the distribution of battle-deaths in interstate conflict over time'. *Journal of Peace Research* 57 (2):221–234.

Czaika, Mathias, Hein de Haas, and Maria Villares-Varela. 2018. 'The global evolution of travel visa regimes'. *Population and Development Review* 44 (3):589–622.

Dahl, Adam. 2020. 'Creolizing natural liberty: Transnational obligation in the thought of Ottobah Cugoano'. *Journal of Politics* 82 (3):908–920.

Dahl, Adam. 2021. 'Oppression and racial slavery: Abolitionist challenges to neo-republicanism'. *Contemporary Political Theory* 20 (2):272–295.

Dahl, Robert A. 1956. *A Preface to Democratic Theory*. Chicago: University of Chicago Press.

Dahl, Robert A. 1970. *After the Revolution? Authority in a Good Society*. New Haven: Yale University Press.

Dahl, Robert A. 1998. *On Democracy*. New Haven: Yale University Press.

Dahl, Robert A. 1999a. 'Can international organizations be democratic? A skeptic's view'. In *Democracy's Edges*, edited by Ian Shapiro and Casiano Hacker-Cordón, 19–36. Cambridge: Cambridge University Press.

Dahl, Robert A. 1999b. 'The shifting boundaries of democratic governments'. *Social Research* 66 (3):915–931.

Dahl, Robert A. 2001. 'Is post-national democracy possible?' In *Nation, Federalism and Democracy*, edited by Sergio Fabbrini, 35–46. Trento: Editrice Compositori.

Dahl, Robert A., and Edward R. Tufte. 1973. *Size and Democracy*. Stanford: Stanford University Press.

Dahrendorf, Ralf. 1959. *Class and Class Conflict in Industrial Society*. Stanford: Stanford University Press.

Damluji, Hassan. 2019. *The Responsible Globalist: What Citizens of the World Can Learn from Nationalism*. London: Allen Lane.

Dante Alighieri. *c.*1312/1996. *Monarchy*. Cambridge: Cambridge University Press.

Davies, Ronald B., and Krishna Chaitanya Vadlamannati. 2013. 'A race to the bottom in labor standards? An empirical investigation'. *Journal of Development Economics* 103 (July):1–14.

de Kraker, Marlieke E. A., Andrew J. Stewardson, and Stephan Harbarth. 2016. 'Will 10 million people die a year due to antimicrobial resistance by 2050?' *PLoS Medicine* 13 (11): e1002184. https://doi.org/10.1371/journal.pmed.1002184.

De Wilde, Pieter, Wiebke Marie Junk, and Tabea Palmtag. 2016. 'Accountability and opposition to globalization in international assemblies'. *European Journal of International Relations* 22 (4):823–846.

De Wilde, Pieter, Ruud Koopmans, Wolfgang Merkel, and Michael Zürn, eds. 2019. *The Struggle over Borders: Cosmopolitanism and Communitarianism*. Cambridge: Cambridge University Press.

Della Porta, Donatella, ed. 2007. *Global Justice Movement: Cross-national and Transnational Perspectives*. Boulder: Paradigm.

Della Porta, Donatella, and Martín Portos. 2023. 'Rich kids of Europe? Social basis and strategic choices in the climate activism of Fridays for Future'. *Italian Political Science Review/Rivista Italiana di Scienza Politica* 53 (1):24–49.

Dellink, Rob, Jean Chateau, Elisa Lanzi, and Bertrand Magné. 2017. 'Long-term economic growth projections in the Shared Socioeconomic Pathways'. *Global Environmental Change* 42 (January):200–214.

Deudney, Daniel. 2007. *Bounding Power: Republican Security Theory from the Polis to the Global Village*. Princeton: Princeton University Press.

Dewey, John. 1946. *The Public and its Problems: An Essay in Political Inquiry*. Chicago: Gateway Books.

Diamond, Larry. 2021. 'Democratic regression in comparative perspective: Scope, methods, and causes'. *Democratization* 28 (1):22–42.

Diehl, Paul F., Gary Goertz, and Yahve Gallegos. 2021. 'Peace data: Concept, measurement, patterns, and research agenda'. *Conflict Management and Peace Science* 38 (5):605–624.

Dietsch, Peter, and Thomas Rixen, eds. 2015. *Global Tax Governance: What's Wrong with it and How to Fix it*. Colchester: ECPR Press.

Dill, Janina, Scott D. Sagan, and Benjamin A. Valentino. 2022. 'Kettles of hawks: Public opinion on the nuclear taboo and noncombatant immunity in the United States, United Kingdom, France, and Israel'. *Security Studies* 31 (1):1–31.

Dingwerth, Klaus. 2014. 'Global democracy and the democratic minimum: Why a procedural account alone is insufficient'. *European Journal of International Relations* 20 (4):1124–1147.

Dingwerth, Klaus, Henning Schmidtke, and Tobias Weise. 2020. 'The rise of democratic legitimation: Why international organizations speak the language of democracy'. *European Journal of International Relations* 26 (3):714–741.

Dion, Michelle L., and Vicki Birchfield. 2010. 'Economic development, income inequality, and preferences for redistribution'. *International Studies Quarterly* 54 (2):315–334.

Dogan, Mattei. 1994. 'The decline of nationalisms within Western Europe'. *Comparative Politics* 26 (3):281–305.

Donnelly, Jack. 2006. 'Sovereign inequalities and hierarchy in anarchy: American power and international society'. *European Journal of International Relations* 12 (2):139–170.

Dooley, Kate, Christian Holz, Sivan Kartha, Sonja Klinsky, J. Timmons Roberts, Henry Shue, Harald Winkler, Tom Athanasiou, Simon Caney, and Elizabeth Cripps. 2021. 'Ethical choices behind quantifications of fair contributions under the Paris Agreement'. *Nature Climate Change* 11 (4):300–305.

Downing, Brian. 1993. *The Military Revolution and Political Change: Origins of Democracy and Autocracy in Early Modern Europe*. Princeton: Princeton University Press.

Doyle, Michael W. 2000. 'A more perfect union? The liberal peace and the challenge of globalization'. *Review of International Studies* 26 (5):81–94.

Dreher, Axel. 2006. KOF Index of Globalization. Konjunkturforschungsstelle ETH Zürich. https://kof.ethz.ch/en/forecasts-and-indicators/indicators/kof-globalisation-index.html (accessed 17 February 2024).

Drury, A. Cooper, and Dursun Peksen. 2014. 'Women and economic statecraft: The negative impact international economic sanctions visit on women'. *European Journal of International Relations* 20 (2):463–490.

Dryzek, John S. 2006. *Deliberative Global Politics: Discourse and Democracy in a Divided World*. Cambridge: Polity Press.

Dryzek, John S. 2011. 'Global democratization: Soup, society, or system?' *Ethics & International Affairs* 25 (2):211–234.

Dryzek, John S., André Bächtiger, and Karolina Milewicz. 2011. 'Toward a Deliberative Global Citizens' Assembly'. *Global Policy* 2 (1):33–42.

Du Bois, W. E. B. 1945. *Color and Democracy: Colonies and Peace*. New York: Harcourt, Brace, and Company.

Dubois, Didier, and Henri Prade. 2009. 'An overview of the asymmetric bipolar representation of positive and negative information in possibility theory'. *Fuzzy Sets and Systems* 160 (10):1355–1366.

DuBois, Ellen Carol, ed. 2022. *The Elizabeth Cady Stanton–Susan B. Anthony Reader*. Third edition. Jefferson: McFarland.

Dubois, Pierre. c.1306/1956. *The Recovery of the Holy Land*. New York: Columbia University Press.

Duchacek, Ivo D. 1986. *The Territorial Dimension of Politics: Within, Among, and Across Nations*. Boulder and London: Westview Press.

Dworkin, Ronald. 1987. 'What is equality-Part 4: Political equality'. *University of San Francisco Law Review* 22:1–30.

Dworkin, Ronald. 1995. 'Constitutionalism and democracy 1'. *European Journal of Philosophy* 3 (1):2–11.

Dziobek, Claudia, Carlos Gutierrez Mangas, and Phebby Kufa. 2011. Measuring Fiscal Decentralization: Exploring the IMF's Databases. IMF Working Paper WP/11/126.

Early, Bryan R., and Dursun Peksen. 2022. 'Does misery love company? Analyzing the global suffering inflicted by US economic sanctions'. *Global Studies Quarterly* 2 (2):ksac013.

Ebeling, Martin. 2016. 'Epistemic political egalitarianism, political parties, and conciliatory democracy'. *Political Theory* 44 (5):629–656.

Eberl, Oliver, and Peter Niesen. 2011. 'Kommentar'. In *Immanuel Kant: Zum Ewigen Frieden*, 89–416. Frankfurt a.M.: Suhrkamp.

Ecker-Ehrhardt, Matthias. 2016. 'Why do citizens want the UN to decide? Cosmopolitan ideas, particularism and global authority'. *International Political Science Review* 37 (1):99–114.

Ecker-Ehrhardt, Matthias. 2018. 'International organizations "going public"? An event history analysis of public communication reforms 1950–2015'. *International Studies Quarterly* 62 (4):723–736.

Egel, Naomi, and R. Lincoln Hines. 2021. 'Chinese views on nuclear weapons: Evidence from an online survey'. *Research & Politics* 8 (3):20531680211032840.

Einstein, Albert. 1946/2007. 'Reply to Sumner Welles's article on the atomic bomb and world government'. In *Einstein on Politics*, edited by David E. Rowe and Robert Schulmann, 380–381. Princeton: Princeton University Press.

Einstein, Albert. 1947. 'Atomic war or peace'. *The Atlantic*, November, 29–32.

Einstein, Albert. 1948/2007a. 'A reply to the Soviet scientists'. In *Einstein on Politics*, edited by David E. Rowe and Robert Schulmann, 393–397. Princeton: Princeton University Press.

Einstein, Albert. 1948/2007b. 'Open letter to the General Assembly of the United Nations'. In *Einstein on Politics*, edited by David E. Rowe and Robert Schulmann, 388–392. Princeton: Princeton University Press.

Eisentraut, Sophie. 2020. *Talking Democracy at the United Nations: Power, Regime Type, and the Democratization of International Rule*. Baden-Baden: Nomos.

Elkins, Zachary, and John Sides. 2007. 'Can institutions build unity in multiethnic states?' *American Political Science Review* 101 (4):693–708.

Elsässer, Lea, Svenja Hense, and Armin Schäfer. 2021. 'Not just money: Unequal responsiveness in egalitarian democracies'. *Journal of European Public Policy* 28 (12):1890–1908.

Elsässer, Lea, and Armin Schäfer. 2023. 'Political inequality in rich democracies'. *Annual Review of Political Science* 26:469–487.

Elster, Jon. 1986. 'The market and the forum: Three varieties of political theory'. In *Foundations of Social Choice Theory*, edited by Jon Elster and Aanund Hylland, 103–132. Cambridge: Cambridge University Press.

Elster, Jon. 2018. 'The political psychology of constitution making'. In *Constituent Assemblies*, edited by Jon Elster, Roberto Gargarella, Vatsal Naresh, and Bjørn Erik Rasch, 207–245. Cambridge: Cambridge University Press.

Ely, John Hart. 1980. *Democracy and Distrust: A Theory of Judicial Review*. Cambridge, MA: Harvard University Press.

Erasmus, Desiderius. 1530/2005. 'A most useful discussion concerning proposals for war against the Turks, including an exposition of Psalm 28'. In *Collected Works of Erasmus*, Volume 64, edited by Dominic Baker-Smith, 201–266. Toronto: University of Toronto Press.

Erman, Eva, and Jonathan W. Kuyper. 2020. 'Global democracy and feasibility'. *Critical Review of International Social and Political Philosophy* 23 (3):311–331.

Escobar, Gabriela García. 2023. 'Norms versus interpretations: Human rights universality revisited'. *Global Jurist* 23 (2):183–205. https://doi.org/10.1515/gj-2023-0001.

Esipova, Neli, Anita Pugliese, and Julie Ray. 2018. 'More than 750 million worldwide would migrate if they could'. Gallup. https://news.gallup.com/poll/245255/750-million-worldwide-migrate.aspx (accessed 17 February 2024).

Esty, Daniel C., and Damien Geradin. 1998. 'Environmental protection and international competitiveness'. *Journal of World Trade* 32 (3):5–46.

Ewing, Alfred Cyril. 1947. *The Individual, the State, and World Government*. New York: Macmillan.

Fader, Marianela, Colleen Cranmer, Richard Lawford, and Jill Engel-Cox. 2018. 'Toward an understanding of synergies and trade-offs between water, energy, and food SDG targets'. *Frontiers in Environmental Science* 6:112.

Fagan, Brennen T., Marina I. Knight, Niall J. MacKay, and A. Jamie Wood. 2020. 'Change point analysis of historical battle deaths'. *Journal of the Royal Statistical Society: Series A (Statistics in Society)* 183 (3):909–933.

Falk, Richard A. 1975. *A Study of Future Worlds*. New York: Free Press.

Falk, Richard A., and Andrew L. Strauss. 2000. 'On the creation of a global peoples assembly: Legitimacy and the power of popular sovereignty'. *Stanford Journal of International Law* 36 (2):191–220.

Falk, Richard A., and Andrew Strauss. 2001. 'Toward global parliament'. *Foreign Affairs* 80 (1):212–220.

Fazal, Tanisha M. 2022. 'The return of conquest? Why the future of global order hinges on Ukraine'. *Foreign Affairs* 101 (3):20–27.

Fearon, James D. 2003. 'Ethnic and cultural diversity by country'. *Journal of Economic Growth* 8 (2):195–222.

Fearon, James D. 2018. 'Cooperation, conflict, and the costs of anarchy'. *International Organization* 72 (3):523–559.

Federation of American Scientists. 2022. 'Status of world nuclear forces'. https://fas.org/issues/nuclear-weapons/status-world-nuclear-forces/ (accessed 17 February 2024).

Felsenthal, Dan S., and Moshé Machover. 1998. *The Measurement of Voting Power*. Cheltenham: Edward Elgar.

Ferejohn, John, and Frances McCall Rosenbluth. 2008. 'Warlike democracies'. *Journal of Conflict Resolution* 52 (1):3–38.

Fick, Carolyn E. 1990. *The Making of Haiti: The Saint Domingue Revolution from Below*. Knoxville: University of Tennessee Press.

Fifth Pan-African Congress. 1947. 'The challenge to the colonial powers'. In *Colonial and Coloured Unity: A Programme of Action: History of the Pan-African Congress*, edited by George Padmore, 5. Manchester: Pan-African Federation.

Fish, M. Steven, and Matthew Kroenig. 2009. *The Handbook of National Legislatures: A Global Survey*. Cambridge: Cambridge University Press.

Fishkin, James. 2009. *When the People Speak: Deliberative Democracy and Public Consultation*. Oxford: Oxford University Press.

Flikschuh, Katrin. 2010. 'Kant's sovereignty dilemma: A contemporary analysis'. *Journal of Political Philosophy* 18 (4):469–493.

Follesdal, Andreas. 2012. 'Cosmopolitan democracy: Neither a category mistake nor a categorical imperative'. In *Global Democracy: Normative and Empirical Perspectives*, edited by Daniele Archibugi, Mathias Koenig-Archibugi, and Raffaele Marchetti, 96–114. Cambridge: Cambridge University Press.

Follesdal, Andreas. 2017. 'Tracking justice democratically'. *Social Epistemology* 31 (3):324–339.

Follows, John William. 1951. *Antecedents of the International Labour Organization*. Oxford: Clarendon Press.

Forsyth, Murray. 1981. *Unions of States: The Theory and Practice of Confederation*. Leicester: Leicester University Press.

Fraser, Donald M., and John P. Salzberg. 1979. 'International political parties as a vehicle for human rights'. *Annals of the American Academy of Political and Social Science* 442 (1):63–68.

Freeman, Michael. 2022. *Human Rights*. Fourth edition. Cambridge: Polity Press.

Frey, Bruno S., and Reiner Eichenberger. 1999. *The New Democratic Federalism for Europe: Functional, Overlapping, and Competing Jurisdictions*. Cheltenham: Edward Elgar.

Frey, Bruno S., and Alois Stutzer. 2006. 'Strengthening the citizens' role in international organizations'. *Review of International Organizations* 1 (1):27–43.

Fricko, Oliver, Petr Havlik, Joeri Rogelj, Zbigniew Klimont, Mykola Gusti, Nils Johnson, Peter Kolp, Manfred Strubegger, Hugo Valin, and Markus Amann. 2017. 'The marker quantification of the Shared Socioeconomic Pathway 2: A middle-of-the-road scenario for the 21st century'. *Global Environmental Change* 42 (January):251–267.

Frost, Isabel, Thomas P. Van Boeckel, João Pires, Jessica Craig, and Ramanan Laxminarayan. 2019. 'Global geographic trends in antimicrobial resistance: The role of international travel'. *Journal of Travel Medicine* 26 (8):taz036.

Fuso Nerini, Francesco, Julia Tomei, Long Seng To, Iwona Bisaga, Priti Parikh, Mairi Black, Aiduan Borrion, Catalina Spataru, Vanesa Castán Broto, and Gabrial Anandarajah. 2018. 'Mapping synergies and trade-offs between energy and the Sustainable Development Goals'. *Nature Energy* 3 (1):10–15.

Gaddis, John Lewis. 1986. 'The long peace: Elements of stability in the postwar international system'. *International Security* 10 (4):99–142.

Gadinger, Frank, and Jan Aart Scholte, eds. 2023. *Polycentrism: How Governing Works Today*. Oxford: Oxford University Press.

Gallagher, Michael, and Paul Mitchell. 2005. 'Introduction to electoral systems'. In *The Politics of Electoral Systems*, edited by Michael Paul Mitchell Gallagher, 3–23. Oxford: Oxford University Press.

Gallup Organization. 1946. Gallup Poll # 1946-0376: Education/Federal Budget. Survey conducted by Gallup Organization. Ithaca: Roper Center for Public Opinion Research, Cornell University.

Gallup Organization. 1947. Gallup Poll # 1947-0409: Universal Military Training Program/Automobile/Political Parties. Survey conducted by Gallup Organization. Ithaca: Roper Center for Public Opinion Research, Cornell University.

Gallup Organization. 1951. Gallup Poll # 1951-0473: Military Draft/1952 Presidential Election/Korea/Communism. Survey conducted by Gallup Organization. Ithaca: Roper Center for Public Opinion Research, Cornell University.

Gallup Organization. 1953. Gallup Poll # 1953-0518: Domestic Issues/Korea/Automobiles. Survey conducted by Gallup Organization. Ithaca: Roper Center for Public Opinion Research, Cornell University.

Gallup Organization. 1955. Gallup Poll # 545. Survey conducted by Gallup Organization. Ithaca: Roper Center for Public Opinion Research, Cornell University.

Ganghof, Steffen. 2015. 'Four visions of democracy: Powell's *Elections as Instruments of Democracy* and beyond'. *Political Studies Review* 13 (1):69–79.

Ganghof, Steffen. 2016. 'Reconciling representation and accountability: Three visions of democracy compared'. *Government and Opposition* 51 (2):209–233.

Ganghof, Steffen. 2019. 'Designing democratic constitutions: The search for optimality'. *Politics and Governance* 7 (4):243–253.

Gardner, Peter, Tiago Carvalho, and Maria Valenstain. 2022. 'Spreading rebellion? The rise of Extinction Rebellion chapters across the world'. *Environmental Sociology* 8 (4):424–435.

Garibaldi, Giuseppe. c.1871/1934. 'Unione europea'. In *Scritti e discorsi politici e militari: Volume III (1868–1882)*, 545–546. Bologna: Cappelli Editore.

Gebeye, Berihun Adugna. 2021. 'Global constitutionalism and cultural diversity: The emergence of jurisgenerative constitutionalism in Africa'. *Global Constitutionalism* 10 (1):40–71.

Geddes, Barbara, Joseph Wright, and Erica Frantz. 2014. 'Autocratic breakdown and regime transitions: A new data set'. *Perspectives on Politics* 12 (2):313–331.

Gelman, Andrew, Jonathan N. Katz, and Joseph Bafumi. 2004. 'Standard voting power indexes do not work: An empirical analysis'. *British Journal of Political Science* 34 (4):657–674.

George, Justin, Dongfang Hou, and Todd Sandler. 2019. 'Asia-Pacific demand for military expenditure: Spatial panel and SUR estimates'. *Defence and Peace Economics* 30 (4):381–401.

Gerring, John, Michael Hoffman, and Dominic Zarecki. 2018. 'The diverse effects of diversity on democracy'. *British Journal of Political Science* 48 (2):283–314.

Gerring, John, Carl Henrik Knutsen, and Jonas Berge. 2022. 'Does democracy matter?' *Annual Review of Political Science* 25:357–375.

Getachew, Adom. 2019. *Worldmaking after Empire: The Rise and Fall of Self-determination.* Princeton: Princeton University Press.

Gethin, Amory, Clara Martínez-Toledano, and Thomas Piketty. 2021. *Political Cleavages and Social Inequalities: A Study of Fifty Democracies, 1948–2020.* Cambridge, MA: Harvard University Press.

Ghassim, Farsan. 2020. 'Who on earth wants global democracy—and why (not)? A theoretical and experimental study of international public opinion'. Thesis for the degree of Doctor of Philosophy (DPhil) in International Relations, University of Oxford.

Ghassim, Farsan, Mathias Koenig-Archibugi, and Luis Cabrera. 2022. 'Public opinion on institutional designs for the United Nations: An international survey experiment'. *International Studies Quarterly* 66 (3):sqac027.

Ghassim, Farsan, and Markus Pauli. 2023. 'Who on earth wants a world government—and why? An international survey experiment'. Paper presented at the Global Studies Seminar, Shanghai University, 25 October.

Ghébali, Victor Yves, Roberto Ago, and Nicolás Valticos. 1989. *The International Labour Organisation: A Case Study on the Evolution of UN Specialised Agencies*. Dordrecht, Boston, and London: Martinus Nijhoff Publishers.

Gilabert, Pablo, and Holly Lawford-Smith. 2012. 'Political feasibility: A conceptual exploration'. *Political Studies* 60 (4):809–825.

Gill-Tiney, Patrick. 2022. 'A liberal peace? The growth of liberal norms and the decline of interstate violence'. *Journal of Conflict Resolution* 66 (3):413–442.

Ginsburg, Tom. 2009. 'International delegation and state disaggregation'. *Constitutional Political Economy* 20 (3):323–340.

Ginsburg, Tom, and Mila Versteeg. 2014. 'Why do countries adopt constitutional review?' *Journal of Law, Economics, & Organization* 30 (3):587–622.

Ginsburg, Tom, and Mila Versteeg. 2018. 'From Catalonia to California: Secession in constitutional law'. *Alabama Law Review* 70 (4):923–986.

Glasius, Marlies. 2006. *The International Criminal Court: A Global Civil Society Achievement*. London: Routledge.

Global Challenges Foundation. 2014. *Global Challenges Foundation Risk Survey: The Pulse of International Sentiment*. Stockholm: Global Challenges Foundation.

GlobeScan. 2004. *What NGO Leaders Want for the Year 2020: Report of the Second Survey of the 2020 Global Stakeholder Panel*. Toronto: GlobeScan.

GlobeScan. 2016. 'Global citizenship a growing sentiment among citizens of emerging economies: Global poll'. Press release, Globescan. https://globescan.com/2016/04/27/global-citizenship-a-growing-sentiment-among-citizens-of-emerging-economies-global-poll/ (accessed 17 February 2024).

Goda, Thomas, and Alejandro Torres García. 2017. 'The rising tide of absolute global income inequality during 1850–2010: Is it driven by inequality within or between countries?' *Social Indicators Research* 130:1051–1072.

Goertz, Gary, Paul Francis Diehl, and Alexandru Balas. 2016. *The Puzzle of Peace: The Evolution of Peace in the International System*. Oxford: Oxford University Press.

Goldberg, Saskia, and André Bächtiger. 2023. 'Catching the "deliberative wave"? How (disaffected) citizens assess deliberative citizen forums'. *British Journal of Political Science* 53 (1):239–247.

Goldman, Ralph Morris, ed. 1983. *Transnational Parties: Organizing the World's Precincts*. Lanham: University Press of America.

Goldsmith, Benjamin E. 2007. 'Arms racing in "space": Spatial modelling of military spending around the world'. *Australian Journal of Political Science* 42 (3):419–440.

Goldsmith, Jack, and Daryl Levinson. 2008. 'Law for states: International law, constitutional law, public law'. *Harvard Law Review* 122 (7):1791–1868.

Goldstein, Joshua S. 2011. *Winning the War on War: The Decline of Armed Conflict Worldwide*. London and New York: Penguin.

Gómez León, María, and Herman J. De Jong. 2019. 'Inequality in turbulent times: Income distribution in Germany and Britain, 1900–50'. *Economic History Review* 72 (3):1073–1098.

Gómez-Reino, Margarita. 2014. 'European integration and an alternative party family: Regionalist parties and the European question'. In *Europe's Contending Identities: Supranationalism, Ethnoregionalism, Religion, and New Nationalism*, edited by Andrew C. Gould and Anthony M. Messina, 118–138. Cambridge: Cambridge University Press.

González, Francisco E., and Desmond King. 2004. 'The state and democratization: The United States in comparative perspective'. *British Journal of Political Science* 34 (2):193–210.

Goodin, Robert E. 2007. 'Enfranchising all affected interests, and its alternatives'. *Philosophy and Public Affairs* 35 (1):40–68.

Goodin, Robert E. 2010. 'Global democracy: In the beginning'. *International Theory* 2 (2):175–209.

Goodin, Robert E. 2012. 'World government is here!' In *Varieties of Sovereignty and Citizenship*, edited by Sigal R. Ben-Porath and Rogers M. Smith, 149–165. Philadelphia: University of Pennsylvania Press.

Goodin, Robert E. 2016. 'Enfranchising all subjected, worldwide'. *International Theory* 8 (3):365–389.

Goodin, Robert E. 2022. 'Proximity principle, adieu'. In *Studies on the Democratic Boundary Problem*, edited by Paul Bowman, 11–31. Stockholm: Institute for Futures Studies.

Goodin, Robert E., and Steven R. Ratner. 2011. 'Democratizing international law'. *Global Policy* 2 (3):241–247.

Gorman, Brandon, and Charles Seguin. 2018. 'World citizens on the periphery: Threat and identification with global society'. *American Journal of Sociology* 124 (3):705–761.

Görres, Joseph. 1798/1979. 'Der allgemeine Frieden, ein Ideal'. In *Friedensutopien*, edited by Zwi Barscha and Richard Saage, 111–172. Frankfurt a.M.: Suhrkamp.

Gould, Carol C. 2009. 'Structuring global democracy: Political communities, universal human rights, and transnational representation'. *Metaphilosophy* 40 (1):24–41.

Graham, Benjamin A. T., Michael K. Miller, and Kaare W. Strøm. 2017. 'Safeguarding democracy: Powersharing and democratic survival'. *American Political Science Review* 111 (4):686–704.

Graham, Benjamin A. T., and Jacob R. Tucker. 2019. 'The international political economy data resource'. *Review of International Organizations* 14 (1):149–161.

Green, Jon, Matthew Baum, James Druckman, David Lazer, Katherine Ognyanova, Matthew D. Simonson, Roy Perlis, and Mauricio Santillana. 2020. *Identifying and Measuring Conditional Policy Preferences: The Case of Opening Schools During a Pandemic*. Northwestern Institute for Policy Research Working Paper Series.

Greig, J. Michael, and Andrew J. Enterline. 2017. 'National Material Capabilities (NMC) data documentation version 5.0'. Correlates of War. https://correlatesofwar.org/wp-content/uploads/NMC_Documentation_v5_0.pdf (accessed 17 February 2024).

Griffiths, Ryan D. 2010. 'Security threats, linguistic homogeneity, and the necessary conditions for political unification'. *Nations and Nationalism* 16 (1):169–188.

Griffiths, Ryan D. 2018. 'The Waltzian ordering principle and international change: A two-dimensional model'. *European Journal of International Relations* 24 (1):130–152.

Grigorescu, Alexandru. 2007. 'Transparency of intergovernmental organizations: The roles of member states, international bureaucracies and nongovernmental organizations'. *International Studies Quarterly* 51 (3):625–648.

Grigorescu, Alexandru. 2015. *Democratic Intergovernmental Organizations? Normative Pressures and Decision-Making Rules*. Cambridge: Cambridge University Press.

Grigorescu, Alexandru. 2023. *Restraining Power through Institutions: A Unifying Theme for Domestic and International Politics*. Oxford: Oxford University Press.

Grimm, Dieter. 2015. *Sovereignty: The Origin and Future of a Political and Legal Concept*. New York: Columbia University Press.

Grossmann, Igor, et al. 2023. 'Insights into the accuracy of social scientists' forecasts of societal change'. *Nature Human Behaviour* 7 (4):484–501.

Grotius, Hugo. 1646/1925. *The Law of War and Peace*. Indianapolis and New York: Bobbs-Merrill.

Gruber, Lloyd. 2000. *Ruling the World: Power Politics and the Rise of Supranational Institutions*. Princeton: Princeton University Press.

Gruffydd-Jones, Jamie. 2017. 'Dangerous days: The impact of nationalism on interstate conflict'. *Security Studies* 26 (4):698–728.

Guasti, Alessandro, and Mathias Koenig-Archibugi. 2022. 'Has global trade competition really led to a race to the bottom in labor standards?' *International Studies Quarterly* 66 (4):sqac061.

Gubler, Joshua R., and Joel Sawat Selway. 2012. 'Horizontal inequality, crosscutting cleavages, and civil war'. *Journal of Conflict Resolution* 56 (2):206–232.

Guillaud, Elvire. 2013. 'Preferences for redistribution: An empirical analysis over 33 countries'. *Journal of Economic Inequality* 11 (1):57–78.

Guinier, Lani. 1994. *The Tyranny of the Majority: Fundamental Fairness in Representative Democracy*. New York: Free Press.

Gülzau, Fabian, and Steffen Mau. 2021. 'Walls, barriers, checkpoints, landmarks, and "no-man's-land". A quantitative typology of border control infrastructure'. *Historical Social Research/Historische Sozialforschung* 46 (3):23–48.

Guzman, Andrew T., and Jennifer Landsidle. 2008. 'The myth of international delegation'. *California Law Review* 96 (6):1693–1723.

Gygli, Savina, Florian Haelg, Niklas Potrafke, and Jan-Egbert Sturm. 2019. 'The KOF globalisation index—revisited'. *Review of International Organizations* 14:543–574.

Haas, Ernst B. 1962. 'System and process in the International Labor Organization: A statistical afterthought'. *World Politics* 14 (2):322–352.

Haber, Stephen, and Victor Menaldo. 2011. 'Do natural resources fuel authoritarianism? A reappraisal of the resource curse'. *American Political Science Review* 105 (1):1–26.

Habermas, Jürgen. 1995. 'On the internal relation between the rule of law and democracy'. *European Journal of Philosophy* 3 (1):12–20.

Habermas, Jürgen. 1996. *Between Facts and Norms: Contributions to a Discourse Theory of Law and Democracy*. Cambridge: Polity Press.

Habermas, Jürgen. 1998. 'Kant's idea of perpetual peace: At two hundred years' historical remove'. In *The Inclusion of the Other: Studies in Political Theory*, 165–201. Cambridge, MA: MIT Press.

Habermas, Jürgen. 2001. 'Constitutional democracy: A paradoxical union of contradictory principles?' *Political Theory* 29 (6):766–781.

Habermas, Jürgen 2006. *The Divided West*. Cambridge: Polity Press.

Hackenesch, Christine, and Julia Bader. 2020. 'The struggle for minds and influence: The Chinese Communist Party's global outreach'. *International Studies Quarterly* 64 (3):723–733.

Haerpfer, C., R. Inglehart, A. Moreno, C. Welzel, K. Kizilova, J. Diez-Medrano, M. Lagos, P. Norris, E. Ponarin, and B. Puranen. 2022. World Values Survey: Round Seven—Country-Pooled Datafile Version 4.0. Data set. Madrid and Vienna: JD Systems Institute & WVSA Secretariat.

Hainmueller, Jens, Daniel J. Hopkins, and Teppei Yamamoto. 2014. 'Causal inference in conjoint analysis: Understanding multidimensional choices via stated preference experiments'. *Political Analysis* 22 (1):1–30.

Hale, Thomas, and Mathias Koenig-Archibugi. 2016. 'Are Europeans ready for a more democratic European Union? New evidence on preference heterogeneity, polarisation and crosscuttingness'. *European Journal of Political Research* 55 (2):225–245.

Hale, Thomas, and Mathias Koenig-Archibugi. 2019. 'Could global democracy satisfy diverse policy values? An empirical analysis'. *Journal of Politics* 81 (1):112–126.

Hanschmidt, Alwin. 1977. *Republikanisch-demokratischer Internationalismus im 19. Jahrhundert: Ideen, Formen, Organisierungsversuche*. Oldenburg: Matthiesen Verlag.

Haworth, Alida R., Scott D. Sagan, and Benjamin A. Valentino. 2019. 'What do Americans really think about conflict with nuclear North Korea? The answer is both reassuring and disturbing'. *Bulletin of the Atomic Scientists* 75 (4):179–186.

Hayo, Bernd, and Stefan Voigt. 2014. 'Mapping constitutionally safeguarded judicial independence—a global survey'. *Journal of Empirical Legal Studies* 11 (1):159–195.

Heater, Derek. 1996. *World Citizenship and Government: Cosmopolitan Ideas in the History of Western Political Thought*. New York: St Martin's Press.

Heimberger, Philipp. 2021. 'Corporate tax competition: A meta-analysis'. *European Journal of Political Economy* 69:102002.

Heinzel, Mirko, and Mathias Koenig-Archibugi. 2023. 'Soft governance against superbugs: How effective is the international regime on antimicrobial resistance?' *Review of International Organizations* Published online 30 September. https://doi.org/10.1007/s11558-023-09510-7.

Helbling, Marc, Rahsaan Maxwell, and Richard Traunmüller. 2024. 'Numbers, selectivity and rights: The conditional nature of immigration policy preferences'. *Comparative Political Studies* 57 (2):254–286.

Held, David. 1995. *Democracy and the Global Order: From the Modern State to Cosmopolitan Governance*. Cambridge: Polity Press.

Held, David. 2004. 'Democratic accountability and political effectiveness from a cosmopolitan perspective'. *Government and Opposition* 39 (2):364–391.

Heldt, Eugénia, and Henning Schmidtke. 2017. 'Measuring the empowerment of international organizations: The evolution of financial and staff capabilities'. *Global Policy* 8 (S5):51–61.

Hellman, Martin. 2008. 'Risk analysis of nuclear deterrence'. *Bent of Tau Beta Pi* 99 (2):14–22.

Henderson, Errol Anthony. 2002. *Democracy and War: The End of an Illusion?* Boulder: Lynne Rienner.

Heritage Foundation. 2022. 2022 Index of Economic Freedom. https://www.heritage.org/index/ (accessed 17 February 2024).

Herman, Lise Esther. 2017. 'Democratic partisanship: From theoretical ideal to empirical standard'. *American Political Science Review* 111 (4):738–754.

Herz, John H. 1959. *International Politics in the Atomic Age*. New York: Columbia University Press.

Hinich, Melvin J., and Michael C. Munger. 1994. *Ideology and the Theory of Political Choice*. Ann Arbor: University of Michigan Press.

Hix, Simon, and Abdul Noury. 2009. 'After enlargement: Voting patterns in the sixth European Parliament'. *Legislative Studies Quarterly* 34 (2):159–174.

Hix, Simon, Abdul Noury, and Gérard Roland. 2007. *Democratic Politics in the European Parliament*. Cambridge: Cambridge University Press.

Hobson, J. A. 1934. *Democracy and a Changing Civilisation*. London: John Lane The Bodley Head.

Höffe, Otfried. 2006. *Kant's Cosmopolitan Theory of Law and Peace*. Cambridge: Cambridge University Press.

Höffe, Otfried. 2007. *Democracy in an Age of Globalisation*. Dordrecht: Springer.

Hoffmann, Stanley. 2003. 'World governance: Beyond utopia'. *Daedalus* 132 (1):27–35.

Holthaus, Leonie. 2018. *Pluralist Democracy in International Relations: L.T. Hobhouse, G.D.H. Cole, and David Mitrany*. Basingstoke: Palgrave Macmillan.

Hooghe, Liesbet, Tobias Lenz, and Gary Marks. 2019. *A Theory of International Organization: A Postfunctionalist Theory of Governance, Volume IV*. Oxford: Oxford University Press.

Hooghe, Liesbet, Gary Marks, Tobias Lenz, Jeanine Bezuijen, Besir Ceka, and Svet Derderyan. 2017. *Measuring International Authority: A Postfunctionalist Theory of Governance, Volume III*. Oxford: Oxford University Press.

Howes, Dustin Ells. 2003. 'When states choose to die: Reassessing assumptions about what states want'. *International Studies Quarterly* 47 (4):669–692.

Hugo, Victor 1848/1875. 'Plantation de l'arbre de la liberté, place des Vosges'. In *Actes et Paroles: Avant l'Exil 1841–1851*, 109–111. Paris: Michel Levy Freres.

Hume, David. 1772/1994. 'Of the rise and progress of the arts and sciences'. In *Political Essays*, 58–77. Cambridge: Cambridge University Press.

Hurrell, Andrew. 2007. *On Global Order: Power, Values, and the Constitution of Global Society.* Oxford: Oxford University Press.

Ibhawoh, Bonny. 2001. 'Cultural relativism and human rights: Reconsidering the Africanist discourse'. *Netherlands Quarterly of Human Rights* 19 (1):43–62.

Ikilezi, Gloria, Orvalho J. Augusto, Joseph L. Dieleman, Kenneth Sherr, and Stephen S. Lim. 2020. 'Effect of donor funding for immunization from Gavi and other development assistance channels on vaccine coverage: Evidence from 120 low and middle income recipient countries'. *Vaccine* 38 (3):588–596.

ILO. 1944. Declaration concerning the aims and purposes of the International Labour Organisation. https://www.ilo.org/static/english/inwork/cb-policy-guide/declarationofPhiladelphia1944.pdf (accessed 6 March 2024).

IMF. 2021. Build Forward Better: IMF Annual Report 2021. Washington, DC: International Monetary Fund.

Inglehart, Ronald, et al., eds. 2014. World Values Survey: All Rounds—Country-Pooled Datafile Version. Data set. Madrid: JD Systems Institute.

International Institute for Strategic Studies. 2022. *The Military Balance 2022.* London: Taylor & Francis.

Isensee, Josef. 2003. 'Die vielen Staaten in der einen Welt—eine Apologie'. *Journal for Comparative Government and European Policy/Zeitschrift für Staats-und Europawissenschaften* 1 (1):7–31.

Ishiyama, John. 2022. 'Has legislative power declined globally?' *Journal of Legislative Studies* Published online 25 July. doi:10.1080/13572334.2022.2103288.

ISSP Research Group. 1998. International Social Survey Programme: National Identity I—ISSP 1995. Cologne: GESIS Data Archive, ZA2880 Data file Version 1.0.0. https://doi.org/10.4232/1.2880.

ISSP Research Group. 2012. International Social Survey Programme: National Identity II—ISSP 2003. Cologne: GESIS Data Archive, ZA3910 Data file Version 2.1.0. doi:10.4232/1.11449.

Jackson, Robert. 2000. *The Global Covenant: Human Conduct in a World of States.* Oxford: Oxford University Press.

Jägermeyr, Jonas, Alan Robock, Joshua Elliott, Christoph Müller, Lili Xia, Nikolay Khabarov, Christian Folberth, Erwin Schmid, Wenfeng Liu, and Florian Zabel. 2020. 'A regional nuclear conflict would compromise global food security'. *Proceedings of the National Academy of Sciences* 117 (13):7071–7081.

James, Patrick, Eric Solberg, and Murray Wolfson. 1999. 'An identified systemic model of the democracy–peace nexus'. *Defence and Peace Economics* 10 (1):1–37.

Jenne, Erin K. 2018. 'Is nationalism or ethnopopulism on the rise today?' *Ethnopolitics* 17 (5):546–552.

Jervis, Robert. 1978. 'Cooperation under the security dilemma'. *World Politics* 30 (2):167–214.

Johnston, Seth, Dan Reiter, John Schuessler, and Richard Ned Lebow. 2011. 'Are democracies aggressive? Is the United States aggressive? An exchange'. *St Antony's International Review* 7 (1):166–188.

Jones, Eric. 2003. *The European Miracle: Environments, Economies and Geopolitics in the History of Europe and Asia.* Third edition. Cambridge: Cambridge University Press.

Jönsson, Christer, and Jonas Tallberg, eds. 2010. *Transnational Actors in Global Governance: Patterns, Explanations and Implications*. Basingstoke: Palgrave Macmillan.

Kahler, Miles. 2005. 'Defining accountability up: The global economic multilaterals'. In *Global Governance and Public Accountability*, edited by David Held and Mathias Koenig-Archibugi, 8–34. Oxford: Blackwell.

Kalm, Sara, and Anna Meeuwisse. 2023. 'Transcalar activism contesting the liberal international order: The case of the World Congress of Families'. *Social Politics: International Studies in Gender, State & Society* 30 (2):556–579.

Kamminga, Menno R. 2006. 'Why global distributive justice cannot work'. *Acta Politica* 41:21–40.

K'ang, Yu-wei. 1902/1958. *Ta T'ung Shu: The One-World Philosophy of K'ang Yu-wei*. London: George Allen & Unwin.

Kant, Immanuel. 1775–76/2012. 'Lecture of the winter semester 1775–1776 based on the transcriptions Friedländer 3.3 (Ms 400), Friedländer 2 (Ms 399) and Prieger'. In Immanuel Kant, *Lectures on Anthropology*, edited by Robert B. Lauden and Allen W. Wood, 43–256. Cambridge: Cambridge University Press.

Kant, Immanuel. 1784/2007. 'Idea for a universal history with a cosmopolitan aim'. In Immanuel Kant, *Anthropology, History, and Education*, edited by Günter Zöller and Robert B. Louden, 107–120. Cambridge: Cambridge University Press.

Kant, Immanuel. 1793/1996. 'On the common saying: That may be correct in theory, but is of no use in practice'. In Immanuel Kant, *Practical Philosophy*, edited by Mary J. Gregor, 277–309. Cambridge: Cambridge University Press.

Kant, Immanuel. 1795/1996. 'Toward perpetual peace'. In Immanuel Kant, *Practical Philosophy*, edited by Mary J. Gregor, 317–351. Cambridge: Cambridge University Press.

Kant, Immanuel. 1797/1996. 'The metaphysics of morals'. In Immanuel Kant, *Practical Philosophy*, edited by Mary J. Gregor, 353–603. Cambridge: Cambridge University Press.

Kant, Immanuel. 2016. 'Fragments from notes on natural right'. In Immanuel Kant, *Lectures and Drafts on Political Philosophy*, edited by Frederick Rauscher, 21–70. Cambridge: Cambridge University Press.

Kaplan, Morton A. 1966. 'The new great debate: Traditionalism vs. science in international relations'. *World Politics* 19 (1):1–20.

Kasuya, Yuko, and Kota Mori. 2022. 'Re-examining thresholds of continuous democracy measures'. *Contemporary Politics* 24 (4):365–385.

Kelemen, R. Daniel, and Laurent Pech. 2019. 'The uses and abuses of constitutional pluralism: Undermining the rule of law in the name of constitutional identity in Hungary and Poland'. *Cambridge Yearbook of European Legal Studies* 21:59–74.

Kelsen, Hans 1920. *Das Problem der Souveränität und die Theorie des Völkerrechts: Beitrag zu einer reinen Rechtslehre*. Tübingen: J. C. B. Mohr (P. Siebeck).

Kelsen, Hans. 1929. *Vom Wesen und Wert der Demokratie: Zweite, umgearbeitete Auflage*. Tübingen: J. C. B. Mohr (P. Siebeck).

Kelsen, Hans. 1942. *Law and Peace in International Relations: The Oliver Wendell Holmes Lectures, 1940–41*. Cambridge, MA: Harvard University Press.

Kelsen, Hans 1944a. *Peace Through Law*. Chapel Hill: University of North Carolina Press.

Kelsen, Hans 1944b. 'The strategy of peace'. *American Journal of Sociology* 49 (5):381–389.

Kelsen, Hans 1946. 'Organization and procedure of the Security Council of the United Nations'. *Harvard Law Review* 59 (7):1087–1121.

Kelsen, Hans. 1955. 'Foundations of democracy'. *Ethics* 65 (1:2):1–67.

Kelsen, Hans 1967. *Pure Theory of Law*. Berkeley: University of California Press.

Keohane, Robert O. 2003. 'Global governance and democratic accountability'. In *Taming Globalization: Frontiers of Governance*, edited by David Held and Mathias Koenig-Archibugi, 130–159. Cambridge: Polity Press.

Keohane, Robert O. 2006. 'Accountability in world politics'. *Scandinavian Political Studies* 29 (2):75–87.

Keohane, Robert O. 2015. 'Nominal democracy? Prospects for democratic global governance'. *International Journal of Constitutional Law* 13 (2):343–353.

King, Gary, Michael Tomz, and Jason Wittenberg. 2000. 'Making the most of statistical analyses: Improving interpretation and presentation'. *American Journal of Political Science* 44 (2):347–361.

King, Gary, and Langche Zeng. 2007. 'When can history be our guide? The pitfalls of counterfactual inference'. *International Studies Quarterly* 51 (1):183–210.

King, Jr, Martin Luther. 1964/2012. 'The greatest hope for world peace'. In Martin Luther King, Jr, *'In a Single Garment of Destiny': A Global Vision of Justice*, edited by Lewis V. Baldwin, 146–149. Boston: Beacon Press.

King, Jr, Martin Luther. 1967. *Where Do We Go from Here: Chaos or Community?* New York: Harper & Row.

Kingsbury, Benedict, Nico Krisch, and Richard B. Stewart. 2005. 'The emergence of global administrative law'. *Law and Contemporary Problems* 68 (3/4):15–61.

Kinne, Brandon J. 2012. 'Multilateral trade and militarized conflict: Centrality, openness, and asymmetry in the global trade network'. *Journal of Politics* 74 (1):308–322.

Kinski, Lucy. 2022. 'Transnational partisanship in the EU: Opportunities, incentives and obstacles'. In *Transforming the Political Union: Reinforcing Europarties ahead of the European Elections*, edited by Ania Skrzypek, 21–53. Brussels: FEPS (Foundation for European Progressive Studies).

Kirikakha, Aleksandra, Gabriel J. Felbermayr, Constantinos Syropoulos, Erdal Yalcin, and Yoto V. Yotov. 2021. 'The Global Sanctions Data Base (GSDB): An update that includes the years of the Trump presidency'. In *Research Handbook on Economic Sanctions*, edited by Peter A. G. van Bergeijk, 62–106. Cheltenham: Edward Elgar.

Kirsch, Werner, and Gabor Toth. 2022. 'Collective bias models in two-tier voting systems and the democracy deficit'. *Mathematical Social Sciences* 119 (September):118–137.

Kitschelt, Herbert. 1994. *The Transformation of European Social Democracy*. Cambridge: Cambridge University Press.

Kitschelt, Herbert. 2000. 'Linkages between citizens and politicians in democratic polities'. *Comparative Political Studies* 33 (6–7):845–879.

Kleingeld, Pauline. 2011. *Kant and Cosmopolitanism: The Philosophical Ideal of World Citizenship*. Cambridge: Cambridge University Press.

Klingemann, Hans-Dieter, Richard Hofferbert, Ian Budge, Hans Keman, Ian Keman, Torbjörn Bergman, François Pétry, and Kaare Strom. 1994. *Parties, Policies, and Democracy*. Boulder: Westview Press.

Klingemann, Hans-Dieter, Andrea Volkens, Judith Bara, Ian Budge, and Michael McDonald. 2006. *Mapping Policy Preferences II: Estimates for Parties, Electors, and Governments in Eastern Europe, the European Union and the OECD, 1990–2003*. Oxford: Oxford University Press.

Klotz, Lynn. 2019. 'Human error in high-biocontainment labs: A likely pandemic threat'. *Bulletin of Atomic Scientists*, 25 February. https://thebulletin.org/2019/02/human-error-in-high-biocontainment-labs-a-likely-pandemic-threat/ (accessed 17 February 2024).

Koenig-Archibugi, Mathias. 2004a. 'Explaining government preferences for institutional change in EU foreign and security policy'. *International Organization* 58 (1):137–174.

Koenig-Archibugi, Mathias. 2004b. 'International governance as new Raison d'État? The case of the EU Common Foreign and Security Policy'. *European Journal of International Relations* 10 (2):147–188.

Koenig-Archibugi, Mathias. 2004c. 'Transnational corporations and public accountability'. *Government and Opposition* 39 (2):234–259.

Koenig-Archibugi, Mathias. 2011a. 'Global polio eradication initiative'. In *The Handbook of Transnational Governance: Institutions and Innovations*, edited by Thomas Hale and David Held, 166–175. Cambridge: Polity Press.

Koenig-Archibugi, Mathias. 2011b. 'Is global democracy possible?' *European Journal of International Relations* 17 (3):519–542.

Koenig-Archibugi, Mathias. 2012a. 'Fuzzy citizenship in global society'. *Journal of Political Philosophy* 20 (4):456–480.

Koenig-Archibugi, Mathias. 2012b. 'Global democracy and domestic analogies'. In *Global Democracy: Normative and Empirical Perspectives*, edited by Daniele Archibugi, Mathias Koenig-Archibugi, and Raffaele Marchetti, 160–182. Cambridge: Cambridge University Press.

Koenig-Archibugi, Mathias. 2022. 'Who are the people? Defining the demos in the measurement of democracy'. *Political Studies* 70 (2):402–424.

Koenig-Archibugi, Mathias, and Kate Macdonald. 2017. 'The role of beneficiaries in transnational regulatory processes'. *Annals of the American Academy of Political and Social Science* 670 (1):36–57.

Kohr, Leopold. 1957. *The Breakdown of Nations*. London: Routledge & Kegan Paul.

Kojève, Alexandre. 1943/2000. *Outline of a Phenomenology of Right*. Lanham: Rowman & Littlefield.

Kokaz, Nancy. 2005. 'Institutions for global justice'. *Canadian Journal of Philosophy* (supplementary volume) 31:65–107.

Koremenos, Barbara. 2016. *The Continent of International Law: Explaining Agreement Design*. Cambridge: Cambridge University Press.

Koriyama, Yukio, Antonin Macé, Rafael Treibich, and Jean-François Laslier. 2013. 'Optimal apportionment'. *Journal of Political Economy* 121 (3):584–608.

Kosinski, Leszek A. 1969. 'Changes in the ethnic structure in east-central Europe, 1930–1960'. *Geographical Review* 59 (3):388–402.

Koubi, Vally. 2019. 'Climate change and conflict'. *Annual Review of Political Science* 22:343–360.

Krasner, Stephen D. 1988. 'Sovereignty: An institutional perspective'. *Comparative Political Studies* 21 (1):66–94.

Krasner, Stephen D. 1999. *Sovereignty: Organized Hypocrisy*. Princeton: Princeton University Press.

Krehbiel, Jay N. 2021. 'Do voters punish noncompliance with high courts? A cross-national analysis'. *Politics* 41 (2):156–172.

Kreppel, Amie. 2014. 'Typologies and classifications'. In *The Oxford Handbook of Legislative Studies*, edited by Shane Martin, Thomas Saalfeld, and Kaare W. Strøm, 82–100 Oxford: Oxford University Press.

Kriesi, Hanspeter. 1998. 'The transformation of cleavage politics: The 1997 Stein Rokkan lecture'. *European Journal of Political Research* 33 (2):165–185.

Kriesi, Hanspeter, Edgar Grande, Romain Lachat, Martin Dolezal, Simon Bornschier, and Timotheos Frey. 2008. *West European Politics in the Age of Globalization*. Cambridge: Cambridge University Press.

Krisch, Nico. 2010. *Beyond Constitutionalism: The Pluralist Structure of Postnational Law*. Oxford: Oxford University Press.

Kroenig, Matthew. 2020. 'Rejoinder: A nuclear exchange on survivable normative biases'. *New Perspectives* 28 (1):123–127.

Kroll, Christian, Anne Warchold, and Prajal Pradhan. 2019. 'Sustainable Development Goals (SDGs): Are we successful in turning trade-offs into synergies?' *Palgrave Communications* 5 (1):1–11.

Krotoszynski, Ronald J. 2011. 'The separation of legislative and executive powers'. In *Comparative Constitutional Law*, edited by Tom Ginsburg and Rosalind Dixon, 234–253. Cheltenham: Edward Elgar.

Kucera, David. 2002. 'Core labour standards and foreign direct investment'. *International Labour Review* 141 (1/2):31–69.

Kuhn, Theresa, and Francesco Nicoli. 2020. 'Collective identities and the integration of core state powers: Introduction to the special issue'. *Journal of Common Market Studies* 58 (1):3–20.

Kukathas, Chandran. 2006. 'The mirage of global justice'. *Social Philosophy and Policy* 23 (1):1–28.

Kumm, Mattias. 2013. 'The cosmopolitan turn in constitutionalism: An integrated conception of public law'. *Indiana Journal of Global Legal Studies* 20 (2):605–628.

Kuper, Andrew. 2004. *Democracy Beyond Borders: Justice and Representation in Global Institutions*. Oxford: Oxford University Press.

Kurz, Sascha, Nicola Maaser, and Stefan Napel. 2017. 'On the democratic weights of nations'. *Journal of Political Economy* 125 (5):1599–1634.

Kushi, Sidita, and Monica Duffy Toft. 2023. 'Introducing the Military Intervention Project: A new dataset on US military interventions, 1776–2019'. *Journal of Conflict Resolution* 67 (4):752–779.

Kuyper, Jonathan W. 2014. 'Global democratization and international regime complexity'. *European Journal of International Relations* 20 (3):620–646.

Kuyper, Jonathan W., and Theresa Squatrito. 2017. 'International courts and global democratic values: Participation, accountability, and justification'. *Review of International Studies* 43 (1):152–176.

Kymlicka, Will. 2001. *Politics in the Vernacular: Nationalism, Multiculturalism, and Citizenship*. Oxford: Oxford University Press.

L'Aurora, Enrico Michele. 1796/1956. 'All'Italia nelle tenebre l'Aurora porta la luce'. In *Giacobini italiani*, Volume 1, edited by Delio Cantimori, 157–189. Bari: Laterza.

L'Ouverture, Toussaint. 1797/2019. 'Address to soldiers for the universal destruction of slavery'. In Toussaint L'Ouverture, *The Haitian Revolution*, edited by Nick Nisbett, 28 London: Verso.

L'Ouverture, Toussaint. 2019. *The Haitian Revolution*. London and New York: Verso.

La Hovary, Claire. 2015. 'A challenging ménage à trois? Tripartism in the International Labour Organization'. *International Organizations Law Review* 12 (1):204–236.

Laborde, Cécile, and Miriam Ronzoni. 2016. 'What is a free state? Republican internationalism and globalisation'. *Political Studies* 64 (2):279–296.

Lacy, Dean. 2001. 'A theory of nonseparable preferences in survey responses'. *American Journal of Political Science* 45 (2):239–258.

Lacy, Dean, and Emerson M. S. Niou. 2000. 'A problem with referendums'. *Journal of Theoretical Politics* 12 (1):5–31.

Lacy, Dean, and Emerson Niou. 2013. 'Nonseparable preferences and issue packaging in elections'. In *Advances in Political Economy*, edited by Norman Schofield, Gonzalo Caballero, and Daniel Kselman, 203–215. Berlin and Heidelberg: Springer.

Lagerspetz, Eerik. 2016. *Social Choice and Democratic Values*. Cham: Springer.

Lauterpacht, Hersch 1950. *International Law and Human Rights*. London: Stevens and Sons.

Law, David S., and Mila Versteeg. 2011. 'The evolution and ideology of global constitutionalism'. *California Law Review* 99 (5):1163–1257.

Leach, Stefan, Andrew Kitchin, and Robbie Sutton. 2023. 'Word embeddings indicate historical growth in moral concern for people, animals, and the environment'. *British Journal of Social Psychology* 62 (4):1925–1938.

Lebow, Richard Ned. 2011. 'Aggressive democracies'. *St Antony's International Review* 6 (2):120–133.

Lee, Hyo Won, and Sijeong Lim. 2022. 'Making sense of citizen desire for IO democracy: An analysis of public opinion across 44 countries'. *European Journal of International Relations* 28 (2):471–494.

Lee, Jong-Wha, and Hanol Lee. 2016. 'Human capital in the long run'. *Journal of Development Economics* 122:147–169.

Leebron, David W. 2002. 'Linkages'. *American Journal of International Law* 96 (1):5–27.

Lefkofridi, Zoe, and Alexia Katsanidou. 2018. 'A step closer to a transnational party system? Competition and coherence in the 2009 and 2014 European Parliament'. *Journal of Common Market Studies* 56 (6):1462–1482.

Lefkofridi, Zoe, Markus Wagner, and Johanna E. Willmann. 2014. 'Left-authoritarians and policy representation in Western Europe: Electoral choice across ideological dimensions'. *West European Politics* 37 (1):65–90.

Lehmann, Pola, Simon Franzmann, Tobias Burst, Sven Regel, Felicia Riethmüller, Andrea Volkens, Bernhard Weßels, and Lisa Zehnter. 2023. The Manifesto Data Collection. Manifesto Project (MRG/ CMP/ MARPOR). Version 2023a. Data set. Berlin and Göttingen: Wissenschaftszentrum Berlin für Sozialforschung (WZB); Institut für Demokratieforschung (IfDem). https://doi.org/10.25522/manifesto.mpds.2023a.

Leinen, Jo, and Andreas Bummel. 2018. *A World Parliament: Governance and Democracy in the 21st Century*. Berlin: Democracy Without Borders.

Lencucha, Raphael, and Shashika Bandara. 2021. 'Trust, risk, and the challenge of information sharing during a health emergency'. *Globalization and Health* 17 (1):1–7.

Lever, Annabelle. 2009. 'Democracy and judicial review: Are they really incompatible?' *Perspectives on Politics* 7 (4):805–822.

Lewis, Gregory, Piers Millett, Anders Sandberg, Andrew Snyder-Beattie, and Gigi Gronvall. 2019. 'Information hazards in biotechnology'. *Risk Analysis* 39 (5):975–981.

Li, Ruisi, Kaiping Peng, Linjia Jiang, Jingjin Li, and Wang Fei. 2022. 'Is the need for autonomy universal? Investigations with three large-scale global datasets'. Psyarxiv.com, 18 January. doi:10.31234/osf.io/rwqbx.

Li Donni, Paolo, Maria Marino, and Christian Welzel. 2021. 'How important is culture to understand political protest?' *World Development* 148 (December):105661.

Lijphart, Arend. 1999. *Patterns of Democracy: Government Forms and Performance in Thirty-six Countries*. New Haven: Yale University Press.

Lim, Adelyn. 2016. 'Transnational organising and feminist politics of difference and solidarity: The mobilisation of domestic workers in Hong Kong'. *Asian Studies Review* 40 (1):70–88.

Lindqvist, Erik, and Robert Östling. 2010. 'Political polarization and the size of government'. *American Political Science Review* 104 (3):543–565.

Linz, Juan J., and Alfred Stepan. 1996. *Problems of Democratic Transition and Consolidation: Southern Europe, South America, and Post-communist Europe*. Baltimore: Johns Hopkins University Press.

Liou, Ryan Yu-Lin, Amanda Murdie, and Dursun Peksen. 2021. 'Revisiting the causal links between economic sanctions and human rights violations'. *Political Research Quarterly* 74 (4):808–821.

Lipset, Seymour M. 1960. *Political Man: The Social Basis of Modern Politics*. New York: Doubleday.

List, Christian. 2006. 'Republican freedom and the rule of law'. *Politics, Philosophy & Economics* 5 (2):201–220.

List, Christian, and Mathias Koenig-Archibugi. 2010. 'Can there be a global demos? An agency-based approach'. *Philosophy and Public Affairs* 38 (1):76–110.

List, Christian, and Philip Pettit. 2002. 'Aggregating sets of judgments: An impossibility result'. *Economics & Philosophy* 18 (1):89–110.

List, Christian, and Philip Pettit. 2011. *Group Agency: The Possibility, Design, and Status of Corporate Agents*. Oxford: Oxford University Press.

List, Christian, and Laura Valentini. 2016. 'Freedom as independence'. *Ethics* 126 (4):1043–1074.

Little, Adrian, and Kate Macdonald. 2013. 'Pathways to global democracy? Escaping the statist imaginary'. *Review of International Studies* 39 (4):789–813.

Lloyd, Lola Maverick, and Roskia Schwimmer. 1942. *Chaos, War, or a New World Order*. Enlarged edition. Chicago: Campaign for World Government.

Lovett, Adam, and Jake Zuehl. 2022. 'The possibility of democratic autonomy'. *Philosophy & Public Affairs* 50 (4):467–498.

Lovett, Frank. 2016. 'Should republicans be cosmopolitans?' *Global Justice: Theory Practice Rhetoric* 9 (1). https://doi.org/10.21248/gjn.9.1.100.

Lu, Catherine. 2018. 'Cosmopolitan justice, democracy and the world state'. In *Institutional Cosmopolitanism*, edited by Luis Cabrera, 232–252. Oxford: Oxford University Press.

Lucena Carneiro, Cristiane, and Laerte Apolinário, Jr. 2016. 'Targeted versus conventional economic sanctions: What is at stake for human rights?' *International Interactions* 42 (4):565–589.

Luhmann, Sybille. 2017. 'A multi-level approach to European identity: Does integration foster identity?' *Journal of Common Market Studies* 55 (6):1360–1379.

Lührmann, Anna, and Staffan I. Lindberg. 2019. 'A third wave of autocratization is here: What is new about it?' *Democratization* 26 (7):1095–1113.

Lührmann, Anna, Marcus Tannenberg, and Staffan I. Lindberg. 2018. 'Regimes of the World (RoW): Opening new avenues for the comparative study of political regimes'. *Politics and Governance* 6 (1):60–77.

Lundgren, Carl. 2013. 'What are the odds? Assessing the probability of a nuclear war'. *Nonproliferation Review* 20 (2):361–374.

Lusseau, David, and Francesca Mancini. 2019. 'Income-based variation in Sustainable Development Goal interaction networks'. *Nature Sustainability* 2 (3):242–247.

Ma, Debin, and Jared Rubin. 2019. 'The paradox of power: Principal–agent problems and administrative capacity in Imperial China (and other absolutist regimes)'. *Journal of Comparative Economics* 47 (2):277–294.

MacAskill, William. 2022. *What We Owe the Future*. London: Oneworld.

Macdonald, Kate. 2012. 'Global democracy for a partially joined-up world: Toward a multilevel system of public power and democratic governance?' In *Global Democracy: Normative and Empirical Perspectives*, edited by Daniele Archibugi, Mathias Koenig-Archibugi, and Raffaele Marchetti, 183–209. Cambridge: Cambridge University Press.

Macdonald, Kate, and Terry Macdonald. 2010. 'Democracy in a pluralist global order: Corporate power and stakeholder representation'. *Ethics & International Affairs* 24 (1):19–43.

Macdonald, Terry 2008. *Global Stakeholder Democracy: Power and Representation beyond Liberal States*. Oxford: Oxford University Press.

Macdonald, Terry. 2012. 'Citizens or stakeholders? Exclusion, equality and legitimacy in global stakeholder democracy'. In *Global Democracy: Normative and Empirical Perspectives*, edited by Daniele Archibugi, Mathias Koenig-Archibugi, and Raffaele Marchetti, 47–68. Cambridge: Cambridge University Press.

Macdonald, Terry, and Kate Macdonald. 2006. 'Non-electoral accountability in global politics: Strengthening democratic control within the global garment industry'. *European Journal of International Law* 17 (1):89–119.

Macdonald, Terry, and Kate Macdonald. 2020. 'Towards a 'pluralist' world order: Creative agency and legitimacy in global institutions'. *European Journal of International Relations* 26 (2):518–544.

Mackie, Gerry. 2018. 'Deliberation and voting entwined'. In *The Oxford Handbook of Deliberative Democracy*, edited by Andre Bächtiger, John S. Dryzek, Jane Mansbridge, and Mark Warren, 218–236. Oxford: Oxford University Press.

Maerz, Seraphine F., Amanda B. Edgell, Matthew C. Wilson, Sebastian Hellmeier, and Staffan I. Lindberg. 2021. *A Framework for Understanding Regime Transformation: Introducing the ERT Dataset*. V-Dem Working Paper 113. Gothenburg, Sweden: V-Dem Institute.

Mangone, Gerard J. 1951. *The Idea and Practice of World Government*. New York: Columbia University Press.

Manheim, David, and Gregory Lewis. 2022. 'High-risk human-caused pathogen exposure events from 1975–2016 [version 2; peer review: 2 approved]'. *F1000Research* 10 (752):752.

Marchetti, Raffaele. 2008. *Global Democracy—For and Against: Ethical Theory, Institutional Design and Social Struggles*. London and New York: Routledge.

Marchetti, Raffaele. 2012. 'Models of global democracy: In defence of Cosmo-federalism'. In *Global Democracy: Normative and Empirical Perspectives*, edited by Daniele Archibugi, Mathias Koenig-Archibugi, and Raffaele Marchetti, 22–46. Cambridge: Cambridge University Press.

Markandya, Anil, Alessandro Antimiani, Valeria Costantini, C. Martini, Alessandro Palma, and M. C. Tommasino. 2015. 'Analyzing trade-offs in international climate policy options: The case of the green climate fund'. *World Development* 74 (October):93–107.

Markkanen, Sanna, and Annela Anger-Kraavi. 2019. 'Social impacts of climate change mitigation policies and their implications for inequality'. *Climate Policy* 19 (7):827–844.

Marks, Gary, Liesbet Hooghe, and Kermit Blank. 1996. 'European integration from the 1980s: State-centric v. multi-level governance'. *Journal of Common Market Studies* 34 (3):341–378.

Marsiglio of Padua. c.1339/1993. 'Defensor minor'. In Marsiglio of Padua, *Writings on the Empire: Defensor Minor and De Translatione Imperii*, edited by Cary J. Nederman, 1–64. Cambridge: Cambridge University Press.

Martens, Wil, Bastiaan van der Linden, and Manuel Wörsdörfer. 2019. 'How to assess the democratic qualities of a multi-stakeholder initiative from a Habermasian perspective? Deliberative democracy and the Equator Principles framework'. *Journal of Business Ethics* 155:1115–1133.

Martí, José Luis 2010. 'A global republic to prevent global domination'. *Diacritica* 24 (2):31–72.

Marx, Karl. 1875/1989. 'Critique of the Gotha Program'. In *Marx & Engels Collected Works*, Volume 24, 75–99. London: Lawrence & Wishart.

Mastanduno, Michael. 2014. 'Realism and Asia'. In *The Oxford Handbook of the International Relations of Asia*, edited by Saadia M. Pekkanen, John Ravenhill, and Rosemary Foot, 25–44. Oxford: Oxford University Press.

Mattoo, Aaditya, and Arvind Subramanian. 2012. 'Equity in climate change: An analytical review'. *World Development* 40 (6):1083–1097.

Maxmen, Amy. 2022. 'Scientists struggle to probe COVID's origins amid sparse data from China'. *Nature* 603 (7903):773–775.

May, Kenneth O. 1952. 'A set of independent necessary and sufficient conditions for simple majority decision'. *Econometrica* 20 (4):680–684.

Mayne, Richard, and John Pinder. 1990. *Federal Union: The Pioneers: A History of Federal Union*. Basingstoke: Macmillan.

McConaughey, Meghan, Paul Musgrave, and Daniel H. Nexon. 2018. 'Beyond anarchy: Logics of political organization, hierarchy, and international structure'. *International Theory* 10 (2):181–218.

McGann, Anthony J. 2004. 'The tyranny of the supermajority: How majority rule protects minorities'. *Journal of Theoretical Politics* 16 (1):53–77.

McGann, Anthony J. 2006. *The Logic of Democracy: Reconciling Equality, Deliberation, and Minority Protection*. Ann Arbor: University of Michigan Press.

McGann, Anthony J. 2013. 'Fairness and bias in electoral systems'. In *Representation: Elections and Beyond*, edited by Jack H. Nagel and Rogers M. Smith, 90–113. Philadelphia: University of Pennsylvania Press.

Mearsheimer, John J. 2018. *The Great Delusion: Liberal Dreams and International Realities*. New Haven: Yale University Press.

Melton, James, and Tom Ginsburg. 2014. 'Does de jure judicial independence really matter? A reevaluation of explanations for judicial independence'. *Journal of Law and Courts* 2 (2):187–217.

Merler, Stefano, Marco Ajelli, Laura Fumanelli, and Alessandro Vespignani. 2013. 'Containing the accidental laboratory escape of potential pandemic influenza viruses'. *BMC Medicine* 11 (1):1–11.

Midlarsky, Manus I. 1995. 'Environmental influences on democracy: Aridity, warfare, and a reversal of the causal arrow'. *Journal of Conflict Resolution* 39 (2):224–262.

Milanovic, Branko. 2012. 'Global inequality: From class to location, from proletarians to migrants'. *Global Policy* 3 (2):125–134.

Milanovic, Branko. 2016. *Global Inequality: A New Approach for the Age of Globalization*. Cambridge, MA: Harvard University Press.

Milanovic, Branko. 2021a. 'Notes on global income inequality: A non-technical summary'. Globalinequality blog. https://glineq.blogspot.com/2021/05/notes-on-global-income-inequality-non.html (accessed 27 July 2021).

Milanovic, Branko. 2021b. 'Towards global progressiveness'. International Politics and Society, 17 August. https://www.ips-journal.eu/topics/economy-and-ecology/towards-global-progressiveness-5338/.

Mill, John Stuart. 1861/1991. 'Considerations on representative government'. In John Stuart Mill, *On Liberty and Other Essays*, edited by John Gray, 205–467 Oxford: Oxford University Press.

Miller, David. 2007. *National Responsibility and Global Justice*. Oxford: Oxford University Press.

Miller, David. 2009. 'Democracy's domain'. *Philosophy and Public Affairs* 37 (3):201–228.

Miller, David. 2010. 'Against global democracy'. In *After the Nation: Critical Reflections on Post-nationalism*, edited by Keith Breen and Shane O'Neill, 141–160. Basingstoke: Palgrave.

Miller, Michael K. 2015. 'Democratic pieces: Autocratic elections and democratic development since 1815'. *British Journal of Political Science* 45 (3):501–530.

Miller, Nicholas R. 1983. 'Pluralism and social choice'. *American Political Science Review* 77 (3):734–747.

Mills, Charles W. 1997. *The Racial Contract*. Ithaca: Cornell University Press.

Mills, Michael J., Owen B. Toon, Julia Lee-Taylor, and Alan Robock. 2014. 'Multidecadal global cooling and unprecedented ozone loss following a regional nuclear conflict'. *Earth's Future* 2 (4):161–176.

Milner, Helen. 1991. 'The assumption of anarchy in international relations theory: A critique'. *Review of International Studies* 17 (1):67–85.

Mitrany, David. 1975. 'A political theory for the new society'. In *Functionalism*, edited by A. J. R. Groom and Paul Taylor, 25–52. London: University of London Press.

Monbiot, George. 2003. *The Age of Consent: Manifesto for a New World Order*. New York: Harper Perennial.

Montanaro, Laura. 2012. 'The democratic legitimacy of self-appointed representatives'. *Journal of Politics* 74 (4):1094–1107.

Montesquieu, Charles-Louis de Secondat. 1748/1989. *The Spirit of the Laws*. Cambridge: Cambridge University Press.

Montesquieu, Charles-Louis de Secondat. 2012. *My Thoughts*. Indianapolis: Liberty Fund.

Monteux, Camille A. 2006. 'Decentralisation: The new delusion of ethnic conflict regulation'. *International Journal on Multicultural Societies* 8 (2):162–182.

Moon, Suerie, Devi Sridhar, Muhammad A. Pate, Ashish K. Jha, Chelsea Clinton, Sophie Delaunay, Valnora Edwin, Mosoka Fallah, David P. Fidler, and Laurie Garrett. 2015. 'Will Ebola change the game? Ten essential reforms before the next pandemic. The report of the Harvard-LSHTM Independent Panel on the Global Response to Ebola'. *Lancet* 386 (10009):2204–2221.

Moore, Margaret. 2006. 'Globalization and democratization: Institutional design for global institutions'. *Journal of Social Philosophy* 37 (1):21–43.

Moravcsik, Andrew. 1993. 'Preferences and power in the European Community: A liberal intergovernmentalist approach'. *Journal of Common Market Studies* 31 (4):473–524.

Moravcsik, Andrew. 1994. *Why the European Community Strengthens the State: Domestic Politics and International Cooperation*. Cambridge, MA: Minda de Gunzburg Center for European Studies, Harvard University.

Morgan, T. Clifton, Navin A. Bapat, and Yoshiharu Kobayashi. 2021. 'The threat and imposition of economic sanctions data project: A retrospective'. In *Research Handbook on Economic Sanctions*, edited by Peter A. G. van Bergeijk, 44–61 Cheltenham: Edward Elgar.

Morgenthau, Hans J. 1954. *Politics among Nations: The Struggle for Power and Peace*. Second edition. New York: Alfred A. Knopf.

Mori, Massimo. 2008. *La pace e la ragione: Kant e le relazioni internazionali: diritto, politica, storia*. Bologna: Il Mulino.

Mortier, Roland. 1995. *Anacharsis Cloots ou l'utopie foudroyée*. Paris: Stock.

Mosley, Layna. 2011. *Labor Rights and Multinational Production*. Cambridge: Cambridge University Press.

Mosley, Layna, and Saika Uno. 2007. 'Racing to the bottom or climbing to the top? Economic globalization and collective labor rights'. *Comparative Political Studies* 40 (8):923–948.

Mousseau, Michael, and Yuhang Shi. 1999. 'A test for reverse causality in the democratic peace relationship'. *Journal of Peace Research* 36 (6):639–663.

Mueller, John. 2013. *The Remnants of War*. Ithaca: Cornell University Press.

Munck, Gerardo L. 2015. 'Democratic transitions'. In *International Encyclopedia of the Social & Behavioral Sciences*. Second edition. Volume 6, edited by James D. Wright, 97–100. Amsterdam: Elsevier.

Munger, Michael, and Georg Vanberg. 2023. 'Contractarianism, constitutionalism, and the status quo'. *Public Choice* 195:323–339.

Murithi, Tim. 2012. 'Towards the metamorphosis of the United Nations: A proposal for establishing global democracy'. In *Global Democracy: Normative and Empirical Perspectives*, edited by Daniele Archibugi, Mathias Koenig-Archibugi, and Raffaele Marchetti, 132–149. Cambridge: Cambridge University Press.

Murray, Christopher J. L., Kevin Shunji Ikuta, Fablina Sharara, Lucien Swetschinski, Gisela Robles Aguilar, Authia Gray, Chieh Han, Catherine Bisignano, Puja Rao, and Eve Wool.

2022. 'Global burden of bacterial antimicrobial resistance in 2019: A systematic analysis'. *Lancet* 399 (10325):629–655.

Musunuri, Sriharshita, Jonas B. Sandbrink, Joshua Teperowski Monrad, Megan J. Palmer, and Gregory D. Koblentz. 2021. 'Rapid proliferation of pandemic research: Implications for dual-use risks'. *mBio* 12 (5):e01864-21.

Nafafé, José Lingna. 2022. *Lourenço da Silva Mendonça and the Black Atlantic Abolitionist Movement in the Seventeenth Century.* Cambridge: Cambridge University Press.

Naitram, Simon. 2022. 'How big are strategic spillovers from corporate tax competition?' *Economic Inquiry* 60 (2):847–869.

Nanz, Patrizia. 2006. *Europolis: Constitutional Patriotism Beyond the Nation State.* Manchester: Manchester University Press.

Nanz, Patrizia, and Jens Steffek. 2005. 'Global governance, participation and the public sphere'. In *Global Governance and Public Accountability*, edited by David Held and Mathias Koenig-Archibugi, 190–211. Oxford: Blackwell.

Nardulli, Peter F., Cara J. Wong, Ajay Singh, Buddy Peyton, and Joseph Bajjalieh. 2012. *The Composition of Religious and Ethnic Groups (CREG) Project.* Champaign and Urbana: Cline Center for Democracy, University of Illinois at Urbana-Champaign.

Neuenkirch, Matthias, and Florian Neumeier. 2015. 'The impact of UN and US economic sanctions on GDP growth'. *European Journal of Political Economy* 40 (December):110–125.

Neuenkirch, Matthias, and Florian Neumeier. 2016. 'The impact of US sanctions on poverty'. *Journal of Development Economics* 121 (July):110–119.

Newcombe, Hanna. 1983. *Design for a Better World.* Lanham: University Press of America.

Nicolaïdis, Kalypso. 2012. 'The idea of European demoicracy'. In *Philosophical Foundations of European Union Law*, edited by Julie Dickson and Pavlos Eleftheriadis, 247–274. Oxford: Oxford University Press.

Noel, Hans. 2014. *Political Ideologies and Political Parties in America.* Cambridge: Cambridge University Press.

Norkus, Zenonas, and Jurgita Markevičiūtė. 2021. 'New estimation of the gross domestic product in Baltic countries in 1913–1938'. *Cliometrica* 15:565–674

Norman, Ludvig, and Wouter Wolfs. 2022. 'Is the governance of Europe's transnational party system contributing to EU democracy?' *Journal of Common Market Studies* 60 (2):463–479.

Norris, Pippa, and Ronald Inglehart. 2019. *Cultural Backlash: Trump, Brexit, and Authoritarian Populism.* Cambridge: Cambridge University Press.

Novicow, Jacques. 1901. *Die Föderation Europas.* Berlin and Bern: Akademischer Verlag für sociale Wissenschaften Dr John Edelheim.

Novus and Global Challenges Foundation. 2020. *Global Catastrophic Risks and International Collaboration: Opinion Poll 2020.* Stockholm: Global Challenges Foundation.

Nozick, Robert. 1974. *Anarchy, State, and Utopia.* New York: Basic Books.

Nussbaum, Martha C. 2006. *Frontiers of Justice: Disability, Nationality, Species Membership.* Cambridge, MA: Harvard University Press.

Nussbaum, Martha C. 2019. *The Cosmopolitan Tradition: A Noble but Flawed Ideal.* Cambridge, MA: Harvard University Press.

Nye, Joseph S. 2002. 'Parliament of dreams'. *WorldLink*, March/April, 15–17.

O'Connor, Kelsey J., Luisa R. Blanco, and Jeffrey B. Nugent. 2018. 'Does oil really curse democracy? A long-run time-series analysis of 127 countries'. *Resources Policy* 57 (August):264–277.

O'Donnell, Guillermo. 1993. 'On the state, democratization and some conceptual problems: A Latin American view with glances at some postcommunist countries'. *World Development* 21 (8):1355–1369.

OECD. 2021. *Managing Climate Risks, Facing up to Losses and Damages*. Paris: Organisation for Economic Co-operation and Development.

Olney, William W. 2013. 'A race to the bottom? Employment protection and foreign direct investment'. *Journal of International Economics* 91 (2):191–203.

Onderco, Michal, Michal Smetana, and Tom W. Etienne. 2023. 'Hawks in the making? European public views on nuclear weapons post-Ukraine'. *Global Policy* 14 (2):305–317. https://doi.org/10.1111/1758-5899.13179.

Oneal, John R., and Bruce Russett. 2000. 'Comment: Why "an identified systemic model of the democracy-peace nexus" does not persuade'. *Defence and Peace Economics* 11 (1):197–214.

O'Neill, Onora. 2001. 'Agents of justice'. *Metaphilosophy* 32 (1–2):180–195.

Ooms, Gorik, Rachel Hammonds, Attiya Waris, Bart Criel, Wim Van Damme, and Alan Whiteside. 2014. 'Beyond health aid: Would an international equalization scheme for universal health coverage serve the international collective interest?' *Globalization and Health* 10 (1):1–15.

Oppenheim, Lassa. 1921. *The Future of International Law*. Oxford: Clarendon Press.

Ord, Toby. 2020. *The Precipice: Existential Risk and the Future of Humanity*. London: Bloomsbury.

Orwin, Alexander I. 2014. 'Can humankind deliberate on a global scale? Alfarabi and the politics of the inhabited world'. *American Political Science Review* 108 (4):830–839.

Overesch, Michael, and Johannes Rincke. 2011. 'What drives corporate tax rates down? A reassessment of globalization, tax competition, and dynamic adjustment to shocks'. *Scandinavian Journal of Economics* 113 (3):579–602.

Padmore, George, ed. 1947. *Colonial and Coloured Unity: A Programme of Action: History of the Pan-African Congress*. Manchester: Pan-African Federation.

Page, Scott E. 2010. *Diversity and Complexity*. Princeton: Princeton University Press.

Paine, Thomas 1791/1995. 'Rights of Man'. In Thomas Paine, *Rights of Man, Common Sense, and Other Political Writings*, edited by Mark Philp, 83–197. Oxford: Oxford University Press.

Paine, Thomas 1792/1995. 'Rights of Man, Part the Second'. In Thomas Paine, *Rights of Man, Common Sense, and Other Political Writings*, edited by Mark Philp, 199–331. Oxford: Oxford University Press.

Pan, Jennifer, and Yiqing Xu. 2018. 'China's ideological spectrum'. *Journal of Politics* 80 (1):254–273.

Panda, Smita Mishra, and Annapurna Devi Pandey. 2022. 'Rural women's self-determination and grassroots resistance movement'. In *Gender, Power, and Non-Governance: Is Female to Male as NGO is to State?*, edited by Andria D. Timmer and Elizabeth Wirtz, 124–149. New York and Oxford: Berghahn.

Parent, Joseph. 2011. *Uniting States: Voluntary Union in World Politics*. Oxford: Oxford University Press.

Parizek, Michal, and Matthew D. Stephen. 2021. 'The increasing representativeness of international organizations' secretariats: Evidence from the United Nations system, 1997–2015'. *International Studies Quarterly* 65 (1):197–209.

Partington, John S. 2003. 'H.G. Wells and the world state: A liberal cosmopolitan in a totalitarian age'. *International Relations* 17 (2):233–246.

Pasternak, Avia. 2012. 'Cosmopolitan justice and the league of democracies'. *Critical Review of International Social and Political Philosophy* 15 (5):649–666.

Patomäki, Heikki. 2011. 'Towards global political parties'. *Ethics & Global Politics* 4 (2):81–102.

Patomäki, Heikki. 2012. 'The problems of legitimation and potential conflicts in a world political community'. *Cooperation and Conflict* 47 (2):239–259.

Paul, Darel E. 1999. 'Sovereignty, survival and the Westphalian blind alley in international relations'. *Review of International Studies* 25 (2):217–232.

Pavel, Carmen 2015. *Divided Sovereignty: International Institutions and the Limits of State Authority*. Oxford: Oxford University Press.

Payne, Rodger A., and Nayef H. Samhat. 2004. *Democratizing Global Politics: Discourse Norms, International Regimes, and Political Community*. Albany: SUNY Press.

Pecqueur, Constantin. 1842. *De la Paix, de son principe, et de sa réalisation*. Paris: Capelle.

Peksen, Dursun. 2011. 'Economic sanctions and human security: The public health effect of economic sanctions'. *Foreign Policy Analysis* 7 (3):237–251.

Pemstein, Daniel, Kyle L. Marquardt, Eitan Tzelgov, Yi-ting Wang, Juraj Medzihorsky, Joshua Krusell, Farhad Miri, and Johannes von Römer. 2021. *The V-Dem Measurement Model: Latent Variable Analysis for Cross-National and Cross-Temporal Expert-Coded Data*. V-Dem Working Paper No. 21. Sixth edition. University of Gothenburg, Varieties of Democracy Institute.

Penrose, Lionel S. 1946. 'The elementary statistics of majority voting'. *Journal of the Royal Statistical Society* 109 (1):53–57.

Peters, Margaret E. 2015. 'Open trade, closed borders immigration in the era of globalization'. *World Politics* 67 (1):114–154.

Pettit, Philip 1997. *Republicanism: A Theory of Freedom and Government*. Oxford: Oxford University Press.

Pettit, Philip. 2010a. 'A republican law of peoples'. *European Journal of Political Theory* 9 (1):70–94.

Pettit, Philip. 2010b. 'Legitimate international institutions: A neorepublican perspective'. In *The Philosophy of International Law*, edited by Samantha Besson and John Tasioulas, 139–162. Oxford: Oxford University Press.

Pettit, Philip. 2012. *On the People's Terms: A Republican Theory and Model of Democracy*. Cambridge: Cambridge University Press.

Pettit, Philip. 2013. 'Two republican traditions'. In *Republican Democracy: Liberty, Law and Politics*, edited by Andreas Niederberger and Phillip Schink, 169–204. Edinburgh: Edinburgh University Press.

Pettit, Philip. 2022. 'Statehood and justice'. *Society* 59 (2):140–148.

Pevehouse, Jon C. W., Timothy Nordstrom, Roseanne W. McManus, and Anne Spencer Jamison. 2020. 'Tracking organizations in the world: The Correlates of War IGO Version 3.0 datasets'. *Journal of Peace Research* 57 (3):492–503.

Pew Research Center. 2007. 'Survey methods in detail: About the 2007 Pew Global Attitudes Survey'. https://www.pewresearch.org/global/dataset/spring-2007-survey-data/ (Accessed 7 March 2024).

Philo. 1993. 'On the unchangeableness of God'. In *The Works of Philo: New Updated Edition*, translated by C. D. Yonge, 158–173. Peabody, MA: Hendrickson Publishers.

Pinker, Steven. 2012. *The Better Angels of Our Nature: Why Violence has Declined*. London: Penguin Books.

Pinker, Steven. n.d. 'Fooled by belligerence: Comments on Nassim Taleb's "The Long Peace is a Statistical Illusion"'. https://stevenpinker.com/files/pinker/files/comments_on_taleb_by_s_pinker_1.pdf (accessed 17 February 2024).

Pogge, Thomas W. 1992. 'Cosmopolitanism and sovereignty'. *Ethics* 103 (1):48–75.

Posner, Eric A. 2006. 'International law: A welfarist approach'. *University of Chicago Law Review* 73 (2):487–543.

Posner, Eric A. 2009. *The Perils of Global Legalism*. Chicago: University of Chicago Press.

Powell, G. Bingham. 2000. *Elections as Instruments of Democracy: Majoritarian and Proportional Visions*. New Haven: Yale University Press.

Pradhan, Prajal, Luís Costa, Diego Rybski, Wolfgang Lucht, and Jürgen P. Kropp. 2017. 'A systematic study of Sustainable Development Goal (SDG) interactions'. *Earth's Future* 5 (11):1169–1179.

Press, Daryl G., Scott D. Sagan, and Benjamin A. Valentino. 2013. 'Atomic aversion: Experimental evidence on taboos, traditions, and the non-use of nuclear weapons'. *American Political Science Review* 107 (1):188–206.

Przeworski, Adam. 2009. 'Conquered or granted? A history of suffrage extensions'. *British Journal of Political Science* 39 (2):291–321.

Przeworski, Adam. 2010. *Democracy and the Limits of Self-Government*. Cambridge: Cambridge University Press.

Rabkin, Jeremy A. 2005. *Law without Nations? Why Constitutional Government Requires Sovereign States*. Princeton: Princeton University Press.

Rae, Douglas W. 1975. 'The limits of consensual decision'. *American Political Science Review* 69 (4):1270–1294.

Ramos, Miguel R., Matthew R. Bennett, Douglas S. Massey, and Miles Hewstone. 2019. 'Humans adapt to social diversity over time'. *Proceedings of the National Academy of Sciences* 116 (25):12244–12249.

Rasler, Karen, and William R. Thompson. 2004. 'The democratic peace and a sequential, reciprocal, causal arrow hypothesis'. *Comparative Political Studies* 37 (8):879–908.

Ravlo, Hilde, Nils Petter Gleditsch, and Han Dorussen. 2003. 'Colonial war and the democratic peace'. *Journal of Conflict Resolution* 47 (4):520–548.

Rawls, John. 1996. *Political Liberalism*. New York: Columbia University Press.

Rawls, John. 1999a. *A Theory of Justice*. Revised edition. Cambridge, MA: Harvard University Press.

Rawls, John. 1999b. *The Law of Peoples: With 'The Idea of Public Reason Revisited'*. Cambridge, MA: Harvard University Press.

Raz, Joseph. 1986. *The Morality of Freedom*. Oxford: Clarendon Press.

Razum, Oliver, Devi Sridhar, Albrecht Jahn, Shehla Zaidi, Gorik Ooms, and Olaf Müller. 2019. 'Polio: From eradication to systematic, sustained control'. *BMJ Global Health* 4 (4):e001633.

Reagan, Ronald. 1987. 'Address to the 42nd session of the United Nations General Assembly in New York'. 21 September. https://www.reaganlibrary.gov/archives/speech/address-42d-session-united-nations-general-assembly-new-york-new-york (accessed 17 February 2024).

Rector, Chad. 2009. *Federations: The Political Dynamics of Cooperation*. Ithaca and London: Cornell University Press.

Reiter, Dan. 2001. 'Does peace nature democracy?' *Journal of Politics* 63 (3):935–948.

Renan, Ernest. 1882/2018. 'What is a nation?' In *What Is a Nation? And Other Political Writings*, 247–263. New York: Columbia University Press.

Reves, Emery. 1945. *The Anatomy of Peace*. New York: Harper and Brothers.

Review on Antimicrobial Resistance. 2016. *Tackling Drug-Resistant Infections Globally: Final Report and Recommendations*. London: Wellcome Trust.

Reysen, Stephen. 2022. 'Globalization and all-inclusive global identities'. In *Globalized Identities: The Impact of Globalization on Self and Identity*, edited by Iva Katzarska-Miller and Stephen Reysen, 219–243. Basingstoke: Palgrave Macmillan.

Reysen, Stephen, and Iva Katzarska-Miller. 2018. *The Psychology of Global Citizenship: A Review of Theory and Research*. Lanham: Lexington Books.

Riahi, Keywan, Detlef P. Van Vuuren, Elmar Kriegler, Jae Edmonds, Brian C. O'Neill, Shinichiro Fujimori, Nico Bauer, Katherine Calvin, Rob Dellink, and Oliver Fricko. 2017. 'The Shared Socioeconomic Pathways and their energy, land use, and greenhouse gas emissions implications: An overview'. *Global Environmental Change* 42 (January):153–168.

Rice, Stuart A. 1925. 'The behavior of legislative groups: A method of measurement'. *Political Science Quarterly* 40 (1):60–72.

Riker, William. 1975. 'Federalism'. In *The Handbook of Political Science*, Volume V: *Government Institutions and Processes*, edited by Fred Greenstein and Nelson Polsby, 93–172. Reading, MA: Addison Wesley.

Riker, William. 1995. 'Federalism'. In *A Companion to Contemporary Political Philosophy*, edited by Robert E. Goodin and Philip Pettit, 508–514. Oxford: Blackwell.

Roberts, Louisa L. 2019. 'Changing worldwide attitudes toward homosexuality: The influence of global and region-specific cultures, 1981–2012'. *Social Science Research* 80 (May):114–131.

Robespierre, Maximilien de. 1793/1979. 'Discours à la Société des Jacobins, séance extraordinaire du 22 frimaire an II (12 December 1793)'. In *Écrits révolutionnaires, 1790–1794*, by Anacharsis Cloots, 653–655. Paris: Champ libre.

Rodrik, Dani. 2000. 'How far will international economic integration go?' *Journal of Economic Perspectives* 14 (1):177–186.

Rodrik, Dani. 2011. *The Globalization Paradox: Democracy and the Future of the World Economy*. New York: W. W. Norton & Company.

Roeder, Philip G. 2009. 'Ethnofederalism and the mismanagement of conflicting nationalisms'. *Regional & Federal Studies* 19 (2):203–219.

Romanello, Marina, Alice McGushin, Claudia Di Napoli, Paul Drummond, Nick Hughes, Louis Jamart, Harry Kennard, Pete Lampard, Baltazar Solano Rodriguez, and Nigel Arnell. 2021. 'The 2021 report of the Lancet Countdown on health and climate change: Code red for a healthy future'. *Lancet* 398 (10311):1619–1662.

Ronzoni, Miriam 2017. 'Republicanism and global institutions: Three desiderata in tension'. *Social Philosophy and Policy* 34 (1):186–208.

Roope, Laurence S. J., Richard D. Smith, Koen B. Pouwels, James Buchanan, Lucy Abel, Peter Eibich, Christopher C. Butler, Pui San Tan, A. Sarah Walker, Julie V. Robotham, and Sarah C. Wordsworth. 2019. 'The challenge of antimicrobial resistance: What economics can contribute'. *Science* 364 (6435):eaau4679.

Rosenblum, Nancy L. 2010. *On the Side of the Angels: An Appreciation of Parties and Partisanship*. Princeton: Princeton University Press.

Ross, Edward Alsworth. 1920. *The Principles of Sociology*. New York: The Century Company.

Rosselli, Carlo. 1930/1994. *Liberal Socialism*. Princeton: Princeton University Press.

Rosset, Jan, and Christian Stecker. 2019. 'How well are citizens represented by their governments? Issue congruence and inequality in Europe'. *European Political Science Review* 11 (2):145–160.

Roth, David F. 1977. 'The global village: Who will represent the villagers, who will run the village?' *International Interactions* 3 (1):27–32.

Rousseau, Jean-Jacques. 1755/1997. 'Discourse on political economy'. In Jean-Jacques Rousseau, *The Social Contract and Other Later Political Writings*, edited by Victor Gourevitch, 3–38. Cambridge: Cambridge University Press.

Rousseau, Jean-Jacques. c.1760/1994. 'Geneva manuscript'. In Jean-Jacques Rousseau, *Social Contract, Discourse on the Virtue Most Necessary for a Hero, Political Fragments, and Geneva Manuscript*, edited by Roger D. Masters and Christopher Kelly, 153–161. Hanover: Dartmouth College Press.

Rousseau, Jean-Jacques. 1762/1997. 'Of the social contract'. In Jean-Jacques Rousseau, *The Social Contract and Other Later Political Writings*, edited by Victor Gourevitch, 39–152. Cambridge: Cambridge University Press.

Rousseau, Jean-Jacques. 1782/2005. 'Judgement of the plan for perpetual peace'. In Jean-Jacques Rousseau, *The Plan for Perpetual Peace, On the Government of Poland, and Other*

Writings on History and Politics, edited by Christopher Kelly, 53–60. Hanover: Darthmouth College Press.

Rovny, Jan, and Gary Marks. 2011. 'Issues and dimensions in public opinion'. Unpublished manuscript. http://garymarks.web.unc.edu/files/2016/09/rovny-and-marks.-issues-and-dimensions.pdf (accessed 17 February 2024).

Rozo, Michelle, and Gigi Kwik Gronvall. 2015. 'The reemergent 1977 H1N1 strain and the gain-of-function debate'. *mBio* 6 (4):e01013-15.

Ruck, Damian J., R. Alexander Bentley, and Daniel J. Lawson. 2020. 'Cultural prerequisites of socioeconomic development'. *Royal Society Open Science* 7 (2):190725.

Ruck, Damian J., Luke J. Matthews, Thanos Kyritsis, Quentin D. Atkinson, and R. Alexander Bentley. 2020. 'The cultural foundations of modern democracies'. *Nature Human Behaviour* 4 (3):265–269.

Rueschemeyer, Dietrich, Evelyne Huber Stephens, and John D. Stephens. 1991. *Capitalist Development and Democracy*. Cambridge: Polity Press.

Russell, Bertrand. 1959. *Common Sense and Nuclear Warfare*. London: George Allen and Unwin.

Sagan, Scott, and Kenneth Waltz. 1995. *The Spread of Nuclear Weapons: A Debate*. New York: W. W. Norton.

Samir, K. C., and Wolfgang Lutz. 2017. 'The human core of the shared socioeconomic pathways: Population scenarios by age, sex and level of education for all countries to 2100'. *Global Environmental Change* 42 (January):181–192.

Sandberg, Anders, and Cassidy Nelson. 2020. 'Who should we fear more: biohackers, disgruntled postdocs, or bad governments? A simple risk chain model of biorisk'. *Health Security* 18 (3):155–163.

Sartorius, Johann Baptist. 1837. *Organon des vollkommenen Friedens*. Zürich: Höhr.

Sathyamala, C., Onkar Mittal, Rajib Dasgupta, and Ritu Priya. 2005. 'Polio eradication initiative in India: Deconstructing the GPEI'. *International Journal of Health Services* 35 (2):361–383.

Saunders, Ben. 2010. 'Democracy, political equality, and majority rule'. *Ethics* 121 (1):148–177.

Schaffer, Johan Karlsson. 2015. 'The co-originality of human rights and democracy in an international order'. *International Theory* 7 (1):96–124.

Schakel, Wouter, and Daphne Van Der Pas. 2021. 'Degrees of influence: Educational inequality in policy representation'. *European Journal of Political Research* 60 (2):418–437.

Scheidel, Walter. 2019. *Escape from Rome: The Failure of Empire and the Road to Prosperity*. Princeton: Princeton University Press.

Schelling, Thomas. 1992. 'The global dimension'. In *Rethinking America's Security*, edited by Graham Allison and Gregory F. Treverton, 196–210. New York: Norton.

Schelling, Thomas C. 2009. 'A world without nuclear weapons?' *Daedalus* 138 (4):124–129.

Scherer, Laura, Paul Behrens, Arjan de Koning, Reinout Heijungs, Benjamin Sprecher, and Arnold Tukker. 2018. 'Trade-offs between social and environmental Sustainable Development Goals'. *Environmental Science & Policy* 90:65–72.

Scheuerman, William E. 2011. *The Realist Case for Global Reform*. Cambridge: Polity Press.

Schimmelfennig, Frank, Thomas Winzen, Tobias Lenz, Jofre Rocabert, Loriana Crasnic, Cristina Gherasimov, Jana Lipps, and Densua Mumford. 2020. *The Rise of International Parliaments: Strategic Legitimation in International Organizations*. Oxford: Oxford University Press.

Schmitt, Carina, Hanna Lierse, Herbert Obinger, and Laura Seelkopf. 2015. 'The global emergence of social protection: Explaining social security legislation 1820-2013'. *Politics & Society* 43 (4):503–524.

Schmitt, Carl. 1932/1996. *The Concept of the Political*. Chicago: University of Chicago Press.

Schmitter, Philippe C. 1999. 'The future of democracy: Could it be a matter of scale?' *Social Research* 66 (3):933–958.

Scholte, Jan Aart. 2005. 'Civil society and democratically accountable global governance.' In *Global Governance and Public Accountability*, edited by David Held and Mathias Koenig-Archibugi, 87–109. Oxford: Blackwell.

Scholte, Jan Aart, ed. 2011. *Building Global Democracy? Civil Society and Accountable Global Governance*. Cambridge: Cambridge University Press.

Scholte, Jan Aart. 2014. 'Reinventing global democracy'. *European Journal of International Relations* 20 (1):3–28.

Scholte, Jan Aart. 2020. 'After liberal global democracy: New methodology for new praxis'. *Fudan Journal of the Humanities and Social Sciences* 13 (1):67–92.

Schrock-Jacobson, Gretchen. 2012. 'The violent consequences of the nation: Nationalism and the initiation of interstate war'. *Journal of Conflict Resolution* 56 (5):825–852.

Schuman, Frederick Lewis 1952. *The Commonwealth of Man: An Inquiry into Power Politics and World Government*. New York: Knopf.

Schvitz, Guy, Luc Girardin, Seraina Rüegger, Nils B. Weidmann, Lars-Erik Cederman, and Kristian Skrede Gleditsch. 2022. 'Mapping the international system, 1886–2019: The CShapes 2.0 dataset'. *Journal of Conflict Resolution* 66 (1):144–161.

Schwartzberg, Joseph. 2012. *Creating a World Parliamentary Assembly: An Evolutionary Journey*. Berlin: Committee for a Democratic UN.

Schwartzberg, Joseph E. 2013. *Transforming the United Nations System: Designs for a Workable World*. Tokyo: United Nations University Press.

Schwarzenberger, Georg. 1951. *Power Politics: A Study of International Society*. New York: Praeger.

Segall, Jeffrey J. 1990. 'Building world democracy through the UN'. *Medicine and War* 6 (4):275–285.

Segall, Jeffrey J. 1991. 'A UN second assembly'. In *Building a More Democratic United Nations*, edited by Frank Barnaby, 93–109. London: Frank Cass.

Sehm-Patomaki, Katarina, and Marko Ulvila, eds. 2007. *Global Political Parties*. London and New York: Zed Books.

Sen, Amartya. 1999. *Development as Freedom*. Oxford: Oxford University Press.

Sen, Amartya. 2009. *The Idea of Justice*. London: Allen Lane.

Senninger, Roman, Daniel Bischof, and Lawrence Ezrow. 2022. 'How transnational party alliances influence national parties' policies'. *Political Science Research and Methods* 10 (3):651–658.

Shaffer, Gregory. 2004. 'Parliamentary oversight of WTO rule-making'. *Journal of International Economic Law* 7 (3):629–654.

Shapiro, Ian. 2003. *The State of Democratic Theory*. Princeton: Princeton University Press.

Shapiro, Ian 2016. *Politics against Domination*. Cambridge, MA: Harvard University Press.

Shaw, Martin 2000. *Theory of the Global State: Globality as an Unfinished Revolution*. Cambridge: Cambridge University Press.

Shmueli, Galit. 2010. 'To explain or to predict?' *Statistical Science* 25 (3):289–310.

Simmons, Beth A., Frank Dobbin, and Geoffrey Garrett. 2008. 'Introduction: The diffusion of liberalization'. In *The Global Diffusion of Markets and Democracy*, edited by Beth A. Simmons, Frank Dobbin, and Geoffrey Garrett, 1–63. Cambridge: Cambridge University Press.

Simmons, Beth A., and Michael R. Kenwick. 2022. 'Border orientation in a globalizing world'. *American Journal of Political Science* 66 (4):853–870.

Singer, J. David. 1969. 'The incompleat theorist: Insight without evidence'. In *Contending Approaches to International Politics*, edited by Klaus Knorr and James N. Rosenau, 62–86. Princeton: Princeton University Press.

Singer, J. David, Stuart Bremer, and John Stuckey. 1972. 'Capability distribution, uncertainty, and major power war, 1820–1965'. In *Peace, War, and Numbers*, edited by Bruce Russett, 19–48. Beverly Hills: Sage.

Skinner, Quentin. 1998. *Liberty before Liberalism*. Cambridge: Cambridge University Press.

Skogstad, Karl. 2016. 'Defence budgets in the post-Cold War era: A spatial econometrics approach'. *Defence and Peace Economics* 27 (3):323–352.

Slaughter, Anne-Marie. 2004. *A New World Order*. Princeton: Princeton University Press.

Smetana, Michal, and Michal Onderco. 2022. 'From Moscow with a mushroom cloud? Russian public attitudes to the use of nuclear weapons in a conflict with NATO'. *Journal of Conflict Resolution* 67 (2–3):183–209.

Smith, Craig. 2006. *Adam Smith's Political Philosophy: The Invisible Hand and Spontaneous Order*. London and New York: Routledge.

Smith, James Andrew, and Jonas B. Sandbrink. 2022. 'Biosecurity in an age of open science'. *PLoS Biology* 20 (4):e3001600.

Sokolov, Boris. 2018. 'The index of emancipative values: Measurement model misspecifications'. *American Political Science Review* 112 (2):395–408.

Solt, Frederick. 2020. 'Measuring income inequality across countries and over time: The Standardized World Income Inequality Database'. *Social Science Quarterly* 101 (3):1183–1199.

Sommerer, Thomas, Hans Agné, Fariborz Zelli, and Bart Bes. 2022. *Global Legitimacy Crises: Decline and Revival in Multilateral Governance*. Oxford: Oxford University Press.

Sørensen, Georg. 2013. 'Book review: *The Realist Case for Global Reform*, by William E. Scheuerman'. *Perspectives on Politics* 11 (3):895–897.

Southwood, Nicholas. 2015. 'Democracy as a modally demanding value'. *Noûs* 49 (3):504–521.

Southwood, Nicholas. 2016. 'Does "ought" imply "feasible"?' *Philosophy & Public Affairs* 44 (1):7–45.

Southwood, Nicholas. 2018. 'The feasibility issue'. *Philosophy Compass* 13 (8):e12509.

Southwood, Nicholas 2022. 'Feasibility as deliberation-worthiness'. *Philosophy & Public Affairs* 50 (1):121–162.

Southwood, Nicholas, and Robert E. Goodin. 2021. 'Infeasibility as a normative argument-stopper: The case of open borders'. *European Journal of Philosophy* 29 (4):965–987.

Spagat, Michael, and Stijn van Weezel. 2020. 'The decline of war since 1950: New evidence'. In *Lewis Fry Richardson: His Intellectual Legacy and Influence in the Social Sciences*, edited by Nils Petter Gleditsch, 129–142. Cham: Springer.

Squatrito, Theresa 2018. 'The democratizing effects of transnational actors' access to international courts'. *Global Governance* 24 (4):595–613.

Starr, Harvey, and Benjamin A. Most. 1978. 'A return journey: Richardson, "frontiers" and wars in the 1946–1965 era'. *Journal of Conflict Resolution* 22 (3):441–467.

StataCorp. 2023. *Stata Lasso Reference Manual. Release 18*. College Station, TX: Stata Press.

Steffek, Jens. 2010. 'Public accountability and the public sphere of international governance'. *Ethics & International Affairs* 24 (1):45–68.

Steffek, Jens. 2015. 'The cosmopolitanism of David Mitrany: Equality, devolution and functional democracy beyond the state'. *International Relations* 29 (1):23–44.

Steffek, Jens, and Kristina Hahn, eds. 2010. *Evaluating Transnational NGOs: Legitimacy, Accountability, Representation*. Basingstoke: Palgrave Macmillan.

Steffek, Jens, Claudia Kissling, and Patrizia Nanz, eds. 2007. *Civil Society Participation in European and Global Governance: A Cure for the Democratic Deficit?* Basingstoke: Palgrave Macmillan.

Stein, Rachel M. 2015. 'War and revenge: Explaining conflict initiation by democracies'. *American Political Science Review* 109 (3):556–573.

Steinebach, Yves, Xavier Fernández-i-Marín, and Christian Aschenbrenner. 2021. 'Who puts a price on carbon, why and how? A global empirical analysis of carbon pricing policies'. *Climate Policy* 21 (3):277–289.

Stemplowska, Zofia. 2016. 'Feasibility: Individual and collective'. *Social Philosophy and Policy* 33 (1–2):273–291.

Stephenson, Matthew C. 2003. '"When the devil turns …": The political foundations of independent judicial review'. *Journal of Legal Studies* 32 (1):59–89.

Stevens, Jacqueline. 2009. *States without Nations: Citizenship for Mortals*. New York: Columbia University Press.

Stevenson, Hayley. 2016. 'The wisdom of the many in global governance: An epistemic–democratic defense of diversity and inclusion'. *International Studies Quarterly* 60 (3):400–412.

Stevenson, Hayley, and John S. Dryzek. 2014. *Democratizing Global Climate Governance*. Cambridge: Cambridge University Press.

Stewart, Blake. 2020. 'The rise of far-right civilizationism'. *Critical Sociology* 46 (7–8):1207–1220.

Stinnett, Douglas M., Jaroslav Tir, Paul F. Diehl, Philip Schafer, and Charles Gochman. 2002. 'The Correlates of War (COW) project direct contiguity data, version 3.0'. *Conflict Management and Peace Science* 19 (2):59–67.

Stoetzer, Lukas F., and Steffen Zittlau. 2015. 'Multidimensional spatial voting with non-separable preferences'. *Political Analysis* 23 (3):415–428.

Stoetzer, Lukas F., and Steffen Zittlau. 2020. 'Vote choice and the nonseparability of economic and social issues'. *Public Opinion Quarterly* 84 (1):158–170.

Streeck, Wolfgang. 2018. 'Taking back control? The future of Western democratic capitalism'. *Efil Journal of Economic Research* 1 (3):30–47.

Streit, Clarence K. 1938. *Union Now: A Proposal for a Federal Union of the Democracies of the North Atlantic*. New York: Harper and Brothers.

Stuurman, Siep. 2017. *The Invention of Humanity: Equality and Cultural Difference in World History*. Cambridge, MA: Harvard University Press.

Suganami, Hidemi. 1989. *The Domestic Analogy and World Order Proposals*. Cambridge: Cambridge University Press.

Sugden, Robert. 1989. 'Spontaneous order'. *Journal of Economic Perspectives* 3 (4):85–97.

Sukin, Lauren. 2020. 'Experimental evidence on determinants of support for nuclear use in response to threats of nuclear retaliation'. *Peace and Conflict: Journal of Peace Psychology* 26 (3):336.

Sustainable Development Solutions Network. 2014. 'Health in the Framework of Sustainable Development: Technical report for the post-2015 development agenda'. https://irp-cdn.multiscreensite.com/be6d1d56/files/uploaded/Health-For-All-Report.pdf (accessed 17 February 2024).

Synovate. 2007. 'IN:FACT (BBC) DEMOCRACY'. Survey questionnaire. http://news.bbc.co.uk/1/shared/bsp/hi/pdfs/08_10_07_democracy.pdf (accessed 20 July 2022).

Tallberg, Jonas, Thomas Sommerer, and Theresa Squatrito. 2016. 'Democratic memberships in international organizations: Sources of institutional design'. *Review of International Organizations* 11 (1):59–87.

Tallberg, Jonas, Thomas Sommerer, Theresa Squatrito, and Christer Jönsson. 2013. *The Opening Up of International Organizations: Transnational Access in Global Governance*. Cambridge: Cambridge University Press.

Tallberg, Jonas, Thomas Sommerer, Theresa Squatrito, and Christer Jönsson. 2014. 'Explaining the transnational design of international organizations'. *International Organization* 68 (4):741–774.

Tallberg, Jonas, and Anders Uhlin. 2012. 'Civil society and global democracy: An assessment'. In *Global Democracy: Normative and Empirical Perspectives*, edited by Daniele Archibugi, Mathias Koenig-Archibugi, and Raffaele Marchetti, 210–232. Cambridge: Cambridge University Press.

Talmon, Stefan. 2005. 'The Security Council as world legislature'. *American Journal of International Law* 99 (1):175–193.

Tamir, Yael. 2000. 'Who's afraid of a global state?' In *Nationalism and Internationalism in the Post-Cold War Era*, edited by Kjell Goldmann, Ulf Hannerz, and Charles Westin, 254–277. London and New York: Routledge.

Tanasoca, Ana, and John S. Dryzek. 2022. 'Determining vaccine justice in the time of COVID-19: A democratic perspective'. *Ethics & International Affairs* 36 (3):333–351.

Tannenwald, Nina. 2007. *The Nuclear Taboo: The United States and the Non-use of Nuclear Weapons Since 1945*. Cambridge: Cambridge University Press.

Tannenwald, Nina. 2018. 'How strong is the nuclear taboo today?' *Washington Quarterly* 41 (3):89–109.

Tay, Louis, and Ed Diener. 2011. 'Needs and subjective well-being around the world'. *Journal of Personality and Social Psychology* 101 (2):354–365.

Taylor, Peter J. 1986. 'An exploration into world-systems analysis of political parties'. *Political Geography Quarterly* 5 (4):S5–S20.

Thacker, Strom C. 1999. 'The high politics of IMF lending'. *World Politics* 52 (1):38–75.

Theiler, Tobias. 2022. 'International functionalism and democracy'. *European Journal of International Relations* 28 (2):312–336.

Thérien, Jean-Philippe, and Madeleine Bélanger Dumontier. 2009. 'The United Nations and global democracy: From discourse to deeds'. *Cooperation and Conflict* 44 (4):355–377.

Thompson, Kenneth W. 1987. *Winston Churchill's World View: Statesmanship and Power*. Baton Rouge: Louisiana State University Press.

Thompson, Kimberly M. 2017. 'Modeling and managing the risks of measles and rubella: A global perspective, part II'. *Risk Analysis* 37 (6):1041–1051.

Thompson, Kimberly M., and Stephen L. Cochi. 2016. 'Modeling and managing the risks of measles and rubella: A global perspective, part I'. *Risk Analysis* 36 (7):1288–1296.

Thompson, William R. 1996. 'Democracy and peace: Putting the cart before the horse?' *International Organization* 50 (1):141–174.

Threlkeld, Megan. 2022. *Citizens of the World: US Women and Global Government*. Philadelphia: University of Pennsylvania Press.

Tibshirani, Robert. 1996. 'Regression shrinkage and selection via the lasso'. *Journal of the Royal Statistical Society Series B: Statistical Methodology* 58 (1):267–288.

Tilly, Charles. 2000. 'Processes and mechanisms of democratization'. *Sociological Theory* 18 (1):1–16.

Tinbergen, Jan, and Dietrich Fischer. 1987. *Warfare and Welfare: Integrating Security Policy into Socio-Economic Policy*. Brighton, UK, and New York: Wheathseaf Books and St Martin's Press.

Tinnevelt, Ronald. 2011. 'Does a world state really lead to a graveyard of freedom?' In *Cosmopolitan Justice and its Discontents*, edited by Cecilia M. Bailliet and Katja Franko Aas, 29–49. London and New York: Routledge.

Tobin, Brendan. 2014. *Indigenous Peoples, Customary Law and Human Rights: Why Living Law Matters*. London and New York: Routledge.

Traber, Denise, Miriam Hänni, Nathalie Giger, and Christian Breunig. 2022. 'Social status, political priorities and unequal representation'. *European Journal of Political Research* 61 (2):351–373.

Truman, David. 1951. *The Governmental Process.* New York: Alfred A. Knopf.

Tschakert, Petra, Jon Barnett, Neville Ellis, Carmen Lawrence, Nancy Tuana, Mark New, Carmen Elrick-Barr, Ram Pandit, and David Pannell. 2017. 'Climate change and loss, as if people mattered: Values, places, and experiences'. *Wiley Interdisciplinary Reviews: Climate Change* 8 (5):e476.

Tullock, Gordon. 2006. 'Comment to strengthening the citizens' role in international organizations by Bruno S. Frey and Alois Stutzer'. *Review of International Organizations* 1 (1):45–46.

Tusalem, Rollin F. 2021. 'Bringing the legislature back in: Examining the structural effects of national legislatures on effective democratic governance'. *Government and Opposition* 58 (2):291–315.

Tuttle, Florence Guertin. 1919. *Women and World Federation.* New York: Robert M. McBride & Co.

Ulaş, Luke. 2013. 'Realising cosmopolitanism: The role of a world state'. Thesis for the degree of Doctor of Philosophy, Department of Government, the London School of Economics.

Ulaş, Luke. 2016. 'Doing things by halves: On intermediary global institutional proposals'. *Ethics & Global Politics* 9 (1):30223.

Ulaş, Luke. 2021. 'Institutionalising Kant's political philosophy: Foregrounding cosmopolitan right'. *European Journal of Political Theory* 20 (3):421–442.

Underdal, Arild, and Taoyuan Wei. 2015. 'Distributive fairness: A mutual recognition approach'. *Environmental Science & Policy* 51:35–44.

Unger, Roberto Mangabeira. 2022. *Governing the World without World Government.* London: Verso.

United Nations. 2019. '2019 revision of world population prospects'. United Nations Department of Economic and Social Affairs, Population Division. https://population.un.org/wpp/ (accessed 17 February 2024).

Valdez, Inés. 2019. *Transnational Cosmopolitanism: Kant, Du Bois, and Justice as a Political Craft.* Cambridge: Cambridge University Press.

Valentini, Laura. 2011. *Justice in a Globalized World: A Normative Framework.* Oxford: Oxford University Press.

Valentini, Laura. 2012. 'Assessing the global order: Justice, legitimacy, or political justice?' *Critical Review of International Social and Political Philosophy* 15 (5):593–612.

Valentini, Laura. 2013. 'Justice, disagreement and democracy'. *British Journal of Political Science* 43 (1):177–199.

Valentini, Laura. 2014. 'No global demos, no global democracy? A systematization and critique'. *Perspectives on Politics* 12 (4):789–807.

Vallinoto, Nicola. 2014. 'Civil society movements and campaigns for international democracy'. In *The Democratization of International Institutions*, edited by Lucio Levi, Giovanni Finizio, and Nicola Vallinoto, 463–475. London and New York: Routledge.

Van der Hout, Eliora, and Anthony J. McGann. 2009. 'Proportional representation within the limits of liberalism alone'. *British Journal of Political Science* 39 (4):735–754.

Van Doren, Carl. 1948. *The Great Rehearsal: The Story of the Making and Ratifying of the Constitution of the United States.* New York: Viking Press.

Van Zanden, Jan Luiten, Joerg Baten, Peter Foldvari, and Bas Van Leeuwen. 2014. 'The changing shape of global inequality 1820–2000; exploring a new dataset'. *Review of Income and Wealth* 60 (2):279–297.

Vanberg, Georg. 2015. 'Constitutional courts in comparative perspective: A theoretical assessment'. *Annual Review of Political Science* 18 (1):167–185.

Vaubel, Roland. 2008. 'A history of thought on institutional competition'. In *Institutional Competition*, edited by A. Bergh and R. Höijer, 29–66. Cheltenham: Edward Elgar.

Voeten, Erik. 2000. 'Clashes in the Assembly'. *International Organization* 54 (2):185–216.

von Arnauld, Andreas, Kerstin von der Decken, and Mart Susi, eds. 2020. *The Cambridge Handbook of New Human Rights: Recognition, Novelty, Rhetoric*. Cambridge: Cambridge University Press.

Von Borzyskowski, Inken, and Felicity Vabulas. 2019. 'Hello, goodbye: When do states withdraw from international organizations?' *Review of International Organizations* 14 (2):335–366.

Waldron, Jeremy. 2006. 'The core of the case against judicial review'. *Yale Law Journal* 115 (6):1346–1406.

Waltz, Kenneth N. 1979. *Theory of International Politics*. Reading, MA: Addison-Wesley.

Waltz, Kenneth N. 1986. 'Reflections on "Theory of International Politics": A reply to my critics'. In *Neorealism and Its Critics*, edited by Robert O. Keohane, 322–345. New York: Columbia University Press.

Walzer, Michael. 2000. 'Governing the globe: What is the best we can do?' *Dissent* 47 (4):44–52.

Wang, Zhiyuan. 2017. 'Democracy, policy interdependence, and labor rights'. *Political Research Quarterly* 70 (3):549–563.

Wang, Zhiyuan. 2018. 'Economic competition, policy interdependence, and labour rights'. *New Political Economy* 23 (6):656–673.

Ward, Hugh, and Albert Weale. 2010. 'Is rule by majorities special?' *Political Studies* 58 (1):26–46.

Watkins, David, and Scott Lemieux. 2015. 'Compared to what? Judicial review and other veto points in contemporary democratic theory'. *Perspectives on Politics* 13 (2):312–326.

Waytz, Adam, Ravi Iyer, Liane Young, Jonathan Haidt, and Jesse Graham. 2019. 'Ideological differences in the expanse of the moral circle'. *Nature Communications* 10 (1):1–12.

Weale, Albert. 2007. *Democracy*. Second edition. Basingstoke: Palgrave Macmillan.

Webb, Adam K. 2016. 'Can the global South take over the baton? What cosmopolitanism in "unlikely" places means for future world order'. *Third World Quarterly* 37 (6):1016–1034.

Weber, Eugen. 1976. *Peasants into Frenchmen: The Modernization of Rural France, 1870–1914*. Stanford: Stanford University Press.

Weber, Matthias. 2020. 'Choosing the rules: Preferences over voting systems for assemblies of representatives'. *Journal of Economic Behavior & Organization* 174:420–434.

Weiler, J. H. H. 2003. 'In defence of the status quo: Europe's constitutional Sonderweg'. In *European Constitutionalism Beyond the State*, edited by J. H. H. Weiler and Marlene Wind, 7–24. Cambridge: Cambridge University Press.

Weinstock, Daniel. 2006. 'The real world of (global) democracy'. *Journal of Social Philosophy* 37 (1):6–20.

Weinstock, Daniel. 2015. 'Integrating intermediate goods to theories of distributive justice: The importance of platforms'. *Res Publica* 21 (2):171–183.

Weiss, Thomas G. 2009. 'What happened to the idea of world government'. *International Studies Quarterly* 53 (2):253–271.

Weitzman, Martin L. 2017a. 'On a world climate assembly and the social cost of carbon'. *Economica* 84 (336):559–586.

Weitzman, Martin L. 2017b. 'Voting on prices vs. voting on quantities in a world climate assembly'. *Research in Economics* 71 (2):199–211.

Wells, H. G. 1933. 'The open conspiracy'. In *The Open Conspiracy and Other Writings*. London: [no publisher].

Wells, H. G. 1942. *Phoenix: A Summary of the Inescapable Conditions of World Reorganization*. London: Secker & Warburg.

Welzel, Christian. 2013. *Freedom Rising: Human Empowerment and the Quest for Emancipation*. Cambridge: Cambridge University Press.

Welzel, Christian. 2021. 'Democratic horizons: What value change reveals about the future of democracy'. *Democratization* 28 (5):992–1016.

Wendt, Alexander. 2003. 'Why a world state is inevitable'. *European Journal of International Relations* 9 (4):491–542.

Wendt, Alexander, and Daniel Friedheim. 1995. 'Hierarchy under anarchy: Informal empire and the East German state'. *International Organization* 49 (4):689–721.

Wesson, Robert G. 1978. *State Systems: International Pluralism, Politics, and Culture*. New York: Free Press.

White, Aaronette, and Shagun Rastogi. 2009. 'Justice by any means necessary: Vigilantism among Indian women'. *Feminism & Psychology* 19 (3):313–327.

White, Jonathan, and Lea Ypi. 2016. *The Meaning of Partisanship*. Oxford: Oxford University Press.

Wight, Martin 1959/2022. 'On the abolition of war: Observations on a memorandum by Walter Millis'. In Martin Wight, *International Relations and Political Philosophy*, edited by David S. Yost, 175–181. Oxford: Oxford University Press.

Wight, Martin 1991. *International Theory: The Three Traditions*. Leicester and London: Leicester University Press.

Wilson, James Lindley. 2019. *Democratic Equality*. Princeton: Princeton University Press.

Wilson, Matthew Charles, and Josef Woldense. 2019. 'Contested or established? A comparison of legislative powers across regimes'. *Democratization* 26 (4):585–605.

Wimmer, Andreas, Lars-Erik Cederman, and Brian Min. 2009. 'Ethnic politics and armed conflict: A configurational analysis of a new global data set'. *American Sociological Review* 74 (2):316–337.

Wintein, Stefan, and Conrad Heilmann. 2022. 'Liberal political equality does not imply proportional representation'. *Social Choice and Welfare* 59 (1):63–91.

Wojczewski, Thorsten. 2024. The international cooperation of the populist radical right: building counter-hegemony in international relations. *International Relations*, published online 13 January. https://doi.org/10.1177/00471178231222888.

Wolf, Klaus Dieter. 1999. 'The new Raison d'État as a problem for democracy in world society'. *European Journal of International Relations* 5 (3):333–363.

Wollstonecraft, Mary. 1792/1995. 'A vindication of the rights of woman'. In Mary Wollstonecraft, *A Vindication of the Rights of Men and a Vindication of the Rights of Woman*, edited by Sylvana Tomaselli, 65–294. Cambridge: Cambridge University Press.

Woodhull, Victoria C. 1871. *The Origin, Tendencies, and Principles of Government*. New York: Woodhull, Claflin, & Co.

Woodhull, Victoria C. 1872/2010. 'A page of American history: Constitution of the United States of the World'. In *Selected Writings of Victoria Woodhull*, edited by Cari M. Carpenter, 7–20. Lincoln and London: University of Nebraska Press.

Woodhull, Victoria. 2010. *Selected Writings of Victoria Woodhull*, edited by Cari M. Carpenter. Lincoln and London: University of Nebraska Press.

Wootton, Barbara. 1943. 'Socialism and federation'. In *Studies in Federal Planning*, edited by Patrick Ransome, 269–298. London: Macmillan.

World Bank. 2021. 'World Development Indicators (WDI).' World Bank: Data Catalog. http://data.worldbank.org/data-catalog/world-development-indicators (accessed 17 February 2024).

World Food Programme. 2022. *Annual Review 2021*. Rome: World Food Programme.

World Health Organization. 2019. *Thematic Paper on the Status of Country Preparedness Capacities: Background Report Commissioned by the Global Preparedness Monitoring Board (GPMB)*. Geneva: WHO.

World Health Organization. 2021. *International Health Regulations (2005): State Party Self-assessment Annual Reporting Tool*. Second edition. Geneva: WHO.

Wright, Erik Olin. 2010. *Envisioning Real Utopias*. London: Verso.

Yesilyurt, M. Ensar, and J. Paul Elhorst. 2017. 'Impacts of neighboring countries on military expenditures: A dynamic spatial panel approach.' *Journal of Peace Research* 54 (6):777–790.

Ypi, Lea. 2012. *Global Justice and Avant-garde Political Agency*. Oxford: Oxford University Press.

Yu, Shi, Chantal Levesque-Bristol, and Yukiko Maeda. 2018. 'General need for autonomy and subjective well-being: A meta-analysis of studies in the US and East Asia.' *Journal of Happiness Studies* 19:1863–1882.

Yunker, James A. 2011. *The Idea of World Government: From Ancient Times to the Twenty-first Century*. London and New York: Routledge.

Zadeh, Lotfi Asker. 1978. 'Fuzzy sets as a basis for a theory of possibility.' *Fuzzy Sets and Systems* 1 (1):3–28.

Zimmern, Alfred E. 1953. *The American Road to World Peace*. New York: Dutton.

Zolo, Danilo. 1997. *Cosmopolis: Prospects for World Government*. Cambridge: Polity Press.

Zürn, Michael 2000. 'Democratic governance beyond the nation-state: The EU and other international institutions.' *European Journal of International Relations* 6 (2):183–221.

Zürn, Michael. 2005. 'Global governance and legitimacy problems.' In *Global Governance and Public Accountability*, edited by David Held and Mathias Koenig-Archibugi, 136–163. Oxford: Blackwell.

Zürn, Michael. 2016. 'Four models of a global order with cosmopolitan intent: An empirical assessment.' *Journal of Political Philosophy* 24 (1):88–119.

Zürn, Michael. 2018. *A Theory of Global Governance: Authority, Legitimacy, and Contestation*. Oxford: Oxford University Press.

Zürn, Michael, and Christian Joerges, eds. 2005. *Law and Governance in Postnational Europe: Compliance Beyond the Nation-state*. Cambridge: Cambridge University Press.

Zürn, Michael, Alexandros Tokhi, and Martin Binder. 2021. 'The International Authority Database.' *Global Policy* 12 (4):430–442.

Index

For the benefit of digital users, indexed terms that span two pages (e.g., 52–53) may, on occasion, appear on only one of those pages.

Tables, figures, and boxes are indicated by an italic *t*, *f*, and *b* following the page numbers.